Hearts on Fire

Mother Mary Joseph Rogers,
founder of the Maryknoll Sisters

Hearts on Fire

The Story of the Maryknoll Sisters

CENTENARY EDITION

Penny Lernoux

with Arthur Jones and Robert Ellsberg

ORBIS BOOKS

Maryknoll, New York 10545

Founded in 1970, Orbis Books endeavors to publish works that enlighten the mind, nourish the spirit, and challenge the conscience. The publishing arm of the Maryknoll Fathers and Brothers, Orbis seeks to explore the global dimensions of the Christian faith and mission, to invite dialogue with diverse cultures and religious traditions, and to serve the cause of reconciliation and peace. The books published reflect the views of their authors and do not represent the official position of the Maryknoll Society. To learn more about Maryknoll and Orbis Books, please visit our website at www.maryknollsociety.org.

Library of Congress Cataloging-in-Publication Data

Lernoux, Penny, 1940–
    Hearts on fire : the story of the Maryknoll Sisters / Penny Lernoux ; with Arthur Jones and Robert Ellsberg.
        p. cm.
    ISBN 0-88344-925-0 (hc); 1-57075-019-X (pbk); 978-1-57075-934-5 (rev. ed.)
    1. Maryknoll Sisters—History.   I. Jones, Arthur, 1936–   .   II. Ellsberg, Robert, 1955–   .
    III. Title.
    BV2300.M4L47   1993
    271'.97—dc20   93-36831
                                                                                                          CIP

To Angela

Contents

～

Foreword to the Centenary Edition

Archbishop Emeritus Desmond Mpilo Tutu

~

PENNY LERNOUX'S RIVETING ACCOUNT of the courageous lives of the Maryknoll Sisters makes me proud to be a Christian. With hearts truly on fire, the Maryknoll Sisters have journeyed for 100 years to "the uttermost parts of the earth" while at the same time through heights and depths of the human spirit.

From its foundation by the spirited and visionary Smith College graduate, Mollie Rogers, who became Mother Mary Joseph, the congregation introduced a new style of being missioners. Inspired by a gospel of love and a firm belief that we humans the world over are family, seven women from disparate backgrounds came together in 1912 in Hawthorne, New York, to assist Father James Anthony Walsh to inform and inspire American Catholics of foreign missions through the nascent publication of the mission magazine, *The Field Afar*.

"Come, let us see what God has in store for us!" Mollie Rogers said to Margaret Shea. These simple words have reverberated through 100 years as the Maryknoll Sisters truly journeyed to "fields afar" and spread in mission from Asia, to Africa, to Latin America, and beyond. These ordinary women who lead extraordinary lives incarnate a God of love and justice and compassion. Knowing no borders or boundaries that separate the human family, they reach beyond the narrow agendas of national interests and rivalries that vie for power over peoples and the earth's abundance. Maryknoll Sisters incarnate the God of the poor and vulnerable, the God of the sick and the lame, the God of the stranger and despised, the God of the human family and the whole of creation as they immerse themselves in cultures not their own and speak in tongues of distant peoples.

These Sisters take the Incarnation seriously. As Jesus walked the dusty roads of Galilee of his day offering to all he encountered a new way of living with each other as sisters and brothers in the human family, so, too, the

Sisters have walked and continue to walk the dusty roads of Dodoma, the jungle paths of Riberalta, the war torn roads of Pusan and Phnom Penh, and the refugee paths of Salvadorans and Zimbabweans carrying and embodying that message of Jesus.

As contemplatives in action, Maryknoll Sisters discern the "signs of the times" in the cultures in which they live. As medical doctors and nurses, as teachers and social workers, as artists and lawyers, as theologians and fiscal managers, they apply their creative imaginations to the needs and dreams of the peoples among whom they live and minister. Because of the forward vision of the congregation's foundress, Maryknoll Sisters today respond to the needs of our twenty-first-century world. With eyes and hearts wide open to the world and all its strengths and weaknesses, we find them at the forefront of responding to the AIDS epidemic, forming interdisciplinary teams and integrating medical treatment for the infected, preventive education, and loving care for AIDS orphans. We see them helping trafficked women free themselves from the shackles of sexual exploitation and become reintegrated into their societies. We all benefit from their reverence and care for the earth and all its creatures through the solid environmental education they offer in ways to act constructively in relation to the earth and the whole of creation.

Although Maryknoll Sisters have seen the worst we humans can do to one another, they ultimately look through the prism of goodness in each person and work with others for solutions to some of our most intractable problems. Their lives are not without risk—some giving their lives for their faith, while others have been detained as prisoners of war or incarcerated for their stand on human rights. Yet, because they have witnessed the realities of the way the vast majority of people are forced to live due to political, economic, social, and religious concerns, they continue on their journey with hearts on fire and minds emboldened to creating a more just and equitable world.

Each person puts a mark on the earth and all creation. How we live with one another matters. My goodness, might we all learn how to live a little more humanely with each other from the Maryknoll Sisters. Never daunted by perilous challenges or even threats to their lives, they live and share their lives with the poorest, most neglected and dehumanized of our human family. Never cautionary or dour in their commitment to justice, the Sisters always exhibit a tremendous sense of fun and with glad hearts know how to laugh and find joy with others and among themselves. With spirited hearts, these Sisters continue to move forward into the future as strong Christian women and responsive global citizens. I promise you, by reading *Hearts on Fire,* you will want to challenge your own heart and open wide your spirit in a loving embrace of our world and all its peoples.

Foreword

Sister Barbara Hendricks, M.M.

∼

IT WAS A COOL day in early September 1989 when the call came from Bogota, Colombia. The voice was Penny Lernoux's, the tone was pure anguish, and her words were a cry for help. "The doctor gives me no hope. He says that I have only a few months, or weeks, to live." There was a plaintive pause and then, "Barbara, I want to finish the book. I want to live and finish it! What should I do?" As we talked, it became clear that she should come to the States for another medical consultation. The plan was quickly put together; she and Denis Nahum, her husband, would fly to New York as soon as possible and, meanwhile, I would locate a cancer specialist in the New York area.

George Black and Anne Nelson Black met the plane and a former Maryknoller, Dr. Patricia McCormick, a highly respected cancer surgeon, graciously offered to handle the consultation and arrange for the treatment. For a week or more there seemed to be hope as Penny and Denis moved into the Maryknoll Sisters' Center in Ossining, New York. Denis bought a computer and we set up an office near Penny's room, gathering all the materials she would need to continue her work on the book about the Maryknoll Sisters' charism and mission. Within two weeks it was obvious that Penny had begun her last journey—a journey to Jerusalem. She was rushed to Northern Westchester Medical Center where she died a few days later on October 8, 1989.

Penny Lernoux was not able to finish her last book, yet the memory of this valiant woman journalist, who was irrevocably committed to truth, justice, and compassionate love, lives on in her writings, and in the relationships that she formed over the forty-nine years of her life. As I look back over that brief year and a half in which Maryknoll Sisters collaborated with Penny in her research, interviews, discussions, and times of sharing hospitality, I realize that strong bonds of friendship and mutual admiration were formed and grew. For those of us who knew Penny and worked with her in the preparation of the book, it was as if we were writing this book with her. I think that we wanted to finish the book as much as Penny herself did. Early on, she told me that this was the only book she actually "had fun writing."

Penny and I became close friends as we worked together. She was the author and I was her liaison with the Maryknoll Sisters and the secretary for the newly formed Sisters' Book Committee. My role was to facilitate her research and interviews and to be the connecting link with the Maryknoll Sisters' Congregation here in the States and, also, in our other mission regions in Africa, Asia, the Central Pacific, and Latin America. As a missioner with over two decades of mission in South America, I had great respect for Penny's writings, which captured the plight of the poor and revealed her respect and love for the rebirth of a new kind of church in Latin America. She was fun to work with, full of enthusiasm, steady, consistent, creative, and able to listen carefully to people. She was extremely careful in recording interviews and always sent transcribed interviews for correction to those she interviewed.

Maryknoll Sisters' confidence in her grew quickly; she understood what our ideals were, respected each one's life commitment, and was able to translate our values into her literary genre. Penny and the Maryknoll Sisters seemed to "click" when they met and talked about women in mission. The Sisters who were interviewed found Penny stimulating, affirming, warm, and loving. Penny felt that the Sisters were amazingly open with her. She was greatly moved by their depth, vitality, commitment, and by the rich experience of global mission they shared with her.

In April 1988, soon after a second round of interviews at Maryknoll, Penny visited the Sisters' retirement residence in Monrovia, California, where she learned more details about the foundation of the Maryknoll Sisters and the early missions in Asia. A week later she was in Los Angeles continuing a lecture tour she was involved in at the time. As she began her talk she took a quick look around the audience and, to her utter amazement, saw a group of retired Maryknoll Sisters from Monrovia who had battled the hazardous freeway in order to cheer Penny on. To make the day complete, they all paraded up to greet her at the end of her talk. When Penny recounted this later, tears filled her eyes. "Those women are saints," she said, "at least that is the way I see them." Her criteria for sainthood: "extraordinary concern for the poor, courage, and deep spirituality."

From the beginning of our collaboration with Penny Lernoux, we insisted that she visit some of our mission regions in both Africa and Asia. Our reason was that the book would not fully represent the charism and oral history of the Maryknoll Sisters unless the author had a wide spectrum of our experience in mission and some knowledge of the peoples with whom we worked. Although Penny had visited several of our mission regions in Central and South America and knew many of the Sisters working there, she had little acquaintance with our other missions in Africa, Asia, and the Central Pacific areas. Penny immediately recognized the need for this kind of exposure. She had interviewed many Sisters at the Center whose missions were in these continents, but she realized that actual on-site interviews and exposure would be extremely valuable for an understanding of our charism and experience. The problem was money for these trips. Pantheon Books, the publisher of the book at that time, had allocated a minimum fee to Penny. Convinced of the importance of her trips, the Central Governing Board of the Maryknoll Sisters offered to cover the cost of the travel to both Africa and Asia. The Sisters in the particular regions would handle the hospitality expenses.

Penny flew to Asia on November 14, 1988, spending a week in Hong Kong and another week in the Philippines where our Sisters had been working since the early 1920s. She worked long days and often late into the nights, listening, asking questions, taping interviews, observing and sharing the life of the Sisters in an intense, interested, and always respectful way.

The trip to Africa was to take place on January 12, 1989. Everything was all set, the tickets were waiting for Penny in New York, and the Sisters in Tanzania and Kenya were alerted. Penny would meet the entire group at the Sisters' Africa World Section meeting in Nairobi. At the last minute Penny called from Colombia to tell me that she was completely exhausted, unable to get back her energy after the Asian trip. The illness that would consume her was not yet diagnosed, but her physician recommended rest without any travel for the time being.

Greatly disappointed, Penny arranged with me to have her interview "questionnaire" mailed to each Sister in the Africa regions as a substitute for the visit. She was, at that point, already behind her deadline.

In her December 9, 1987, proposal to the Central Governing Board of the Maryknoll Sisters, Penny wrote that she wanted "to write a book that will convert hearts through the examples of the Maryknoll Sisters." For Penny "conversion" meant turning to God in a deep spirituality based on an extraordinary concern for the poor and courage to live out that kind of concern. She understood that the witness of conversion was love and solidarity with the poor. Her objective for the book was "to tell a story of charisms and a call to conversion."

In order to do this, she wanted as much material on our founder, Mother Mary Joseph Rogers, as we had on hand. She read everything made available to her and gleaned the most moving material from the older Sisters who shared their memories of Mother with her. Penny felt that Mother Mary Joseph was still alive in the charism she was experiencing in the Sisters she was meeting. In chapter two her description of Mollie Rogers rings true to those who knew Mother Mary Joseph. This is a tribute to Penny's careful research and listening heart because, of course, she had never met Mollie Rogers, who died in 1955.

How did Penny Lernoux describe the book that she wanted to write? This is the proposal she sent to the Maryknoll Sisters' Central Governing Board in December of 1987:

I am writing to ask the Maryknoll Sisters' Central Governing Board to reconsider a proposal for an oral history of the Maryknoll nuns. The reasons for this request are:

1. When George Black of Pantheon Books first proposed the idea in July 1986, it was not known who would write the book or how the material might be handled. Since then, Pantheon has contracted me to write a book about American nuns which I would very much like to recast as the original proposal of an oral history of the Maryknoll Sisters.

My reasons for wanting to write about Maryknoll are personal and have to do with my faith commitment. I admire women and men from other religious orders, but I owe a special debt to Maryknoll because it was through your missioners in Chile that I regained my Catholic faith. Although I was educated in Catholic schools, I began to drift away from the church after I arrived in Colombia in the early 1960s, before Vatican II. The institutional church in Colombia was/is wedded to the upper classes, particularly the Conservative Party, and I was shocked to hear priests in the pulpit threatening to excommunicate anyone who voted for another party. My experience of this near-feudal institution was so painful that for years afterward I was estranged from the church. But in the early 1970s I came in contact with Maryknoll missioners in Chile, who showed me a different church—the church of the poor. It was also through them that I became aware of and entered into another world—not that of the U.S. embassy or the upper classes, which comprise the confines of most American journalists, but the suffering and hopeful world of the slums and peasant villages. The experience changed my life, giving me new faith and a commitment as a writer to tell the truth of the poor to the best of my ability.

There is a saying in this church of the poor: "You make your path by walking it." But I walked a path that your people had already made. Wherever there was a Maryknoll missioner, I was welcomed, informed and encouraged. Sometimes I wrote about them, as in the chapter in *Cry of the People* about the Maryknoll nuns in Somoza's Nicaragua. But mostly I tried to convey your ideals, faith and courage as reflected in the struggle of the poor for justice and peace. Along the way I made many friendships with Maryknoll nuns, priests and lay people; enjoyed several stays at Maryknoll; and developed a lasting relationship with *Maryknoll* magazine and Orbis Books, which have published my work. As your people can attest, I have also defended the Maryknoll Sisters in dealings with the secular press, which is often unable to understand our commitment to the poor, and tried to be helpful whenever possible, as in my support for Judith Noone during her writing of *The Same Fate as the Poor*. I think of Maryknoll as my spiritual family. Maryknoll nuns are my heroines.

I have gone into so much background detail because it helps explain my desire to write about Maryknoll. It also indicates how I would handle the material: I do not want to write a sensational exposé but a work that will convert hearts through the examples of the Maryknoll Sisters.

2. An oral history by a sympathetic author who is known to Maryknoll and who considers herself a member of the family is a quite different proposition from an agreement with a publishing house to let an unknown author write such a book. Oral means spoken history, a recent example being Studs Terkel's book on work. My idea is for Maryknoll Sisters to tell the history of the congregation through the stories of their lives. I'm not suggesting a massively detailed study but the interweaving of charisms in a story from the heart to the heart "as told to Penny Lernoux"—much like an autobiography ghosted by a professional writer. My job would be to edit and focus the material, but the voices would be those of the Maryknoll Sisters. I see this as a cooperative effort in which I would be guided by your suggestions and advice, with a committee of Sisters to review the material. I would not use anything the committee objected to, nor would I use any material that would endanger the lives or work of your people, since protection of sources has been a lifelong rule for me. Editing of the final manuscript by Pantheon would be solely stylistic—adding a period or changing the order of a sentence, for example. I should add that Pantheon is one of the most reputable publishing houses in the United States.

The book would be about 200 pages, possibly with pictures, and would include interviews with several generations of Sisters, from the oldest to the youngest. Third World emphasis would be on Latin America, because of my own experience and a limited travel budget, but I would hope to interview sisters from other parts of the world who visit or live at Maryknoll or elsewhere in the United States. I would also rely on your personal histories, files and the *Maryknoll Magazine's* library, including tapes and videotapes.

3. The book would be a positive influence. As we all know, there is a negative knee-jerk reaction in certain quarters regarding Mary-

knoll nuns in Central America. I believe that is a minority opinion in the United States, as shown by my research for the book I have just finished on the church. Nevertheless, I think we could make a positive contribution by showing that the commitment made in Central America did not just suddenly occur but was the logical continuation of the prophetic vision of Mary Joseph Rogers and that small band of women who comprised the first missioner. Americans have no idea of the scope of that history, so they can't understand why Maryknoll nuns are on the cutting edge. I see a direct line between the heroic stories of your sisters in the Far East in earlier decades and those in Latin America in this decade. The role of the missionary may have been different because the times and needs were different, but the charisms were the same as those exhibited by your people today.

And what has the role of the religious order historically been if not to show the way—to prove, as Dom Helder Camara says, that roses bloom in the desert? As our prophets—our reverse missionaries—I think you have a special role to play in U.S. society. Instead of trying to avoid the limelight, which is impossible in any case, why not use it to convert people? Such would be the aim of the book. I know that other books have been written about Maryknoll, but they dealt primarily with the Maryknoll men and/or were written prior to Vatican II. I think the women are the prime pushers and movers and that you have a great deal to say to women and men in our country. Sr. Judith Noone's book was a moving story of martyrdom in Central America. I would like to enlarge the picture and, in the process, dispel the half truths and lies, not by confrontational tactics but by letting the Sisters' stories tell it as it really was. By seeing the whole tapestry, readers might better understand individual events and motives.

4. If such a project were approved, what would I ask from you?

a. Guidance and suggestions about how to proceed with the material.

b. Access to histories, files on same and any tapes and videotapes that would contribute to the oral history.

c. Letters of introduction and contacts with your regional governing boards in order to carry out possible interviews with individual Sisters, provided they agree to the interviews. Same for retired and active Sisters in the United States, where pertinent.

d. Establishment of a committee of Maryknoll Sisters to review my work.

I'm very grateful for any consideration you may give this project.

Attached are a summary of my past work and some sample articles. It would be a joyful service to write the book.

Penny Lernoux

Why did the Maryknoll Sisters Congregation agree to a collaborative effort with Penny Lernoux in the writing of this book? Long before any particular author was located, George Black first proposed the idea of interviewing eight to ten Maryknoll Sisters in Latin America for a book with Pantheon Books. The Sisters considered the project and declined. Our Congregation was still suffering from the uninformed negative publicity that had surfaced with the murders of the four churchwomen in El Salvador, two of whom were Maryknoll Sisters. But when Penny Lernoux not only expressed interest but also sent her proposal to the Maryknoll Sisters, something happened. Her proposal touched our hearts.

Sister Luise Ahrens, President of the Congregation at that time, expresses the reasons for the final acceptance of Penny's proposal in a letter written to the Maryknoll Sisters, February 25, 1988: "After some discussion about focus and content, we on the Central Governing Board feel privileged to have accepted the offer and will do all that we can to facilitate Penny's work. . . . We are honored to be asked to work with her on this project and look forward to close collaboration. . . . This book may well be a chance to speak of our reality and the reality of Third World peoples to an audience we could not otherwise reach." In a note posted on the bulletin board at the Sisters' Center two days earlier, Sister Luise had said, "Please give Penny all the support you can in this project that will serve both Maryknoll and the people to whom we have committed ourselves in mission."

And that is precisely why, even after Penny's unforeseen death, we Maryknoll Sisters continued to collaborate in the completion of this book.

Preface

Arthur Jones

∿

WHEN PENNY LERNOUX DIED in October 1989, she had written an eighty-thousand-word preliminary draft of the first five chapters and the introduction to this book. She had a thorough chapter outline prepared for the remaining eleven chapters. Her reporting and interviews were all completed and nearly all transcribed.

I stepped into the picture reluctantly. A group of Penny's friends and professional colleagues—her husband, Denis, her Maryknoll Sister friends, her agent, editor, publisher, and so on—wanted to see the book completed. I was by no means my own first choice and had suggested possible writers. When, after six months, it appeared there was difficulty in deciding on a writer, I faxed Denis in Bogota, Colombia, and offered my services. At the same time, Pantheon Books, who had originally contracted with Penny for the book, agreed to cede the project to Orbis Books, which, as the publishing arm of the Maryknoll Fathers and Brothers, appeared to be a natural home for the book.

The National Catholic Reporter and Penny Lernoux were a mutual adoration society, in the finest sense of that expression. As editor at the time, I had hired Penny. I edited her work as she made the transition from secular writing to primarily religion-based sociopolitical coverage, and assigned her the ten-part series that led to her second book. It was because I knew her as an editor as well as a friend that I offered to complete this volume; that and the fact that it was dedicated to her daughter, Angela, who deserved something uniquely meant for her.

I had several stipulations. The main three were that I not be paid, that my name not appear in or on the book, and that I not be out of pocket. I was prevailed upon to change the second stipulation when it was drummed home to me that unless my name appeared somewhere, there would be no explanation of how the book's completion had come about.

The National Catholic Reporter has borne some of my incidental expenses and conferred a particular blessing. This book was written in the evenings, on weekends, and during vacations. However, during two of the three summers, because the *NCR* is published only every second week for eight weeks, I was given the "off" weeks to work on the book, for which I am extremely grateful to both the editor, Tom Fox, and the publisher, Bill McSweeney.

The task itself was both easy and complex. Easy because everything was in place. Denis would mail up the box of Penny's notes for each chapter, and I would go to work. But some chapters had more than a million words of notes. Digesting the chapter material for the first rough draft was formidable. I knew what was in Penny's outline, but I didn't know what was in her head.

Two issues have to be dealt with in fairness to the reader. The first is, what was the involvement of the Maryknoll Sisters? The second, how much of the final two-thirds is Penny, and how much Arthur Jones, and how much Orbis Editor-in-Chief, Robert Ellsberg?

Penny had approached the Maryknoll Sisters and asked for their cooperation, fully and openly. She received it, along with access to their archival information and to Sisters willing to be interviewed. Penny wanted the Sisters to form a Sisters' Book Committee and to see the first draft of the book. The reason was quite simple. They would have no control over editorial direction, but they would be a tremendously helpful resource in facts, names, dates, spellings, and suggested nuance.

This was never intended as a "cozy" in-house title and has never been that type of book. Penny speaks for herself on these matters in the Introduction. A line in a March 14, 1989, letter to Penny from the then-Maryknoll President Sister Luise Ahrens, though it dealt with a specific topic, spoke to the whole enterprise: "We do not have control over your use of that material—you are writing the book."

The Sisters formally reviewed the Introduction and first five chapters before Penny's death and shared their observations with her. They have reviewed the first draft of the ten final chapters with me and Robert Ellsberg and shared their observations. The second and final draft of the concluding ten chapters is, however, Penny's and mine and Robert Ellsberg's. I submitted a second draft to Robert and he sat down with the book committee for review and completed the final draft. In the latter chapters particularly, the extent of Robert Ellsberg's contribution must not be underestimated, and it can rightly be said that the final draft is Lernoux, Jones, and Ellsberg. At the same time, the contributions of the two book committees deserve full recognition—the three drafts of the manuscript, mine completed at Easter 1992 and January 1993, and Robert's completed in August 1993, were read line-by-line by the book committee Sisters.

So, how much of chapters six to the end is Penny Lernoux? From the start, this book was unlike previous Penny Lernoux titles. She was usually so intense, so anxious to get the word out, that her books are moving, challenging, gripping, frightening, and insightful accounts of the immediate story and recent history. They are tight, frequently a relentless staccato of facts supporting each claim she makes.

Here the reader meets not Penny the front-line journalist, though there is more than a touch of that, but Penny the storyteller: more relaxed, insightful yes, but calm and reflective, reconciled perhaps, though never fully content.

Now for the acknowledgments. I apologize to any writer whose material is quoted without acknowledgment. Chapter twelve relies heavily on Maryknoll Sister Judith Noone's book, *The Same Fate as the Poor*. On Penny's behalf, thanks to all those who helped. I am certain Penny's listed acknowledgments, especially in the light of the enormous work undertaken by him after her death, would have begun with her husband, Denis Nahum. As the book is dedicated to Angela, I have nothing to add except that I did the best I could, Angela. To Penny's closest early supporters for this book that I know of, her agent, Charlotte Sheedy, her friend and the original editor for Pantheon, George Black, and others whose names I do not know, I can add my thanks to hers.

To Penny's extended family, most especially to her mother, Mrs. Beatrice Lernoux, whom I do not know, I am certain she would have extended thanks. This book deliberately touches on her faith, and one does not do that outside of family. And to the individual Sisters, the women of Maryknoll, Penny would have given not merely thanks but abrazos, hugs, and echoes of joy and laughter for the tears and intimacies, the friendships, and the constant flow of letters and mutual support. These are obviously too numerous to name. But some will be mentioned by the back door.

There were two Book Committees of Maryknoll Sisters on this project because there was a change in Maryknoll leadership in 1990 when the make-up of the Book Committee also changed. "Penny's" Book Committee was the hard-working team of Sisters Luise Ahrens, Dolores Rosso, Barbara Hendricks, Betty Ann Maheu, Marion Hughes, Camilla Kennedy, and Mary Bowes.

As far as I was concerned, I could not have completed this project without "my" book committee: Maryknoll Sisters Rose Marie Franklin, Sandy Galazin, Rose Guercio, Marion Hughes, Camilla Kennedy, Claudette LaVerdiere (current president), and Ms. Beth Yakel. They were as dedicated to the project as I was, and gave enormous time to it—helping me literally line by line, because I knew so little at the outset. To my everlasting good fortune, archivist Beth Yakel was undertaking the direction of the consolidated Maryknoll Mission Archives, a collaborative effort of the

Congregation and the Society. I also appreciate the assistance of Maryknoll Sister Margaret Mary Bradley when I first undertook the task, and Father Leo Sommer, M.M., who read the manuscript in its several drafts. All credit then to Penny's outline, her notes, and the two Book Committees.

My personal thanks are extended to Dawn Gibeau, through whom I first met Penny, to Tom Fox, editor, and to Bill McSweeney, publisher, all of *NCR*. To Denis, yes, and to all the Sisters who greeted me at Ossining during Holy Week, 1992. To Orbis Editor-in-Chief Robert Ellsberg, for seeing the project through to completion. To my wife, Margie, who had to put up with me writing yet another book.

Is it maudlin to thank Penny with whom, in effect, I have gone every step of this way? I think not. She was present, her photograph is always to my left on the narrow windowsill alongside where I work and where I balance my constant cup of tea. But I'll thank her in a telex, for old time's sake:

LERNOUX BOGOTA STOP MSS DONE STOP
ORBISWARDED STOP CONGRATS STOP JONES NCR

I have one regret, and it is that the book, in the final analysis, was not written by a woman. I do not mean in the selection of material. The regret has to do with the special insights of a woman writing about women. I think I did not inhibit or interfere with Penny's insights as a woman when I edited her *NCR* copy. I hope I haven't here.

I used no information from copies of personal letters to Penny from Sisters she interviewed, only the interview material. Although Robert interviewed a number of Sisters to round out the story, particularly in chapter fourteen, I did no reporting myself. I made a few telephone calls when I needed direct clarification on a point. And here is the exception to that statement. What joy Penny lived in doing this research around the world. What joy and hope she gave, as the letters show. So I feel obliged to quote, anonymously, from one Sister on behalf of the many: "Yes, my journey is often dark and lonesome and the God I experience is rarely kind and gentle. Then out of the blue, came someone special like you who made me feel understood and appreciated. I am so grateful that your book brought us together. I am sure we shall be friends for a long time to come . . . Do keep well."

But Penny did not keep well. She probably had cancer when that letter was written. Penny and the Maryknoll Sisters had become the closest of friends and family. And, with Denis and Angela, it was to the Maryknoll Sisters in Ossining that Penny went to die.

Through them, with them, and in them, she had come home. Home spiritually, home as a Catholic, home as an American, home as a woman. Safe, in death, among family and friends. And a writer to the end.

Introduction

~

THEY SAY ADVENTURE IS dead—that we've been everywhere and done everything. But our subconscious knows that's not true, else why do we dream of unknown lands, people, and experiences? Somewhere in that pantheon of dreams, the psychoanalysts tell us, lies the key to unexplored dimensions of life.

That adventure is still possible I know from researching this book, which is about the dream of a group of idealistic American women—the Maryknoll Sisters. Many saw themselves as the woman on horseback who would go forth to do battle with the forces of evil. But as in most myths—dreams—they discovered that the real objective of their often perilous journeys was not to change the world, or even a small portion of it, but to go beyond themselves and do something important in life. So my journey in search of these women was a dual adventure—to places that aren't on most maps and, in the psychic realm, to another dimension of life that is the source of inner peace and happiness even in the most difficult physical circumstances.

In our history books we read about the almost mythical pioneer American women who underwent incredible hardships and adventures in the opening of the country's frontiers. But these Maryknollers are flesh-and-blood pioneers—women who are still on the world's geographical frontiers while also moving toward new understandings of the human condition. Founded in 1912, they were the first congregation of *American* Catholic women to go abroad in mission, and I emphasize American rather than Catholic because their history reflects the "American Century" of economic, political, and religious expansion, and the traits that distinguish them—individuality, courage, generosity—are American characteristics. But these Maryknollers are different as well, because they stand outside the mainstream: Like others who seek a different dimension of life, they beckon us to that part of the American dream that does not depend on material success but is inspired by religious ideals.

That idealism is not dull but the stuff of adventure is shown by the Sisters' eventful lives in missions as diverse as Nepal and the Amazon. There are, of course, packaged tours even to such places, but tourists are unlikely to enter the real world of those far-away mountains and jungles—the world of the poor, the world's majority. How different the Maryknoll world is from that seen by most travelers forcibly struck me on the ninth hour of a roller-coaster ride over the Guatemalan mountains in a small, rickety bus, three passengers packed into a space meant for one. At the tenth hour, during a turning in the dirt road, I glimpsed my objective across the mountains—a small Mayan village where a group of Maryknoll Sisters live and that was only another hour away. "From a distance it looks like Shangri-la," a Sister had told me before I embarked on the journey. I guess it did look magical, but at that point all I cared about was getting there.

Close up, the village of Jacaltenango could be any poor Indian town in the Guatemalan highlands, except that one side of the plaza is bordered by a hospital with flowering gardens. The fifty-bed hospital was constructed in the early 1960s through the efforts of a Maryknoll Sister medical team and fifteen hundred Indians, who carried the building materials and hospital equipment over the mountains. In those days there were no roads in the region, and to get to Jacaltenango from the nearest city meant a six-hour mule ride. Prior to the Sisters' arrival, women had routinely died in childbirth, and whooping cough, measles, and other diseases had frequently decimated the population. Desperate for a hospital to serve the surrounding region, the Jacaltecos had beseeched the Maryknoll Sisters' superior to give them a Sister-doctor when she visited the town in 1959. One thousand Indians had affixed their thumbprints to the petition, and they were among those who spent thousands of grueling hours hauling materials and equipment on their backs to build the hospital.

But all I knew when I got off that bus was that every bone in my body ached. At the age of forty-eight, I asked myself, what am I doing spending eleven hours in a junk heap to get to this forsaken village? Such thoughts were soon banished, however, on meeting the town's original Sister-doctor. "Rosie," as everyone calls her, is a vigorous seventy, and the other sisters, my age or older, are even more energetic. Travel is so easy now, they say. Just imagine what it was like when we had to go by mule. One Sister tells me she enjoys spending ten hours a day on horseback visiting outlying villages. Maybe it's the mountain air or the simplicity of the lifestyle, or the Sisters' obvious sense of fulfillment—whatever, there is a Shangri-la quality about life in this remote place.

Jacaltenango turned out to be one of the more luxurious places I visited—the Sisters actually had a hot shower, even if the water only came out in drips. I thought of it while standing inside a tiny mud enclosure on the arid Yucatan Peninsula, the black sky above me, taking a "shower" from a small hand bucket while keeping an eye out for a large rat that fancied the soap in my hand. Again the question, this time more plaintive: What am I doing here? Me, middle-class American, used to comfortable hotels, flush toilets—there's a mud hole next to the shower that serves as a toilet—and who hates rats, snakes, flying cockroaches and the other nasties that inhabit this place.

One obvious reason was to hear the stories of two Maryknoll Sisters who live there. But the real impetus was curiosity. During the early 1980s, when the Guatemalan military had adopted a scorched-earth policy to put down a guerrilla rebellion, nearly two hundred thousand Indian peasants had fled across the northern border to Mexico. I had heard about the people's terrible sufferings, but it was only at the refugee camp at Quetzal Edzna in southeastern Mexico that I was able to put faces on the statistics. Many refugees were still traumatized by their violent experiences in Guatemala—the military frequently massacred whole villages—and all showed signs of weariness. Forced to abandon their homes in Guatemala, they established new communities in Chiapas in southern Mexico, only to be relocated by the Mexican government to the barren plains of the Yucatan Peninsula. The uprooting meant rebuilding homes for a third or fourth time with almost no resources.

At Quetzal Edzna, where five thousand people subsist, everyone, including the Sisters, lives in two-room stick houses with asphalt roofs. The tiny houses are jammed one against the other, so that anyone who coughs in one can be heard in the next. The mud-baked gardens are too small for extensive planting, and water, which must be carried in buckets from communal faucets, is rationed. There is no electricity, and communal latrines are several blocks distant from the houses. The men work in fields lent to the refugees by the Mexican government. But because of the lack of water and insect plagues, bean and corn crops often fail, and it is difficult or impossible to grow fruits and vegetables. In the months before I arrived, eight refugees, mostly young men, had killed themselves by drinking pesticides.

The Sisters aid the refugees through community projects, such as a nutritional program for the children and the weaving of hammocks, the sale of which brings in a little money from England and the United States. But they are there primarily to accompany—to show the refugees they are not entirely forsaken and to help provide religious services that give the people hope as well as consolation. What do the Sisters get out of it? Nothing in a material sense. But it is clear from the way the people greet them that they have earned the community's love. That, and knowing they can be of some small help, make the heat, rats, and lack of water seem small inconveniences. One of the Sisters had previously worked in an upper-class girls' school in the city of Mérida, a four-hour drive from the camp. Mérida is a lively town with well-stocked shops, lush gardens, and, in the wealthy areas, a swimming pool in every backyard. But Sister Mary had hated her lifestyle there, which seemed meaningless and restricted by the social ambitions of the rich. The two-room stick house in Quetzal Edzna is certainly restrictive—two people have trouble not bumping into each other. Yet Mary feels free because she is able to help the truly needy. "The refugees are my friends and family," she explained, "and their way of bearing suffering, their prayers and celebrations have given meaning to my being. I remember, when I was fifteen and thinking about Maryknoll, I had this strong conviction about the shortness of a life span and the need to do more than gather things around me. I didn't know it would be the opposite: Instead of giving, I've received."

Three months and several thousand miles later, I was on a tour of Manila, capital of the Philippines. The first part was your ordinary packaged deal—sort of—in which the Sisters took me around the city's colonial section and the wealthy residential areas. I was particularly interested in Fort Santiago, a Spanish colonial fortress on the Pasig River, because a Maryknoll Sister had been imprisoned and tortured there during World War II. The well-to-do neighborhoods are sealed off by barbed wire, and there is a guard at each entrance. "Do you have a camera?" one asked before waving us through. I lied. "Why no cameras?" I asked the Sisters. "Because too many foreign journalists have taken pictures of these wealthy mansions and then published them next to photos of the slums."

I could understand the rich Filipinos' dislike of such comparisons when, in the next stage of the tour, I found myself on a mountain of garbage. We were at Smokey Mountain, the Manila garbage dump, where several thousand people live. They survive by picking over the newest layer of garbage thrown on these man-made mountains that have grown up beside the Pasig. The view of the river is breathtaking; the stench, incredible. Shacks built from scavengings cling precariously to the sides of the hills, below which are swamps of oozing garbage. Halfway over the second mountain, as we were passing a swamp, my companion said sharply, "Watch where you step, or you'll fall into the garbage." A previous visitor had done just that and was up to his neck in filth before being pulled out. Freed of the slime, he turned heel and was never seen again. I could understand his feelings. The Sisters come here often, but what am I doing here? I don't need the smell, the muck, the misery. I just want to get out, to somewhere that's air-conditioned and comfortable (of which there is no hope, because I'm staying with Maryknoll Sisters).

It's all in the mind, of course. If you stop worrying about the discomforts, you begin to experience the good things, like the hospitable Filipinos who invite you into their homes and joke about the garbage outside the window. But I didn't discover that until I went to the Bolivian Amazon, again in search of Maryknoll Sisters. Headwaters of the Amazon river basin, the northern Bolivian regions of the Beni and the Pando are still large-ly untouched by the voracious settlement schemes that have destroyed much of the Brazilian Amazon. But when I boarded a Bolivian air force plane in La Paz for the three-hour flight to the Beni, I didn't see anything romantic in the trip. It had been freezing cold at the 12,500-foot-high air-port in La Paz, and when I stepped off the plane in Riberalta on the banks of the Beni River, I staggered physically from the jungle heat—it seemed as if the whole sky were pressing downward. The Sisters immediately took me on a tour of the local sights, starting with a wild rubber factory where peas-ants from outlying jungle settlements bring huge balls of wild rubber formed after days of cooking the tree latex over a wood fire. Frankly, I didn't pay much attention to the foreman's explanation of the process be-cause I was overwhelmed by the smell of burnt rubber and the sweat pour-ing off me. Down the red dirt road was another factory, this one for crack-ing and sorting Brazil nuts harvested by the jungle settlements. We made our way through hills of unshelled nuts to a huge shed where more than a hundred women were cracking and sorting nuts, their kids milling about. For fifteen hours a day of this boring, grinding labor in the hot, overcrowd-ed shed, the women received less than $2. Still, they considered themselves lucky to have jobs, and at least the children could eat the broken nuts on the floor, which may not have been sanitary but at least were nourishing.

When at last we trudged back to the Sisters' small house, and I was given a cold drink (they had a refrigerator!) and a rocking chair, and the sweat began to congeal, I noticed that, in addition to the mud all over my pants, there were swarms of small black insects. "Those are just fleas," shrugged Ann Catherine Ryan. Fleas! "What will my husband say?" I wailed. "We've just spent two months trying to get rid of our dog's fleas. The expense—we sent out all the carpets—and now I bring back Bolivian fleas! What am I going to do?"

Ann Catherine, a lanky Sister in her early seventies who can remember what it was like to wear a nun's full habit in the awful heat, stopped her rock-ing chair, drew, herself up to her considerable height, and gave me an impe-rious stare. "What are you going to do?" The rocking resumed. "Suffer!"

And we burst into laughter. As if by magic, the fleas ceased to be impor-tant, I stopped worrying about the heat, and I discovered I was having a good time. Ann Catherine had said something that was obvious: I was so preoccupied with my middle-class hang-ups that I was missing the beauty and adventure of the place. Here I was on the edge of a two-thousand-mile chain of rivers and lakes, where orchids, parrots, and monkeys are not plas-tic but real; where the sunsets fill the sky with purple and orange flame; and where the "folks," as the Sisters call the peasants, are overwhelmingly hos-pitable and kind—and I'm worrying about a few fleas. Later, when I was sitting on Riberalta's plaza with Phyllis Martin, a Maryknoll Associate Sister and a member of Ann Catherine's community, and we were watching the teenagers motorcycle round and round the park, in a jungle version of the Spanish promenade, I wondered what it would be like to travel those rivers with the Sisters. The Maryknollers have houseboats on which they spend weeks on the rivers and lakes, helping people in remote settlements organize authentic Christian communities. The life is hard. The Sisters sleep in hammocks or on the ground and eat whatever is available in the communities, which usually is very little—perhaps some rice, a bit of fruit, and occasionally smoked meat. Poisonous snakes are common, malaria is rampant, river rapids are lethal, and trees can come crashing down on unsuspecting travelers. Yet imagine yourself steering the houseboat, said Phyllis, through the pages of the *National Geographic,* exploring fifty-three thousand square miles of tropical rain forests that are almost entirely as they were centuries ago. Imagine being with people, she said, who have nothing but will give you their last cup of rice.

I left Riberalta with a different perspective. I wished I could have stayed—the Sisters were going on a three-week trip to the Madidi River in the jungles of north-central Bolivia. Now that I had talked with those who had been there, the turquoise lakes I glimpsed from the airplane took on a romantic aura. I guessed there were fleas there, too, but because of Ann Catherine's insight, I no longer cared. I think, too, I captured something of the Maryknoll myth. The late Joseph Campbell, the noted expert on mythology, said that all adventure stories about the discovery of a hidden world are marked by the appearance of a herald, "the loathly, underestimated carrier of the power of destiny"—for instance, the frog king in the fairy tale about a lovely princess. The herald "represents the repressed instinctual fecundity within ourselves." The joyousness of Ann Catherine and the other Maryknoll Sisters I met in my travels around the world comes, I believe, from the discovery of the herald—in the poor, tattered Bolivian peasants along the distant jungle rivers, the Filipinos on top of a mountain of garbage, or Guatemalan Indians marooned on a desert peninsula. In giving to the poor, the Maryknollers received in return, and because of the uncluttered lives of the poor, who have few material possession to distract them, it was clear what the Sisters were getting—love without any strings attached. Through that gift they gradually realized that saving souls for a particular church was not what the Reign of God was about, but finding God in themselves and in others and, in so doing, becoming more human.

∼

That, too, was the reason they went to China, although the Sisters could not have known in the early 1900s that the "pagans," as Americans called the Chinese, embodied the herald. At the time, Americans saw themselves as the "chosen people," the Israel of the century that would "bear the ark of the liberties of the world." They had "won the West," and the last frontiers of Indian territory would soon become states. Society still basked in the glow of the "Gilded Age"—nothing seemed beyond the grasp of the young nation. Missionary fever was at a high pitch—the religious element in Americans' sense of "Manifest Destiny." "As goes America," wrote one Protestant missionary leader, "so goes the world, in all that is vital to its mortal welfare." Symbolic of the faith in the "imperialism of righteousness" was President William McKinley, who headed the country at the time of the Spanish-American War in 1898, when the United States made its debut as a world power by annexing Puerto Rico, Guam, and the Philippines. A fervent Methodist, McKinley told a group of missionaries that his decision to retain the Philippines had only come after much soul-searching.

I walked the floor of the White House night after night until midnight; and I am not ashamed to tell you, gentlemen, that I went down on my knees and prayed to Almighty God for light and guidance more than one night. And one night late it came to me this way—I don't know how it was, but it came: . . . that there was nothing left for us to do but to take them all, and to educate the Filipinos, and uplift and civilize and Christianize them, and by God's grace do the very best we could by them, as our fellowmen for whom Christ died.

To the modern ear, McKinley's piety sounds uncomfortably simplistic, but at the time many Americans really believed they had a divine mandate to save the world and "take up the white man's burden," as Rudyard Kipling urged. "Civilizing the natives" was not only God's work, of course, since it also aided the expanding political and economic interests of the United States. In annexing the Philippines, for example, McKinley gained a bridge to China; in the same period, Secretary of State John Hay proclaimed his famous "Open Door Policy" for China. A year later, in 1900, American troops were sent to China to help end the Boxer Rebellion, which had targeted foreign Christian missions, among other symbols of foreign interference.

Although the Protestants took the lead in sending thousands of missionaries to the "darkened Orient," Catholics began to catch up in the second decade of the 1900s, following the founding at Ossining, N.Y., of the Maryknoll Society, which was designated the country's Catholic missionary organization by the American bishops. Early Maryknoll supporters, such as Cardinal James Gibbons, saw the fledgling organization as a means to compete with the zeal of "the Protestant brethren." "The prestige of our country has become widespread," Gibbons wrote, "and Protestants, especially in the Far East, are profiting by it, to the positive hindrance of Catholic missioners."

As shown by the cardinal's remarks, the delay in catching up with the brethren was not due to any hesitancy about taking up the white man's burden but, rather, to American Catholicism's internal problems. Still largely a poor, immigrant institution, the American Catholic Church had been overwhelmed by new waves of European immigrants at the turn of the century, and it was not until 1908 that the United States was officially removed from the Vatican's list of mission territories. The Maryknoll Fathers and Brothers were founded a mere three years later, to be followed, almost immediately, in early 1912, by the group of women who were to become the Maryknoll Sisters. Although Catholics were viewed with suspicion by Anglo-Saxon Protestants, their immigrant status made them more American than the Americans. As one early Maryknoll missioner wrote:

> The world is looking to America for leadership. Asia particularly hangs on our words with flattering attention. Asia is all eagerness to learn our mechanics, to wear our clothes . . . and to dance to our music. How much more important for them if they could learn to know and love our God!

While Americans may have been confident of a divine mandate, Rome was not. The Vatican had been appalled by the upstart's easy victory over Catholic Spain in the war of 1898 and was not at all happy about U.S. control of the supposedly Catholic Philippines. Then as now, certain Roman authorities assumed that the streets of American cities were paved with gold. Such luxury-loving people were too soft to make zealous missionaries, the Curia believed, although the Vatican was prepared to allow a few Maryknoll priests to prove themselves in China. Maryknoll women, on the other hand, should stay home and stick to their female duties—cooking, cleaning, and sewing for the men while the latter prepared for missionary work in China. The prejudice against women was not limited to Catholics but reflected the belief at the time that women's place was in the home. "I cannot recommend bringing women into this work," said the foreign secretary of the American Board of Protestant Missions. Even after Protestant women forced the men to recognize them by forming their own mission societies, they were still regarded as second-class citizens, and after 1910, when most women's agencies were merged into general denominational boards, they were dominated by men. The prevailing sentiment, expressed by the secretary of the American Baptist Missionary Union, was that "woman's work in the foreign field must be careful to recognize the headship of man in ordering the affairs of the Kingdom of God."

Mary (Mollie) Josephine Rogers, the founder of the Maryknoll Sisters, never doubted the headship of the Fathers in mission work, but she was determined that the Sisters not be permanently relegated to the role of domestic helpmates in the United States. After four frustrating years of repeated petitions, the Vatican (Congregation for Religious) gave approval for the Maryknoll Sisters to be established as a missionary Congregation (or Institute) under the Archdiocese of New York. A year later, in 1921, the first group of Maryknoll women set out for China.

Two things soon became clear. One was that, contrary to Rome's misgivings, the Americans were often better suited for such work than European Sisters in China, because the latter were hemmed in by Old World traditions that prevented any but formal contact with the Chinese. More open and adaptable, the Maryknoll women had no qualms about going out to live in Chinese villages, away from convent and the protection of priests—much to the horror of their European Sisters. The second was that, because they were women, these Maryknoll women were welcomed into Chinese homes, whereas the men were prevented from such contact by strict Chinese customs. In 1923, when Mollie Rogers, then Mother Mary Joseph, visited China, she was instantly accepted by the peasants despite her foreign religious garb, white skin, and inability to speak the language. A large woman with a ready smile, she "saw China from the inside of kitchens and the interior of the family quarters, cooed in unison with babies and smiled her way into the hearts of women folk," a Maryknoll priest wrote. "She saw family life as we cannot see it, women smiling without restraint and unbashful girls that are not 'flappers.' The women guiding boats or doing coolie's work would chat with her unreservedly, fully confident that she could divine their thoughts."

An uncomplicated American-Irish girl whose warmth attracted trust, Mollie conveyed the same undemanding love shown decades later by Mary at the Guatemalan refugee camp and Ann Catherine in the Bolivian jungle. And it was that quality that opened homes and hearts. As a Chinese teacher told one Sister, "It will not matter to us if you don't understand our customs, religion or way of doing things. What will matter is your friendship and love for us."

It was largely an illusion, of course. Although individual Chinese loved the Sisters, and some were even willing to die for them, Maryknoll had as much impact on China as did American Protestant missionaries—almost none. The idea that a few thousand American missionaries could convert a four-thousand-year-old civilization with hundreds of millions of people reflected the romantic beliefs of a society that assumed the "heathen" needed, or wanted, the Americans' religion. "It was like two ships passing in the night," remarked a Chinese Sister of the American missionaries' experience in her country: Neither understood the motivations, history, or cultural differences of the other. Perhaps most ironic, Americans were both attracted by the romance of the Orient and repelled by its appearance in their own country. Although large-scale Chinese immigration was encouraged in the mid-1800s, when contract laborers laid the tracks of America's first transcontinental railroad, the Chinese subsequently became the scapegoat for a declining economy. Deprived of basic civil rights, massacred in anti-Chinese riots, and confined to Chinatown ghettos, they suffered the ultimate humiliation when, in 1882, the U.S. government for the first and only time in its history passed legislation forbidding the entry of an entire ethnic group into the country. The exclusion acts were not repealed until after World War II. Yet at the same time, the American people were generally supportive of mission efforts in China, as shown by the huge outpouring of funds for U.S. missionary efforts there, the interest in Chinese culture, and Hay's Open Door Policy, which attempted to shore up the disintegrating Chinese empire by preventing further partition by Europe and Japan.

Even though Washington sent troops to help put down the Boxer Rebellion, Hay tried to limit the objective by telling the European powers that the United States aimed "to preserve Chinese territorial and administrative entity [integrity]"—a phrase that became a cornerstone in U.S. policy toward China. As pointed out by American historians, the Open Door Policy was not disinterested, being a device to prevent other powers, such as Russia, from absorbing Chinese territory. It also reflected a patronizing attitude toward a weaker nation—Hay thought he had "done the Chinks a great service." Still, China's independence corresponded to deep-rooted American feelings about self-determination. Similarly, American missionary efforts in China may now seem unrealistic and romantic, but we have the advantage of hindsight—most of those who left home and country were motivated by idealism. That the idealism was overlaid with Western culture and false beliefs about paganism does not obscure the principal driving force—"the love which Christ feels for us, the love which he placed in us, the love which is life," as one missioner wrote. Maryknoll Bishop James E. Walsh, who served many years in China and was later imprisoned there, described the discovery of such feelings in a Chinese rice field:

> "I choose you," sang in my heart as I looked at my awkward farmer boy, perfect picture of the underprivileged soul . . . the overworked and overlooked, the forgotten and despised . . . I choose you and dedicate myself to you and I ask no other privilege but to devote the energies of my soul to such as you . . . Shine on, farmer boy, symbol to me of the thousand million like you who drew the Son of God from heaven to smooth and bless your weary anxieties and puzzled brows . . . Teach me that souls are people. And remind me everlastingly that they are magnificent people like you.

The Maryknoll Sisters felt the same love for the Chinese poor. The pioneer women knew nothing about the country's history or political conditions, and they learned the language and customs on the job. There was no training in "inculturation." One Sister recalled how, while still at headquarters in New York, she practiced drinking tea; another tried to learn Cantonese (neither, it turned out, went to China). However naive, the desire to share God's love was real. The products of large middle- and working-class families in which love held a higher priority than material possessions, they wanted to give what they had received. They didn't have grand expectations of massive conversions. Most hoped to save Chinese babies, especially girls, who were routinely abandoned in ditches and on streets, often naked in a paper bag and suffering from smallpox or some other disease. The tragedy was not imagined. "Babies would be left on our doorstep," remembered Sister Monica Marie Boyle, an early pioneer. "I'm a nurse, and I had to do something about them. I paid more attention to taking care of babies than learning the language. I even smuggled a couple to bed with me to give them medication. My heart would break because so many died."

The stories of such sufferings were vividly depicted in *The Field Afar*, later renamed *Maryknoll* magazine. The "saving of Chinese babies" was the most prominent theme, and Americans responded overwhelmingly: Mite boxes containing nickels and pennies to "buy" a Chinese baby from starvation and death became a standard item in Catholic schools and churches. And Maryknoll was soon flooded with applications from young women. Typical of these earnest Americans was the young aspirant who, on arriving at the Maryknoll Motherhouse in New York, announced to the startled Sister who opened the door, "I've come to go to China."

Most were in their late teens and early twenties; few had professional degrees. Had they not joined Maryknoll, they probably would have become part of the generation of Catholic families that climbed the social ladder and migrated to the suburbs. That Maryknoll was a way out of an unhappy home, or the answer to a lack of suitors, may have been true for a few, but many were remarkably handsome girls, and most came from loving families. The religious life was not the drawing card but mission work in China, particularly saving girl babies. In those days there was no Peace Corps or lay missionary group, so if a young Catholic woman wanted to become a missionary, she joined a religious order. Few who entered Maryknoll had traveled beyond their own towns; they thirsted for a different experience, for a chance "to make a contribution to the world." Television and jet travel were in the future, and there was considerable attraction in sailing across the world to the mysterious Orient. Some women joined because they pictured themselves riding horses across the backlands of China in a crusade for God. Although most who went to China had to walk from village to village, and life in the impoverished countryside was stark, they never lost the call to adventure—the feeling that they were on new frontiers—or a sense of joy: We are "gloriously happy," reads the entry in an early diary. They saved countless Chinese lives, comforted the sick, and fed the hungry, converted a few "pagans," and were loved. The last was the most important, because it taught the women the secret of the China myth: "*They* do not need Sisters here," admitted a Maryknoll diarist in Manchuria, "but maybe *we* need them." Such, too, was the discovery of their successors in Guatemala, the Philippines, Bolivia, and elsewhere, who found that the third-world poor were the heralds of a new dimension in their own lives. Although the pioneer Maryknoll women could not have articulated it, they had become missioners, said Barbara Hendricks, former president of the Maryknoll Sisters, because of "a desire, a compulsion, to search for the 'other'—someone else who needs you. China was the symbol of the completely other—the one who lives at the other end of the world. But it is only through that other person that you find out who you really are. In the end you are searching for another dimension of yourself."

The search was heroic precisely because it was mythical—it did not depend on quantifiable facts and figures but on a faith that transcended the rational and that conveyed the Good News that God is love. Despite the many changes that have occurred since those early mission days, mission life remains heroic, not because of the places or conditions in which Maryknollers live—all of us are capable of putting up with mud, heat, even fleas—but because it depends on faith. In a world in which the secular state predominates, rendering life spiritually significant is an audacious undertaking. "Most people suppose a different challenge," observed Maryknoller Anastasia Lott, who works with poor people in a remote region of Kenya. "Foreign languages, living conditions, dangers, violence—those difficulties exist. But what's really heroic is the willingness to keep coming together to reconstruct a vision of God's love for all of us when faced over and over again with our own failures and loss of hope."

~ 1 ~

Revolution in China

═══════════════════════════════════

Because a draft blew through a crack in the bathroom door, the paper had dried and crinkled. I figured if we removed it carefully enough, perhaps we could break in to get some supplies. It felt like a daring adventure to rob your own house, but each time I went to the bathroom, I gave the paper a little tug. Finally came the day for the robbery. Paulita was always making things, and she was to be at the entrance to the convent singing and hammering and warn me through a code if anyone came. I had to put the paper back with egg white. The Communists were in the rooms next door, and there were only supposed to be rats in that part of the house. So I tiptoed in—the boards creaked—and got more kerosene for the lamps, tea, canned meat, peas and a can of cheese. I could have taken more but was afraid. We got rid of the cans by throwing them into the chimney of the smoke house at the entrance to the compound.

IT WAS EARLY 1951, and Edith Rietz and Paulita Hoffmann were slowly starving in the enforced confinement of their South China house. Most of the convent had been sealed off by the Chinese Communists when they had placed the Maryknoll Sisters under house arrest. Although it would have been an easy matter to tear off the tissue seals, which had been pasted on with egg white, neighbors had been executed for less. Still suffering from the trauma of a violent public trial, the women were not about to anger their captors by removing even a shred of paper. Well, not so they'd notice. The Communists had taken all the Sisters' money, and the women's eight-cent daily allowance for food and fuel was insufficient to feed Paulita, much less her tall, young companion. Edith knew that on the other side of the bathroom door was a stock of canned food hidden beneath the floor boards. All that barred the way was that tissue seal on the door.

Edith, who was to raid the secret food stores on several occasions, also proved ingenious in inventing distractions during the tense, thirteen-month-long siege—they had nothing to read, neither newspapers nor letters, and their only contact with the outside world was through a neighbor who brought their small allotment of food. Long hours were spent playing pool after Edith made a pool table out of a bed mat, with chopsticks for cues and marbles for balls. "We were forbidden by the bishop to play cards. Well, forget it, we're under house arrest. So I made a deck of cards out of holy cards." On another occasion, while staring at the linoleum floor, Edith wondered, "What's under this?" "Newspapers," replied Paulita. "Newspapers! We tore up the linoleum and got them and reread the old newspapers and played the crossword puzzles."

The need to keep their minds off the awful things happening around them drove the pair to a variety of tasks—at one point Edith made a bread oven out of a large tin can; Paulita was engaged in growing bean sprouts in a hidden box. Since the public trial that January, Edith's nerves had been stretched to the breaking point. Her whole body had broken out in pus, and try as she might, she could not pray. "The only time I felt a relief from the tension was at sunset, when I went out to our little porch and listened to the sound of a Chinese flute that drifted over the rice paddies. To listen to the flute was prayer—God is in this somewhere." Several times she thought she was going to die, either of the strange illness that had attacked her body or in the dawn executions that occurred almost daily. Twenty-nine and unsophisticated, the young Chicagoan had been in China less than three years, knew only a smattering of the language, and was much less self-confident than the older Paulita, who sang her way through any ordeal, even the prospect of martyrdom by the "Reds." Paulita was worried, but Edith was physically afraid. What saved her during the seemingly endless confinement and constant insults and threats was a cheeky sense of humor. Though scared, she enjoyed the joke of the tissue paper, and the Chinese guards were never the wiser.

The ability to laugh even in the most awful circumstances is a Maryknoll trait, and it helped the Sisters survive one of the most turbulent periods in their history, when they were uprooted from China—which had been Maryknoll's *raison d'être*—and where, through thirty years of war, starvation, floods, and epidemics, they had lived and loved.

Storm clouds had been gathering since 1947, when Mao Tse-tung's forces began to expand their control from Manchuria on the Russian border to the imperial city of Peking, which they reached the following year. Even then, the Maryknollers did not believe the Communists would seize all China, and those in the South, where most of the missioners were concentrated, carried on a normal life. Faced with a fait accompli in 1949, they still held to the conviction that they would be able to continue their mission work. The illusion was fostered by the initially circumspect behavior of the soldiers of the People's Liberation Army and the lack of harassment—save for brief questioning and a house search at the time of the takeover, the Maryknollers were left in peace. But the atmosphere changed markedly after mid-1950 and the start of the Korean War, which pitted China and North Korea against the United States and South Korea. The

Chinese Communists were already hostile to Americans because of U.S. support for the ill-fated Nationalist regime of Chiang Kai-shek—a support publicly endorsed by the Maryknoll bishop in South China, Francis X. Ford. Because of the Vatican's official condemnation of Communism and the church's identification with Chiang Kai-shek, Maryknollers were doubly suspect. Between October 1950, and January 1951, almost half of the ninety-nine Maryknoll priests and Brothers and the thirty-eight Sisters in South China were placed under house arrest on suspicion of being American spies. Some Sisters were jailed, and a few, such as Edith and Paulita, endured public trials.

The two women lived in the village of Hingning, two hundred miles inland from the South China Sea, in an undeveloped rural area where poverty and ignorance were widespread. Like the other Sisters in the region, they spent their days walking to and from villages, giving religion classes and sharing the people's simple lifestyle. Often, they spent the night in a peasant hut, sleeping under the family's single quilt. The beds were thin boards without mattresses, a bucket at the foot for a toilet. During the winter months the weather was bitterly cold; in the summer the Sisters sweltered in the humidity, the hat pins in their bonnets rusted, and they suffered from prickly heat. "We had to wash those crazy religious habits," Edith grimaced—full-length robes with capes, high white collars, bonnets, and veils. "You were so hot, and by the time you finished washing the habit, you were soaking wet and ready to wash the one you were wearing." There was no electricity. Ice cubes were unknown, and all water was hauled from wells. Like the local people, the Sisters took bucket baths at sundown. For Edith the evenings were the best time, the people crowded around a kerosene lamp, listening to stories from the Bible. "We would say night prayers in Hakka [the local dialect], and the Chinese would roll with laughter at our pronunciation. People had sores, indicating malnutrition, and you saw a lot of babies with boils on their heads and children with extended bellies. The women wore trousers and a shirt, and they were real patched. Yet they were so generous. The villagers always gave us eggs, rice, cakes, chickens."

Although life was Spartan, the young Sister gave little thought to the discomforts—"you just accepted them." "Edi," as her family called her, had been brought up in Chicago during the Depression, and the experience made her undemanding of luxuries. The Rietz family had eight children, and sometimes they barely had enough to eat. Her father was a policeman who worked nights in the family basement carving intricate doll houses to sell at Christmas time in order to buy presents for his own children. To make ends meet, he mended all the family's shoes. Edith's mother earned money by making bouquets of wax flowers in the family's small dining room. Her father didn't want her to enter Maryknoll, but when he saw Edith in the missioners' gray habit, he admonished her, "You're in a habit now. You behave like a lady!" Father knew daughter: Edith had a look in those blue eyes that promised mischief, and there was a determined tilt to the chin—a "rarin' to go," as she'd say. But she was a worrier, too, and during World War II, when four brothers were in the army, Edith worried herself to skin and bones. She was still thin as a rail when she embarked for China in 1948, and a strenuous life of hours on the road, tramping through rice paddies and over dirt roads, did not add any flesh to the tall frame. Still, she got enough to eat, even if it was strange food, and though there were bandits in the area and Nationalist troops were frequently seen in the villages, Edith paid little heed, living for and enjoying each day.

Into this stark but placid existence burst a political hurricane that upended the Sisters' rural world. From being objects of curiosity or hospitality, they were suddenly the butt of scorn and hatred as President Truman's supposedly hand-picked spies. Although many peasants remained loyal to the Sisters, those who showed sympathy were likely to be arrested, tortured, and shot.

In November 1950, the Sisters were confined to their convent in Hingning's small church compound; the Chinese priest, Father Aloisius Au, was arrested. During the first weeks of their confinement, crowds of hostile Chinese invaded the women's quarters, examining every stick of furniture and ridiculing the Maryknollers as "American dogs." But other Chinese felt the Sisters and priests were unfairly treated. Among them was an elderly, impoverished woman who lived next door to the Maryknollers and kept them informed of what was happening in the village. Thus they knew there would be a public trial, and as the event approached they could hear the villagers rehearsing in the church. "We knew our bonnets and veils would be torn from us," recounted Edith, "and in an effort to keep some vestige of dignity I put up my hair the night before." At 10 A.M. on a cold January Sunday, Father Au, preceded by a clamor of drums and cymbals, was led past the convent in soiled flannel pajamas stained in front with large blotches of ink. Ropes were tied around his neck, arms, and body, and he was escorted by policemen with drawn revolvers. Edith and Paulita were ordered to fall into line, and during the half-mile walk to the open trial site they were stoned by a jeering crowd. At a prearranged signal a woman behind Paulita yanked off her veil. "I turned quickly and picked it up from the dirt just before the guard's heavy boot trampled it, said Paulita. "This was an unexpected move on my part, and they didn't know what to do next. Edith took hers off at the same time."

At last the group reached a public ball court where a dais had been erected. The Sisters were told to sit on one side, but the priest was forced to stand. For six hours under a blazing sun he was accused of dozens of sins, all fabricated, including sexual relations with the Sisters. When Chinese Catholics tried to defend the priest, they were arrested on the spot—by the end of the trial twenty were in prison. Pushed and slapped, Au eventually gave up trying to respond. "Death, death, death," chanted the crowd to a crescendo of cymbals and drums.

Edith, who could not understand what was being said and was faint from the sun and noise, was eventually led away with Paulita to the local prison, where they were told to wait. Mesmerized by a grim-looking official who watched their every movement, Edith was convinced they were about to be hung or shot in what she took to be the execution room.

Eventually, the Sisters were marched back to the convent, but Au, who had been sentenced to hard labor, was taken to the church, which had been converted to a prison. Day and night the Sisters heard the screams of people being beaten and tortured there. Edith broke out in a fever, her body covered in pus. A doctor was finally found, but he was so frightened by the armed guard hovering over her bed that he trembled throughout the examination. Edith survived, but with physical scars she would carry all her life. She had suffered sun poisoning to the bone, which had been aggravated by the emotional strain. "It was all mixed up, the physical and emotional, and it came out in festering sores."

Indomitable Paulita, who was herself suffering from a hemorrhoid and needed surgery, talked and sang and sang and talked, until Edith could stand it no longer. "My stomach kept getting tighter and tighter, and I thought something's going to burst, I've got to tell her to stop. How can I tell her? What will I say? I don't remember where we were. I can only remember saying, 'Sister Paulita, could you not sing any more because it makes me sick.' That's what came out after thinking for days about the best way to say it. It came out like a telegram: Stop! It was really tragic. Her face fell as though I had insulted her, and she walked away. I went to my room and cried. What did I do? Fortunately—I don't know how long I was kneeling there—she came, and that was enough. When she saw me on my knees, she forgave all."

Paulita's singing notwithstanding, Edith was fond of the short, energetic Sister. Each woman kept a small "runaway bag," with tennis shoes, toothbrush, and a few other items, in case they were suddenly taken away. Edith was upstairs in the convent when she heard the arrival of yet another government interrogator, and she didn't like the sound of the soldier's harassment of Paulita. Donning the tennis shoes—"I don't know what possessed me"—she rushed to the rescue, tripped at the top of the staircase and fell down the wooden stairs with a crash that sounded "like an invading army. It frightened the life out of the soldier. Gun at the ready, he was crouched at the door, waiting for he knew not what to appear. In staggered a flustered young Sister trying to look composed and courageous. I hobbled over to Paulita and stood stolidly and tall, thinking, 'Here I am, you have to deal with me as well as Paulita.' Should I burst out laughing or cry in frustration? No, just adopt an enigmatic expression, and let the scene roll on."

Though barefoot and in rags, Father Au gave the women hope by sending messages to keep up their courage. Chinese friends smuggled food into the convent, and whenever they encountered the Sisters without guards, they insisted on giving the women everything they had on them—money, eggs, a piece of salt pork. But the scene daily grew uglier. Communist guards killed and ate Au's beloved dog, whom they called Tulaman— Truman. They tore down the wooden crucifix in the church and used it for firewood. New waves of Chinese soldiers repeatedly tried to break into the convent, and one day Au disappeared, transferred to another prison. He later died of starvation and tuberculosis at a hard labor camp on the edge of the Gobi Desert.

In the neighboring city of Wuchow, meanwhile, soldiers arrested the Maryknoll Sisters' local superior, Rosalia Kettl, after planting opium in her room. Mary Diggins, among the Sisters present at the time, said that when Rosalia was confronted with the contraband, one of the younger soldiers interjected, "But we put that there!" "Shut up!" his superiors said. When Rosalia entered the police station, three men rushed at her, tearing off her habit and leaving her only in a slip.

A thin woman in her forties, Rosalia had been in China seventeen years and knew the local dialect. Her cell was near the torture rooms, and she was forced to listen to the round-the-clock interrogations, which were usually followed by the screams of those tortured. (Among the most common methods were hanging by the thumbs and the water torture, in which water and gasoline were forced into the prisoner's mouth and nose until he or she nearly asphyxiated.) Rosalia herself was frequently questioned, and sometimes tied up and gagged, the unspoken threat being that she, too, would be tortured. Toward the end of the first week she heard the ravings of an American Baptist doctor, whom the Sisters held in high regard and who had been arrested at the same time with Rosalia, a Maryknoll priest, and the local Maryknoll bishop, Frederick Donaghy. The doctor had been badly tortured, and Rosalia asked permission to talk to him—his mind was so deranged by his sufferings that he did not recognize her. He later hanged himself, but the guards and other women prisoners kept his death from Rosalia—one of many kindnesses in the midst of brutality.

Ill from the tension, cramped quarters, and lack of hygiene, Rosalia was nursed by the Chinese women prisoners, who saved their own small portions of rice to feed her. They also hid her rosary during periodic searches by the guards because they knew how much it meant to her. Rosalia, in turn, comforted those who returned hysterical from the torture sessions. When she was transferred from one jail to another, she was tied to a prisoner who was too ill to walk. Somehow, Rosalia managed to drag herself, the woman, and their bedding through the streets, much to the wonder of the townspeople, who were impressed by the American's courage. As Rosalia was approaching the prison, an unknown woman darted out and insisted on carrying the baggage into the jail despite the guards' protestations.

The aim of such harsh treatment was to force the Maryknollers to seek permission to leave China, but the missioners were determined to stay on as long as possible. Sister Mary Diggins, a tall, green-eyed Californian with a ready laugh, was still young enough to be unafraid, and on several occasions she and the four other Sisters who were still free attempted to visit Rosalia in prison. Pete Reilly, the local Maryknoll pastor, was furious with the women. Like Mary, he had escaped arrest, apparently because the Communists did not understand his position in the local church, but Reilly was much more apprehensive, said Mary, "because he had a better understanding of what was happening." "Don't you realize," he would thunder at the Sisters, "that every time you go to that prison you risk arrest?" The women ignored him. Being in a group gave them courage, whereas the priest was alone. To add to the tension, all mail and newspapers had been stopped. Despite the lack of communications, telegrams regularly arrived for the Sisters on the feast days of their patron saints from the Maryknoll convent in Hong Kong. The unsigned cables always carried the same message: "Loving Feast Day Greetings." Reilly would grumble, "Another one— Loving Feast Day Greetings!" "At least we know our Sisters are in Hong Kong and safe," the women retorted. "The Chinese didn't know what we were saying to each other," Mary explained, "but on both sides of the border we knew we were thinking of and praying for each other."

The Sisters sent food, clothes, and medicine to Rosalia, and messages were regularly passed back and forth through guards who were secretly sympathetic to the women. Rosalia several times asked for "the Sweet Bread," which was smuggled into her in bread rolls. The "Sweet Bread" was the most important part of her sustenance during the five-month-long confinement because the tiny wafer, or consecrated host, was Christ. The symbolism in the Blessed Sacrament, as Catholics call the host, was extremely powerful—it conferred a healing reassurance that God was with Rosalia and that she would not be forsaken, no matter what happened. Edith and Paulita also received consolation and courage from the "Sweet Bread," which was smuggled into them hidden in the basket with their small rations of food.

Although the Chinese Communists derided such beliefs as mumbo-jumbo, their own cultural heritage, which was both religious and heavily superstitious, gave them some inkling of the power of such symbolism— hence, rosaries, medals, and other items of religious significance were always confiscated. Thus, Maryknoller Monica Marie Boyle was told on her arrest that she was forbidden to pray (though she did so throughout her imprisonment).

Originally charged with spying for the American government, Monica Marie was later accused of murdering two thousand babies at the Loting orphanage, which she supervised. For over a hundred years a rumor had circulated in China that foreign missionaries killed abandoned babies in order to gouge out their eyes to make magic medicine. The tale was widely believed, and in 1870 angry mobs in northern China had dragged ten Catholic Sisters into the streets, killed them, then burned their convent. At the Loting orphanage, which had been in existence since the early 1920s, the Sisters received nearly two thousand abandoned infants a year in the period after World War II when hunger was widespread. A gentle soul whose only ambition in life had been to go to China to save such babies, Monica cried every time one died—the fate of many, who were beyond medical help by the time they reached the orphanage. Still, the evil story persisted, and Chinese women, after bringing dying babies to the orphanage, would often carefully examine the corpses to make sure they had not been mutilated. In the endless interrogations that Monica endured after her arrest, the questions always returned to the same rumor: "How many babies did you kill? Why did you kill them?"

Monica gave up trying to answer. Weak from the lack of food and water and confined to an overcrowded, rat-infested cell, she contracted malaria and would have died but for the other prisoners, who nursed her. After a particularly bad bout of malaria, her tongue was so swollen she thought she would choke to death. "Please," she begged the guard, "give me some tea. I'm dying of thirst."

"If you die, we won't have to shoot you," he scolded. "Why should I give tea to our enemy?" Continuing to shout, he furtively filled her cup with tea.

Other guards were less charitable. One spat in her face, and Monica, who was handcuffed, could do nothing but say, "Thank you." She was sick and worn and tears were running down her face: "My Lord and God was spit upon like this. You have made me more like him. For that, I am grateful."

The effect was dramatic—the young soldier himself burst into tears.

Monica also had a profound effect on the women prisoners. "Why," they kept asking, "are you alone forbidden to pray? What is your prayer that they should be afraid of it? She told them. Although no conversions occurred, Monica's message brought consolation to the prisoners, particularly those who were taken away for execution.

By the fall of 1951, most of the Sisters had been released and deported to Hong Kong. But for several months it was touch and go, and some Maryknollers were convinced they would be shot. The situation began to change in Wuchow after Mary and Moira Riehl went to Father Reilly for help. Chinese Catholics had told the Sisters that the only solution was to leave China—indeed, their presence endangered local Catholic communities—and Moira and Mary were determined to get Sister Rosalia out of jail. Reilly did not want to sign a request for permission to leave because he thought he would be abandoning Bishop Donaghy, although such a request would open prison doors. "Moira started to cry—deliberately," recalled Mary. "She's not a crying woman. But she cried, and he couldn't bear it, so he signed the papers."

A month later Rosalia, the bishop, and the other Maryknoll priest were released. Rosalia said that, on the day she was told to collect her few belongings, she was convinced she would be shot—such was the standard procedure. But it was the storm before the calm. Returned to the Wuchow convent, she could hardly walk because of the months of cramped incarceration, and Mary and Moira massaged, fed, and cared for her, until she regained some normalcy. But Rosalia faced still another trial. Three of the Wuchow Maryknollers had already departed for Hong Kong, which left Mary, Moira, and Rosalia, until Mary and Moira were told to leave by the authorities. Not wanting to abandon Rosalia, but aware that staying would complicate her situation, the Sisters packed their bags. Rosalia cried. "We all cried," said Mary. "But I told Rosalia, when you're coming out, send us a cable. Just say, 'Loving Feast Day Greetings,' and we'll know to meet you at the border." In September 1951, a month after Mary's and Moira's departure, a cable arrived at the Maryknoll Hong Kong convent: "Loving Feast Day Greetings." The next day Mary and the others were waiting for Rosalia at the border. And there she was, sick and frightened but alive.

In Hingning, meanwhile, Edith and Paulita began a two-month process of filling out forms and more forms in order to get permission to leave. After several last-minute reroutings by the local authorities, made presumably in the belief that the women were dangerous spies who might escape, they eventually reached the border. Along the way they underwent frequent body and baggage searches, the last of which was the most bizarre. After the contents of the women's baggage were dumped on the floor, police officials carefully went over every item. "What's this?" demanded one inspector, pouncing on a notebook, the title of which was "The Three-Legged Mouse."

"It's a Chinese translation of a children's story in English," Edith explained.

The inspector was not persuaded. "Have you ever seen a three-legged mouse?"

"No."

"Then why have you written it down? Have you three-legged mice in Hingning?"

"No."

"Are there three-legged mice in America?"

"No."

On and on, until convinced at last that the mouse was not a code, and that Americans were stupid enough to believe three-legged mice existed, the inspector let them go.

Flying with the Eagle

Although the Maryknollers suffered harassment and imprisonment under the Communists, and Maryknoll Bishop Ford died in a Chinese prison, the passage of time and changing political attitudes enabled them to see that the situation had not simply been a case of good against evil, as they had originally perceived. The Chinese could not be entirely faulted for their assumption that foreign missionaries were agents of Western imperialism, and in the atmosphere of mutual mistrust the Communists had assumed that Maryknoll priests and nuns were spies for the U.S. government. The missioners thought the charge absurd, but they were unconscious of their role as the harbingers of foreign values and political interests or their contribution to revolutionary ferment through the introduction of liberal ideas about social and political reform. As a Maryknoll Sister pointed out, "All of us are a product of our countries. When I came out, my thinking was geared to what the U.S. government thought of China. We were not analytical and didn't understand the political situation. We just lived day to day."

The Sisters knew about the Opium Wars in the nineteenth century and the unjust treaties forced on China by foreign powers, but they failed to grasp the depth of resentment against foreigners that fed the rising tide of nationalism. Nor were they trained to distinguish between political opportunism and Christian principles. Because Chiang Kai-shek was a Christian and against Communism, Washington, the Vatican, and Maryknoll supported him, although he espoused fascist ideas and had been deeply involved in China's opium trade. Corrupt local officials were tolerated as inevitable, but the Maryknollers exonerated Chiang from wrongdoing because he favored foreign missionaries and the U.S. government supported him. "In those days," explained a Maryknoll Sister, "we traveled on the wings of the American eagle"—Edith, for example, flew to China on a U.S. military cargo plane that was part of a fleet that would become a CIA airline. She didn't know it, of course; nevertheless, such identification labeled her politically. Traveling on a U.S. military plane was a small matter compared to Bishop Ford's public exhortations on behalf of Chiang's Nationalists and invitations to Nationalist officials to speak at church functions. (Some churches went so far as to hang the Nationalist flag on their altars.)

Still, flying with the eagle reflected the women's unrecognized assumption that "we go where the U.S. government goes."

Maryknoll was not the only religious group to blur, at times, the distinction between cross and flag. On the contrary, the overwhelming majority of missionaries in China believed they were doing the Chinese a service by bringing—or imposing, in the Chinese view—the "more advanced civilizations" of the Western nations to the heathen Orient. They were unable to see that their cultural superiority was limited—Western bathrooms may have been superior to squatting in a rice field, but the religious ideals of Buddhism and Confucianism predated those of Christianity by several centuries. Nor did they realize the extent to which their religious message was identified with the unequal treaties imposed by the Western nations and from which the missionaries themselves benefited. Moreover, for all the sincerity of its religious idealism, the missionary enterprise in China suffered from a fatal flaw. It was because of the Western countries' engagement in the opium trade that the missionary presence was allowed and even encouraged.

Although the Jesuits were allowed to enter China at the end of the sixteenth century, China again closed its doors in the late 1700s. Meanwhile, a triangular trade developed among British India, China, and England that was originally based on tea but soon expanded to include opium produced under the protection of the British Indian government and transported to China by private British, American, and Indian traders. Although opium was illegal in China, the traders flouted the law, to their profit and that of the British Indian exchequer, which depended on opium to offset the vagaries of the tea market. When the Chinese authorities attempted to suppress the drug traffic, the British declared war on the Chinese, with British opium traders supplying vessels and other support as well as helping to plan strategy. A second war, in which the French joined the British, forced the Chinese in 1858 to accept a series of treaties that gave the Europeans control of enclaves, or mini-states, in five, and eventually more than eighty, Chinese ports. Under a system of extraterritoriality, foreigners were not subject to Chinese laws but only to those of their own countries. It was due to the privileges conferred by extraterritoriality, and the Western powers' willingness to use arms to guarantee them, that foreign merchants and missionaries were able to penetrate the heretofore closed world of China. France undertook the protection of Catholic missionaries; Britain and the United States, that of Protestants. The treaties remained in force until 1943, when the Allies abolished them in order to gain support for the war against Japan. Missionary groups, Maryknoll included, were therefore tainted by association with a system of foreign domination that had originated with the opium trade.

The treaties, which served to carve up the country like a "Chinese melon," were hated by Chinese of all ideologies. At the same time, Western ways and ideas, the spread of which were aided by zealous missionaries, helped pave the way for the fall of a decadent dynasty and the emergence of a more modern state headed by Sun Yat-sen. A widely traveled medical doctor, Sun owed his introduction to the outside world to British missionary schools. Although Chinese conversions to Christianity were few, the influence of missionary schools and hospitals, as well as missionary idealism, did have an impact by stimulating change. To some extent, therefore, the missionaries "were the Communists' predecessors," in the words of John K. Fairbank, the noted American expert on China. Ironically, a key factor in the success of Sun's nationalist revolution in 1911 was his ability to capitalize on widespread animosity against foreigners. But though a republican government swept away the old order, it proved incapable of dealing with centuries of injustice, particularly in the countryside, or with the foreign powers that dominated China.

Two leaders emerged to claim Sun's mantle in the ensuing power struggles—Chiang Kai-shek and Mao Tse-tung. Chiang dominated the stage from the late 1920s through World War II, but despite his abilities as a political strategist, he never came to grips with China's massive social problems, preferring alliances with opium overlords and foreign bankers and merchants. In the late twenties he destroyed Shanghai's leftist labor movement by using gangs controlled by the city's opium chief, who subsequently became a major general in Chiang's Nationalist army. Chiang then legalized the drug traffic to obtain taxes to finance his military campaign, but the popular outcry was such that he was forced to abolish the scheme. In the 1930s, under the guise of the "New Life" movement, which was supposed to stop the traffic, the opium trade was rerouted from territory controlled by Chiang's warlord opponents to the Shanghai monopoly. Instead of destroying the drugs it seized, Chiang's government hoarded the opium, making an estimated profit of 500 million Chinese dollars. After World War II, the Nationalist forces quickly returned to Shanghai, where corruption and vice, including narcotics, again flourished with their connivance.

Chiang was also an advocate of fascism, and in the 1930s Nazi German officers trained Nationalist troops. The Nationalist version of the German shock troops was called the Blue Shirts, and they operated with impunity in stamping out all dissent. Chiang's American advisers apparently did not question such tactics, and during World War II he received massive aid from the United States, with no strings attached. Among the few dissenters was General Joseph W. Stilwell, commander of U.S. troops in the China-Burma-India area, but Washington chose to back Chiang, not Stilwell.

By the end of the war, however, the Truman administration realized the Nationalists were losing ground to Mao Tse-tung's Communists. Hoping to achieve a truce, the president dispatched to China his wartime commander, George C. Marshall. Thanks to his personal prestige, Marshall was able to achieve a cessation in hostilities, but it did not endure, and by 1947, when he became Secretary of State, China was in the grip of a bloody civil war. While some U.S. political leaders urged intervention, Marshall and Truman recognized the futility of such an undertaking in the world's most populous nation.

The Nationalists were demoralized by corruption and desertions and had nothing to offer the impoverished masses; in contrast, the Communist ranks swelled, particularly in the countryside, where the peasantry responded to the call for change. Inept military strategy combined with a disastrous economic policy destroyed public confidence in Chiang's government, and by 1948 his army was in shreds. In January 1949, the Nationalists surrendered. Although American historians, including military experts, believe Chiang's overthrow was inevitable, given his refusal to heed the advice of able military tacticians and the chaos that engulfed the country in his last years in power, at the time many Americans blamed allegedly disloyal China experts in the State Department for "losing" China to the Communists. Having idealized Chiang Kai-shek and his wife, they found it impossible to believe them capable of stupidity and corruption. Thus the stage was set for a Cold War hysteria symbolized by Senator Joseph Mc-Carthy's infamous witch hunts for supposed "Reds."

Among those who might have presented a more realistic assessment of the situation in China were the Maryknollers. But because of blind allegiance to Chiang Kai-shek, the Catholic church's fierce opposition to Communism and the missionaries' imprisonment and expulsion by Mao Tse-tung's government, theirs were among the loudest voices in denouncing the Communist threat. Maryknoll's magazine, *The Field Afar*, frequently printed articles on the evil Reds, including comic strips depicting the Sisters' confrontations with Communist-indoctrinated youths. Even as late as 1962, when the Catholic church was beginning to reexamine its attitudes toward "paganism" and atheism, the magazine was still publishing diatribes against the Chinese Communists and arguing against recognition of China. "Negotiations with Communists are not possible," said an editorial in *The Field Afar*, dismissing disarmament talks as "the epitome of naive simplicity." Maryknoll books also portrayed a negative image of China. *Nun in Red China*, published in 1953 under the auspices of the archconservative cardinal of New York, Francis Spellman, provided an account of the sufferings of Edith, Paulita, Rosalia, and other Maryknoll Sisters during their imprisonment and expulsion. Though true, the stories were presented in a simplistic manner, with American heroines pitted against "rat-faced" Commies, who were the agents of "Satanism, a super-intelligent force of pure evil." Most Chinese, said the book, were too simple, their "brains muddled by paganism," to understand that they were being used as instruments of hate. *The Bamboo Cross,* a fictionalized version of the experiences of Sisters Rosalia and Monica Marie, was similarly simplistic in style, but the film version, which starred Jane Wyman and was directed by John Ford, was a popular hit.

Wyman and Ford were not the only celebrities to take the Maryknollers' part. Leo Durocher, manager of the New York Giants, sent baseball equipment to the Sisters in Hong Kong for refugees from mainland China, and Gene Autry visited Maryknoll headquarters in New York to teach the missioners how to ride a horse. The cowboy star likened Maryknoll to the West Point of the Catholic church, whose soldiers would go forth to defend American ideals.

But undoubtedly the most important influence was that of Cardinal Spellman, an intimate of presidents and cabinet ministers who exercised such political power that he was known as the "American Pope." Spellman, who was Maryknoll's official "protector," was outraged by the Maryknoll missioners' expulsion from China, which reinforced his support for Senator McCarthy, also a Catholic. During the fifties, "McCarthy became a big hero to most of us for his anti-Communist crusades," recalled a former Maryknoller who said that at one point he thought of leaving the seminary to join the Army in order to fight Communists. The Sisters were no less vehement, and some reported the threat made by minor Chinese officials that they would "liberate America in ten years." The idea was of course absurd, but in the emotional atmosphere of the early fifties Americans took the threat seriously.

Maryknoll was by no means the only Catholic organization to support McCarthy, who remained a Catholic hero long after Protestant churches had denounced him. Although the Protestants had also suffered in China, as had Buddhists and Muslims, the Vatican elevated the struggle against Communism to a holy crusade. Concerned about the possibility of a Communist victory in Italy's 1948 elections, Pius XII in 1947 began holding special services to save the world from Communism, and these were copied by the churches in China. Six months after the Communists took power in China, Rome issued a decree forbidding Catholics to collaborate with the Communists on pain of sin and excommunication. The decree, combined with the intransigence of the papal ambassador to China, confirmed the Communists' belief that the Vatican was a temporal power determined to impose Western ideological beliefs on their country.

The Communists had a point in that Rome regarded itself as a temporal power, and had undoubtedly acted like one for most of its history. Until the Second Vatican Council in the early 1960s, Catholicism was indistinguishable from Western culture—Asians and Africans, for example, had to become "little Europeans," in the words of one theologian, in order to become Christians. Symbolic of such cultural colonialism was the insistence of

Catholic missionaries that Chinese converts destroy shrines to their ancestors, which were synonymous with paganism, although a reverence for the
dead is common to all great religions, including Christianity. In the Chinese culture, which places heavy emphasis on respect for family hierarchy
and ancestors, such an act required Catholic converts to cut themselves off
from the rest of society, thereby disrupting the social harmony so prized by
Chinese. The Jesuits who proselytized in China in the 1700s had not demanded that converts renounce their culture—Catholic rituals were conducted in the vernacular, and Catholics were allowed to participate in ceremonies honoring their ancestors. But these innovations were frowned on
by other missionary orders, which were jealous of the Jesuits' influence,
and in 1742 Pope Benedict XIV condemned such practices in a papal decree. The Chinese reacted by expelling all foreign missionaries, including
the Jesuits, whose work of two centuries was thus destroyed by Western
cultural prejudice. At the turn of the century, and again in the early 1900s,
when the Chinese secretly invited the Vatican to reestablish diplomatic relations, the French government, backed by the French bishops and mission
superiors in China, dissuaded Rome from accepting the olive branch. Relations were finally established in the 1920s, and in the following years increasing numbers of Chinese were appointed bishops to replace foreigners.
Yet there was always the stigma of second-class citizenship because the
Chinese were not white and Western. As remarked by Cardinal Costantini,
the enlightened papal delegate to China in the late 1920s, the Catholic
church was a foreign presence—*in* China but not *of* it. During a walk with
Costantini along the parapets of the great wall surrounding Peking, a
Maryknoller recalled, the cardinal sadly pointed to the huge Catholic mission compounds, each encased in high walls and cut off from the adjacent
houses. "That is our great weakness," Costantini said. "These mission compounds are tiny foreign islands in the cities of China. They belong to a day
that is gone. If only we could abolish them and make the church truly belong to the city and the people."

Maryknoll attempted to do so. The missioners lived as much as possible
with the people. This was especially true of the Sisters, whose tiny convents
were usually part of a Chinese house in an impoverished village and whose
lives were dedicated to the poor. But the missioners could not overcome
the cultural prejudices of the times—they did not even know they were
prejudiced. Not only did they accept Christianity's traditional understanding of the Chinese as pagans, they believed that anything, even the corrupt
Nationalists, was preferable to Communism. And being Americans, they
were convinced that the eagle was China's savior. Such were the reasons for
reports by Maryknoll Bishop Ford to the American consulate in Swatow on
Communist troop movements, economic conditions, communications,
and transport facilities in his area. These and other incriminating writings,

which were found by the Communists in Ford's files, convinced them that Maryknoll was "the biggest spy ring in China." Neither side understood the other's motivations, each believing the other guilty of evil instincts and acts. Yet both were ultimately concerned with the same goal—to better the lives of the Chinese masses.

The Maryknoll Sisters, who were less politically aware than the priests and whose work was almost exclusively in remote areas with the illiterate poor, were caught in the gulf of misunderstanding and paid heavily for their political innocence. Typical of the false conceptions existing on both sides was the obsession of local Communist officials with an old radio discovered in a Maryknoll convent. Even though the radio was covered with mold and did not work, the officials were convinced it was a high-powered transmitter through which the Sisters sent messages to the State Department. Open the radio, open the radio, they insisted. What they meant was, turn on the radio. But even if the Sisters had understood, they could not have complied because the radio was broken. Absurd as the charges against the Sisters may have seemed, there was a certain logic in Chinese thinking. If the Maryknollers were spies—and the government said they were—then the Americans had to be communicating by radio with President Truman. Much the same logic operated in the United States and Rome: The Chinese were in contact with Moscow; ergo, the order to expel the Maryknollers came directly from Stalin. That the radio was broken and the Sisters were politically naïve—and hence unlikely spies—did not enter into Chinese thinking, any more than Americans took into account the importance of Chinese revulsion against foreigners as a motivating factor in the Communist revolution.

Even had there been more understanding, however, the outcome would have been much the same since Mao Tse-tung and his followers were determined to make religion subservient to the state, regardless of whether it was Christian, Buddhist, Muslim, or Taoist. All those who did not cooperate were persecuted, including Chinese Catholics, thousands of whom were arrested and sentenced to hard labor. By late 1951, when relations between the Vatican and China were severed, most of the country's five thousand Catholic foreign missionaries had been expelled. Missionary schools, universities, hospitals, and orphanages were occupied by the Communists, and religious services forbidden. The Communists could afford to ignore Vatican protests because the country's 3.5 million Catholics represented less than one percent of the population. (Protestants numbered 1.5 million Chinese; Orthodox Christians, two hundred thousand.) Maryknollers left behind sixty-six thousand Catholics in five different missions.

Although Maryknoll had been founded specifically for mission to China, its expulsion did not lead to its demise, as some feared, but to a new flowering in other parts of the globe, particularly Latin America. The experience there put the Chinese revolution into a different perspective, by teaching the missionaries the error of confusing cross with flag. While it is unlikely that Chinese Christians could have escaped persecution, given Mao Tse-tung's dogmatism, the charge most frequently laid against them—that they were disloyal to China because they were lackeys of the Americans and Europeans—would not have held up had Western missionaries not associated religion with the ideological and cultural ambitions of their own countries. Moreover, to be *of* and not just *in* China, Christianity must be genuinely Chinese, in its leadership and cultural outlook, whereas most churches in China at the time of the missionaries' expulsion were "foreign islands" dependent on Rome, as Cardinal Costantini had bemoaned. If China had turned to Communism, wrote one Maryknoller, it was in large part the fault of the Christian West, which had not known how to help China but had introduced the opium traffic and profited from the country's weakness through unjust treaties: "The complaints and curses which the East utters against us are inspired not only by hatred but also by profound disillusion."

A Vision

On Edith's first Sunday in Hong Kong after her expulsion from China, she attended Mass in a church packed with hundreds of people. For the first time in more than a year, she found herself at a public religious function where Christians could express themselves openly and without fear. Suddenly, Edith, who had been unable to pray during her imprisonment, found herself on her knees, praying not through words but tears—tears for what she and the others had suffered, for a China that had been and could no longer be. "Forever" was a word often stamped on the Chinese expulsion orders received by the Maryknollers. But forever is a make-believe word, and there would come a time when the gates of China would reopen. Still, a chapter had ended, both for the Maryknollers and the United States. Catholics and Protestants would soon reject the outdated notion that non-Christians were simply pagans, while large numbers of Americans would question their parents' belief in "my country, right or wrong." Though marred by Cold War hysteria, the fifties marked a social and political turning point—the last period of national complacence in modern American history, when many still believed, as Boston's Cardinal Richard Cushing said, that "America is destined to lead the world to sanity and sanctity." On the morrow loomed the Vietnam War, the countercultural revolution and the Second Vatican Council, all of which would challenge the "imperialism of righteousness." China would undergo its own social upheaval in the Cultural Revolution. And in the end, President Nixon, the political ally of the Red-baiting McCarthy, would normalize relations with China.

Maryknoll went through a similar period of soul-searching in trying to comprehend the full import of its experience in China. Among the lessons learned was the importance of being of, and not just in, a country by identifying with and respecting the cultural traits of the people. Another was the need to maintain a cautious distance from corrupt and unpopular governments, even if they were pro-American. Although Bishop Ford made a fatal error in tying Maryknoll's fortunes to those of the Nationalists, he hit upon an original idea that would be a key factor in the missioners' future by sending the Sisters to live with the poor in rural villages. The experience, which was unheard of in Catholic missions of the time, permanently marked the Maryknoll women, who would seek out the poorest and neediest wherever they traveled. Through such identification they learned that cross and flag were not inseparable, and that only by challenging their society would they live up to Christianity's prophetic ideals. In less than two decades the same missioners who were expelled from Communist China were suffering right-wing persecution in Latin America and elsewhere for their defense of human rights. Although they still flew with the eagle, the vision was different—broader, freer, because it was no longer bound up with Washington's political ambitions. China had been the test of that vision, showing the Maryknollers that the Christian message of love would be understood only when it transcended ideologies and cultural prejudices.

Edith captured the vision, even as she was suffering at the hands of the "Reds."

The young Communist sitting on the edge of my bed while his comrade rifled through my personal things in the cupboard, that fellow could as easily have been my brother. He was comparable in age, highly motivated for the cause, striving to level society and make things "right." Yet he could not prevent friendliness from breaking through the austere exterior. It was like play-acting. We were supposed to be enemies, yet beneath the ideological differences were human beings—brother and sister.

I could understand the young people's feelings because my oldest brother briefly joined the Communist Party. We were living through the Depression in Chicago, and he had to quit high school to work to help support our family. He would go to meetings for young Communists and come home quoting Marxist slogans. There was a lot of Robin Hood romance in it, just as there was for the young Communists in China—they were going to take from the rich to give to the poor. At the same time you felt the hysteria, an idealism gone berserk in the cruel punishment of the landlords, and in the way we were ill-treated and humiliated. I think they had to work through their rage against the poverty they had suffered for so long. Yet at heart they were more Chinese than Communist: Underneath the soldier's uniform with all its insignia was a human being formed in the values of a civilization that had endured for thousands of years.

Edith traveled a long way to find her brother in a Chinese soldier. The journey may have seemed heroic to those who read the articles and books about the Sisters' sufferings in China or saw Jane Wyman gallantly defy a Communist commissar in *The Bamboo Cross*. But the real heroism was different because it recognized human frailty. The Maryknoll Sisters of the pop books and movies never cried, were never afraid, though in fact the women suffered from the same weaknesses that any human being endures when threatened, imprisoned, and abused. They survived sorrow and despair not because of superhuman qualities but because of the kindnesses and love of countless Chinese—neighbors, prisoners, even guards—and the power of faith. "God is in this somewhere," Edith had told herself at the end of another day of confinement, the tension gradually subsiding with the twilight call of a peasant flute.

"God is in this somewhere." One person who would have understand this insight was Mollie Rogers. Over forty years earlier, living in the carefree atmosphere of Smith College, she had been far removed from the poverty and suffering of China, which was merely a place on a map with strange-looking people. But it was because of Mollie Rogers—later known as Mother Mary Joseph—that Edith went to China. For one day Mollie had a vision of a force that would soar across the seas and circle the globe. She called it love.

2

Pioneers on the Hudson

It was a warm June evening, sweet with the fragrance of the flowering campus. I was a junior at Smith College, and as I walked toward the Students' Building, I dreamed of the future. My reveries were suddenly broken by shouts of joy as the doors of the Students' Building were flung open and floods of light poured out upon the paths. A crowd of girls rushed out, forming a circle around five of them and singing "Onward, Christian Soldiers."

The five had just signed the Student Volunteer pledge to go to China to teach in mission schools or work in hospitals. Everybody in college knew what the Student Volunteer pledge meant, but this was our first experience in the actual offering of girls, and they were the college's best.

Something—I do not know how to describe it—happened within me. I forgot my errand; I was no longer mindful of the beauty and joy about me. I passed quickly through the campus to St. Mary's church, where, before Jesus in the tabernacle, I measured my faith and the expression of it by the sight I had just witnessed. From that moment I had work to do, little or great, God alone knew.

SO BEGAN MARY JOSEPHINE ("Mollie") Rogers' long, often difficult, and eventful journey of faith. Sensitive and idealistic, the young Bostonian was impressed by the fervor and self-sacrifice of the Protestant students. In the early 1900s everybody but the Catholics seemed excited about foreign missions, and there was no Catholic mission club or counterpart to the Protestants' Student Volunteer pledge. No sooner had she arrived at Smith in 1901—"even before I had unpacked my trunk"—than a group of girls had arrived to ask her to join one of the mission study classes sponsored by Protestant churches. "I told them I couldn't unless there was a Catholic one. There wasn't, of course, so they went off, unwittingly leaving in my mind a seed that would germinate."

Though nonsectarian, Smith, like most colleges of the day, strongly encouraged religious activities (church and college chapel attendance were compulsory). While the energies of American Catholicism were absorbed by floods of European immigrants, the Protestants were expanding abroad on the wave of an emerging national power. American colleges and universities, Smith included, played a major role in such expansion through the Student Volunteer Movement, which recruited young Americans for missions in China and elsewhere "for the evangelization of the world in this generation."

Aglow with optimism and humanitarian crusading, the times encouraged such idealism. The first Smith volunteers included the idol of the senior class—a beautiful, rich, and talented girl—as well as other popular students. (A year later one of them would die of a fever contracted in a foreign mission.) Mollie, who had gone to public schools in Massachusetts and had no formal religious training, was inspired by their example, not out of a sense of religious competition but from a desire to share the love of God she had experienced in her own Catholic family. The parish priest had thought she was "on the road to perdition" by attending a non-Catholic college, but as Mollie later admitted, she would never have become involved in foreign missions had she not gone to Smith.

The "lovely Northampton experience," as she called her years at the Massachusetts college, were the most influential in her life, because they provided "a sense of self-reliance and responsibility to take up our work in the world." Smith had been founded to give young women the same educational opportunities as those enjoyed by men and was thus in the forefront of a nascent feminist movement. Like Wellesley, Radcliffe, and other such women's colleges, Smith taught its students to retain their individuality and to value professional competence—lessons Mollie would remember when founding the Maryknoll Sisters, the United States' first Catholic women's mission congregation. At the time, however, a religious life seemed the last thing on the horizon: While keenly interested in missions, Mollie "never cared for nuns. They wore black habits, and I thought, 'I certainly wouldn't want to go around dressed that way.'"

Though she was not a notable beauty, and already showed a tendency to stoutness, Mollie was tall and carried herself with regal bearing. Her most attractive features, in addition to a mass of copper-colored hair worn in a Gibson girl pompadour, were enormous blue-gray eyes and a hearty, infectious laugh. Her serious side was balanced by a frivolity that enjoyed new clothes and was prepared to experiment with beauty fads to enhance her appearance. For a time she and a cousin at Smith ate raw onions nightly, believing they would improve their complexion. On another occasion, she went to a dance looking like a broiled lobster after she was unable to peel off the turpentine with which she had doused herself in order to whiten her skin, a pearly white face and shoulders then being the height of fashion. Mollie was able to laugh at her predicament—a sense of humor, kindliness, and ability to dance well ensured that she never lacked for boyfriends. Life at Smith was not all prayer and work, of course. Although the students

were always chaperoned and visiting privileges by young men were restricted, afternoon teas and receptions and evening dances, plays, and parties made for an active social life. "Dressing for dinner" was still customary,
but in an effort to make the poorer students feel less uncomfortable, some,
including Mollie, wore a simple long skirt and shirtwaist instead of more
elaborate gowns. The gesture was typical of Mollie's sense of justice—a trait
she exhibited from early childhood by fighting and besting the neighborhood bully and later, at Smith, by befriending a Washington girl of mixed
blood at a time when racial prejudice was widespread.

Born into a prosperous Irish-American family with loving parents,
Mollie did not experience the slurs and insecurities suffered by her friend
from Washington. The Rogers home was a warm, hospitable place where
generosity was taken for granted. As the first girl among eight children,
Mollie enjoyed a special regard as her father's favorite daughter. The family had a wide circle of friends and relatives that provided a sense of
belonging, even though the Irish were still looked down upon by many
Massachusetts Protestants. While Mollie and the other children learned
their catechism, went to weekly Mass, and received Holy Communion,
religious training was informal, and the values she learned were less the
result of schooling than of the Christian atmosphere in her home. Indica-
tive of her ability to cross the still rigid lines that separated Protestants
and Catholics, she chose "Toleration" as the subject of her talk at com-
mencement exercises at her largely Protestant public high school in Rox-
bury. The opening quote in Latin could have been the motto for her entire
life: "In what is essential, unity; in what is indifferent, liberty; in all things,
charity."

A Crucial Meeting

After Mollie graduated from Smith in 1905, she returned to the college as
an instructor in zoology in order to continue her studies. But one afternoon a professor of English invited her to tea and changed her life. The
college was concerned about the lack of religious activities for its Catholic
students, said the professor, herself a fervent Episcopalian, and would Mollie be willing to start a group, perhaps a mission club? Mollie's first reaction
was to demur—she knew nothing about Catholic missions—but remem-
bering her earlier experience on the night of the Student Volunteer pledges,
she accepted. A few months later she was standing outside the entrance of
the Boston office of Father James Anthony Walsh, the local director of the
Society for the Propagation of the Faith and her primary source of information for the budding mission club:

Such a surprising ready-to-tumble-down-place it was! Narrow, rickety stairs and a dark hall led to the "rookery," as he called his office, and it was with a sense of relief that I saw in the sun's revealing light a room lined with books, here and there on the wall bright splotches of color, a large desk, on the table beside it, a globe, and at the desk, smiling a welcome, the director himself.

An Irish American like Mollie, Walsh was in his late thirties, of medium build, with a prominent nose and long upper lip—an ordinary-looking man, until he began to speak and his small eyes lit up with a lively wit. Walsh felt passionately about the need for an American Catholic missionary movement, and Mollie was a willing listener. He showed her the galleys for the first issue of *The Field Afar*, a missionary monthly patterned after the popular magazine *Life*, telling her of his hopes to awaken American interest in Catholic missions. Time flew, and Mollie suddenly realized she may have overstayed her welcome. "I really must be going now."

"No, no," Walsh insisted. "Sit down again. I'm trying to form an opinion of you."

Though she felt "dead silly" to be so scrutinized, Mollie stayed. When she eventually left, Walsh shook her hand and smiled, "I think we are going to be very good friends."

"Can I help you, Father, in my spare time?" Mollie had innocently inquired during a later meeting with the priest, and when she descended the rickety stairs, she was loaded with photo albums. That night the Rogers' bathtub was afloat with bearded missioners, children with pathetic faces, temples with swooping roofs, solemn groups of First Communicants in borrowed finery—photos soaked from cardboard backing that would form the beginnings of *The Field Afar*'s archives. Mollie was also busy with translations of letters from French missioners and editing and writing for *The Field Afar*—Walsh had given her not only photographs to sort but a host of other assignments as well. Every minute of her free time was spent on the little magazine, the entire Rogers family sometimes pitching in to help. Each month brought new subscribers. People liked the interesting layout, the lavish (for then) use of pictures, the stories from foreign lands and the vein of irrepressible humor running throughout. Though Mollie could not have known it when she visited Walsh's "rookery," she had begun to fulfill her promise to God of "work, little or great," made on the night of the Smith Student Volunteer pledges.

Walsh, meanwhile, had joined forces with Father Thomas Frederick Price, a saintly priest from North Carolina known as the "Tar Heel Apostle" because of his work among the South's impoverished people. Like Walsh, Price believed the best way to encourage a missionary spirit among

American Catholics was by sending their own people abroad, thereby establishing a personal link with foreign missions. At the time, only sixteen American priests of the seventeen thousand in the country were serving overseas, most with European religious communities. A few American Sisters also worked abroad but not in a distinct missionary enterprise. The Catholic church in the United States had no official organization dedicated to the recruitment and training of foreign missioners, men or women, and Walsh and Price were determined to provide one, at least for men.

The lack of a mission society reflected the unstable nature of American Catholicism, which was overwhelmed with the social and economic needs of millions of European immigrants. Dependent on Europe, particularly France, for money and personnel, the American church was itself a missionary enterprise until 1908, when the Vatican upgraded the United States to a self-supporting national church. Three years later, the American bishops approved Price and Walsh's proposal to establish a mission seminary, thereby launching the Catholic Foreign Mission Society of America, soon to be known popularly as Maryknoll. Pope Pius X gave his blessing to the project two months after the bishops' announcement.

Mollie, meantime, had given up her teaching at Smith to teach in Boston in order to give more time to *The Field Afar*. Walsh insisted on paying her for the work, and after Mollie refused, the angry Irishman announced, "If you don't take this, you can't come any more!"

Mollie meekly accepted the money, only to receive a call the following day from a still irate Walsh, who accused her of sending the money back to him. Having received the exact amount in the morning mail from an anonymous donor, he was convinced she was fibbing. But Mollie had the last word: How, she sweetly asked, could Father question providential aid, probably from St. Joseph himself? Walsh gave up arguing.

Such diplomatic skills later proved useful in dealing with the problems that immediately beset the new Mission Society, including the anti-Catholic sentiments of New York property owners. Walsh had tried to buy a property in Pocantico Hills adjoining the estate of John D. Rockefeller, but the latter, having no liking for such a neighbor, effectively blocked the purchase by offering a higher price. (Two years of litigation ensued, resulting in an out-of-court settlement of $8,000 for the Mission Society.) Walsh then furtively looked at a property in Ossining on the Hudson River twenty-five miles north of New York City. The ninety-three-acre farm was selling for $44,500, and Walsh liked the look of the place, with its woodlands and sweeping view of the Hudson and the blue Catskills beyond. But after the experience with Rockefeller he was taking no chances. Mollie was therefore enlisted to make the purchase, posing as a wealthy Bostonian looking for a country estate. She appeared for the event in a large hat and veil and driven by a goggled Walsh, who was disguised as a chauffeur—

fortunately, it turned out, because the lawyer responsible for closing the deal immediately asked Mollie if she'd heard about "the interesting lawsuit between Rockefeller and that priest who was trying to buy a site for his seminary." Once the land was secured, Mollie transferred it to the Mission Society for one dollar. The sale was celebrated with a supper of Boston baked beans.

By the time of the purchase in 1912, four young women helpers were already living in Hawthorne near Ossining, their main job being to package and mail *The Field Afar*. Among the four was a lovely, dark-haired girl, Mary Louise Wholean, who, like Mollie, had attended a prominent women's college, in her case, Wellesley. But Mary Louise, who was sickly and often in pain, would not live to see the fruits of those early labors, dying of cancer only five years later.

The women were a courageous group: They had no money, did not know one another, and were bound only by a common interest in foreign missions. The first time they met was in New York City en route to Hawthorne, and when they got off the train at the small village, it was a wintry January evening. The cottage Walsh had rented for them was cold and drafty, and pieces of furniture were stacked here and there in bare, uncarpeted rooms. Mary Louise felt numb. Expecting to enter a furnished house with a hot meal on the stove, she kept telling herself "for God and souls" as she stoically climbed the narrow stairs to make the beds. Some bags of food lay on the kitchen table, but on examination they turned out to contain only bread. Father Price then appeared to welcome them, bringing an armful of bread. Sisters from a nearby convent also sent them a welcome gift—bread! Their supper that first night was "creamed toast."

The morning light did not improve the women's impression of the cottage, which was so cold that they ate breakfast with their coats on and sat on the radiator in the evenings. The plumbing was primitive, and they were often reduced to a quick splash from a basin half-filled with murky water. Sometimes there was no water for drinking, cooking, or bathing—more than once they resorted to "washing" their hands on the dew-covered grass. Nevertheless, they rose every morning at six for a long day of work on *The Field Afar*, interspersed with prayers and manual labor. Walsh tried to help: He hired a cook, a boy to unfreeze the pipelines and pump water, and a laundress willing to wash with almost no water. But their work was erratic and short-lived—the first cook departed because she was convinced the house was haunted. The group tried to maintain their enthusiasm, but they were homesick and discouraged by the hard living and working conditions. The glorious adventure for God "did not feel so glorious after all."

Had Mollie been with the women from the beginning, things might have been different—no matter how difficult the situation, she always made it seem an amusing adventure. When she visited the Hawthorne cottage, the women's spirits rose, and even the house cat, which scratched and bit the other women, gave up his wild ways, sleeping contentedly in Mollie's lap. She not only did office work but also the cooking and cleaning, chores that had seemed so wearing to the others but which she carried lightly. But much as she wanted to, she could not stay, because the Rogers family had fallen upon hard times through unwise business investments. Her father had been forced to mortgage the family home, and Mollie's salary as a teacher, which once would have meant little to her parents, was now needed. Walsh badly wanted Mollie's help at Hawthorne—he could see the women's group disintegrating and doubted it could survive without her leadership. But he did not have the financial means to free Mollie from family obligations, as he told Mother Alphonsa, the head of a nearby Dominican religious community that ran a hospital for poor cancer patients.

The aging, white-habited nun knew all about hard beginnings, having given up a glamorous life to start a nursing home for the poor. The daughter of Nathaniel Hawthorne, Mother Alphonsa had been a beautiful and imperious young woman, "a peach blossom in the sun," as one admirer had described her, and it had not been easy to renounce a life of luxury for a vow of poverty. Mollie held the older woman in high regard, a feeling returned by the Dominican, who urged Mollie to move to Hawthorne. When she hesitated, Mother Alphonsa insisted, "What is it? Financial?"

It wasn't only financial, Mollie thought. Her father had suffered a stroke because of the family's economic difficulties, her mother was getting older, and there was that big house to manage. The other children had gone off to marry and make their own homes, but she, the eldest girl, "the old reliable," as even Walsh called her, was a mainstay. Torn between family loyalties and the desire to continue her work for foreign missions, Mollie saw financial need as the balancing factor in the equation.

"Yes," she said, "it is financial. There are obligations."

"How much do you need?"

"If I had two thousand dollars, I could stay," Mollie laughed ruefully, thinking she might as well be asking for the moon.

"Two thousand dollars, repeated Mother Alphonsa, saying nothing more.

A few days later Walsh gave Mollie a note from Mother Alphonsa.

She read it, at first surprised, then upset. "I can't take it."

"She says it is a thank offering," he reminded her gently.

"Oh, but I couldn't think of accepting it. Look at her own burdens, caring for all those sick people, trying to build, supporting her own Sisters. If I had ever guessed what she had in mind . . ."

But Mother Aiphonsa was adamant. Her community had received generous contributions in recent months, she told Mollie, and she had promised to make a thank offering. By accepting the money, Mollie would be offering herself to God. How could she refuse? It was a difficult decision—"My heart is a ragged old thing," she wrote Mother Alphonsa of the pain in leaving her family—but she went.

Of Berries, Beans, and Other Things

Mollie was packing her bags when Margaret Shea came calling. "Little Miss Shea," as she was quickly dubbed, was all of seventeen, her hair down her back, tied with a neat bow. She wanted to become a Sister, and after hearing of Walsh's work with foreign missions, she had screwed up her courage to visit Mollie. Half expecting to find her in a convent, Margaret was dressed all in black with long sleeves, a mourning outfit relieved only by a small bunch of violets on her hat. Mollie, who was wearing a summer dress with short sleeves, thought perhaps Margaret was a widow; still, she looked so young. But Margaret insisted that she was very grown up: "Why, I'll be eighteen in December!"

She wasn't trained for anything, Margaret anxiously explained, but she would be glad to help in any way at Hawthorne. Mollie, who had already gained the young woman's confidence, smiled at her. "Let's go together and find out what God has in store for us."

They arrived at Hawthorne by train and made their way to the cottage by horse and buggy. With her sweet smile and gentle disposition, Margaret quickly gained the women's confidence. "It's perfect, just perfect," she told the amazed group after seeing her tiny attic room.

Margaret's youthful enthusiasm and Mollie's steadying presence soon lifted everyone's spirits. The women still had to work so hard that "it was a positive pleasure to be able to lie down in bed at night," but it no longer seemed a drudgery. Although money was scarce, providence always came to their aid—Walsh gave the women his last five dollars to spend at the local church fair, and the next morning a substantial gift arrived in the mail. There were funny incidents, too. Brother Thomas, one of the early Maryknoll Brothers, often visited the women en route from the village, where he customarily bought himself a coconut custard pie. Walsh did not approve of such snacks, so Brother Thomas always indulged himself when the boss was away. One lunchtime, Mollie recalled, he appeared at the women's cottage with a custard pie to share with them—Walsh was supposed to be on a trip:

> I can see the scene very well—he gave each of us a piece of pie— we used our hands, not even a plate—and there we were, standing around eating this delicious custard pie when in walked Father Walsh—not only himself but with a bishop and a priest! At the back

of the stairs was a window, and it was open, and when Brother Thomas heard them coming he bolted through that window and went out the back door and left us standing there with our pies.

Custard pie or not, Walsh had absolute confidence in Mollie, and shortly after her arrival he asked the women whether they wanted to be under her direction. All said yes, and so it was that Mollie, who had just turned thirty, became the leader of the group of seven women who moved to Maryknoll's Ossining property in the fall of 1912. They took over one of the old farmhouses, a leaky, run-down place infested with bugs; nevertheless, it had twenty-two rooms for *The Field Afar* offices and the women's living quarters—a veritable palace after the cramped cottage at Hawthorne. They christened their new home St. Teresa's Lodge, for the Spanish mystic who was said to have saved more souls through her prayers than most missionaries had. Soon the "secretaries," as Walsh had first called them, became the "Teresians." Among the first to welcome them was Father William Cashin, the chaplain at nearby Sing Sing Prison. A gentle soul, Cashin had adopted the family of his widowed sister-in-law (two nieces would later join Maryknoll), and from the time of the women's arrival at Ossining, he was always on hand with gifts and kindly advice.

Aided by the small group of seminarians who had already gathered at Maryknoll, the women scrubbed floors, moved furniture, painted walls, sewed clothes for themselves and the men, cooked, and prayed. But the center of their busy lives was *The Field Afar*. Every issue had to be hand-wrapped, the paste of a consistency that would flow but not soak the paper. There was a special technique to yanking the top wrapper from under the paste pot and, with a flip of the wrist, rolling the magazine inside the wrapper to show the address. Each week the magazines piled higher to the accompaniment of a din of typewriters and multigraph and addressograph machines—circulation would soon top ninety-two thousand. Inevitably there was a crisis—the unwrapped magazines arrived late, the roof fell in (literally), or the seminary's cook quit. The last happened frequently, and Mollie often volunteered to feed the men. An excellent cook who could make a mouth-watering clam chowder or a succulent chocolate cake, Mollie was remembered by the aspiring priests as the "queen of cuisine." But they didn't always seem so appreciative at the time.

One evening, after she had prepared the third meal of the day, Mollie was sitting, tired and hot, on the back steps of the seminary, hoping the cool air would refresh her before she washed the dishes. Around the corner of the house came a file of priests and students out for their evening constitutional. The priests tipped their hats to her and bowed, the students nodded, and "the well-fed line passed on down the hill and out of sight." None had thought to mention the meals she had so laboriously prepared. "Oh men," she said to herself, getting up to go back to the kitchen. But she never forgot the experience, always ensuring that cooks received sufficient praise.

As the seminary grew, so, too, the women's work. Wanting his small group to be self-sustaining, Walsh established a farm with livestock and fruits and vegetables planted by the seminarians. In addition to office work, sewing for the seminary, and making its bread, the women fed the animals, drew water from their rain-filled well, did the laundry, cared for the gardens, and picked and canned so many vegetables and fruits that they came to hate the sight of beans and berries. Though their number had doubled, they were still woefully understaffed. "The month ended with an after-supper strawberry-picking and hulling shift," read an early entry in the women's diary. "Nearly every day of every month not only ends with a shift of one kind or another but has several throughout some days." Reported another entry: "We had a lecture today on the boiling time for beans to prevent them from exploding when canned. Wouldn't it be nice if they did?"

"We worked very hard for the priests and students, but we revered them and did whatever we could to help them reach the priesthood and eventually to get to the missions," Margaret Shea recalled. Mollie saw nothing unusual in the arrangement. The Maryknollers were like a family, and "the woman's part was quite naturally ours."

In those days few women had professional careers, and women's liberation was unheard of. Although suffragettes were gaining momentum, most women still took for granted a male-dominated society. Herself a professional, Mollie encouraged other women to acquire such skills, yet she was no snob about work. Washing floors and baking bread were as important to the missionary endeavor as writing articles or giving a lecture, she felt. Margaret, who would lead an extraordinarily varied and adventurous life, shared Mollie's adaptability. "When I entered Maryknoll, everything was change, change, change. And I thought that was fun."

Well, most of the time. Even the enthusiastic Miss Shea was sometimes overwhelmed by the work—running the multigraph one minute, cutting up five chickens in the next, to say nothing of her fingers. One night, after a long day in the laundry, she was about to tackle the dirty kitchen floor. "Oh, leave it," said Mollie. "Go to bed." Margaret went gratefully, then began to worry that Mollie would do the floor herself. But when she heard her coming upstairs shortly afterward, she fell asleep. The next morning Margaret found a sparkling kitchen floor. "The angels did it, no doubt," smiled Mollie. Much later, Margaret learned that Mollie had washed the floor in less than half an hour in her own efficient way, by boiling a pail of soap scraps, flooding the greasy floor with it, rinsing it with hot water and sweeping the water out over the back porch.

They had fun, too, even if it was only singing to the rhythm of combs and tissue paper. Christmas was always celebrated with a turkey dinner, tree, and Christmas stockings; Halloween was the occasion for apple-dunking and a masquerade party, often with ghosts and devils. The most popular costumes were of nuns, priests, and even a bishop, dressed up in purple, his crozier a broom handle, his mitre a fancy cockade. In 1915 Mollie started a Maryknoll tradition by celebrating St. Teresa's feast day with ice cream sodas. She secretly set up a soda fountain and booths in the garden, but Margaret, who was unaccustomed to handling such a large bottle of soda, managed to spray it all over the kitchen before the party started, and another had to be purchased. The soda fountain offered such tempting concoctions as "Ningpo Sundae" and "Chop Suey," Mollie and Margaret serving as soda jerks. In what also became a Maryknoll custom the party was followed by three-legged and sack races and dancing.

There were birthday parties as well, and plays, picnics, and outings to Rye Beach, where the women went swimming in the ugly tank suits of the period. Once a week the local undertaker took the women for a drive. Visiting missionaries also gave lectures, some enlightening. One guest, for example, dispelled the popular myth that the people of Borneo were "wild." The only "wild man from Borneo," he said, was an Irishman who worked for the Barnum and Bailey circus.

While no birthday passed without gifts, they were simple and inexpensive—a bouquet of violets gathered from the woods or funny items from the Five-and-Ten. Once they had lobsters for dinner, a treat from a wealthy woman friend, but worried that they had scandalized a visitor by such a "worldly" meal. The women's dresses were always patched and mended, their coats second-hand, the soles for their shoes paper-thin. "We had no radios, television, newspapers, magazines—things that are necessary now but were not then," Margaret recalled. "Still, we were joyous because we were giving to God. I never knew we were poor—I was so happy. It was only later, when I looked back, that I realized how few material things we had."

Even in those hectic early years Mollie was thinking of the future—to a time when Maryknoll women, as well as men, would serve in foreign missions. Walsh's original idea had been to use the Teresians as auxiliaries to keep the seminary going, much as similar women's organizations helped European missionary societies. But since her days at Smith, Mollie had always nurtured the hope that young women would go overseas. The idea of starting a new community of religious women for foreign missions evolved naturally from the first goal. As Mollie admitted, she had been attracted to foreign missions since childhood but not to the Sisterhood. Nevertheless, the atmosphere at Maryknoll, with the heavy emphasis on spirituality, encouraged the women's religious sensibilities. Some, such as Margaret, were more interested in a traditional religious life, whereas others, including

Mollie, were primarily concerned with adapting religious life to mission. These differences would later surface, and nearly divide, the Maryknoll Sisters, but at the time it seemed a logical step to evolve from auxiliary lay-women to Sisters with religious vows.

Mollie's trip to Europe in 1914 on the eve of World War I encouraged that vision. Among the Teresians' friends was a well-to-do fashion designer, Julia Ward, whose name frequently appeared on New York theater programs and whose clients included such popular stars as the actress Maude Adams. The older woman greatly admired Mollie, and she helped the Teresians with generous gifts, including the famous lobsters, as well as such practical items as winter hats and screens for St. Teresa's Lodge. She wanted Mollie to accompany her on a trip to Europe, and Walsh, who saw how hard Mollie worked, thought it would be a good change for her. Knowing that she would refuse, he insisted she accept the invitation, signing the order "commander-in-chief."

They arrived in France less than a month after the murder of the heir to the throne of Austria-Hungary, Archduke Ferdinand, and his wife Sophie by a Serbian nationalist. Unaware that the assassinations would spark an international war, the women journeyed with other pilgrims to Lourdes. A few days after their arrival, they heard the mayor read mobilization orders for the war with Germany. Trains were immediately requisitioned to transport soldiers, and the sick who had traveled to Lourdes in the hope of a miraculous cure had to wait for hours on the station platform until trains could be spared for them. The women eventually made their way to Italy. By the time they reached Rome, Pope Pius X was dying, and they were present for his funeral and the election of a new pope. Because of the war, they had to wait for a return passage to the United States, and during that time Mollie gained a sense of the grandeur and history of the Roman Catholic Church. Among her most vivid impressions was the Colosseum, where so many early Christians had been martyred and which, unknown to Mollie, symbolized the fate of future Maryknoll Sisters. Another was a Catholic chapel, where white-veiled novices prayed around the clock for their Sisters' work with the poor and sick. An idea took hold that would later bear fruit in a small cloister where Maryknoll Sisters would pray for the missionaries and their families. When Mollie left Europe, she had a better understanding of the sacrifices and gifts of a religious life.

Shortly after the women had arrived at Maryknoll in 1912, Walsh had given them a schedule that was nearly as exacting as a formal novitiate—the day started at 5:30 A.M. and continued with prayers, work, and recreation till 9:30 at night when the exhausted women fell into bed. But there was always a certain flexibility—if *The Field Afar* had to be mailed that day, prayers had to wait. Mollie herself encouraged pragmatism as well as ladylike behavior and polite restraint in relations with the seminary. In those days priests and nuns were strictly separated, and even though the women were not yet religious, Walsh kept them at arm's length—he would not even walk alone with his own sister. The mystical Price was even more reticent. Although he prayed constantly to St. Bernadette of Lourdes, and believed himself spiritually united with the French saint, he often avoided the Teresians. Yet he was less authoritarian than Walsh, who acted the part of a strict Irish father and frequently became involved in the most minute decisions, such as the brand of sewing machine the women should use. When Margaret first went to work in the seminary kitchen, he spent fifteen minutes every morning instructing her about nutrition. Sometimes he scolded Mollie for spoiling the seminarians by giving food to them when they worked for the women. But though stern and uncompromising, Walsh "had an understanding heart," said Margaret. Mollie loved him like an older brother, and they were best friends. Often, he would visit the Teresians' lodge to tell the women about his travels or events at the seminary. His sharp wit may have sometimes seemed sarcastic, but friends knew better, delighting in his skills as a comic mimic.

Some of the funniest—and most frustrating—experiences involved the women's appearance. Early on, Walsh ordered them to discard their stylish pompadours for a sedate bun at the neck. He also thought they should wear a uniform, something similar to a gray dress Mollie occasionally wore. But when they obediently appeared all in gray, he joked, "I am strongly reminded of my visit to Sherburne Prison."

Brother Thomas couldn't stop laughing. "Who are these old ladies in gray?" he hooted.

On another occasion, when Mollie modeled a newly designed bonnet and veil for Walsh, he agreed that all the women should wear the same. But when he next came upon the bonnetted group, he was taken aback: "Everybody has a headache today?"

"A headache?"

"Yes. Aren't those headache bands?"

"Father," said Mollie ominously, "those are bonnets just like the one which I wore and you approved."

"I did?" He seemed genuinely surprised. "It certainly looks different in dozens."

Miss Ward eventually came to the rescue by designing a simple gray habit with a cape and a small toque covered with a veil. Compared to many religious habits, which featured high-pointed bonnets with elaborate fluting or enormous starched wings, pointed cornettes and outsized bibs, the Maryknoll uniform was restrained and practical—as was a distinguishing silver ring with the Greek sign for Christ, Chi-Rho, that completed the outfit. Still, the uniform was anything but smart, as one Maryknoll priest undiplomatically observed. Years later, Mollie experienced the same indignation when a priest in Hawaii contrasted the life of the Sisters with that of an actress who had committed suicide. "She had money, attention, beauty," said the priest, "but she was so unhappy she killed herself. Now you see before you"—they were in the first row—"the Maryknoll Sisters. They are poor, they are not noticed, they are not beautiful, but they are happy." Mollie's retort: "My Sisters *are* beautiful."

Although relations between the Maryknoll men and women were occasionally strained—at one point the women demanded and got from Walsh a raise from two to five cents a quart for the strawberries they picked and preserved—the keynote was humor. The seminary men were prepared to go to any lengths to avoid washing dishes, and when a heavy snowfall prevented the women from reaching the seminary, the seminarians took considerable trouble to rig up a horse-drawn sled to bring them to the kitchen, even though it would have been easier and quicker to do the dishes themselves. The women took the incident good-naturedly, and in the spring of 1919, when men and women succumbed to the Spanish influenza that had been raging throughout the country, the seminarians more than repaid the favor. With most of the Sisters sick, the women's laundry had piled up, so the seminarians did it for them. The first results were startling. First an apologetic young man showed up at the women's door with something that looked like a small tent. It was a habit, starched and scorched to a dapple brown. "I washed it twice over, but it still comes out this color," said the perplexed student. Then a neat little grey package arrived—a clean habit folded in careful creases to the size of a handkerchief. The sheets, too, were carefully ironed and folded into minute squares. Subsequent efforts produced less exotic though still impressive effects: When the Sisters were able to return to the laundry, they found "clean clothes hanging in full driers; boxes of clean, sorted clothes on tables and floor; shirts beautifully ironed hanging on horses; and here and there a smooth, spotless petticoat."

A Valentine's Day Gift

By the end of the decade, illness had become a familiar companion. Mary Louise Wholean, the pretty pioneer from the Hawthorne trio, agonized through a long, painful illness from incurable stomach cancer, and Mollie had to be twice hospitalized for surgery, which marked the start of periodic illnesses during the rest of her life. Some of the sickness could be attributed to overwork, but there was also the strain of two different novitiates and Rome's long refusal to give the Maryknoll Sisters legal recognition.

As Mollie readily admitted, there was "hardly a group more ignorant of spiritual ways" than the Maryknoll women, and it came as a shock to discover how rigid was traditional religious life. In 1914, three Sisters from the Servants of the Immaculate Heart (IHM) came to Maryknoll to form and direct the Teresians in a novitiate, the first step in a process they hoped would lead to formal vows. But it was hard to adjust to Old World disciplines. Most religious communities in the United States were offshoots of a European order or had been founded by a European, whereas the Maryknoll women were totally American in outlook and without any set idea of how things should function. Although the women tried to live up to the demanding obligations imposed by the IHM Sisters, the relationship was often strained. The more democratic Teresians found it difficult to accept a situation in which there was no discussion and the superior's command was absolute law. Meals and recreation were governed by a strict hierarchy, from oldest to youngest; demeaning penances, such as kissing the superior's feet, were often demanded. Walsh favored a program that allowed ample time for prayer but also provided uninterrupted periods of work, for without the women's help the development of the fledgling mission society would be severely hampered. The IHM superior, in contrast, wanted them to have the same customs and observances that European convents had. In European-style convents the summoning of a bell to prayer meant the Sisters instantly had to stop what they were doing—to drop pencil, chalk, or spoon, cut a word in half, leave a letter unfinished, a "y" without its tail, a "t" without its cross. These seeming idiosyncrasies of conduct were a type of gymnastic training for the Holy Rule of monastic life, but they were totally impractical in an office that was trying to publish a monthly magazine, and none of the Teresians ever learned to drop paste and wrapper in mid-air.

Other conflicts arose over family, personal attachments, and the women's behavior. In the traditional convent, relations with the Sisters' families were severely restricted—visits were discouraged, and they were allowed to write only four letters a year to their relatives, no letter being longer than four pages. But Mollie, who came from a warm, loving family, believed in strengthening family ties through weekly letters and frequent visits by relatives to Maryknoll. Personal friendships were a gift from God, she thought, not something to be rejected, as was the traditional practice in women's religious orders. That a woman had an affection for a kitten or kept a photograph of her parents seemed perfectly natural to her, whereas the IHM superior predicted a dire fate for those who did not give up such attachments—they would be "buried on a dunghill" and publicly denounced. Mollie, whose ideas and tastes were quite different, obediently submitted to the superior, but as she later ruefully confided, the former "thought I was proud, and no doubt she was right."

And of course, the Maryknoll women were so exuberant—they loved parties and jokes, and during free periods they had a good time talking and singing, even though recreation consisted of stringing beans or darning the seminarians' socks. Recreation in traditional convents was much more for-mal—everyone sat in a circle facing each other, making polite talk about the weather while sewing, but never voicing their personal feelings. The Maryknoll women felt no such constraints and were often entertained by a young Teresian nicknamed "The Clown," who had an ample repertoire of song and dance and operatic burlesque. Irrepressible, she once presented Walsh with a bouquet of vegetables after he had given a talk on martyrs. Then there was the incident of the piglet. When one of the IHM Sisters came to breakfast on her feast day, she found, in addition to the usual gifts, a tiny, pink and white piglet, bedecked with bows and an Easter hat, occu-pying the place next to her at the table. That night the Maryknollers cele-brated with a costume ball with kimonos trimmed with ribbons and tinsel. Mollie, who was supposed to be the austere founder of a strict religious order, showed up with giant emerald earrings made from Christmas tree candle holders. Although the IHM Sisters were good-humored about such partying, the experience must have been nerve-wracking for such sedate, earnest women.

They departed less than two years later, when it was learned that the novitiate had not been valid under church law because of a new ruling that made Rome's approval necessary to start a religious community. Disheart-ened but unwilling to give up, the women then petitioned the Vatican for approval for a novitiate, only to be refused. Mollie was shocked and pained by the decision but encouraged the women to keep up their spirits. Even though they had not made formal vows, many made private ones and even took religious names, Mollie becoming Mother Mary Joseph; Margaret, Mary Gemma (for an Italian saint); and the others, various additions to Mary, such as Dominic and Bernadette.

The Vatican's delay in recognizing the American women's community was due in part to bureaucratic error—the petition was sent to the wrong congregation, and went back and forth for several months between New York and Rome. But the primary reason, as the women later learned, was the belief of authorities in Rome that "American girls would not make good missioners," in Mollie's words. "They thought we were too soft, too inured to luxury, that we didn't have the right kind of faith."

In the following decades, Americans would often voice Mollie's com-plaint that the "Europeans did not think much of Americans as Catholics," in large part because the Vatican officials had little first-hand experience of the United States. She thought that the courage and self-sacrifice of Ameri-can women who had served in the front lines during World War I might have given Rome "a new and truer appreciation of the American character." But undoubtedly the deciding factors responsible for the Vatican's change of heart were the death of the cardinal in charge of religious petitions and his replacement by a more amenable bishop, support by American bishops and the establishment of financial autonomy for the women's community. When the women in mid-1919 sent a third petition for legal recognition, the reaction in Rome was more positive, and on Valentine's Day, 1920, they received Vatican approval for the formation of the Maryknoll Sisters, officially to be known as the Foreign Mission Sisters of St. Dominic. (The title was later changed to Maryknoll Sisters of St. Dominic.) They were thirty-five women, among them Mollie's younger sister Louise. A year later, she, Mollie and twenty-one others would make their formal religious vows of poverty, chastity, and obedience, and Mollie would become Mother Mary Joseph, the superior. She was thirty-eight and ready at last for God's "great work."

"Large Virtues"

Among the blessings received by the Maryknollers during the trying time of rejection and waiting for Vatican approval was the arrival of a Dominican nun from Wisconsin, Sister Fidelia. A gentle and kindly person, she continued the instruction begun by the IHM Sisters, only hers was less rigid, and there were none of the earlier constraints. Though she looked like a severe school-mistress, with big glasses, small eyes, and a long, pale face, Sister Fidelia was able to distinguish between the essentials of religious life and unnecessary formalities. Nearly sixty, she insisted on joining in the women's fun—"I never saw a community that could get a party going so quickly"—ably juggling the demands of work, recreation, and religious training. Sister Fidelia loved Mollie, and the affection was returned.

The decision to affiliate with the Dominicans reflected several influences, among them the unwavering support and friendship of the Dominican, Mother Alphonsa, whose gift to Mollie had been critical to the Maryknoll women's survival. At the time, new religious communities usually attached themselves to one of three international women's orders—Franciscans, Carmelites, and Dominicans—although Maryknoll, as a mission organization, need not have done so. While the women felt a special devotion to St. Teresa, the Spanish Carmelite, and admired the Franciscans' missionary heritage, study of the constitutions of the three orders persuaded them that the Dominican best suited their needs. The most flexible and the broadest, the Dominicans' six-hundred-year-old constitution had weathered all sorts of crises without needing any changes, and it was sufficiently apostolic to allow the future missionaries to be "contemplatives in action." It also encouraged a down-to-earth practicality, and Mollie was a strong believer in common sense. For example, religious rules held that no Sister could go out without another, but since the Maryknollers often lacked the money to send two women to New York City, she sent only one, who could do the job as well as two. Unable to afford a chauffeur, the Sisters often drove to town in a battered old car. They welcomed visiting nuns to their table, another unconventional practice. And with Mollie's encouragement they retained their natural spontaneity. Refusing to be "hampered by an over-regimented and parceled-out prayer life," she insisted that prayer schedules be adjusted to the demands of mission and that work itself was a form of prayer. She didn't want a bunch of "unnatural goody-goodies" or "ascetics concerned strictly with bodily mortification" but "generous, unhypocritical women whose lives reflect the love of Christ." To her mind there was "altogether too much talk about being 'nailed to the cross' by vows when they are energizing forces which under God's grace make it possible to fulfill our vocation—the constant seeking for union with God."

While sensible, such attitudes were ahead of the times, and Maryknoll Sisters were sometimes criticized by more traditional religious congregations because of their openness and individuality. "We were unknown, suspect, unsought," Mollie said, "and in trying to make ourselves known and our work loved and aided, we were by some considered not a little forward."

As "little Miss Shea," or Sister Gemma, said of her lifelong friend, "Everything about Mother Mary Joseph was large. She was a large person with a large heart and very generous. She had all those large virtues. I remember one time, when the father of one of our Sisters died, she went crying to Mother, asking for the Sisters' prayers, because the family was in terrible financial straits. Mother Mary Joseph had had her own financial problems at Hawthorne, and she found out how much money the family needed to get by on, and she got the money for them. Later, when the family wanted to repay her, she said, no, that's God's gift. She always encouraged us to eliminate 'I,' 'my' and 'mine,' from our vocabulary."

She also urged the women to overlook each other's faults and to be good sports. Under her supervision a more balanced schedule was instituted, with long walks, free afternoons on Wednesdays, simple family entertainments, and home vacations—activities that were taken for granted during her college days at Smith but that were highly unorthodox for women's religious communities of the time. Typically, the Sisters staged their own Broadway productions and saw Hollywood's early movies at Maryknoll, thanks to generous benefactors (films were forbidden to most nuns). Even after the projector blew up, along with a Harold Lloyd film, Mother Mary Joseph was not deterred from providing more movies, which she thought an innocent form of relaxation. Out for a hike through the woods one day, she was leading the Sisters in a game called "stumping" when she stepped on a stone in the brook and fell full length into the muddy stream. Undaunted, she got up and continued to "stump" because the women were enjoying the sport.

But perhaps her greatest gift was her free American spirit. "She didn't believe in training, because that was for animals," said Gemma, "but in teaching through ideas." Mother Mary Joseph's ideas "were not entirely religious," as Gemma pointed out, because she was educated in the public school system and brought up without dogmatic beliefs and rigid religious practices. Valuing individuality, she urged the Maryknoll women to retain and develop their personal gifts as a service to others. She didn't want "every Sister cut to a pattern" or "docile plastic in the hands of her superiors," because she knew they would have to go out to foreign lands and use their ingenuity, their gifts, to make friends with people "who will be suspicious of us, who will not like us, who will respect us only when we have proven our virtue, sincerity and usefulness to them."

"No matter who we were as professional people—doctors, teachers, social workers—she always stressed that our gift was not for ourselves but for the people with whom we were going to share it," said a Maryknoll Sister. "She constantly challenged us to learn foreign languages and do anything to improve ourselves, not for us but for the sake of the people with whom we were going to be in mission. She also stressed adaptability, to do whatever was at hand, whether scrubbing floors or attending a university. She believed deeply in the dignity of each person, in equality. That was another reason for the tension between European and American, between a hierarchical class model and one in which the superior would gladly peel a potato."

"I like to feel," Mother Mary Joseph said, "that people see reflected in our eyes the charity of Christ, and on our lips the words that speak of the charity of Christ and are closed to gossip and scandal, but ever sympathetic to the grief and sorrows of others. I like to feel that they see in us the spirit of mutual love and tenderness which certainly existed in the early ages of the church, when the pagans were forced to say, 'See how they love one another.'"

A Dream Fulfilled

In 1920, the same year the Sisters received Vatican recognition, four, including Gemma, set out for the West Coast to work with Japanese communities in Los Angeles and Seattle, and in 1921 six sailed for China. The first foreign departure was a traumatic experience for the women and their families—in those days missionaries went abroad for life, and faraway China was the last place parents would have chosen for their beloved daughters. But the occasion was lightened by noisemakers, which became a Maryknoll custom for departure ceremonies, and Mother Mary Joseph's consoling words to the parents. This should not be a sad affair, she told them, because "it's the start of a wonderful adventure." The Maryknoll Fathers were already in China, and they would look out for the young women, she said, promising that she herself would carefully monitor the situation there.

Meanwhile, the women's numbers were growing—they were seventy-six by the end of 1921—and more kept coming, some in response to the suffering caused by a world war, others because of the novelty of an American women's mission community. Soon they would overflow five houses at Maryknoll, including a carriage house and a converted barn. The farm now had a sizeable dairy as well as sixty acres of corn, hay, truck gardens, vineyards, and orchards, and the women, though many more than the original band of Teresians, still worked long hours picking and canning, in addition to putting out *The Field Afar* and a new magazine for young people, *The Maryknoll Junior*. But everyone's sights were on China, and the women would wait breathlessly during the announcement of coveted mission assignments, which were made at mealtimes following the tinkling of a bell.

A pioneer band of four Maryknoll priests had opened the first mission in China in 1918, but Father Price, who led the men, died less than a year later of a ruptured appendix. In 1923 the women suffered their first casualty when a Maryknoll Sister, nurse Gertrude Moore, died of typhoid in Yeungkong after nursing sick patients. The first women missioners looked after an orphanage and homes for the elderly and blind and crippled children, but the emphasis was always on women, particularly the poor. Mother Mary Joseph strongly opposed "westernizing Oriental women," and from the start she encouraged the missioners to eat the local food and learn the language and customs. "If there is any conversion as far as customs go," she said, "we are the ones who should change."

In March 1921, less than a month after she had made her religious vows, Mother Mary Joseph visited the Sisters on the West Coast, the first of many trips to distant missions. She returned to Maryknoll with a small, smiling Japanese woman, who would become the first of a number of Asian women to join Maryknoll. Two years later Mother Mary Joseph sailed for China with seven other Maryknoll Sisters, the third group to depart for the Orient.

China in the twenties was in the midst of a civil war, and it was no time for visiting the interior, where war lords and pirates preyed on travelers. But Mother Mary Joseph was determined to see how her Sisters were faring in South China, even if she had to travel on bug-infested junks and overcrowded trains. Then a large, heavy woman, she nevertheless managed to crawl into the dark holes that served as sleeping quarters on the junks and negotiate the wobbly gangplanks from deck to shore. Though often tired and dirty, she brought laughter to the missions and was an instant hit with women and children, who hung on her, fingered her rosary, and chattered away at her in unintelligible Chinese. She ended the journey in Korea, where she made her final vows in a bare, wintry room that served as a chapel.

The experience in China helped nuance her mission vision. At Yeungkong, where the hills rise up in barren, brown knots, she experienced a sense of desolation—everything was so unfamiliar, and the strangeness was compounded by the isolation of the tiny mission in a sea of non-Christian Chinese. "I experienced the awful sense of loneliness that overwhelms our missioners," she later told the Sisters. "Hitherto, I had viewed the whole mission life with the exaltation of the enthusiast, and I found myself appreciating for the first time what perseverance in a vocation like ours entails."

But it was at Chusan, a small island off the mainland, that she found the balm for such loneliness. A well-born English Sister headed the mission there, which included two hospitals and an orphanage. The only foreigner in the community, she had few visitors from her own world—the last had been Father Walsh, the Maryknoll superior, and that had been over six years earlier. When Mother Mary Joseph asked her how she survived such isolation, the woman gestured toward the chapel. "If it were not for Him, I could never have done it," she said.

Mother Mary Joseph returned to Maryknoll convinced of the missioners' need for a strong spiritual and professional formation before going abroad. Such skills as nursing and teaching would enable the women to serve the people, but without an inner sense of God's presence, they could easily give in to fatigue, sickness and self-pity. Hence, two of her earliest ambitions were to establish a college, where the Sisters would receive a solid academic foundation, and a cloister branch, where a small group of Maryknoll women would pray constantly for the missioners and encourage the Sisters' spiritual development. Both were established at Maryknoll in the early 1930s, the cloister in a small hilltop farmhouse where ten Sisters were officially "enclosed" behind a locked grille, there to spend their days in prayer and meditation.

Mother Mary Joseph also fulfilled a long-time dream by constructing a large Motherhouse for her rapidly expanding community. The impressive brick edifice, which was completed in 1932, was a tribute to the generosity of American Catholics during the height of the Depression. Mission circles had been formed by women friends of the Sisters, and every month they sent small checks to help support the missioners and finance the Motherhouse. Although the well-to-do and famous helped—Shirley Temple turned up at a tea party for the Los Angeles Japanese mission—most contributors were working-class Catholics who went without lunch or walked to work for a week to send a few dollars to the Sisters. Children saved pennies and nickels to give to the Maryknoll mite boxes, and many families sent bags of cancelled stamps to the Sisters, who earned money by selling them. The Maryknoll Fathers, who had expanded their holdings with an additional sixty-two-acre farm opposite the seminary, sold the Sisters part of the land and gave them the rest, and *The Field Afar* frequently solicited funds for the construction of the Motherhouse. Eventually a three-story structure emerged among the pine and magnolia trees, a sedate building with none of the Chinese touches that ornamented the men's seminary.

Crossing the road from the familiar Maryknoll seminary grounds to the new Motherhouse was an emotional experience, because it symbolized the Sisters' independence from the men. Due to the rapid growth in both communities, Walsh and Mother Mary Joseph no longer saw each other so often, and the women had begun to develop their own distinctive mission style. Walsh viewed the women's departure with a certain sadness, but as Mother Mary Joseph hastened to reassure him, the Sisters were still his daughters in Christ. Four years after the move Walsh, then a bishop, died in 1936 at the age of sixty-nine, leaving Mother Mary Joseph the only survivor of the three Maryknoll founders, Price having died in Hong Kong many years earlier. Unlike Price, who had never had a close relationship with the Sisters, Walsh's death was keenly felt by Mother Mary Joseph. "You would have loved him," she later told the young seminarians, reliving for them her first meeting with the Irishman in his Boston "rookery."

Although the Maryknollers continued to flourish, Mother Mary Joseph suffered other heartaches—the sickness and death of beloved Sisters, her mother's passing, the sometimes sharp criticism of other religious orders, and a public tongue-lashing by the Catholic magazine *America*. During a visit to Columbia University, she had given a lecture on the origins of the Maryknoll Sisters in which she had said that Smith College had been "instrumental in turning my thoughts to Catholic missions." *America's* editors were shocked by the idea that a Catholic vocation could be nourished in a secular college, and Mother Mary Joseph was roundly condemned for such heresy. But throughout the ensuing controversy she stuck to her conviction that "had I not gone to Smith, I would not now be Mother Mary Joseph."

Nor would the Maryknoll Sisters have developed a pioneer spirit that set them apart from other religious communities. As an American bishop would later say to her, Mother Mary Joseph "made popular the idea that American religious women can give any service required by the least of Christ's brethren. It was something revolutionary in the concept of Sisterhoods to see the smiling faces of the Sisters in photographs, proving that they could keep their spontaneity and individuality."

∼ 3 ∼

To the Orient

===========================

The steamboat at last left Kongmoon—only five hours late. We had been going about four hours and were eating our supper when suddenly we heard shots and a fearful scramble at the other end of the deck. A group of men whom we recognized as fellow-passengers came along, brandishing revolvers, looting our baggage and demanding our money. We learned later that they had killed the captain and the purser and had taken possession of the boat. We were in the hands of river pirates.

A COMMON, AND SOMETIMES lethal, hazard in pre-Communist China, pirates were often endowed with a romantic aura by novices at Maryknoll, who dreamed of a "glorious martyrdom" in the pagan Orient. But the real-life, adventure was an "experience one would not wish one's worst enemy," reported Sister Francis Davis, the leader of a troupe of six Maryknoll Sisters and five Chinese women who in late 1926 were set upon by ten different bands of pirates when returning to their South China mission. Such was the women's fright that one, a Chinese catechist, suffered a nervous breakdown. But what most rankled Francis, a hardened missioner from Jersey City, was the loss of her shoes:

> During the first excitement bullets screamed through the air, and all passengers were forced to give up their money and valuables. When our turn came, the bandits were infuriated because we had so little money. We overheard them discussing our fate. To be held for ransom; a Sister and one of the Chinese women to be taken as prizes by one of the young bandits; all to be shot—these were possibilities. Meantime, we sought shelter in the cabin, where our Maryknoll pastor gave us all general absolution. We recited the rosary non-stop.
>
> As soon as darkness broke the next morning, another band of bandits boarded the boat. The first group, which had sailed the steamer onto a sandbar, had left with the loot they had acquired. The second group extorted from the passengers what few coins they had

dared hold back the night before. From us they took our medals, rosaries, and crucifixes. In all, ten bands of pirates boarded the boat, one after the other, each taking what remained to be plundered, until we were left with only the clothes on our backs.

On the second morning our Chinese companions, unharmed, were brought back under escort, with a decree from the pirate chief on shore that no harm was to be done to any of our party. From the Chinese women we learned that the chief, to whose quarters they had been taken, had once lived in Chicago. There he had formed a favorable impression of the Catholic church, and when he learned that we were Catholics, he ordered the women returned and also issued a decree in our favor.

Looting continued, but we enjoyed several hours unmolested, seemingly because the looters respected the chiefs decree, which had been posted on our door. The last band, however, did not recognize this particular chief. Angrily they demanded more money. They searched us none too gently, then insisted I give them my new shoes. Guns or no, I refused, but the other Sisters were afraid I'd be killed. I don't know which was harder to forgive—the bandit who took my shoes or the Sister who took them off my feet!

This was followed by a brief and bitter debate among the bandits that ended in a decree that we should die. When we pointed to the chiefs edict, they laughed scornfully.

We were lined up against the rail on the deck, and for the second time the priest gave us general absolution. Suddenly the sound of an approaching vessel was heard, and, as if by magic, our would-be executioners were over the side of the boat.

Breathlessly we waited. Did this forebode fresh trouble or relief? Our prayers were answered. The boat proved to be a "rescue boat" sent by our ex-Chicagoan to pull us off the sandbar and set us free.

As was customary among women religious at the time, the Sisters downplayed their brush with death, emphasizing amusing incidents instead—"at one point a pirate shook a packet on the floor, thinking it might contain something valuable, but it was full of pepper, and everyone began to sneeze." Nor was poor Francis allowed to forget that she had lost her shoes: "Have you got your shoes safe, Sister Francis?" other Maryknollers would tease her.

But the robbery was no joke—the women lost a year's supply of food for their mission in Yeungkong, in addition to all their clothing and books. At a time when money was scarce, and the Sisters endured a hand-to-mouth existence, Francis was not exaggerating when she complained that "we are really paupers now."

Hard Beginnings

When the first band of six Maryknoll Sisters departed for China in 1921, their only thought was of the wonderful adventure that awaited them in "blazing a trail to Christ." The Maryknoll Fathers, who had already established mission centers in South China and Hong Kong, wanted the Sisters to evangelize among Chinese women, who were inaccessible to priests because of the rigid separation of the sexes. But the goal was vague, and the Sisters, who had had no training in Chinese languages, culture, or history, had nothing to guide them save "faith and simplicity," in the words of Sister Mary Paul McKenna, the leader of the pioneer group:

> Mother Mary Joseph knew nothing about China. She had never been there. And Father Walsh, the Maryknoll superior, who was traveling with us, knew China only from a general tour. He had not seen the Fathers there since 1918, and this was 1921. When we got to China, I asked him, "What should we do?" He said, "Didn't Mother Mary Joseph tell you?" I said, "No." Mother Mary Joseph had said, "Oh, Father General will be with you." So that was all we knew.
>
> I never even thought about financial arrangements, and consequently we made none before we left [the United States]. We had a certain amount of money when we arrived, but we soon found ourselves in debt.

Nor did Hong Kong, the site chosen as the Sisters' South China center, give the women a warm welcome. Although two communities of European Sisters were already established there, the Americans were viewed with suspicion by the Portuguese inhabitants, who comprised a majority of Hong Kong's Catholics. The Maryknollers were Americans, and America was synonymous with Protestant. The European Sisters also distrusted the new arrivals, believing them "unfit for mission life." The Chinese looked on them as curiosities; the British colonials ignored them as socially unimportant. Even the Maryknoll Fathers were reluctant to seem too friendly because of possible disapproval by the stiff-necked Portuguese. "We felt like strangers," Mary Paul ruefully admitted.

Living in a small rented cottage that overlooked the Canton railroad tracks, the women had to contend with a difficult new language, exotic—and to them, inedible—food and bewildering customs. The Chinese carried their food—meat or vegetables—hung on a piece of string, so the Sisters did likewise. But one day, when returning home with a fish on a string, they ran into Father Walsh, who was horrified. Foreigners did not carry anything in the Orient, he said. Frederick Simpich, an American journalist who covered China in the twenties, agreed with Walsh: "No white person of dignity would be seen carrying even a package of books through the streets, lest he lose caste in native eyes. This was not snobbish but wise. It inspired native respect in a land of sharp social distinctions." As Simpich observed, labor had no dignity for the Chinese, who saved money to achieve an easy life, symbolic of which were long fingernails, a long gown, and the leisure to read Chinese classics. But the Sisters, who had been taught to value labor, had no idea that carrying a fish meant "losing face."

For all the strangeness the women found Hong Kong "a storybook" adventure. "I can remember waking on my first morning there," said one, "and hearing this 'click-clock,' 'click-clock' and thinking, what in the world is that? Later, I found out it was the wooden shoes of the people on the street."

Outside the French windows of their European cottages was a teeming world of coolies, rickshaws, and amahs and, beyond in the harbor, colorful sampans and square-sailed junks—a forest of yellow and brown sails. Alleyways and streets overflowed with stalls selling silks, jade, smoked ducks, crude bamboo kitchen utensils, and bouquets of tiny tropical flowers. Around the stalls eddied the human traffic—sweating coolies in mushroom hats balancing heavy loads on bamboo poles, emaciated beggars pleading for a few coins, trousered women hurrying across the cobblestone streets in tiny cloth shoes, old men with long beards smoking water pipes. Here and there the foreigner's white sun helmet bobbed above the crowd. Over all "drifted smoke, plus odors—Chinesey ones"—of fried fish and incense mingled with wisteria and garbage. "I enjoyed every bit of it," remembered one young Sister, "even the dried fish and rice for breakfast."

Mary Paul enjoyed it, too. In later years acquaintances would say that she had adapted so well, in her use of Chinese facial expressions and gestures, that she "began to look Chinese." But in the first months, when she was trying to keep her small group afloat, there was little time to reflect on her experience. Although the Maryknollers lived frugally, the women soon ran out of money, and Mary Paul had to borrow from Walsh. The Fathers had paid the rent and furnished the women's house, but when Mary Paul got the bill, she found to her horror that $5,000 was due. Writing to Mother Mary Joseph for help, Mary Paul forgot to say that the debt was in Hong Kong dollars, and when the money arrived, it turned out to be in U.S. currency. "The exchange being five to one, that put us on our feet for the time being."

Mary Paul knew the Sisters had to have an income, and soon they were organizing a small "factory" in their dining room to make priests' vestments, which were sold in the United States. The work provided jobs for poor, unskilled Chinese girls who were trained by a young Chinese woman, Teresa Yeung, who later became Maryknoll's first Chinese Sister from Hong Kong. The income from this mail order business enabled the Sisters to open a small kindergarten in their garage that eventually grew into one of Hong Kong's most prestigious schools. In 1922, six additional Sisters arrived from Maryknoll, and more kept coming. By 1924, the women were well enough known to be asked by Hong Kong's British governor to staff a local hospital, but the news caused an uproar in the local British community, which was outraged that jobs should be given to the American upstarts when nurses in England were unemployed. Although Mary Paul was secretly relieved by the reaction—at that point the Sisters did not have the resources to staff a good British hospital—typically she refused to withdraw, leaving the governor in the embarrassing position of having to renege on the offer. The Sisters did not lose face—an issue of prime importance to the Chinese—and the governor felt bound to make amends by showing the Maryknollers favor in other ways, such as approval for the lease of a government property for the construction of a convent and school. But Mary Paul was shrewd and tough, and when it was to Maryknoll's advantage, she drove a hard bargain.

Known in her earlier life as Grace Anselma McKenna, Mary Paul had been a school teacher and principal in Pennsylvania before joining Maryknoll in 1917, and she never lost her schoolmarm manner. Short and bespectacled, with a prominent chin and prim-looking mouth, she showed no shyness or hesitancy. Many who came in contact with her were overawed, whether young Sisters, bishops, or Japanese military commanders— her long and often imperious rule came to be known among Maryknollers as the "Manchu dynasty." Even the first Maryknoll pioneers were subdued in her presence—Gemma Shea remembered that when Mary Paul rang a bell, absolute silence ensued, none daring to speak as she gave orders. Nor did she mince words when dealing with church and government officials: "I see no reason for it and no advantage in it," she told a bishop, dismissing his proposal for another Maryknoll center.

Although many Sisters smarted under Mary Paul's rule, her strong personality was important in gaining the Sisters a foothold in China. Nor did she ever ask them to do what she would not—she often made the same dangerous river trip on which her Sisters had been pirated; hence her attitude to the attack was, it's too bad, but don't make a tragedy of it. In the 1920s religious life, even among easygoing Maryknollers, was ruled by the superior, whose job was to lead; the subjects were to follow unquestioningly. Thousands of miles from Maryknoll headquarters, Mary Paul often had to make decisions on her own, some of which were not popular with the other Sisters. That she sometimes experienced loneliness and anxiety was revealed in her letters to Mother Mary Joseph that ended with the lament, "if only I could talk to you." For all her determination, she had a soft spot for the frightened newcomer. "When I first came to Hong Kong," remembered one Sister, "I was so lonely, I couldn't take it. I went to Sister

Mary Paul and put my head in her lap and cried and cried. She comforted me—she understood people."

Yin and Yang

Although the Sisters' earliest works were aimed at obtaining an income, Mary Paul never lost sight of the Maryknollers' primary purpose in coming to China—to evangelize among women. Poor Chinese factory girls, peasants, university students, or the wives of upper-class government officials—all were potential converts to Catholicism, though the largest number would come from the poorer classes, particularly the peasantry.

Then as now, a Chinese woman's identity was determined by her relationship to a man—first as her father's daughter, then as her husband's wife, and later as her son's mother. Parents arranged the girl's marriage, often when she was still a toddler, and once married she was subject to the tyranny of both husband and mother-in-law. Although upper-class women enjoyed more leisure, they suffered numerous humiliations, including the imposition of secondary wives and concubines, and could be repudiated for a variety of reasons, such as failure to provide a son. Symbolic of women's subjugation was the practice of footbinding, which was not outlawed until the 1930s. From age five to fifteen a girl's feet were tightly wrapped, thereby producing a broken arch and curled toes, or the "lily feet" prized by Chinese men for their erotic attraction. Peasant women were less likely to undergo footbinding because it limited their ability to walk and work, and the peasant woman was the principal beast of burden in rural China. Not only did she plant, water, and harvest the fields, she was also expected to collect firewood; cook, wash and clean; weave cloth and mats; and care for her children and her husband's parents and grandparents. Illiterate, undernourished, and overworked, she received no income for her labors and had few or no property rights.

Because wives were expected to live with their husbands' families, and most girls married between the ages of twelve and fifteen, only the in-laws benefited from their adult labor. Thus girl babies were less welcome than boys, for economic as well as social reasons. Boys would continue to work for the extended family when they grew up, and sons were a status symbol. In the Chinese world the social order devolved on two complementary elements, *yin* and *yang*. *Yin* represented the female, dark, passive, and weak; *yang* symbolized the male, bright, strong, and active. In actuality, little complementarity was recognized in regard to male and female status, worth, and dignity. Added to such social prejudices were superstitions that protected the male offspring but could lead to the death or abandonment of a girl baby. In some rural areas, for example, superstition held that if a girl infant was killed, the next child would be a boy. If a woman had several girls in succession, she was believed to be possessed by a devil, and only by killing the last girl baby could she rid herself of the spell.

The most common form of infanticide was suffocation, by putting the baby in a crock and covering it with ashes or dirt or wrapping it so tightly in rags that it could not breathe or cry. Many were abandoned in ditches and temples, there to die. The mother often had no say in the matter, although some tried to save their infant daughters by giving them to foreigners. Maryknoller Monica Marie Boyle, who ran an orphanage in South China, recalled how one afternoon, when she was walking home and had stopped to rest beneath a large tree, she discovered a bundle nearby that turned out to be a tiny waif:

> On examining the child more closely, I found its clothing to be of a better quality than that in which most babies in our area were abandoned. On its outer garment was a note which read: "Precious Joy. Born June 16." Six weeks old, and quiet as if in her mother's arms, the infant continued her slumbers while my companion and I ate lunch. As no one was present to claim the baby, I decided she was meant for the mission.
>
> A year later we received a letter from Precious Joy's mother inquiring about her daughter. The father and mother, with two other children, had been refugees on their way to Kwangsi the previous summer. The mother was not well at the time and was unable to make the long journey on foot and to care for the child, too. Consequently, the father had demanded that the baby be abandoned. The mother's letter continued:
>
> "For several days I tried to leave her behind, but always lost heart. One day I saw a Sister coming across the field, towards the tree where we had been resting. I felt that, if we left the baby there, Sister would pick her up and care for her. This we did, and then fled into a rice field nearby. We watched until Sister picked up the child and carried her away. Then something happened within me—for the first time in my life I felt the desire to pray. I knelt down as I had seen the Christians do. I did not know any prayer, but I cried out from my heart, 'O God of the Sisters, be good to my little Precious Joy!'"

Precious Joy grew into a sturdy child, but many girl infants were dead or dying by the time they reached Monica's orphanage. Although some had been abandoned, most were victims of unsanitary care at birth. In South China, for instance, a piece of rice straw or hemp was used to tie the umbilical cord, which was then cut with a broken glass and dressed with the ashes of old rags. Consequently many infants died from lockjaw. Those that survived frequently contracted a deadly disease such as smallpox or typhoid.

Orphanages for girls were among the first works undertaken by the Sisters when they expanded from Hong Kong to the Chinese mainland in 1922. Though a traditional form of charity, they gave testimony to the Maryknollers' belief in the equal value of female life. Women's dignity was the keynote from the start, not only shaping the Maryknoll Sisters' work in China but, later, in Latin America and Africa. Protestant missionaries also played an important role in upgrading women's status, through orphanages and schools, but among the Catholics only the Maryknoll Sisters went into the villages to live and work with the women in an unprecedented outreach to the poor. "I think we were aware of the dignity of women long before it was talked about," said a Maryknoll Sister who served in South China. "It was hammered into us by our superiors, who would read us articles and books about women that gave us a sense of women's rights."

While the aim was to evangelize, religion itself became a means of women's liberation. Like missionaries before them, the Maryknoll priests soon discovered that they could make little headway by converting only men. Forbidden contact with Chinese women and hampered by a lack of women catechists, they baptized a few men, but the families remained "pagan" because the mothers, who were responsible for the children's upbringing, had no women to instruct them. If the father died, the entire effort was wasted. Moreover, many men lapsed back into the old ways because of lack of family support. The Sisters were supposed to change this situation—and did—by going into fields and kitchens, where they gained the women's confidence and friendship, eventually kindling their desire for religious instruction and baptism. "Some of the priests in China were excellent speakers," recalled a Maryknoll Sister, "but they could never talk about the humdrum things of life like we Sisters could. I think that's true of women on the whole—we can get down into our skins. Men tend to be loners and want to be administrators and directors. In China it was often more lonesome for the priests. We brought joy to the women's lives. When they came to the mission, we'd have games and fun. They didn't know joy but only hard work. Excitement? Forget it, except when a new baby was born."

The Maryknollers also gave Chinese peasant women a sense of worth, with their emphasis on the belief that all people were equal regardless of sex or color. Constant stress on the Christian ideal of womanhood led to greater cooperation among the village women, including wives and mothers-in-law. Husbands were encouraged to show greater respect for wives, an ideal put into practice in Catholic lay associations in which women had the same voting rights as men. That wives could receive communion together with husbands and mothers-in-law at the same altar was itself a revelation in a society in which wives traditionally walked several steps behind husbands and mothers-in-law, usually carrying the heaviest burdens.

The relationship between the Maryknoll Sisters and priests and Brothers also provided small lessons in women's dignity. Although the pastor was supposed to be the boss, the missioners usually worked as teams, and the men were "most thoughtful, concerned for our welfare, kind and appreciative," as one Sister observed. They even helped the women bring in the laundry when rain threatened, an example that caused no little consternation among the Chinese men who worked with the Maryknollers and felt bound to do likewise.

Through schools for orphans and poor girls, the Sisters provided role models at a time when China was about to undergo profound social and political changes that would offer women new opportunities. Because they were literate, and knew how to cook and sew, the Maryknoll orphans were much sought after as wives and were often able to attract good husbands. The Sisters served as surrogate parents, providing a wedding trousseau and party. But the Maryknollers never forced any of their charges to marry, and some did not, preferring to become midwives or nurses or to join local novitiates of Chinese Sisters.

Yet, however much they loved and sacrificed for the orphans, the missioners were sometimes blind to human need in their zeal to evangelize. In order to care for the babies they received, the Sisters paid Chinese women a small fee to breast-feed them. Sometimes the nurses were the babies' own mothers—an arrangement approved only if the mother agreed that the child belonged to the mission. In most cases the relationship proved satisfactory: The child was adequately fed, clothed and educated—luxuries poor mothers could not afford—and the family visited the girl or took her home during Chinese festivals. Occasionally, however, the wet nurses decided they wanted to keep their daughters. But because they were non-Catholics, the Sisters insisted on the return of the baptized children, even threatening the parents with a court action and imprisonment. Conditioned by the prevailing Catholic belief that souls were more important than bodies or feelings, they "made a terrible social mistake," as one Sister later conceded, by refusing to compromise.

The mistake was one of many. Though more involved in village life than other Catholic missionaries, the Sisters shared the same cultural and religious prejudices, and sometimes they were hopelessly ignorant—they wore white habits, for example, although white for the Chinese is a symbol of death. Undoubtedly, the most serious error of foreign missionaries was the demand that converts renounce important cultural practices, such as Chinese festivals and rites in honor of the dead, which were part of the social fabric of community life. In order to become Catholic, the Chinese were expected to adopt Western ways, even when they destroyed the harmony of social relations so important to the Chinese way of life. Catholicism divided villagers, parents and children, husbands and wives, undermining a cultural code that subordinated the individual to the social conventions of the extended family or clan. Defying a clan elder, father, or husband over ancestral rites, for example, was unacceptable conduct that led to a loss of face and set the person adrift from a system in which he or she had previously enjoyed stable relationships.

The Maryknollers' American prejudices against a society with strange habits and food were more quickly overcome than Catholic ones. Living with the Chinese, they came to love and respect them, adopting many of their ways. Much harder to deal with was the existing model of the Catholic church, which denigrated other religions as barbaric cults and recreated eurocentric copies of the church in overseas missions. Unable to understand that Confucianism was a code of moral conduct, Rome confused nonreligious rituals with religious ones. The principal sticking point was so-called ancestor worship. Most clans had a wall shrine, some enclosed in glass, with tablets containing the names and histories of their ancestors and a bowl of incense burning in front of the shrine. Clan cemeteries showed similar reverence for ancestors: Located on a slope facing hills and water, they were laid out in the form of a horseshoe, each grave with its name, the first ancestor's resting place facing and guarding the rest. Foreigners mistook incense, colored scrolls, and ritual processions as signs of superstition, not realizing the difference between kneeling in front of ancestral tablets, which was a sign of remembrance and an expression of hope for the clan's continuity, and the same act in front of a wind god. Incense burning also had different meanings—filial piety in front of the tablets, worship in front of gods or, in a house, a way to eliminate bad odors or keep away mosquitoes. Nevertheless, the Sisters routinely destroyed ancestral shrines and forbade burning incense or praying at a coffin because they could be interpreted as signs of superstition. The incongruity of condemning rituals common to both Christians and Confucians was not lost on a Maryknoll priest who, at his first Chinese funeral,

> immediately blessed the place, knelt down and said a couple of prayers for the dead man. After the funeral Father Meyer, our superior, told me that the catechist had reported I performed a superstition at the funeral by kneeling beside the man's coffin and saying a prayer. He laughed at me and said, "Well, you are excommunicated."

That one person's religion was another's superstition was clear to educated Chinese. They thought it absurd that they should be accused of superstition because they put food on the graves of their ancestors when

Westerners covered their relatives' graves with flowers. "When do they come up to smell the flowers?" they asked. "So why should our ancestors come up and eat the food? We make such offerings as a symbol of sharing. They have shared their lives with us, and we want to show our continuous gratitude for what we have received from them."

Although some Chinese rituals were tinged with superstition, from the perspective of those outside, the same could probably be said of such Catholic rituals as the sprinkling of holy water on village livestock. If the Sisters found Buddhist virgins strange, because they shaved their heads and worshiped idols, the Chinese thought the bonneted and veiled Americans even more so. Sometimes the Sisters overheard their whispers: "Are they men or women?" "The big one is the husband, and the shorter one is the wife." "No, they're Buddhists. Look at their prayer beads!"

By the end of the thirties, when Rome officially recognized its error in condemning Confucian rites of filial piety, the Maryknollers were more flexible in their demands of Catholic converts, who were no longer forced to renounce community customs in order to be baptized. Had they done so earlier, they might have had more success in encouraging a Chinese version of Christianity. But very few missionaries understood the common values in Christianity and Confucianism. One was the Italian Jesuit Matteo Ricci, who, in the late 1500s, opened China's doors by adopting the dress, language, food, and customs of the Chinese mandarins and becoming a learned commentator on Confucius. Because of his open appreciation of the local culture, Ricci's gifts, including a knowledge of mathematics, philosophy, astronomy, and map-making, were welcomed by the Chinese. When he died, the emperor of China decreed that he be buried as a high mandarin; his successors became advisers to the Manchu dynasty. Ricci did not attempt to proselytize among the poor, believing the mandarin class the key to religious conversion. Nor did he give any thought to women. But as an example of "inculturation," or presenting Christianity within an indigenous framework, he was a brilliant pioneer.

Even though China was again closed to foreign missionaries at the end of the eighteenth century, the seeds planted by Ricci endured, as Maryknollers discovered in South China, where Catholic families still remained faithful to their beliefs. Unlike his twentieth-century successors, Ricci was not interested in counting the number of baptisms or catechism classes— all Maryknollers had to issue such monthly statistical reports—but in sharing values and knowledge. His account of life in China, published in 1615, caused a sensation in Europe. His treatise on friendship, *Jiaoyou Lun*, was equally popular in China. As pointed out by a Maryknoll priest, "Chinese intellectuals forgave Ricci's incomplete knowledge of their religious thought because they sensed his earnest attempts to understand their culture." The same could be said of the Maryknoll Sisters, who, despite their mistakes, were welcomed and loved by Chinese women.

Yeungkong

That the Maryknoll women received such a warm reception was due in large part to the makeup of the people in rural South China, where they began their missions. The Chinese peasants were simple, unschooled folk who patiently coaxed a sustenance from the "good earth." Comprising four-fifths of China's population, the largest number lived in the tropical south, where annual monsoons drenched the hills and valleys. Crescent-shaped rice paddies covered most of the arable land, each enclosed by a stone embankment along which ran a narrow footpath. Clusters of huts crowded together on the edge of the rice paddies, never occupying more land than necessary. With less than a half acre of food-producing soil per person, space was, and still is, a luxury few could afford. While richer peasants used water buffalo to supplement their work, most of the farming was done by hand, including the back-breaking labor of transplanting rice seedlings one by one in the muddy, ankle-deep water.

Dependent on sun and rain for survival, the peasantry passively accepted as inevitable such calamities as droughts, floods, starvation, and disease. Unlike Europe and the United States, where ample land was available and agriculture could be supplemented by hunting and fishing, there was little opportunity for initiative in the overcrowded south. The Chinese farmer did not expect change—was suspicious of it—and was encouraged in such conservatism by Confucianism, which emphasized the virtues of patience, pacifism, and compromise. Living in such close proximity, the Chinese were extremely sociable people—even the poorest would welcome the Sisters with tiny cups of tea. The presence of the American women offered a change from the tedium of village life, and when the peasants visited the Maryknoll mission, they were entertained by such novelties as staircases, glass windows, colored pictures, and a hand-wound Victrola. "They all wanted to learn English," Mary Paul recalled. "They knew about America and California—that gold had been found there!"

The Chinese's frank curiosity about the Americans' lifestyle was reciprocated by the unsophisticated young Sisters, who found much to wonder about in their exotic surroundings. Travel, even for short distances, was always an adventure because of inevitable mishaps. Steamboats were stranded on sandbars; junks were commandeered by soldiers or could not sail because of pirates. Although the Sisters' first mission at Yeungkong was only one hundred miles south of Canton on the South China coast, it often took three or more days to reach it by junk, steamer, and sampan. "We have had our first junk experience," reported Mary Paul of the Sisters' maiden voyage to Yeungkong, "and all that we had read and thought paled before the reality":

> Our first glimpse of the old unpainted hulk showed us boxes, crates of ducks, mats and Chinese everywhere. The top deck was piled high, and when we reached it, there seemed to be no room. But a little space, about two feet square, was cleared of ducks—feathers were abundant and blew in all directions. Sampans, with their bits of cargo, stood three deep around the junk. Women were loading and unloading. Children walked perilously near the edge, staring at the curious group on the deck. It grew dark—black—early, and we turned down to our cabins.
>
> The descent was alarming at first—down to a narrow ledge from which we swung around to the kitchen, where Chinese were cooking and eating their rice. Our cabin was at the end of an aisle formed by baggage and sleeping Chinamen. We were next door to a pagan shrine before which a vigil light burned. The door slid open, and we saw our apartment "de luxe"—two shelves, one big enough for four people; the other, for three.
>
> There was no lock on the door; after the seven of us Sisters got inside, there was hardly room for a lock. A little oil lamp hung on the wall and sent an invitation through our three-by-four-window openings to all the mosquitoes' in the neighborhood, and they came.

So did spiders, cockroaches, and rats. Packed head to foot and fearful of the nasty things that scurried over them, few slept. The Chinese, meanwhile, were having an all-night party playing Mah-Jongg, a popular game in which slender tiles serve as cards and are noisily slapped down amidst much laughter and talking. When the burst of firecrackers announced the dawn's arrival, the Sisters dragged themselves topside. "There was a common toilet which was nothing but a hole in the deck," recalled Mary Paul. "You dipped dirty water from the river to wash yourself. There was very little privacy."

Yeungkong was reached on a cold, windy morning. The sampans that were to take the Sisters ashore tossed dangerously in the water, and women had to jump, in full habits, to the pitching boats below. All shared Mary Paul's relief on reaching the shore: "How happy we were to have arrived!"

Mother Mary Joseph, by then a large woman, traveled the same route the following year but made light of the discomforts of crawling down black, slimy holes. "Can you picture me disappearing through a coal scuttle?" she wrote her Sisters at Maryknoll. "Well, that's about what I did on the junk."

The Sisters' cabin opened onto the ship's galley, where ducks and chickens were killed, plucked, and cooked; close by were cages with live skunks and lynx, adding to the odors. The noise never stopped—the junk was a bedlam of soldiers, who were sailing to Yeungkong under the flag of Sun Yat-sen to protect it from a local warlord. When Mother Mary Joseph's group reached the walled town late at night, they had to batter on the gates to gain admittance. "You must open the gates," insisted the Maryknoll priest who accompanied them. "With us is a very large woman from the beautiful country of the West."

Yeungkong, as Mother Mary Joseph discovered the following morning, was no tourist spot. A country town in Kwangtung (now Guang Dong) province, it had a few narrow streets where pigs rooted among the garbage. The thatched huts were made of gray bricks, and there was little foliage to relieve the monotonous view of bare, brown hills. The shops were "interesting but not attractive," wrote Mother Mary Joseph—she found little to buy save some brass scissors and pigskin boxes. But the people were friendly and followed the large American everywhere: "Where are you going? Where did you come from? What did you buy?"

By comparison with the mean, one-room hovels, the Sisters' yellow, three-story convent was a palace; it excited considerable interest among the Chinese, who frequently visited the house to admire the staircases—an architectural innovation—and the view of the river harbor from the upper verandas. The house, which had been built under the supervision of the local Maryknoll superior, Father Francis Ford, was, the Sisters felt, too grand and European, setting them apart from the people—an opinion Ford himself would later share when he sent the Sisters to live in Chinese villages. But at the time "he thought it was too much to ask of us to live in a Chinese-style house," Mary Paul said. The priest was probably right, because the Sisters had enough to contend with in learning the Yeungkong dialect and taking charge of an orphanage, old folks' home, dispensary, and schools for blind girls and peasant women. The weather was humid, and the missioners either sweltered or froze. Typhoons were not uncommon; insects and rats were ever-present. Dressed in white or gray habits, depending on the season, the Sisters had to drag their long skirts through the mud and were often soaked in perspiration. Prickly heat, diarrhea, and rheumatism were frequent complaints, but the worst scourge was bedbugs, which sometimes lodged themselves inside the Sisters' bonnets. Vermin, unhygienic living conditions and little or no preventive medicine or vaccinations led to frequent outbreaks of cholera, malaria, and typhoid, and it was while nursing typhoid victims that the first Maryknoll Sister died in China.

Known to the Chinese as the "doctor," Maryknoll nurse Gertrude Moore had been among the first six Sisters to arrive in Yeungkong in the fall of 1922. A jolly, plump woman, the New York City nurse not only attended the crowded dispensary but went out to the villages on sick calls. There was no doctor in the area, and in Gertrude's first ten months at the mission she treated six thousand cases of worms, blood poisoning, skin disease, and eye afflictions. When a typhoid epidemic struck the town, she was treating fifty to one hundred patients daily until she herself contracted the disease, dying a few weeks later.

One reason Mother Mary Joseph had gone to China in 1923 was to comfort the Sisters and visit Gertrude's grave. The brick-enclosed mound where she was buried was located in a small Christian cemetery barren of trees or grass—a desolate place, Mother Mary Joseph thought, until several curious peasants and children approached. A woman carrying a large load of faggots paused to watch the scene, then was joined by a group of small boys herding water buffalo and a man minding a flock of geese. A leper slunk by, hiding behind a bush. Suddenly, Mother Mary Joseph was glad Gertrude's grave was in that spot, so close to the lives of the poor Chinese whom she had served.

Adding to the drama of the visit was the seizure of the town by a local warlord. Some six thousand soldiers loyal to Sun Yat-sen were guarding Yeungkong, but shortly after Mother Mary Joseph's arrival the hirelings decamped, leaving the town to the mercy of the warlord's soldiers. Refugees poured into the Sisters' compound, and for two nights the Maryknoll Fathers stood guard. As one of the priests told it:

> When the outsiders entered, all hell broke loose. Fires started in about five different parts of the city, guns were banging, people were screaming and, through it all, one could hear the smash, smash of doors as the soldiers got closer on their pilgrimage of loot. The poor souls inside the convent walls were so frightened that one could hear a pin drop. They could not cry out, even if they had wanted to, and strange as it may seem, even their babies were too frightened to cry ... The Sisters could see the soldiers making the rounds and carrying off the loot that had not been stored away before the trouble began. Fortunately, it was just stealing they had to look at. The soldiers did not enter the convent. They just passed it by, and it was not even necessary to tell them it was foreign property.

Eventually, Father Ford, a local Protestant minister, and the town mandarin ventured forth to negotiate peace with the warlord's men, and the refugees were able to return to their homes. The Sisters had prominently displayed the American flag on the convent, and the flag provided protection because of the extraterritorial rights of foreign missions. Such protection was welcomed, and often used, by the Chinese peasantry, which was caught in the middle of a civil war between warlords and the national government that raged throughout the 1920s and 1930s. But a foreign identity was not always a guarantee of physical safety, particularly in the big cities, where anti-foreign outbreaks were common. Maryknoll Sister Rosalia Kettl told of one such incident during a visit to neighboring Canton:

> In those days the cities were walled, with narrow alleyways in which the rickshaws went up and down. Sister Mary Paul had taken a group of us Sisters to see the Maryknoll Fathers' Canton mission, which was a little house at the end of a long alley. When we came out, we were met by a stone-throwing mob. We were too far away from the mission to go back, so we started running—we didn't know what else to do. There was a bus at the end of the alley, and we could see the bus driver waving frantically at us. We jumped in the bus, and even though the mob broke the bus windows, we escaped unhurt.

Matters came to a head in the spring of 1925 when, during a textile workers' protest in Shanghai, British soldiers shot several dozen Chinese. The incident rekindled Chinese hatred of the unjust treaties imposed on them by Europe and Japan and that had reduced the once proud nation to a semi-colonial status. Students and workers led anti-foreign riots throughout China, including Kwantung province, where the Maryknollers were located. Fearful of another Boxer Rebellion, foreign consuls urged their nationals to evacuate the interior, and Maryknoll's superior in China, Father James E. Walsh, responded by recalling priests and Sisters in Yeungkong and Loting, where a second Maryknoll mission had been established. The Maryknollers in Loting arrived in Hong Kong without mishap, but those in Yeungkong could not be reached because the telegraph was down. Walsh first approached the American consul about sending a ship to rescue the missioners, but as no U.S. vessel was available, the British were enlisted to send a gunboat, *The Stanley*. Two Maryknoll priests joined the crew. Surviving the tail end of a typhoon, *The Stanley* arrived at the Yeungkong harbor on a Sunday morning, and the priests went off to fetch the stranded missioners. Though promising to return the same evening, they found on reaching shore that no boatmen would take the group to *The Stanley* until the following morning. At dawn the next day, the Sisters and priests set out in a sampan but, because of contrary winds, were unable to reach the ship, although in sight of her for seven hours. Not realizing that the sampan contained the Maryknollers, the captain decided to return to Hong Kong since his coal supply was nearly exhausted and pirates lurked nearby. The arrival of the ship sans Maryknollers caused considerable consternation, and the U.S. destroyer *Simpson*, which had just entered the harbor, was sent to the rescue.

When the *Simpson* arrived at the mouth of the Yeungkong River, a high sea was running, and the captain was reluctant to launch a boat, but eventually two boats were lowered. Walsh and another Maryknoll priest, Father Anthony Paulhus, boarded a motor launch with twelve sailors, while two others manned a whaleboat. On reaching the breakers, the whaleboat overturned and the launch was swamped. Unable to reach land, the launch returned to the *Simpson* with the news that two seamen had drowned.

The next day, Father Paulhus set off alone in a native sailboat, landed below the mouth of the Yeungkong River, walked eighteen miles to the town gates, finally gained admittance, and, after an hour of drinking tea with the local mandarin, was able to reach the Maryknoll mission with the message that the *Simpson* had come to rescue the Americans. Father Ford, meanwhile, had been called to the mandarin's house, where a bedraggled American sailor was being held prisoner—the mandarin thought he was an Englishman, and popular sentiment against Britain was strong because of the Shanghai incident. Ford was able to convince the official that the sailor was one of the Americans who had been washed overboard when the whaleboat had capsized. When the Maryknollers eventually reached the *Simpson*, they found that the second sailor had also survived. After being in the water six hours, he had been washed ashore near a village where he met a Chinese recently returned from the United States who helped him return to his ship.

As the Sisters' diary observed, the Maryknollers were "willing to lay down our lives for our faith, but no one cares to be killed simply because she is a foreigner." Yet on reflection the missioners realized they had made a mistake by abandoning their posts and becoming too closely identified with the U.S. consulate. When Maryknoll's cofounder, James Anthony Walsh, had first visited China, he had told the American consul in Canton that "it is our intention never, if we can help it, to call on you for any political assistance in carrying out our religious mission." As Walsh knew, too many religious endeavors in China had been tainted by gunboat diplomacy in which foreign arms were used to protect the privileges of missionaries. But Walsh only belatedly realized that the evacuation of the missionaries would be interpreted as a sign of weakness or cowardice. Fortunately, the well-publicized story of the capture and release by bandits of two Maryknoll priests diverted attention, and the Fathers were quickly reassigned to their missions. Although the Sisters were slower in returning, because of Walsh's fear for them, they, too, went back to their missions. In the meantime, the founder of the Loting mission, Father Daniel McShane, continued the Sisters' work in caring for sick babies. In the spring of 1927, he died from smallpox after baptizing a baby with the disease.

From their experience in China Walsh and other Maryknollers in China learned a lesson they would not forget: No matter how difficult the political situation, the Sisters and Fathers would never again willingly abandon their posts. Most stayed on after the bombing of Pearl Harbor in 1941, although they knew they would be interned by the Japanese. Nor would they leave when the Communists took power in 1949—Walsh himself suffered long imprisonment under the Communist regime and, when released in mid-1970, was the last foreign missionary to leave China.

Hakkaland

In the early 1930s, the Sisters expanded to the northeastern section of Kwantung province, where the Hakka people lived. In contrast to earlier missions, where the Maryknollers were engaged in traditional institutional work, such as schools and orphanages, they pioneered a new approach by going out to the people, often living for weeks at a time in the homes of the villagers. That Sisters should live away from their convents without daily Mass and sacraments caused considerable criticism by traditional religious orders. But Maryknoll, and eventually Rome, viewed the experiment as the key to successful mission. Long before the 1960s, when religious orders made a "preferential option for the poor," the Maryknoll Sisters were living it. Although they could not have named that option, nor explained its theological significance, it set them on a different path in which evangelization was to become linked to a large extent with identification with the poor.

The center of this new endeavor was Kaying City, later called Meihsien, or Plum Blossom City, though it hardly merited the name, being only a small market town with a few streets and primitive shops. Most of the town was a maze of alleys where vegetable and fruit vendors somehow squeezed their wooden stands against the overhanging walls. Few ventured out at night, because the cobblestone streets were pocked with dangerous holes, and the only light came from small kerosene lamps inside the houses. The poorest inhabitants lived in the walled section of the town in "family ancestral buildings," where rooms could be rented and work found. Crowding out the little light and air that entered the buildings were giant wooden looms, worked by hand and foot power. Never cleaned, the looms were clogged with lint from the weavers' cotton thread, and the massive beams of the ancient houses were white with lint. "In that conglomeration of dirt and crowded quarters," a Sister remembered, "somebody loved flowers. In the sky-well huge white blossoms filled the musty air with fragrance."

From Kaying the mission spread over fifteen thousand square miles of arid, mountainous land in which some 2.6 million Hakka Chinese lived.

Originally from the north, the Hakka people had migrated south in search of better farming land, but though intelligent and industrious, few could derive more than a sustenance from the grudging earth. The Maryknollers had inherited Hakkaland, as they called it, from French missionaries, and they found pockets of Catholic families scattered among the area's two hundred villages, though most were so remote it proved impossible to visit them more than once a year. Francis Ford, the Maryknoll priest who had been in charge of the Yeungkong mission, opened the Kaying mission with only four priests, two Americans and two Chinese, and it soon became obvious that they would make little headway unless they encouraged lay people to take responsibility for their own church. For such an apostolate Ford sought Maryknoll Sisters. He wanted them not for institutional work, since the mission had neither the money nor personnel to support it, but for direct evangelization by preaching the Gospel—the Hakkas, he believed, would respond to a spiritual call without the inducements of medical facilities or schools. "The reason for emphasis on preaching," he said, "is the logical one that first things come first."

From his earliest days in China Ford had realized the importance of Chinese women as the core of family life, and wherever he went, he invited Maryknoll Sisters to join him to work among the women. Even at Yeungkong, where he had built an impressive convent for the Sisters, he had encouraged them to go out into the villages, and later, in the Hakka missions, he would travel with them, sometimes bicycling over the mountains or riding in the back of a truck piled high with beans or charcoal. A "Sisters' priest," Ford had shown regard for the women from his pioneer days at Maryknoll, where he was among the first group of seminarians. He was often on hand to help Mother Mary Joseph hang out the laundry, particularly on wintry days when such labor was "real suffering," and when other seminarians complained about the women's cooking, he was the first to defend it, declaring he had never had such good food, even at home. But it was only after Mother Mary Joseph's visit to China that he realized that the Sisters did not need to be pampered—despite the hardships of travel, she was always the "life of the party"—and that women could communicate without cultural barriers. "I always thought that it was the foreign face and clothes that frightened them [women and girls]," he wrote of Mother Mary Joseph's visit. "But I look and dress more Chinese than the Reverend Mother did, and yet they ran to her and lost their bashfulness. Her whole trip emphasized the hold our Sisters will have on Chinese women and the utter need of such influence to gain such hearts."

When Ford approached Mother Mary Joseph with his idea of direct evangelization, she proved equally enthusiastic. It was, she felt, the "essence" of Maryknoll's mission vision, because it would allow the Sisters to share God's love in the Chinese home. After his experience at Yeungkong, said Sister Mary Paul, he "didn't like mission compounds, with the church, convent, orphanage and other, institutions all within a wall like a little city. He felt we Sisters should be out among the people, on the road like the priests. And he said he saw no reason why 'Sisters shouldn't be like the priests in everything but administering the sacraments.' He didn't want all our Sisters concentrating on orphans and babies because that was work lay people could and should do. He wanted the Sisters to go out and preach."

He also wanted them to learn the language well and have an appreciation of the culture, and the quickest way to do so was by living in people's homes. Always open to new ideas and methods, he expected the women to take the lead in their own work but not to complain when things did not turn out as they hoped, or when some inconvenience threatened such as a military invasion. During the Sino-Japanese war in the 1930s, the villages in which the Sisters worked were frequently threatened. On one occasion, a Sister recalled, they were advised that the Japanese were about to seize the town and that they should leave immediately. They took the morning bus to Kaying, where Ford lived in a farmhouse. "Are you glad to see us?" the women inquired. "You are as welcome as the flowers in spring," he replied. Then, looking out the window at the falling rain, he added, "And as soon as it stops raining, you can go back to your mission."

"We did," said the Sister, "and the Japanese never came."

Ford thrived on pioneer conditions, difficult travel, exotic food, and weather extremes, and he imbued the Sisters with the same sense of adventure. Going out—instead of waiting behind convent walls for others to come to them—was, he stressed, an American trait born of the frontier. Ford thought that "just by showing yourselves as you are," the American women would make friends and converts. While admitting that "no one is so blind as when talking of his or her national characteristics," he thought the Maryknoll women could influence their Chinese sisters by

showing that you appreciate humor and a good laugh and are not pharisaically scandalized by normal, healthy love of a happy life; showing that you appreciate the fact that lay folk have their own life to lead and are not wax dolls cast in a rigid form of prim severity; showing the American philosophy that leads to use nature's gifts as something to be admired, not disdained as vanity; showing you understand that children must play as well as pray, and eat as well as fast; that the curse on Adam was not meant to take away the joy of life; that a girl can dance and still be a saint; and that God expects us to be neat and clean and attractive. And if we Americans appear to exaggerate the natural virtues, it is only an attempt to balance the scales against those who would make religion too heavy a burden for lay folk.

A slight, ascetic-looking man with a gift for sketching and a poetic turn of phrase, Ford looked frailer than he was—priests as well as Sisters had a hard time keeping up with the rugged-living American. Though a demanding leader, he encouraged those about him to have fun, and his Chinese students learned to sing and dance as well as pray. His only personal indulgences were a pipe and good books, the latter acquired from his father and uncle, who in the early 1900s published Brooklyn's *Irish World*. Several brushes with Mao Tse-tung's Communist followers, who made frequent forays into the Kaying area, made him a lifelong supporter of Chiang Kai-shek, although such partisanship would lead to his arrest and death in a Chinese prison after the 1949 revolution. Although Ford showed no originality in his political analysis—like most Americans in China, he turned a blind eye to Chiang Kai-shek's stupidities and corruption—his missionary vision was far ahead of the times. He discouraged the use of the demeaning word "pagan," preferring "non-Catholic" instead. He constantly extolled the virtues of the Chinese culture and people, and like the sixteenth-century Jesuit Matteo Ricci, was a strong believer in and practitioner of "inculturation." Americans, he often said, could learn as much from the Chinese as they from the Americans. He insisted that "we were not there to preach Western ways or the superiority of any Western science," a Sister recalled. "We were in China to preach only the Word of God."

Ford's primary concern was a church not simply in China but of it, and to that end he worked unceasingly to promote Chinese seminaries, novitiates, and lay organizations, for they had the means to evangelize as foreigners could not. "A native is in his element in treating with fellow nationals," he would say, dismissing any "unholy sense of superiority" on the part of foreign missionaries. He believed that the laity had a right and responsibility to take an active part in their church's development, and he gave women the means to achieve leadership roles, even though some of his priests objected. Such a church began to take form in the early 1960s after the sweeping reforms of the Second Vatican Council, which radically changed Catholic concepts of evangelization. But Ford did not live to see the Council—his ideas stemmed from a remarkable open-mindedness to a foreign culture that enriched his own.

Undoubtedly his greatest contribution was the invention of the two-by-two method, later to be copied by European religious orders. Instead of living in a mission compound, Maryknoll Sisters were sent into the villages in twos. Their convent was actually a rented part of a peasant home, usually one or two rooms, from which the Sisters would go out to other villages. While one stayed at the "convent" to provide religious instruction for those in the area, the other traveled with a Chinese woman catechist to preach the Good News, walking four, five, sometimes thirty miles a day to meet with Chinese women in outlying regions. On her return the other Sister went out.

The "Kaying experiment," as it came to be known, captured the mythical romance of the woman on horseback, and consequently any Maryknoller assigned to Kaying was the envy of her Sisters—they "are all clamoring to be assigned," Mother Mary Joseph wrote Ford. But as Ford himself admitted, only the most "athletic" could endure such a life. Since bicycles often were impracticable on the muddy potholed roads and buses were uncertain or nonexistent, most of the traveling had to be done by the "number eleven bus," as the missioners called two legs. Their rented "convents" in the villages were usually part of a one- or two-story mud-brick house with a few sticks of furniture—in one village the Sisters were forced to accept a Chinese coffin as part of the deal because local superstition held that the coffin could not be moved. In another they lived in a "haunted" hut shunned by the Chinese until it was discovered that the "ghosts" were rats. Sister Magdalena Urlacher, a small, gentle New Yorker, remembered living in a house in which the downstairs served as a gambling and opium den for six months of the year—"the owner would be arrested and spend six months in jail, then it was back to the gambling den."

> We lived in one long room upstairs. It had no windows but wooden slats that closed. The first morning the children were there, looking in through the slats. There was a porch around the house, and we fixed a kitchen at one end with a coal-burning clay stove. Baking was done in a portable oven made from an empty four-gallon kerosene can; for yeast we had a small ball of rice used to ferment rice wine. There was no electricity or running water—we got our water from a well. Our living quarters were always open, and the children played there. It was a way of making friends.
>
> When we went out to the villages, we stayed in Chinese homes, sometimes sleeping in the same bed with grandma or the catechist who accompanied us. We'd always bring our own rice, and we had vegetables from their gardens and occasionally fish. Sometimes vegetables were scarce, and we'd eat a soybean cake called *toufou*, and large red beans. After several days of rice, *toufou*, and red beans I couldn't eat any more. But the people were always very kind. When they saw I couldn't eat, this lady took me into a corner of the house and gave me a bowl of wine with two hard-boiled eggs in it. It was good, but you can imagine trying to pick up those slippery eggs with chopsticks!

The Sisters' work followed the seasons. During planting and harvesting times, the peasant women only had free time at night after the supper had been cooked, the animals fed, and the children bathed. So the Maryknollers would often accompany them in the fields or the kitchen, teaching them a rudimentary catechism and talking about their hopes and woes as they picked peanuts together or prepared the evening rice. The humid weather, unhygienic living conditions, and long treks took a toll of even the most rugged constitutions, yet the Sisters found beauty not unlike that which Christ must have encountered in his wanderings. As one Sister wrote:

> There were holes in the mountains for the foxes, and nests fixed on the walls of the houses for the swallows of the countryside; there were hawks hovering low, where the hens sensed danger and rounded up the little chicks under the spread of motherly wings; there were caves on the mountains for the sheltering of young shepherds who pastured the family buffalo or the herd of goats; there were lilies on the hillsides, glowing sunsets of red, long hedges of prickly cactus, cedar trees and clusters of palms as well as an abundance of annoying insects and a minimum of orderliness, neatness or sanitation.

And there were the women:

> One day we went to the village of the Well, a few houses snuggled together on a cliff. On all sides were rice fields, where the women were plowing, ankle-deep in mud, driving the water buffalo before them.
>
> Someone spied us. "The Sisters are here! The Sisters are here!" arose the cry from fields, kitchens and gardens. Immediately appeared a little group of Catholic women to welcome us. They came spattered with mud from the rice fields or laying down heavy loads of firewood which they had carried from the mountains. Some had babies strapped to their backs or led shy children who clung to them and peeked fearfully at us from places of safety.
>
> Fires were being lighted in dark kitchens to cook the rice for the evening meal, and a woman brought us steaming tea in tiny cups. One family had taken it upon itself to provide for us during our visit. Supper was waiting. It was a meal of rice, vegetables, and meat, served in bowls and eaten with chopsticks as we sat at table with this simple family, chatting and enjoying their hospitality.
>
> Their house has a special room set apart as an oratory, where the Catholic members of the clan gather every evening to chant their night prayers, and where Mass is said when the priest makes a visitation of this section.

After supper we went to that room and joined with the group of twenty or more women and girls who knelt in prayer after their hard labor in the fields to ask God's blessing on their homes. Round, brown youngsters lisped the prayers with their mothers, and babies went to sleep, lulled by the chant. When the last litany was finished, the eager audience seated themselves on the floor on mats while we opened our charts—beige colored pictures depicting the life of Christ. We showed picture after picture, explaining each one in the simple language of the women folk. This was followed by an informal chat, in which our friends told us their troubles, hopes, and joys.

It was late according to village reckoning when we went to our room—but even then not to rest, because everybody wanted to talk and visit with us there. At last the bare feet pattered away and quiet fell on the household, and we managed to get some sleep before the new day began with its adventures.

Occasionally the Sisters visited the homes of the local gentry, who lived in high-walled compounds with many courtyards and gates and large storehouses for grain and salted vegetables in case of a pirate siege. Some were well furnished, boasting jade screens and lacquered furniture, though often covered in dust. Dozens of people, including servants and relatives, lived in these well-protected beehives—the "big houses" celebrated in Chinese and Western novels of China.

Some of the most memorable trips were by sedan chair, the Sisters riding "like the Queen of Sheba" on the backs of coolies, or by sampan and raft along the rivers, passing "picturesque villages and quaint temples perched on commanding points, flanked by low-lying hills that changed colors a thousand times in the lights and shadows of sun and clouds. Boats laden with matting, cinnamon, wood, and other cargoes passed up and down ceaselessly, and numerous rafts made of great bamboo poles floated down the river on their way to market. Women washed clothes at the water's edge, their children filling their water pails or giving their buffalo a refreshing dip in the cool stream."

Looking back on those days in Kaying, Magdalena recalled the discovery of such trips:

We had this darling old grandma who had become Christian, and she would take us to visit non-Christian villages. One evening, when we were crossing a river on a raft, there was a beautiful sunset. We got off the little raft and were going toward our house on this narrow, rough path. I was keeping my eyes on the path when she suddenly touched my arm to stop me. "Look!" she said. We looked at the sky and the people in the boats, everything was tinged with this glorious color. She said, "I think the angels and the saints are having a party."

The Hakka Christians had parties, too, on major feast days and during the months after the rice had been planted, when the women had more free time. Dozens would flock to the Maryknoll mission centers, where they stayed for six weeks, using lofts above the Sisters' rooms for sleeping, and cooking and eating with the Maryknollers. The women brought their children, firewood, and vegetables, and the mission contributed rice, which was a way of returning the villagers' hospitality to the Sisters. During the catechumenates, as they were called, the Sisters taught the women the principles of Christianity through pictures, charts, and stories that could be understood by the illiterate peasants. In those days, few books existed for such instruction (the first Chinese translation of the Catholic Bible was not published until 1920). The Sisters therefore developed their own teaching materials, using Chinese examples to illustrate Christian doctrine. Eventually they produced twenty-four books with simple tales about Chinese children washing clothes in a stream or watering their buffalo—in the Sisters' stories no Hakka child bicycled down a street, since none could afford one and the villages had no streets.

The catechumenates and frequent visits by the women to the Sisters' small "convents" forged a special bond between Chinese and Americans, who, by living together, became friends. As Ford observed, the Sisters' homes were rallying points for the poor, downtrodden peasant women, who there met other women outside of their village clan. Such encounters offered them an opportunity to break out of the narrow confines of a closed social order, by giving them a glimpse of other horizons. But undoubtedly the best times were on such feast days as Christmas when whole villages would converge on the Kaying City mission center for two or three days. "We didn't have enough space for them to stay," recalled Magdalena, "so we just spread straw on the floors and mats on top of that and blankets. And we would get down under all that with the people and the children and talk and sing carols. After prayer they'd stay up until midnight, and that's how they made their marriage arrangements—friend to friend, village to village—I've got a son; you've got a daughter. The people really knew each other and were a community."

Although the results of the missioners' labors were not spectacular—there were no massive conversions—Kaying showed a steady increase in the Catholic population. Despite the buildup of World War II in Asia the work continued, and by the 1940s twenty-six Maryknoll centers dotted the Hakka countryside. Several were staffed by Chinese Sisters from a novitiate begun and nurtured by the Maryknoll women. As at Yeungkong and Loting, where other novitiates were started, Kaying's native Sisterhood was a crucial part of the Maryknollers' work, because it represented a genuinely indigenous church. Educated and encouraged by the American women, the Chinese Sisters were hard-working and courageous, and it was they, together with Chinese priests and the laity, who kept the flame alive during World War II and after the Communist takeover in 1949. Dressed in simple gray tunics with black leather belts, the Chinese Sisters "reminded us of soldiers in battle array," a Maryknoll Sister fondly recalled. "When they mounted on bicycles, they looked like valiant crusaders of the Lord."

Symbolic of the success of the "Kaying experiment" was a seven-story Christian pagoda constructed in Kaying City with the contributions of local Catholics. Topped by a cross that could be seen for miles around, the yellow pagoda was to have served as a spire for a cathedral that was never built—Ford laid the cornerstone just before he was imprisoned by the Communists. Although the pagoda was later vandalized and the cross torn down, it still stands as a testament of Ford's vision and the labors of dozens of Maryknoll missioners. In 1935, Rome recognized the priest's contribution by naming Ford a bishop; he was consecrated at Maryknoll in the last public ceremony attended by the ailing Bishop James A. Walsh. Walsh himself performed the consecration, which took place in the Maryknoll Sisters' chapel. Four years later the Vatican wrote Mother Mary Joseph to praise the contribution made by the Sisters in going out in twos to the Hakka villages. Such work, said the Vatican's Society for the Propagation of the Faith, showed the American women's "courage and devotion. Let us hope that this work may grow and that God may bless it with abundant fruit."

And the work did grow, even after Ford's death and the expulsion of the Maryknollers from China. Among the seeds that scattered and bore fruit were the Sisters' missions in El Salvador, where the same methods of evangelization were used and where Ford's cousin Ita would suffer a martyr's death in 1980.

Manchuria

At the same time that the Sisters were moving into the Hakka villages, others were opening missions in Manchuria, a vast, mountainous region in northeastern China that occupies one-quarter of the country and that for many years was contested by China, Russia, and Japan. When the first Sisters arrived at the port city of Dairen (later renamed Lüta) in 1930, the Japanese controlled Dairen and other parts of southern Manchuria as well as the South Manchuria Railway. The latter had been built by the Russians, but after their defeat in the Russo–Japanese War in 1904–1905, the Japanese acquired their treaty rights with the Chinese. Still a primitive, underpopulated region at the turn of the century, Manchuria suddenly awoke under the dual impetus of cheap, efficient railroad transport and Japanese investments in mining and industry. Millions of Chinese migrated to the land of opportunity, and Dairen became the wonder city of the Orient, with fine buildings and parks and the most modern port facilities in the Far East. By 1930, more than thirty million Chinese had resettled in Manchuria, plowing the land to the frontiers of Siberia and even encroaching on the outer limits of Mongolia. From nowhere Manchuria came to account for one-fifth of China's total trade, exporting soybeans, coal, and iron, and Dairen and satellite cities boasted an industrial base that outstripped all the rest of China put together.

Manchuria's chief attractions were large tracts of virgin land, ample mineral deposits, and a strategic location on the Yellow Sea adjacent to Korea and Russia. But it was not a gentle place. Summers on the Manchurian plains were often as hot as those in Kansas and Missouri. In winter temperatures fell to sixty degrees below zero—to prevent frostbites the Sisters wore muffs of white flannel, inside which were small metal boxes with sticks of lighted charcoal. Yellow dust storms swept down from the Mongolian plains, epidemics of cholera and typhoid were common, and throughout the time the Sisters lived there Manchuria was convulsed by war and banditry.

As in South China, the Sisters learned to live with physical hardships and political uncertainties, soon expanding from Dairen to the coal-mining center at Fushun and the prosperous border town of Antung, where American and other foreign traders were cashing in on the Manchurian boom. Although the Sisters at Fushun ran a rural outpost for Chinese peasants, unstable political conditions confined the Sisters to the cities, where they started schools, orphanages, dispensaries, and a native novitiate for Chinese Sisters. Some worked with the Chinese; others with the Japanese, Koreans, and Russians who populated Manchuria's coastal areas.

Among the early arrivals was Margaret Shea, now Sister Gemma, who had been one of the first Maryknoll pioneers. In 1920, a year before the first band of Sisters set out for China, Gemma had opened a Maryknoll mission in Seattle for Japanese immigrants, and this work had been followed by sojourns in Korea, Manchuria, and Japan. A decade later, she arrived in Dairen to start a kindergarten for Japanese children and to evangelize among Japanese women. Although Gemma was accustomed to Oriental food, the other Sisters were not. "You do not have to eat raw fish in order to start Oriental mission work," one wrote, "but that is how we started in Dairen." Met by a delegation of Japanese ladies, the Sisters were welcomed with a multicourse banquet:

We all sat on our heels on the floor around low tables fifteen to sixteen inches high. At that meal I ate raw fish for the first time in my life. Though not everything served at the meal was fish, nearly everything tasted of fish.

The day proved a double first—in addition to Japanese cuisine, the Sisters were introduced to dial telephones that, while known in the United States, were not yet widely used.

Other surprises followed. Manchurian women smoked briar pipes, and it took some while to discourage the habit among the Chinese novices. Cooking also proved an adventure. The first time the Sisters tried to make a meal at the Fushun mission, they nearly burned down the kitchen; the second day, a clogged chimney filled the house with smoke; on the third the stove collapsed just when the stew was ready, and the dinner went sliding onto the floor. They ate it anyway.

The Maryknollers' dispensaries were always crowded, but though the Sister-nurses saw every kind of disease and suffering, even they were occasionally stunned. One winter evening, when the temperature was subzero, an old man in rags appeared at the women's small dispensary at Fushun. His feet were frozen beyond recovery, but the Sister-nurse cleaned them and gave the man medicine. While wondering how best to tell him that his feet would have to be amputated, he suggested the operation himself. A rickshaw was then called to carry him home, and while trying to get into it, he knocked off one foot, which fell to the ground. The old man felt nothing, but the horrified rickshaw driver cried out, "*Ai Yah!* Is that your foot?"

By that time a crowd of curious Chinese had gathered to observe the proceedings, and the Sister hurriedly bandaged the stump, sending the man home in the rickshaw. The following day, when she visited her patient, a large delegation was waiting for her. The people had heard of her kindnesses to the old Chinese and were sufficiently impressed to want to learn about her religion. Some were later baptized.

Although conversions in Dairen were few, the Sisters gained the gratitude and respect of the White Russian community, which turned to the Sisters for help when the Japanese authorities closed their school. After the Communist revolution, the Russians had poured into Dairen, where many were forced to work as coolies. Stateless and impoverished, they hoped their children might better themselves through education and begged the Maryknollers to teach them. Most of the students were Russian Orthodox or Jewish (including the local rabbi's children), and none spoke English, whereas the Sister-teachers spoke nothing else. Nevertheless, the Sisters agreed to take on the challenge. The "bedlam" of the first days soon changed to orderly classes, and six years later, when five Russians graduated from Maryknoll Academy, all achieved 100 percent on exams sent from an American university with which the academy was affiliated.

Among those who helped the academy was future film star Yul Brynner. He was living at the home of his uncle, who was the Dairen representative of a shipping concern and the Swiss consul. The man's daughter was a Catholic, and through his cousin Brynner met the Sisters. In 1940, while awaiting a visa for the United States, Brynner coached the school production of *Hansel and Gretel*. "It was the best school play any of us had ever seen in Dairen," boasted the Sisters.

Storm Clouds

In the fall of 1931, when the Sisters went to Fushun to open a mission, they traveled over a section of the South Manchuria Railroad only recently reopened. Three weeks earlier, a bomb had derailed a train and crippled transport between Dairen and Fushun in what came to be known as the "Manchuria Incident." Using the explosion as an excuse to seize Manchuria, the Japanese military swept across the border from Korea, which Japan also dominated, to take over key seaports and rail centers. To legitimize the new puppet state of Manchukuo, the Japanese installed as its head the last Manchu emperor, Henry Pu Yi, who had abdicated in 1912 when China became a republic.

Although the Maryknoll missioners tried to maintain strict neutrality and stay out of the political and military battles between Chinese and Japanese, the United States' refusal to recognize Manchukuo cast suspicion on all Americans. The Maryknollers were accused by the Japanese of spying for the U.S. government, their mail was intercepted, and they were kept under constant police vigilance. The Maryknoll superior, Bishop Raymond Lane, and other foreign bishops in Manchuria tried to improve the situation by encouraging the Vatican to declare Manchukuo a mission field independent of China, which it did in 1934, thereby giving the puppet state tacit political recognition. Like other Catholic missions, the Maryknollers celebrated the crowning of Emperor Pu Yi by flying Manchukuo and Vatican flags. The Maryknoll Sisters in Dairen gave their students a holiday. Pu Yi reportedly responded by making a large donation to the Catholic church.

Under the new order relations between the Maryknollers and the government temporarily improved, the missioners cooperating with local authorities in charitable programs, such as relief aid for the victims of flooding, and even providing street preachers to give patriotic pep talks. Any mention of Japanese brutalities, such as the massacre of three thousand Chinese at Fushun, was deliberately omitted from Maryknoll publications in the United States, including *The Field Afar*, which even as late as 1942 was still giving a euphemistic picture of conditions in war-torn China.

One reason for such reticence was Maryknoll's fear that criticism might provoke the Japanese to deport its missioners, who were working in Japan and Korea as well as Manchuria. But many Maryknollers also approved of the way the Japanese ran things. They were industrious, upheld law and order and had brought unprecedented prosperity to Manchuria. Symbolic of such efficiency, the trains ran on time, whereas "with the Chinese you didn't know when they would arrive," said one missioner. Then, too, the Chinese resistance was heavily infiltrated by Communists. For purposes of evangelization, the missioners felt, it did not matter whether Manchuria was run by Japanese or Chinese so long as they were not Communists.

Maryknollers in South China, who were suffering with the people from Japanese bombings and other depredations, did not share such pro-Japanese sentiments, and their clear identification with the Chinese cause gained the local church the respect of non-Christians. That many were converted on that basis is unlikely, but the missions in South China did experience stronger growth than those in Manchuria. Some of the difference could be attributed to evangelization methods, particularly in Kaying, where a direct apostolate was emphasized. But the Maryknollers' failure to speak out against Japanese atrocities in Manchuria may have also been a factor. Moreover, by failing to take a stand, the Catholic church left the leadership of the Manchurian resistance to the Communists. Although Christians joined the resistance, the churches did not provide any guidance, nor did they deal with the question of nationalism, a key factor in the Communists' success. The Maryknollers' argument that the Catholic church should remain politically neutral did not suffice, because the church, in trying to appease the Japanese, did not appear so.

Years later, Maryknollers would face similar dilemmas in places like Central America and the Philippines—to denounce government repression, and risk the destruction of their work and possible expulsion, or to remain silent, and be accused of cooperating with the repressors. But in Manchuria the situation was complicated by the resistance's makeup—many who joined were professional bandits—and the difficulty of distinguishing thieves from patriots. Bandits had plagued Manchuria for decades, working in gangs of at many as three thousand men. Rich Chinese were frequently kidnapped for ransom; if it was not paid, the victim was killed. Known as "Red Beards," because some of the earliest marauders were red-bearded cossacks from Siberia, the bandits included members of the Big Sword Society, an offshoot of the anti-foreign Boxer Rebellion and much feared by the missioners. After the Japanese erected a puppet state, bandits and Big Sword members joined regular Chinese soldiers in a National Salvation Army. Although the Japanese tried to destroy the resistance, they were unable to crush the guerrilla fighters. A scorched earth policy did seriously weaken the guerrillas' base of popular support and sources of food, however, and many bandit units resorted to looting and

percent of the labor force, were unemployed. Cities sprouted soup kitchens, bread lines, and shanty towns on the edge of garbage dumps, where the jobless picked over the leavings. Once prosperous agricultural centers took on the air of ghost towns, such was the number of farm evictions. Two million men roamed the country seeking jobs or handouts, and more than one hundred cities reported the exhaustion of relief funds.

Maryknoll suffered, too. Rich donors suddenly became poor, and many of the working class, who provided the bulk of Maryknoll's income, were reduced to paupers. To ask to collect at church doors was no longer possible because many churchgoers were themselves on relief or helping relatives who were. In desperation the Sisters tried to collect offerings at Yankee Stadium, but when they came away with only $31.86—all in nickels and pennies—they gave up.

Saddled with an enormous debt for the construction of a Motherhouse at New York headquarters, the Sisters took out a second mortgage and prayed to God. Although unable to pay any of the principal, they did manage to meet interest payments through constant economies. To earn money, the women did the seminary's laundry, crocheted toy dogs, and collected used stamps for resale. Some supporters continued to send money to the Sisters, even if only five cents in a "mite box," and the mission circles that had formed in the twenties to finance the Sisters' work valiantly struggled to meet monthly commitments. The Little Flower Circle, which had started in San Francisco to aid Sister Gemma's work with Japanese immigrants in Seattle, loyally sent her $25 every month, even during the hardest times. The money proved crucial to the Sisters' survival when they opened the mission in Dairen.

Even when the economy began to pick up, Americans did not show the same interest in foreign mission lands that they had in the twenties, as reflected by a sharp drop in *The Field Afar* subscriptions. Racial prejudice was still widespread, and if the unfortunate "Chinks" were starving, that was their problem—what else could be expected of a backward race that worshiped idols, bound their girls' feet, and threw away their babies? Despite the writings of Bishop Ford and other Maryknollers in China, who constantly stressed the virtues of the Chinese people, few Americans listened. Not until war clouds burst over Pearl Harbor would they begin to renew their interest in China. By then, Maryknoll had 450 missioners in East Asia, more than half in China. Most would suffer internment, starvation, and mistreatment. But none would willingly abandon their mission.

~ 4 ~

War

Suddenly we heard shouting, "The Japanese are coming! The Japanese are com-
ing!" The Chinese were running down the beach, but we could see no sign of the
Japanese. So Sister Candida and I started walking back to our mission. As we
were climbing a hill, a Japanese airplane appeared, circling overhead, but we
didn't pay much attention because many planes had done that and never land-
ed. There was no place they could land on Sancian Island, because of the hills
and large boulders. Nervous but not overly concerned, we continued to climb
until we reached the crest of the hill—and there, marching up the other side,
was the Japanese army!

We were immediately surrounded by about a hundred men with drawn
bayonets. "What will we do if none of them speaks English?" Sister Candida
whispered. At that, a Japanese officer in white gloves and with a tasseled sword,
stepped forward. "Don't be frightened," he said in perfect English. "We are not
going to harm you."

The first thing he asked me was, "Where is your father?"

"He died when I was young, in America," I told him.

I didn't know what I was saying—I was that scared—but he meant the
priest. "He went to Hong Kong."

"When?"

"Yesterday."

"Who told him we were coming?"

"Nobody. If he had known you were coming, he would have taken us with him."

AT THE TIME OF the hilltop conversation in late 1937, Maryknoll Sisters
Monica Marie Boyle and Candida Basto were among a handful of people
who had not fled to hiding places in Sancian's hills or across the sea to
mainland China. A Chinese priest was supposed to be looking after the
Sisters while Maryknoll Father Robert Cairns was away, but he, too, had
decamped.

A small, barren island south of Macao and eight miles from the South
China coast, Sancian (or Changchuen in Chinese) was bounded on one
side by the China Sea and on the other by the Pacific. The Sisters had

thought the shallow waters would prevent the approach of a Japanese cruiser, but they hadn't reckoned with motor launches. Not that there was anything to hide—Sancian had neither towns nor military installations, most of the people being poor fishermen. No car could traverse the rough mountain paths that linked the thatched-roof settlements studding the base of the hills—to get from one side of the island to the other, people either walked or sailed around in a small junk. Once a week a ferry departed for the trip to Hong Kong; otherwise there was little contact with the outside world. But the Japanese, who had launched a military invasion of China that summer, were taking no chances. The Sisters could return to their mission, the Japanese officer informed them, but he would inspect the two churches marked on his map. One was a small building that Cairns had renovated; the other, a tall-spired landmark on the spot where St. Francis Xavier had died four centuries earlier when trying to reach the mainland. Xavier was a hero to foreign missionaries, so when Maryknoll acquired Sancian as part of its first China mission territory, it was considered a mark of honor.

Monica decided the Japanese officer must be a Catholic if he wanted to visit Xavier's sanctuary. At least it was a comforting thought as they returned to their mission:

We were really scared now! The village where we lived was deserted. Everybody was gone. The doors of the houses were all wide open, and the dogs were barking. We didn't know what to do. "We must hide the money," Sister Candida said, though we didn't have that much to worry about. "Get the geranium pot and put it in there. They'll never think of that." But when they came, they didn't go through anything.

Meanwhile, a Maryknoll priest on the mainland had learned of the Sisters' plight and hurried to the rescue in a sailboat. As the small boat neared Sancian, a huge troop ship loomed into view, so terrifying the Chinese boatman that only by threatening to throw him overboard was the priest able to persuade him to continue. After some parleying, the Japanese agreed to let the Sisters leave with the priest, provided they took nothing with them. "All we took," said Monica, "was our prayer book and the clothes we were wearing"—and the hidden money. The sea was rough, and when their boat neared the mainland, it began to leak badly. "Father was trying to bail out the water as fast as he could, but we were sinking. Just then, the Chinese coast guard appeared. If it hadn't been for them, we would have had to swim ashore."

Although Father Cairns returned to Sancian, the women went on to other missions and adventures. Monica was sorry to leave, even though she had cried when Mary Paul, the Maryknoll regional superior, had assigned her to the isolated island in early 1937. A small woman with a big heart, she had been a nurse in Philadelphia before joining Maryknoll, and within weeks of her arrival on Sancian she was battling a cholera epidemic that took eighty lives in the first days. Monica and Cairns spent a month hiking through the hills in order to bring vaccine to the island's thirty-two villages, but the effort was worthwhile: not another person died.

As things turned out, the Sisters were safer on the China mainland despite constant Japanese bombings. Cairns' associate, Father John Joyce, was nearly killed in early 1941 when an angry Japanese officer shot at the priest at point-blank range after he protested a Sancian fisherman's arrest. Joyce, startled and shaken, tried to make an Act of Contrition, but could think only of the Grace before Meals. When the bullet missed, the officer walked off in disgust. Cairns, who in December was taken prisoner aboard a Japanese destroyer, was less lucky. A few days after his arrest his pith helmet was found floating in the water. The Maryknollers learned that he had been trussed up in a big basket and thrown into the sea to drown.

Monica, meantime, had resigned herself to daily bombings at the Maryknoll mission in Loting in South China. During one attack a Maryknoll priest was struck by shrapnel from an exploding bomb. Monica ran to him with cotton and a bottle of peroxide, but as she was dressing the wound, another bomb fell, knocking the bottle out of her hand. The patient lived to report:

> This was a real calamity as medicine is scarce these days. We both prayed. Heaven seemed to be our destination. Then, as a heap of earth went up in the air, Sister said, "There goes your house." I put up my hand, fearing the debris would bury us alive. As the atmosphere cleared some, Sister remarked, "Never mind, the flag is still there."

In July, 1937, a clash between Japanese and Chinese troops near Peking triggered an eight-year war, the so-called "China Incident" that provided the Japanese government with a pretext to unleash its military machine on the weakened giant. Cities and villages alike were bombed, causing a mass exodus to China's west. Millions were displaced, many dying of starvation and disease. Although the United States had not yet entered the war, the Japanese tried to drive its missionaries, teachers, and traders from China. Despite clear American markings on their roofs, U.S. mission compounds and schools were often bombed, leading one observer to remark that the most dangerous place in an air raid was an American mission. But people back home were uninterested. In a Gallup poll in 1938, more than two-thirds of those interviewed favored a withdrawal from China by all Americans, missionaries included. Nor was there much concern about developments in Europe despite Hitler's increasing aggressiveness. An isolationist mood still lingered, fed by the exhaustion of economic collapse, and few remembered Woodrow Wilson's warning that the only way to prevent American involvement in another world war was to prevent it from starting.

On the spot in East Asia the Maryknollers had no doubt war was coming. "Buy rice. Buy plenty rice," their Chinese friends had advised within days of the "China Incident." A month later, when the first Japanese planes appeared over the Kaying missions, the Maryknollers were stocking rice to provide relief for a swelling tide of refugees. At the time there were 240 Sisters in the Pacific region, including the Philippines, Japan, Korea, and Hawaii, the largest number being in China. Covering an area twice the size of New England, the Maryknoll mission territories were populated by twenty-five million people, and many would turn to the churches to feed, clothe, and protect them.

Shanghai

Three weeks before Monica and Candida's encounter with the Japanese army, eight Maryknoll Sisters working at a Shanghai mental hospital were caught in the crossfire between Chinese and Japanese when the latter attacked the city. The American consul had warned the Sisters to leave Mercy Hospital, which was located ten miles outside Shanghai, but they had refused to abandon the four hundred patients.

During her trip to China in the early twenties, Mother Mary Joseph had stopped in Shanghai, where she had been the guest of Lo Pa-hong, a wealthy Catholic philanthropist responsible for numerous charitable institutions. One of his hospitals had a section for the mentally ill, and Mother Mary Joseph was shocked to find that the patients were chained to prevent them from running away or hurting themselves—it was all that could be done, her host explained, because China had no modern facilities for the insane. A decade later, when Lo requested Maryknoll Sisters to staff the women's section of China's first modern mental asylum, Mother Mary Joseph sent nurses, a lab technician, and an occupational therapist. Only one had any psychiatric training, but she gave the other Sisters good advice: "If you do what you're told to do, God will help you."

Opened in 1935, Mercy Hospital not only boasted the latest equipment and a good medical staff—it was also well laid out, with airy pavilions, flowering gardens, even a gothic church! Convinced that the patients would respond to such pleasant surroundings, Lo refused to heed the staff's requests for locks on the doors and window gratings, until a patient escaped and drowned in a nearby ditch. Sister Herman Joseph Stitz, the

Maryknoll lab technician, admitted that the first days and nights were "scary." Some of the patients were violent, and the Sisters soon acquired scars from bites. But there were funny incidents, too. After Dominican friars visiting the hospital said Mass one Sunday, the Sisters found their patients wandering up and down the halls, heads draped in towels and mumbling and intoning loudly.

A large, easygoing woman, Herman Joseph had been fascinated by foreign missions since a child in Oregon, when her German immigrant mother read to her from German mission magazines. Mercy Hospital lived up to the most exotic expectations—the patients included a variety of nationalities, American and European, as well as Chinese, and even before the Sino-Japanese War started, there was hardly a dull moment, with patients swinging from light fixtures and brandishing mops. The Chinese staff took a philosophical attitude toward the pandemonium. "Why for make a worry," the hospital gatekeeper told Herman Joseph after one patient had escaped. "Plenty more like them inside."

Many patients brought to Mercy Hospital were not mentally ill but starving or dying from some disease, and there were "plenty more like them" in Shanghai, an overcrowded metropolis at the mouth of the Yangtze River. But they were rarely seen in the city's foreign enclaves, or "concessions"—luxurious ghettos with fine houses and manicured lawns; swimming pools; country clubs; smart shops; and broad, paved avenues. The only Chinese who lived there were servants, for the concessions were little bits of Europe grafted onto China, with their own laws and governments. Some were physically separated from the city, such as the French Concession, which was guarded by a bridge that kept the Chinese from entering, even after the Japanese attacked Nantao, the Chinese section of Shanghai.

Unlike the Europeans, the Chinese disdained straight lines, and Nantao typified the local preference for mazes and turnings. As one Sister described it:

> Coolies, children, peddlers, beggars and dogs pushed and shoved their way through the narrow streets. Shops opened on both sides and swarmed with salesmen who could talk price until they wore you down. Exquisite ivories and jade were sold in one; right beside it would be a shack selling chickens. Carved furniture graced a shop next to a place reeking with meat and long-gone fruit. The ragged and dirty rubbed shoulders with those clad in silks, some were pushed in peculiar wheelbarrows, while others glided along in Rolls-Royces, though a car could barely honk its way through the crowds without dragging someone's wash from overhead.

In August 1937, when war was imminent, Herman Joseph and another Sister visited a Shanghai bank to withdraw all the Maryknollers' money in gold. The tree-lined avenues in the concessions were banked with sandbags and fenced by barbed wire, tractors were throwing up barricades, and machine guns "were everywhere in evidence." The bank clerk advised the Sisters to return home immediately as an air raid was expected.

During the first days of the attack, when the bombing was still a mile from the hospital, an endless stream of refugees passed by, trying to reach Shanghai before the oncoming Japanese army. Most of the hospital's Chinese staff joined them after two thousand Chinese soldiers arrived at the hospital gate, digging trenches around the buildings for a last stand against the Japanese. The Maryknoll Sisters and six German Brothers of Charity, who were caring for the men patients, carried on despite bombings of nearby fields. Patients replaced the lost personnel, Herman Joseph taking charge of the cooking. Hoping that one might protect them, the Sisters and Brothers prominently displayed three different flags—a swastika above the Brothers' house, the stars-and-stripes above the convent and, floating from the church spire, a yellow-and-white Vatican flag. Whether God or the flags saved them—the Sisters were convinced of divine intervention—the hospital survived three months of aerial raids without a scratch. In the second month, a spy was caught in a nearby village and confessed to having dug a trench behind the Sisters' convent that marked the spot where bombs were to fall that very night. "He was to give the location signal at nine," the Sisters' diary reported. "A plane kept the rendezvous and hovered over the hospital for two hours. But that day the men from the hospital by pure chance had filled in the trench, and it could not be located!"

By November the battle was nearly over. Three hundred Chinese soldiers who had sought protection near the hospital wall were machine gunned by Japanese airplanes, and the hospital was swamped by twelve hundred refugees, many wounded. The next afternoon eight Japanese soldiers suddenly appeared, dug a trench in front of the hospital, then shouted, "Open the gate!" Expecting to be mowed down by machine guns, the fearful Brothers opened the door as refugees and patients fled in all directions. But nothing happened—the Japanese looked around for Chinese soldiers, then left.

Throughout the week the Sisters went to bed fully clothed, each outfitted with a candle, matches, a bottle of holy water and a clean handkerchief in case they had to abandon the convent. At 2:30 A.M. on November 12, when a bomb exploded at the back door, they rushed to the patients' pavilions as bombs fell and machine guns rattled. Above the racket sounded bugles and the shouts of Chinese soldiers, "Sah! Sah!" "Kill! Kill!" Women and children were wailing, dogs barking. Then, abruptly, silence. Eventually a few boys inside the compound ventured out, finding more than five hundred Chinese soldiers dead, their bodies strewn over the fields. At noon a Japanese major appeared at the hospital gate—carrying flowers and a camera! The Sisters and Brothers took the opportunity to ask if they could care for wounded soldiers and bury the dead, but while assenting to the first request, the major dismissed the second as unnecessary—"They have already been taken care of."

When two Sisters went to Shanghai with a Japanese escort to cable Mother Mary Joseph that the Maryknollers were safe, they saw a tragic picture. Nantao was in flames, and thousands of Chinese were trying to get into the French Concession. A small safety zone had been established next to it by a French priest, and, as the Sisters watched, people in the concession threw bread to the hungry mob. It was wet and cold, and the women's hearts went out to the desperate refugees. Back at the hospital, after countless Japanese checkpoints, the Sisters reported that the bodies had not been buried after all. That was obvious, said Sister Herman Joseph, because the stench had filled the countryside. In a week's time the Brothers buried six hundred bodies, the Sisters searching nearby huts for survivors—they found only four, plus a cow, three sheep, and a goat, all starving.

By then, the hospital compound was overflowing with three thousand refugees. Herman Joseph was at wit's end trying to feed so many of the people; to add to her problems, the electricity had been cut off and most of the water supplies commandeered by the Japanese. The Sisters and Brothers daily drove out in a truck to forage for food, but homes and farms had been ransacked by the Japanese, and all they found were a few stray animals, a piano, and a violin. Thinking the instruments might amuse the patients, they took them, picking up five Chinese refugees on their return and hiding them behind the piano. At each inspection point a Japanese guard mounted the truck to play the Japanese national anthem. None noticed the Chinese crouching behind the piano. "We had a lot of miracles," said Herman Joseph. On one occasion, she obtained a large shipment of rice from a ship forced to return to port because of gunfire on the Yangtze River; on another, a priest showed up with a carload of cabbages and canned milk and a large rasher of bacon.

Herman Joseph, who often went to Shanghai to get money or medicine, took the tensions in stride, thanks to a sense of humor that relished a laugh in the midst of danger. One day at a checkpoint a Japanese soldier, spotting a blunt object protruding from her coat, yelled, "Gun! Gun!" The other guards laughed at his chagrin when Herman Joseph produced her mission crucifix. She was inventive, too. When she learned that Maryknoll Sisters would be stopping in a ship at Shanghai en route to another mission, she faked four travel passes, using pictures from look-alikes at the Mercy Hospital, which the Japanese merely glanced at when the visitors disembarked.

Knowing that Mercy Hospital badly needed medicines, the Sisters had brought supplies hidden in their mantles and camera cases which they removed in a telephone booth, leaving the stock with a triumphant Herman Joseph.

Despite their commitment to the patients, the Sisters opted to leave in 1938. Lo Pa-hong, the hospital's patron, had been assassinated at the end of 1937, and the local bishop wanted the Maryknoll Sisters to assume the hospital's running costs and sizeable debt. Because the Maryknoll community in New York was itself struggling under a large debt and the effects of the Depression, the Sisters told the bishop that all they could provide was trained personnel. For political as well as financial reasons the work was turned over to a community of Sisters from Luxembourg who ran the hospital until the Communist takeover in 1949. Herman Joseph was heartbroken at leaving: "Our work was just beginning to take hold, and we loved the Chinese people very much." But she would soon be back in the trenches, in another war in Korea.

Troubled Interlude

As the uneven contest progressed, whole provinces came under attack by the Japanese. By the end of 1937, Yeungkong's river route to the sea was sealed off. In the next months four bridges and a nearby village were destroyed by bombings. So frequent were the air raids that the blind girls at the Maryknoll mission became expert in estimating the timing and location of bomb strikes. As one Sister wrote:

> What was at first a stunning catastrophe eventually became an ugly routine. It ate into the nerves nonetheless: the frequent alarms, sometimes seven to ten in a day; the interrupted work of teaching and healing; the unfinished or omitted meals; the moonlit nights with ears tuned to the sound of the alarm and the drone of the planes; the shepherding and soothing of crying babies, frightened children, and young girls; the sheltering of fear-driven, dispossessed families; the running for refuge in fields, in caves, on river boats; the crouching under flimsy tables in flimsy houses deafened by the crescendo of diving planes and the falling bombs; the facing up to the residual maimed and dead. Terror itself, and grief, too, became in time routine.
>
> Warfare brought its ugly fellowship—hunger—riceless days for people already existing on a marginal diet; thievery and banditry—depredations by callous opportunists and desperate army deserters; epidemics—measles, polio, cholera, smallpox; growing lists of sick

and wounded and dwindling medical supplies on clinic shelves; increasing isolation because of disrupted mail service, dismantled bridges, torn-up roads; depressing news—great Canton had fallen, the Pearl, the West Rivers were in Japanese hands; tormenting rumors—the Chinese town officials had all fled, the Japanese were already at the bend in the river; and, last but not least, the sudden overwhelming panics. Sometimes by night the whole population of a town silently slipped away. Sometimes by day some insignificant occurrence touched off widespread consternation. A thief chased by the owner of a stolen chicken was suddenly joined by ten, twenty, a hundred, a thousand men, women and children all crying, "Run! Run! Run" until the entire city was emptied into the countryside.

Letters from the isolated missioners occasionally reached Hong Kong, and once in a while priests and Sisters slipped through the Japanese cordon. Sister Mary Paul, the Sisters' intrepid regional superior, decided to see the situation first-hand, managing to visit some of the Sisters' houses in the Kaying area. Describing her distress at the air raids, she wrote Mother Mary Joseph: "The Sisters' trick is to wrap themselves in *mintois* [Chinese quilts] and crawl under the bed—the *mintois* to break the force of any heavy object and the bed to protect them from falling walls. Those houses in Kaying make me ill when I consider them as protection." Such reports increased Mother Mary Joseph's anxiety, and in the spring of 1940 she set out for the Orient to see her Sisters. Midway through the Pacific, her ship was hit by a 120-mile-an-hour hurricane—an omen of the future. The vessel eventually limped into Shanghai, where Mary Paul awaited her. "The poverty on all sides was appalling," Mother Mary Joseph wrote her Sisters at home, "and seemed worse in the cold torrential rain, which added to the suffering of those who live night and day on the streets. Soldiers—British, French, Japanese and U.S. Marines—were everywhere, and there was over all a tenseness that made living in the troubled sections very trying on the nerves."

Nor was the news from Europe good. Hitler's forces had steamrolled across Europe and taken Belgium and France. A British expeditionary force sent to their aid narrowly averted disaster through the courageous small-boat rescue at Dunkirk. "We have just one more battle to win," announced Hitler's propaganda chief Joseph Goebbels, as the German *Luftwaffe* began bombing London into expected submission. President Roosevelt, who had been warning Americans of an international war since the "China Incident," followed developments with increasing dismay. In June 1940, he pledged "the material resources of this nation" to Britain's aid. France's fall had shocked Americans, most of whom desired Hitler's defeat; Japan's formal joining of the European Axis in September was another blow. The Japanese navy exceeded the combined strength of those of the Netherlands, Great Britain, and the United States, and Japan was already turning its sights south, to the U.S.-controlled Philippines and the Dutch territories of Indonesia. But Americans were not yet ready to fight, many agreeing with Roosevelt's critics that the United States should not "be dragged into a war to save England."

When Mother Mary Joseph reached Hong Kong, she found the British colony readying for war, with blackouts and mock battles. Thousands of Chinese refugees were pouring into the enclave, and she saw them everywhere, in lines at soup kitchens or outside the Maryknoll convent gate; in the streets, wandering aimlessly, babies strapped to their backs; in gutters, where they slept at night. Worried about her Sisters on the mainland, Mother Mary Joseph realized it would be impossible to attempt to cross Japanese lines. She was fifty-eight and suffering from malaria, and even had she been physically up to such travel, there were no boats to take her. Three of the Sisters did run the gauntlet from Kaying to Hong Kong to obtain medical help for one of them, who was dying of cancer. Mother Mary Joseph and Mary Paul saw the other two off on their return journey that November. "We'll be all right, Mother," they told her reassuringly. "This will just take time."

It took two weeks, but neither Sister could have known how dangerous it would be. Following the same route as that used by the hard-pressed Chinese army, they found that everything that could float had been requisitioned. Bicycling north to Tamshui, they took refuge in a Catholic meeting hall when bombing began. As they crouched under the house's rickety stairs, they heard the windows shatter, the dust and debris of a nearby Buddhist shrine swirling about them—it had been destroyed by a direct hit. At Waichow, another river town, they met some Presbyterian missionaries who offered to share their sampan with them. Fifteen minutes after the boat scuttled out of Waichow, twenty-six Japanese airplanes hurtled across the sky to bomb the town, leaving giant plumes of fire and smoke in their wake.

Every morning after that, the passengers left the sampan to walk along the tree-lined riverbank, until the planes had ceased their morning sorties. At the sound of a plane the brown-backed sampan burrowed into the river's bamboo overhang, those on shore diving for cover. One morning, as the Sisters were wading ashore ahead of the others, a plane burst from behind the river bank, so low that they could see the pilot's face as he turned in their direction. Terrified, they stumbled breathlessly through mud and stones as the guns blasted away. One Sister fell in the shallow water and disappeared. Looking back, the other saw a machine gun tracer racing along the water toward her and the sampan. Desperately trying to avoid its path, she fell headlong, just as the bullets splashed between her and the other Sister a foot away. Scrambling to their feet, they staggered up the bank, where a group of Chinese women had been watching. Immediately they took pity on the trembling foreigners, bringing hot water for their bleeding feet and cups of tea. The anxious Presbyterian women soon arrived with red socks for the Sisters; thus attired, they continued to Kaying. Before leaving, Mother Mary Joseph learned of their safe arrival.

The Rock

As Mother Mary Joseph sat in her room at Maryknoll, writing letters to her faraway Sisters late into the night, she could feel events moving toward a climax. In July 1941, the United States, Britain, and the Netherlands froze Japan's financial assets, cutting the island nation off from vital oil, iron, and rubber supplies. Without fuel Japan would be forced to "eat her own tail" and withdraw from the Chinese mainland, a loss of face the Japanese militarists would not contemplate. War with the United States was therefore inevitable.

Washington knew a Japanese attack was likely, and in late November, when Japanese warships were sighted south of Formosa, "war warnings" were sent to Pearl Harbor and Manila. The government expected the Japanese to strike, not against Pearl Harbor but the Philippines, Thailand, or the Malay Peninsula. American strategists thought it inconceivable that the Japanese would be so foolhardy as to drive the United States into a war through a direct attack. But Japan's militarists wanted the United States out of the Pacific at whatever cost, and the quickest way to achieve that end was to destroy the Pacific Fleet before hostilities officially began. On December 7 at 7:40 A.M. the first Japanese bombers reached the Hawaiian Islands. "Pearl Harbor was asleep in the morning mist," wrote the commander of the lead attack formation. "Calm and serene inside the harbor . . . important ships of the Pacific Fleet, strung out and anchored two ships side by side."

Hearing the ground-shaking explosions, the children from a Maryknoll parish in Honolulu climbed the trees to see what was happening. A wave of Japanese fighters passed overhead. "Jap planes!" they shouted in astonishment to the disbelieving teacher. "Jap planes, Seesta! Honest! For real! Jap planes!"

Within hours of the attack the Japanese had bombed Manila and Guam and landed troops on the Malay Peninsula. Listening to the news, at breakfast in Hawaii or dinner in New York, Americans were incredulous, then angry. The isolationist mood snapped, and even the most outspoken advocates of nonintervention acknowledged that "oceans are no longer moats around our ramparts." On December 11, Congress declared war on Japan;

three days later Germany and Italy, supporting their ally, did likewise against the United States.

Meanwhile in Hong Kong, a savage blitz was under way. Known as "The Rock," the mountainous island was part of a British colony that included Kowloon Peninsula on the nearby Chinese mainland. A ferry service connected island and peninsula, but when the Japanese launched an attack on Kowloon in early December, the British immediately cut off all communications. Kowloon was the weaker half of the crown colony, its docks, airfields, and oil stations prime targets for Japanese bombers, which demolished them in ten days. Among the casualties was the famous China Clipper anchored in Hong Kong Bay; eight newly ordained Maryknoll priests had disembarked from the gleaming ship the previous day.

While the Maryknoll priests were headquartered on the island, the Sisters' center was in Kowloon at the Maryknoll Convent School. The imposing brick edifice was the successor of the small kindergarten begun in the Sisters' garage on their arrival in Hong Kong—by 1941 it had grown into a large primary and high school. A second Maryknoll school had been opened on Hong Kong island, and when the last ferry departed, the twenty-six Sisters were left divided between island and mainland. Among the ferry passengers was an Irish-American priest, Maryknoller Maurice Feeney, who would serve as the Kowloon Sisters' protector when the Japanese arrived.

Sister Mary Paul had stocked food, blankets, and other items at the Kowloon convent-school, and all the Sisters had taken first-aid courses, though plans to use the school as a first-aid station came to naught when the ambulance service broke down. Japanese planes repeatedly circled the school, trying to destroy a British antiaircraft gun nearby; one bomb actually hit the north side of the building, filling it with smoke, glass, and flying tiles. Miraculously, no one was hurt.

Built atop a natural terrace, the convent offered a clear view of the surrounding area, and the Maryknollers could see the Japanese "coming in a huge wave." Candida Basto, who had returned to Hong Kong after her brush with the Japanese army on Sancian Island, remembered the fear they all felt. "Father Feeney was there, and when he saw those thousands of soldiers, I thought he would faint. But he had guts—he stayed."

Retreating to the basement laundry, the missioners lay in the darkness behind locked doors. As one told it:

> Throughout the night we heard the Japanese marching with steady tread and in grim silence. Tanks and trucks altered the cadence, but never a human voice. The sounds coming out of the darkness gave the uncomfortable suggestion of something uncanny, implacable, relentless, grim. We could not sleep.

Japanese officers soon appeared to announce that the army had requisitioned the convent and school buildings. Although the Sisters were allowed to remain in the basement, Feeney sleeping on a cot outside the entrance, the situation remained tense. Soon after, a detachment of soldiers peremptorily demanded to see the 120 Japanese women said to be interned in the school, departing only after searching school and convent and finding none of their kinswomen. The officers themselves were usually courteous, no doubt because Mary Paul made it impossible not to be. From the beginning she made clear her position as one "also subject to authority"—not that of the Japanese. Coolly confident and determined to achieve her own ends, she was abetted by an unflappable Kentuckian, Maryknoller Anne Clements, who spoke fluent Japanese and was skilled in Japanese social niceties. Mary Paul's fearless demands, translated with flourishes and bows by Anne, were usually accepted as right and fitting, for Mary Paul was like a general in her own army. In the evenings, Mary Paul, Anne, and Feeney would leave the others in the basement for a chat with their captors—about the relative merits of various soy sauce recipes, the folks back home, and Japan's great victories, which the Americans dismissed as "tall tales." Anne also gave one officer English lessons. Keeping a poker face, she would translate copies of the signs he had seen in town: "Peninsula Hotel," "Drink Two Beers," "No Parking." At the end of the class, the Japanese would make a stiff bow and present her with a chocolate bar.

Common danger led to a tenuous truce. On the school veranda one morning, a Sister heard a shell whistle over one corner and bury itself in the neighbor's property. As surprised as the American, the Japanese guard gestured, "Down!" When he rose to run, she followed at his heels. "We were pals for the time being. Along the veranda we dashed, then down the stairs. On the first floor he turned to the Japanese offices, and I left him to rejoin my community. It was an English shell from Hong Kong, and the next one killed a horse."

Such incidents, later laughed over, helped lessen the tension, at least for an hour or two, but chocolate bars and evening chats could not compensate for cruelty. Just before Christmas seven hundred military prisoners, British, Canadian, Chinese, and Indian, were lodged under the Sisters' roof, all in terrible conditions:

> The soldiers were a sorry lot of sick and wounded, starved and famished men. For three days they had not tasted food; for twenty-four hours not a drop of water had slaked their thirst. Most of them had dysentery; some had shed so much blood that their clothes were as stiff as boards. Yet we were not allowed to minister to them.

Nor were these poor fellows to receive a meal that night! Father Feeney was permitted to hear confessions and give communion to about thirty Catholic lads. The following day our Sister-doctor and Sister-nurses were admitted. While they were tending the very ill and dressing the wounded, a victrola blared out "Home Sweet Home." For a moment, some of the men thought it an American's bad idea of a joke. The Japanese had parked an army truck in the driveway with a victrola with a huge horn. Undoubtedly it was an effort to break down the morale of the foreigners. It only succeeded in making everyone angry. By night the men had moved on to permanent prison.

The Sisters, too, moved on. At the end of January 1942, the Japanese announced they needed all space, including the basement, for a military hospital and that the Americans would be sent to an internment camp in Hong Kong, which by then had surrendered. Feeney escaped detention because of his Irish ancestry, as did Candida, who had been born in Portuguese Macao, and four other non-American Sisters. But with no place to sleep, dwindling food supplies, and little money, they were little better off than the others. One of the Japanese guards tried to express his sympathy: With a small English-Japanese dictionary, he pointed out words to Feeney: judgment—remove—heart—wail—suffering—sorry—like—lightning—peace.

Saved at the last minute by the offer of a small apartment nearby, the dispossessed Maryknollers packed what they could. "Bread was baking in the convent oven, and the dinner was cooking on the stove," Candida related. "With steaming dinner in hands, and our two dogs on leashes, we walked to our new home. It was there that Sister Mary Paul later met us."

While the Maryknollers were camping out in the Kowloon basement, their Sisters in Hong Kong were under siege at Queen Mary's Hospital, where they were working as volunteers. The hospital was near Fort Davis, which guarded the entrance to the harbor, and the Sisters could see the men firing the guns and the Japanese bombs exploding all around them. The seventeen-day battle was a "blur of guns blasting, planes diving, bombs exploding, and endless streams of bleeding humanity."

On Christmas Day, the Maryknollers watched from the hospital windows as a soldier slowly raised a limp white flag over the fort. Others were carrying out guns and ammunition and laying them on the lawn. The Rock had fallen. Somewhere nearby, they heard a cockney voice softly singing, "There'll Always Be an England."

A month later, the Japanese officials ordered the hospital evacuated and the staff interned in a camp at nearby Stanley. "Everyone was to go, regardless of splints, casts, unconsciousness," recounted an angry Maryknoller:

Large trucks were brought in front of the hospital, and the patients were loaded in. One Canadian had just had his eye removed, and while he was still under the anaesthetic, I rolled him down to the unpadded, springless car. He had false teeth, which had been removed before the operation. I was afraid that they might be lost, so I wrapped them in a piece of gauze, which I pinned to his gown. Just in case any attendant might think the bag held money, I took time out to show the teeth all round. In lifting him to the truck, the blankets had come undone, and I knew it would be dangerous should he get a chill. I was in a quandary. We had been instructed by the British hospital authorities to make a "scrounge" and take what supplies we could into internment. My mantle, therefore, was the receptacle for many things, personal and otherwise. If I put the cape down on the ground, the curious guards would be sure to do a thorough inspection. So I walked up to the sentry, pushed aside his bayonet and thrust my mantle into his hands, motioning him to mind it. An officer came over to intervene. I had noted that the truck was high, and though I knew I could make the leap, despite my long skirts, I had an idea it might be too conspicuous. Assuming that my dealing with the sentry was just in the ordinary routine of his life, I gently guided the officer to the lorry, and used his shoulder as a prop to clamber aboard the car. I covered up the patient. The Japanese officer waited and offered his shoulder in my descent. We bowed deeply, gravely, to each other; I retrieved my belongings from the sentry, bowed to him and decamped. I didn't see the funny side until much later.

Reunited with her Sisters at the Stanley internment camp, along with three thousand other Americans, Mary Paul immediately began plotting escape. Candida was sent scurrying around the city, doing errands for Mary Paul, who smuggled out messages to her. Walking the streets of Hong Kong was not a pleasant experience. Lines of a quarter mile or more were everywhere—for rice rations, wood for cooking, sugar, ferry or bus transport. Too weak to stand, starving Chinese lay in the streets crying for help. Others were tied naked to poles—they had displeased the Japanese in some way. "If you met any Japanese," said Candida, "you had to bow to them. They were very strict about it and slapped those who didn't."

War, the disruption of transport, and the seizure of food supplies by the Japanese army had aggravated China's perpetual food shortages, and to make matters worse, South China had been inundated by one of the worst Yangtze floods in memory. To deal with food scarcities in Hong Kong and Kowloon, the Japanese simply mandated that four hundred thousand Chinese leave the twin cities. The sale of rice was stopped, and only those who departed received a pint of rice for the journey. Ten thousand daily set out from Kowloon into the wasteland of ravaged China; a fraction survived.

The Maryknollers were not valuable prisoners but more mouths to feed, and Candida had heard there might be a chance of their release. "Do you want us to try to get you out?" she wrote Mary Paul. "Of course!" came the reply. At Hong Kong's Peninsula Hotel, where the Japanese had their headquarters, Candida became friendly with several officers and eventually obtained an interview with the Japanese governor. A small, ingratiating woman with a warm smile, Candida came from a well-to-do Portuguese family and had all the polish of a foreign finishing school. Her courteous manners and knowledge of flattering Japanese phrases, combined with the governor's need to get rid of hungry prisoners, produced the desired results. In April 1942, Mary Paul, Anne Clements, and two other Sisters were released because of their Irish ancestry. They were gradually followed by all but two Sisters, who volunteered to remain in the Stanley camp to accompany the women and children until the following year.

The Long Trek

No sooner was Mary Paul free than she began reorganizing the missions. One of her first acts was to negotiate the release from Stanley of the Maryknoll priests. As many learned from experience, it was difficult to say no to the diminutive Sister when she put her mind to something. Typical of such determination, she had refused to give up her plans to assign two Sisters to Kweilin, on the northwestern border of Maryknoll's South China territories. Kweilin was relatively peaceful during the early part of the war, and after the Sisters left Hong Kong many made their way there. But in 1939, when Mary Paul set off with two young Sisters, it proved impossible to reach the city. Traveling through French Indochina, they got as far as Hanoi, where they had to turn back because the Japanese had cut the road. They spent eighteen days dodging the Japanese army before regaining Hong Kong. A year later another attempt was made, this time in a single-propeller plane. The Sisters were allowed only forty-four pounds of luggage each, and they were going to open a convent. Unfazed, Mary Paul instructed them to wear all their clothes—several slips and summer and winter habits—so they could carry additional luggage. "The other Sisters were so ashamed of these blimp-like nuns," said one of the martyred pair, "that they surrounded us and wouldn't let anyone see us at the airport. When we got on the plane, we took up two seats each." Landing in a pasture, after flying through four terrifying storms, the women staggered forth. The place was deserted, since no one expected them, but eventually a truck turned up, and they heaved themselves aboard. "When the priests at the Kweilin mission saw these huge Sisters, they were quite taken aback. It was so hot, and we had to plead with them to let us go to the convent. There was no furniture in the place, and they wanted us to wait while they tried to fix it up, but all we wanted was to take off those clothes!"

Under the terms of their release from Stanley, the Sisters could not stay in Hong Kong, so Mary Paul sent some back to the United States for medical treatment and rest, the others accompanying her to Macao and the war-torn missions in South China. Like the Chinese, they became refugees, stopping temporarily to provide services at one place or another but always moving westward ahead of the advancing Japanese army.

Meanwhile, twenty-one Sisters from Hong Kong, Manchuria, and Korea returned home aboard the Japanese ship *Asama Maru*. At Mozambique in Portuguese East Africa they were exchanged for Japanese nationals arriving from the West on the Swedish ship *Gripsholm*. The brightly lit vessel sailed up the Hudson River in August 1942, and there, waiting at the dock, was the familiar figure of Mother Mary Joseph. They returned to a joyous welcome at Maryknoll—too joyous, some thought—after all, the country was at war, many Maryknollers were still at risk, and much of the painstaking work they had built up over the decades had been destroyed by the war. Though privately worried about her Sisters in the Orient, and often ill herself, Mother never let her anxiety show. The Sisters should not waste time worrying about the wreckage of past accomplishments, she said, but look to the future—to the missions the Maryknollers would open in Latin America and those they would rebuild in the Orient. The Motherhouse at Ossining overflowed with young candidates and Mother Mary Joseph wanted them to feel the joy of mission. She also wanted the survivors from the *Gripsholm* to eat, relax, and have a good time. "Come on, sing it," she'd say, sitting down at the piano. "You all know it. Of course you do."

Soon the house was ringing with "Mairzy Doats and Dozy Doats and Liddle Lamzey Divey."

In Macao, where Mary Paul and the others gathered, there was no piano, and little cause for joy. Still, they were alive and free. Three Sisters had already established a mission there—in pigsties—and there was plenty of work for more Maryknollers, Mary Paul decided, increasing the number to six. A small enclave on the Pearl River estuary forty miles from Hong Kong, the neutral Portuguese colony, swarmed with starving refugees. Destitute themselves, the Sisters took in five small children found roaming the streets, setting up housekeeping in abandoned pigsties. Soon there were four hundred children sleeping five and six to a bed in roughly converted dormitories. Anne Clements, who was among those assigned there, remembered a rice gruel diet with an occasional sliver of pork and vegetables. "We were on filled-in land, and when the tide came in, water seeped through the earth floors, becoming at times knee deep. We very early left off wearing shoes, stockings, and habits, opting for short, simple dresses."

In addition to the children's home, the Sisters provided a daily meal for five hundred refugees for whom there was no shelter in the pigsties and daily visited a nearby refuge with nearly a thousand beggars. The Macao government supplied funds to feed one hundred orphans, and it was only through hard work and imagination that the Sisters were able to stretch their meager budget to care for the others. Teresa ("Tessie") Yeung, a Hong Kong Chinese who had joined the Sisters when they first came to the Orient, played a crucial role in staving off starvation. A savvy woman who knew her own people, she did all the marketing, with the result that Chinese merchants often found themselves inadvertently contributing to the Maryknoll charity. A typical encounter, described by an admiring coworker, ended in the merchant's defeat:

"If I give you all that rice for such a miserable sum, I shall be a beggar!" the old man cries.

"Well, our religion teaches that it is hard for the rich to enter the kingdom of heaven," states Sister. "Have you any children?"

The old man's face grows sad. "My sons were killed in the war."

"There are over four hundred children in our home," suggests Sister.

"You win, you win!" he exclaims. "In memory of my sons I will give you food to raise up other sons for China. But you will make me a beggar yet!"

"Then you can come and live in our refuge," Sister promises.

From her early days with Maryknoll, when she had taught embroidery to impoverished Chinese girls at the Sisters' small vestments factory in Hong Kong, "Tessie" displayed a love of young people and children. The Macao youngsters willingly went daily with her to market and to collect dry grass to feed rabbits the Sisters hoped to exchange for rice. They helped plant vegetables, looked after the community's three pigs and nine chickens, and kept the dormitories clean under her watchful eye. While they never ate their fill, and hunger was a frequent companion, none starved. When the war ended, Tessie took two orphan girls to Hong Kong with her, where she raised them like daughters.

Candida Basto loved children, too. After Mary Paul's release Candida returned to the Sisters' war-torn mission in Yeungkong to help look after the orphans. Accustomed by now to penury and danger, she nevertheless suffered loneliness and a longing for the more familiar life in Hong Kong. Lacking any common interests with the other two Sisters at the mission, she turned to the children for affection. "The little ones were my lifesavers. There were five of them, aged three, four, and five, and so sweet. I would play with them and take them to chapel. I couldn't have survived that period without the children."

She had to leave them behind when, late one night, the Sisters were warned that a Japanese cruiser was at the mouth of the Yeungkong River:

We took the older girls and walked forty-two miles to a farm that Father Feeney was running. It was dark, and many other people had already heard that the Japanese were coming, and they were leaving, too. The highway was torn up, so we had to follow a narrow, zig-zagging path beside the trees. The only light came from the moon, and it was very eerie. We were expecting the Japanese to appear from behind the trees. Every time we saw a shadow, we thought it was a soldier. Everyone spoke in whispers, we were so afraid.

Feeney's farm brought some compensations. The priest had one bar of chocolate and a little flour left, so Candida baked a chocolate cake. A visiting priest gave her two new toothbrushes—"mine was wearing out, and I so wanted a new one!"—then a Chinese couple presented her with a pair of new shoes. "The Lord provides."

The Sisters kept moving, fleeing next to Loting, where Candida again cared for orphans, this time with Monica Marie Boyle, her partner on Sancian. Soon after Candida's arrival, the Sisters had to leave Loting because of the Japanese advance, going to Kweilin, where other Maryknollers had gathered. A G.I. at the U.S. air base there gave Candida the first butter and coffee she had tasted in years.

By the beginning of 1944, the Maryknollers found themselves surrounded on three sides by the Japanese army and, on the fourth, by the Himalaya Mountains. Japan held the Yangtze Valley, all the China Sea ports, Manchuria in the north, and Indochina and Burma to the south. Refugees, Maryknollers included, were pushing three hundred miles inland, beyond China's western mountains to Szechwan Province, an immense, densely populated plain with fertile rice paddies, citrus groves, and fat cattle. Szechwan's principal port was Chungking, China's wartime capital, and when Kweilin became untenable, the Sisters fled there.

Travel was often harrowing, as two Sisters discovered on the way to Kweilin. Thousands of people were hurrying down the road, frequently scanning the skies for Japanese bombers. When they came, the people rushed for the nearby ditches, lying flat on their faces. "I remember trying to pull a bush with a few leaves on it over our heads as camouflage," said one of the Sisters. "Six bombs were dropped nearby. Sister and I said the act of contrition aloud. An old lady in the ditch looked at us inquiringly. I pointed to the sky and joined my hands in prayer. She seemed to understand."

The site of an American air base, Kweilin was a frequent Japanese target—the city underwent four years of bombings. It had a natural advantage, however, in huge limestone caves that provided shelter for the inhabitants. Situated on a tableland littered with giant limestone columns, Kweilin looked from the air, said one Sister, like an Indian fakir's spike bed. Although the caves provided protection, many people were injured by shrapnel when venturing out too soon. Most of the buildings were flattened—one of the few to survive was the Sisters' small bamboo and mud house with paper windows. Ten Maryknoll Sisters lived in the house, some sleeping on tables because there were not enough beds. Three later went "over the hump" to India to work there.

Because of the war, the city's population had quadrupled to half a million, and many refugees were starving and sick. The Sisters set up dispensaries, treating nearly 160,000 cases in the first nine months of 1944. The Fathers distributed food and funds to the refugees provided by the American and British armies; when a bomb destroyed the central mission, they continued their work from a houseboat. Sometimes the Maryknollers were nearly stormed by hungry mobs:

When 1,300 had passed through the [the gate] and gotten their rice, I decided to go as far as possible to help the others outside. Before long the stronger were trampling the weaker under foot; old women and children as well as the weak were in imminent danger of death, so we called off the distribution . . . It was a most unpleasant task, for they were either swollen from beriberi or were skin and bone.

In the midst of suffering were many acts of charity. One woman who came daily for a cup of rice was found to be sharing her pittance with two blind women. In an abandoned one-room hut the Sisters found a half-starved couple, the husband's aged mother and two strangers who had sought shelter—one a leper, the other a lunatic.

By the fall of 1944 Kweilin was on the march, thousands fleeing by train and boat from the oncoming Japanese army. Mobs of Chinese milled about the train station, and it took the Sisters three days camping out to get tickets:

At 7:30 in the morning the train pulled in, bulging with humanity. People were hanging out the windows and already sitting atop the cars. After much struggling some of our Sisters managed to get standing room near a window, while I and two others, the very last passengers to board the train, got a foothold on the platform.

Late in the afternoon the train went off the track. Derailing is a frequent occurrence, but when it happened this time, there were some who suspected sabotage. The spot was ideal for it—a curve, a mountain, a stream below. While the train was being hauled back onto its tracks, many enterprising Chinese washed their clothes.

We were due to arrive at Liuchow at four that afternoon. Instead, we spent a wearisome night on the train. There was no water, and the air was stifling. Children slept on the section tables, men in the luggage racks. Sixteen hours later, the train wheezed into Liuchow. We got off—tired, dusty, hungry, and thirsty but thankful to be a jump ahead of the Japanese.

The next leg of the trip was even worse. What should have been a twenty-three-hour run turned out to be three days, because of landslides, washouts, and broken-down engines. All the passengers were muddy and exhausted from walking up perpendicular mountains in the rain to get from train to ferry to train. Without water or food, the Sisters stood crushed in the wagons for three appalling nights. At last they arrived at the French Canadian mission of Kweiyang. Never imagining that the trip would take so long, the women had packed a precious ham with their luggage. "When we got to Kweiyang," said one, "only the bone was left—the rats had eaten it. We didn't want to claim it because it looked so terrible, but the Canadian Sisters took it home, and we had bean soup from it."

Forced to leave Kweiyang within a few days, they went to Chungking with a U.S. military convoy, then to Kunming near the Indochina border, where they found work on a U.S. military base. Throughout, Mary Paul traveled back and forth, checking that the Sisters were safe or moving out of danger zones. The only Maryknoll mission territory not devastated was remote Hakkaland, which suffered aerial raids but was not overrun by the Japanese. Getting in and out of such areas was not easy, however, and even the redoubtable Mary Paul occasionally admitted fear and exhaustion. "Unfortunately," she wrote of her trip to the mission at Wuchow in early 1944, "I chose the full moon period for my visit. We spent last night from 12:15 until 5:30 a.m. on the hillside, with planes calling on us and dropping a few cards . . . Just three nights ago, we were up from 1:30 until 4:30, and we had spent the early part of that evening on the hillside . . . We all looked like wrecks."

Among the worst hit of the Maryknoll missions, Wuchow was on the eastern end of the road through Liuchow to Kweilin and underwent frequent bombings. During one raid the Maryknoll mission suffered a direct hit. Two Sisters were in the front part of the church while a third was in the rear with a group of children. Seconds before the bomb struck, she and the children approached the altar, a move that saved their lives. "The flickering sanctuary lamp seemed to beckon to me," she later explained. "I thought we would be safer nearer the tabernacle."

Crashing down behind them came ten-foot-high doors, which were hurled across crumbling pews and benches. Stout beams smashed downward, splintering beside the cowering women and children. Metal candlesticks on the altar were bent and twisted by the impact. At the very place where the Sister and children had knelt a moment before, three stories of wreckage toppled in chaos. Choking with dust, they ran from the ruins, only to discover that a Maryknoll priest had been buried in the debris. Ignoring the bombers passing overhead, they tore frantically at the mountain of rubble until they uncovered him, badly hurt but alive.

The North

Like the Maryknollers in Hong Kong, the missioners in Manchuria were interned after Pearl Harbor. Two Sisters were sent briefly to the dread Mukden camp, where two thousand American soldiers were later imprisoned, but most were held hostage in their own convents. Living conditions in Manchuria were never easy because of the extreme weather conditions, but the Sisters also suffered long interrogations, constant surveillance, sickness, and hunger—so scarce was food in some missions that they willingly ate rice with worms in it.

Although the Maryknollers' Chinese friends were forbidden to visit them, some managed to sneak by the guards. A few months before the war, Lao Chi, a Chinese woman who worked with the Sisters at the Dairen mission, had bought some ducks, on which she lavished care in the hope they would produce eggs. On Christmas Eve, when the Sisters were interned in the cold convent, they saw their friend waddling down the street with a basket from which protruded the roasted ducks. She had wrapped them in rare cellophane and put paper flutings on their legs, as she had seen the Sisters do. But when she asked the Japanese guard at the Sisters' house for permission to leave the basket for them, he brusquely refused. As the Sisters watched from their window, Lao Chi slowly trudged out the gate to the road. Putting down the basket, she covered her face with her hands and cried. "We too wept—not for ourselves, nor the loss of the ducks, but for faithful, generous Lao Chi."

But Lao Chi was not to be defeated so easily. Early the next morning a Chinese boy appeared at the convent's front door, carefully observed the sleeping guard, then retrieved a basket hidden in a bush and slipped into the convent. When the Sisters entered the kitchen later that morning, they found Lao Chi's ducks on the table.

Not all the Sisters' guards were cruel. After one of the women contracted typhoid at the mission near Fushun, the local police chief obtained permission for a Sister-nurse from another mission to attend her.

He also saw to it that the Sisters there got sufficient flour, sugar, rice, and coal.

The official knew a little English, of which he was quite proud. During one visit to the Sisters, he noticed a portable organ, and asked one of them to play. "A booklet of 'Songs the World Sings' was handy," she recalled. "He made his own selection. So I played, and he sang 'God Save the King'!"

Although all the American Sisters had been repatriated by the end of 1943, the Dairen mission continued to function, thanks to four non-American Maryknoll Sisters—two Japanese, a Korean, and a German—and Chinese Sisters trained by the Maryknollers. Cut off from Maryknoll, deprived of funds, and with little food or water, they nevertheless took care of the entire Catholic community in Dairen. Their leader, Sister Sabina Nakamura, was a small, courageous Japanese who held the group together despite sickness, hunger, and considerable danger, particularly when the war ended and marauding Russian soldiers tried to break into the convent. "Don't let them forget us," she told the last American Sisters to depart. "We are Maryknollers, too."

"When I looked back from the bus window," said one, "there was Sabina, fragile, wind-blown, snow-covered, standing erect and composed—for the sake of us who were going and for the Chinese women with her." One was Lao Chi, weeping inconsolably.

A similar scene was enacted in Kobe when Maryknoll Sister Rose Ann Yasuko Nakata bade farewell to her American Sisters. A Japanese like Sabina, Yasuko had been working in Tokyo with Maryknoll pioneer Gemma Shea when Pearl Harbor occurred. After Gemma was interned in a prison camp, Yasuko was reassigned to Dairen, but before leaving, she went to Kobe to see the Sisters waiting for the exchange ship that would take them to Mozambique. She appeared at the internment camp, not in the Maryknollers' traditional gray habit but in a richly embroidered kimono, with a blue butterfly obi—a costume denied ordinary folk because of the war. Carrying a pass from the proper Japanese authorities, she looked and acted the lady of high position, and the guards had little choice but to allow her some conversation with the American women. To meet with and embrace her country's declared enemy took moral and physical courage, but Yasuko, who had given up a promising singing career to become a nun, had never been afraid of hard decisions.

Gemma shared the same qualities: Regardless of the war and her internment, she loved the Japanese people, just as the American-educated Yasuko did the Americans. Gemma had worked all her mission life among the Japanese, in Seattle, Dairen, and Japan, and she had a special attachment for Japan's "poor and homey people." For her sufferings she blamed not them, but a militarism that idolized a superracial and supernational character—a fantasy not limited to Japan. She saw the worst side of such nationalism at the internment camp near Tokyo. Although the prisoners were not beaten or tortured, they suffered from overcrowding and lack of food. At the camp were one hundred nuns and forty Protestant missionary women. They gave Gemma a bed and shared their small portions of food. "The first night we had shredded cabbage with a handful of tiny shrimps and a cup of tea," she said. "We waited for more to eat, and instead an officer got up and said, 'If any of you dare escape, you will be shot.' We laughed, and he got mad. But where would we run to?"

Underweight and nearly fifty, Gemma suffered from ulcers, and her eyes were permanently damaged by malnutrition. Yet she found a "marvelous spirit that permeated the place. Most of the prisoners were teachers, so we formed classes. I studied psychology and Spanish, and taught English to French Sisters from Canada. We had a glee club and put on concerts for our guards. They thought it marvelous that women of our ages could sing so well."

The Other Side

While Japanese in the United States did not suffer the same rigors as Gemma, they were interned nonetheless—an injustice only belatedly recognized by the U.S. government, for the Japanese were also Americans. Maryknoll's earliest work had been among the Japanese on the West Coast, and the missioners and their magazine *The Field Afar* had tried to dispel racial prejudice against Orientals. Such feelings were deep-rooted, however, and after Pearl Harbor whites vandalized Japanese-American properties while newspapers and radio called for their internment. That Japanese-Americans were just as loyal citizens as whites was ignored in the national rage over Pearl Harbor. Within a week of the attack the government froze the financial assets of all those of Japanese ancestry. Hard-working and successful, they lost all their property—money, houses, businesses, and land. "I was an American," said a Japanese-American who later became a Maryknoll priest, "and my draft classification was 1A. I went to the draft board to enlist; ironically, they told me I was reclassified as an enemy alien and would be put into a camp."

In 1942, he and one hundred thousand others were evacuated from the West Coast to hastily erected camps in remote inland areas, such as the California and Arizona deserts. Maryknoll had a large school and mission center in Los Angeles' Little Tokyo and similar institutions in Seattle, and when the people were forced to leave, the missioners closed the schools and went with them. Japanese and American Sisters lived in the camps, while Mother Mary Joseph ensured that Japanese novices enjoyed the safety of the Motherhouse. Although the FBI questioned one, Mother's intervention prevented further reprisals. During the height of the war she arranged a Japanese dinner at Maryknoll for the Japanese Sisters then present. The act spoke volumes of her concern and understanding, as did her hiring of an uprooted Japanese-American landscape gardener, Ryozo Kado, who made a home for his family at Maryknoll. Mother Mary Joseph's kindness was repaid with splendid gardens, including a replica of the Lourdes shrine in the natural rock formation near the Motherhouse.

The first and best known internment camp was constructed at Manzanar in the eastern California desert. More than ten thousand Japanese-Americans lived in roughly made barracks, one family to a room. Meals were served in a mess hall, and there were common, unpartitioned showers and latrines. Known as the "Dust Bowl" because of frequent sand storms, the area was surrounded by barbed wire and guarded by sentries. Maryknollers Susanna Hayashi and Bernadette Yoshimochi volunteered to live in this stark setting for the duration of the war, camping out in one room. They taught catechism, visited the sick and instructed the children in Japanese manners.

Life in the Manzanar wasteland was hard. The days were hot and dusty, the nights freezing, the desert abounded in rattlesnakes, food scarcities sometimes occurred, and once there was a riot in which a Japanese-American was killed. Although the older people accepted the situation with resignation, younger ones were resentful of "being in prison for no good reason." Still, the people were resourceful, creating beautiful gardens in the desert, inventing their own cooling system, constructing furniture and churches. The Maryknoll Sisters and priest were welcome members of the family. "Maryknoll meant more than a Catholic organization," said an internee. "It was the name of a friend."

Mother Mary Joseph herself visited Manzanar and other camps, but Sister Regina Johnson, who worked in a camp in Minidoka, Idaho, observed that it was only after the war that the missioners realized the full extent of the injustice done to Japanese-Americans:

They were gentle, loyal Americans, yet everything was taken from them. All they could bring to the camps was what they could carry. I remember one family with thirteen children—even the smallest who could barely walk had bags tied on their backs.

The day we arrived it was one hundred fifteen degrees in the shade, not unusual, Minidoka being in the middle of a desert. Because of the heat, we didn't go to bed till 11 or 12 p.m., to be awakened at 4 the next morning by the extreme cold. The food was poor, brought in boxcars. Sometimes a trainload of fish would be left standing, and before long the odor was terrible. It was worse to eat it.

Despite the many inconveniences, poor food, extremes of heat and cold and sand storms, I was glad to be there. I thought that sharing their life would somehow convince them that there were those who loved and trusted them.

Quite a few were convinced. Both Manzanar and Minidoko reported a record number of baptisms, and several young Japanese-Americans later joined the Maryknollers. Some went to Japan, among them a Sister who served as a guide for religious communities visiting Hiroshima.

A Woman Called "Church"

Within hours of the attack on Pearl Harbor, Japanese planes destroyed the American air fleet on Luzon, the northernmost island in the Philippines chain and the site of Manila, known till the Japanese conquest as the "Pearl of the Orient." After China the Philippines comprised the Maryknoll Sisters' largest mission, and fifty-three were caught on Luzon when the bombing began. Most were in Manila, where they ran schools and St. Paul's Hospital, a huge colonial building that backed onto the cathedral. St. Paul's was located in Intramuros, the old walled section of the city that had been the first Spanish settlement and that remained Manila's administrative center after the United States annexed the colony in 1898. With its narrow streets and crowded tenements, it was a tinderbox, and fires started by Japanese bombs soon spread from houses to adjoining government buildings and colonial churches, devouring whole sections of the old city. For five days the Sisters attended the wounded at St. Paul's, then fled the smoke-filled walls to a makeshift hospital set up by the U.S. Army on Taft Avenue, the main artery of modern Manila. "So many of the boys came in badly hurt," said one Sister. "The driveway and street in front of the building were crowded with stretcher cases. Some lying on the cement driveway had bloody stumps where a leg or arm had been amputated scarcely an hour before. It was terrible."

By Christmas it was clear the Americans could not hold the city. General Douglas MacArthur, Roosevelt's army commander in the Far East, declared Manila an "open [undefended] city," retreating west to Bataan and Corregidor. Army officers offered to take the Sisters with them, but the Maryknollers, who did not want to abandon their Filipino nurses and students, refused. "We all realized how empty the huge place would be with only our two priests, ourselves, the nurses and some two-score Filipino patients," related a Sister. "But our duty was to remain. The Army must be on its way. As the last one departed, the priests bolted the doors."

Such loyalty probably saved their lives, for Bataan Peninsula and Corregidor Island proved impossible to defend. In May 1942, 12,500 Americans and over sixty thousand Filipinos surrendered unconditionally. MacArthur had already left for Australia, promising to return, as indeed he did. But twenty-five thousand of the captives died on the brutal sixty-five-mile march to a Japanese prison camp from beatings, disease, starvation, and execution. Another twenty-two thousand would die during the first two months there. By then, the Japanese had already taken Manila: "The trucks came up Taft Avenue from the south; flags flying, soldiers grim and quiet, and very orderly. We Sisters heard from them the following morning at 2 A.M. They interned us and left guards."

The Maryknollers at the Taft building were a sizeable group—forty-three of them plus two Sisters from other communities and twenty-four students. After the Japanese told them they would have to vacate the hospital, the missioners advised the Filipino nurses to return home. But the guards misinterpreted the exodus as a mass escape and called for reinforcements. Soon the building was overrun by soldiers with bayonets and hand grenades. When a Sister tried to telephone the Jesuits for help, a soldier dashed the phone from her hand:

> Two Sisters, together with two doctors and the Filipino house boys, were lined up in the patio. The rest of us were kept in the foyer which opened on the garden. We were all ordered not to stir, or it would be our last move. A machine gun was set up on the threshold and trained on the group in the patio. When a soldier squatted behind it, I decided it was all over for us. This scene remained unchanged for two hours—it seemed an eternity. Finally a Japanese colonel arrived with a Protestant minister as interpreter, and the matter was cleared up.

The next day the Maryknollers were interned in Assumption College, a large convent-school with tree-shaded grounds that was run by French Sisters. Others of their group were brought in from Baguio, a mountain resort north of Manila where the Sisters had a retreat house and convent. Only four remained free, in Baguio—two who were too ill to travel, a nurse, and an Irish Sister. During their eighteen-month stay at Assumption conditions were relatively tranquil despite overcrowding and lack of food. Filipino friends smuggled in rice, vegetables, and an occasional chicken. One even went to her home province, collected her rice crop, and brought back the entire harvest—fifteen sacks—to give the Maryknollers. Two of the Sisters worked on doctoral dissertations; others served as volunteer nurses in Manila hospitals. "We always had to wear red arm bands and bow to the Japanese," said a Sister "Otherwise, they would slap you."

Venturing out of the cloistered convent into occupied Manila was often dangerous, for, *as* one Sister wrote:

Lawlessness was rampant. Robberies were going on twenty-four hours a day; graves were opened and corpses relieved of jewelry, clothing, and gold teeth; people were murdered and their bodies thrown in front of the police station to taunt the authorities; for the sake of a few pesos, friend betrayed friend to the Japanese secret police. And there was the constant threat of Japanese brutality. One of their most feared acts was the occasional roundup of hundreds of civilians, rich or poor, who were taken to the torture house at Fort Santiago.

Among those imprisoned in the infamous fort were the Maryknoll regional superior Trinita Logue and Brigida Keily, a pretty, red-haired Sister. During Easter week of 1944, the military police arrived at Assumption, taking Trinita away after carefully searching her room. Two weeks later Brigida was arrested.

A remnant of Spanish colonial times, the circular fort was surrounded by thick walls protected by a moat in front and the Pasig River at the rear. The dungeons were located on both sides of the rear end, and those nearest the river sometimes filled with water, drowning prisoners inside. Trinita's cell was a small dungeon below ground level, and, though not on the river, it was slimy, dark, and overcrowded. During her eight and a half months there, she shared the floor with twenty-four other women, communicating through sign language because they were not allowed to talk. Food consisted of a saucer of rice three times a day, later reduced to twice a day and then to a few sweet potatoes. But physical deprivations were nothing, said Trinita, compared to the mental anguish of facing another torture session: "The sound of the keys in the hands of the guards was enough to make one's heart stop, until he passed your cell, and then you heaved a sigh of relief. How we all prayed for each other, as our turn came to be interrogated!"

A self-possessed New Yorker with the same determination that drove Mary Paul around war-torn China, Trinita had been a New York City telephone supervisor before joining Maryknoll, and she retained an air of authority. Because of her administrative abilities and discretion, she became a focal point for gathering and passing along medicine, clothing, and food to American soldiers in prison, on the run, in the hills—a network of activity about which little was said, nothing was written, and the names of those involved were carefully guarded. A main concern was the camp that housed the survivors of the Bataan Death March, and Trinita saw to it that supplies filtered in. Medicine was sent to those hiding in the hills via the Baguio mission. On one occasion she smuggled four ragged American prisoners of war into the Assumption convent to feed them, with the complicity of a sympathetic Japanese guard. "I often tried to hint [to Sister Trinita] that she 'lay off,' for the risks were great," said an American priest who worked with the underground. "My reward was a smile and a murmured 'poor boys.'"

As the priest feared, the Japanese had been watching Trinita, and when an underground courier was arrested en route from Baguio to Manila, they found a suspicious letter addressed to her from the Baguio Maryknollers about roses and goats. Convinced that seemingly innocent talk about gardens was actually a code, the Japanese charged her with "espionage, guerrilla activities and keeping up the spirit of the Filipinos, crimes punishable by death."

The interrogations were long and brutal. After her first session, when she refused to admit any wrongdoing, the interrogator shouted something in Japanese, faithfully imitated by the translator, who shouted after him, "You don't deserve to wear a religious habit. Take it off!"

"I can't. I have nothing else to put on."

One of the men thrust a coverall apron at her. Deprived of habit, rosary, medal, ring, watch, and eyeglasses, she was locked in a dungeon until 2 A.M., when another three-hour interrogation began. The sessions continued for two weeks, during which she was taken out two or three times a day and as often at night for questioning and torture. "Church! Church!" the guard would shout. "Come! Church!" And Trinita would slowly struggle to her feet to meet her doom.

She was beaten, struck with clenched fists and bamboo rods, thrown down, and kicked. When she still refused to give names, she suffered the water torture. Stretched out on her back with a cloth over her face, and wrists, knees, and ankles tied with heavy electric wire, she tried to turn away from the jet of water directed straight into eyes, nose, mouth, ears. But her head was held firmly in place until she thought she would drown. Coughing, vomiting, she gradually regained consciousness. More questions, then the splash of water. "Sometimes persons die under the water torture—give us names!"

Terror. And the urgency to breathe, breathe deeply while she still could. Water filled her mouth, nostrils.

"Wait," said one of the interrogators. "She said a name."

"It is nothing," replied the other. "She says that all the time. Jesus is the name of her god."

That she survived torture and so many months in the hot, filthy dungeon she attributed to the power of prayer. "I managed to get my hands on a small piece of twine, which I used for one decade of the rosary, by tying one large and ten small knots in it. It was inconspicuous and not detected by the guards." She passed Christmas thus, but on December 31 was released from Fort Santiago and interned with the other Maryknollers.

Before her imprisonment Trinita had been a homely woman who showed her age—she was then in her late forties—but carried her stocky frame with a soldier's ramrod discipline. When she emerged from Santiago, she had lost eighty pounds, looked seventy, and could hardly walk. "She had the guarded, anxious look of the starved," said one of her Sisters, "with eyes overlarge in a shrunken face. But she came back to her own with a heart at ease in the knowledge that she had never revealed any information that could be used to hurt anyone."

High-strung and less robust, Sister Brigida did not fare as well, physically collapsing under repeated interrogations. She was in the cell next to Trinita, but the older woman was powerless to help her. In August 1944, when she seemed likely to die, Brigida was transferred to the Philippine General Hospital. "For a long time afterward," said another Maryknoller, "she had screaming nightmares."

Los Baños

The Sisters welcomed Trinita back, not to the Assumption convent but to Los Baños internment camp, where forty-six of them had been taken in July 1944. By New Year's, when the lice-ridden scarecrow appeared, many of the camp's twenty-one hundred inmates looked no better than Trinita. Nevertheless, they brought her small bits of food hoarded from rare Red Cross packages—a can of spam, another of chocolate balls, two bars of soap, some powdered milk. Though little enough, the offerings demanded tremendous sacrifice from people who were starving to death.

Had the Japanese camp authorities been more humane, the inmates need not have suffered so severely, for Los Baños was located in a lush valley forty-two miles southeast of Manila on the grounds of the Agricultural College of the University of the Philippines. Local farmers would have gladly sold or given food to the hungry Americans, and the camp's storehouses were bulging with rice and corn. But because of one Japanese warrant officer's sadism, the food ration was reduced every time the Japanese suffered a defeat in battle, until all the inmates received was a little unhusked rice. Too weak to forage for wood to cook the rice or even to pluck out the kernels, many starved—in the last month the death rate was two a day.

By then, Los Baños was crowded with the second largest concentration of Allied internees in the Philippines—men, women, and children from ten countries, the majority Americans. The camp was divided into two sections—one containing 250 priests, Brothers, and Sisters and a similar number of Protestant missionaries; the other housing families and single people, including twelve U.S. Navy nurses and eight hundred soldiers captured on Corregidor, as well as doctors, lawyers, engineers, a baker, a journalist, even a concert violinist. The nuns christened their area "Vatican City"; the lower part of the camp, where the unattached males lived, was known as "Hell's Half-Acre." Housed in thatched-roofed, bamboo barracks with dirt floors, the prisoners lived crowded together in groups of seventy-five to one hundred, each with a total living space of 3 by 3 by 7 feet. Primitive washing facilities and latrines were located in separate huts between the twenty-eight barracks, the whole surrounded by barbed wire, bamboo fences, and eight guard towers.

The inmates' days followed a monotonous sameness: roll-call at 7 A.M., during which they were harangued by the Japanese about their conduct, followed by long lines for breakfast, which in the beginning consisted of corn-rice mush and coconut milk. "We practically lived in one or another of the various camp lines," related a Maryknoll Sister:

> If you chanced upon a line the purpose of which you were ignorant, you claimed a place; afterwards you inquired as to the why and wherefore. Bit by bit, we acquired our outfits—straw hats, wooden shoes, wash tubs, tin pails, enamel plate, knife, fork, and spoon, native stoves [made from broken pipes], earthen water jugs, trays, stools—these were all necessary parts of our equipment. Our collection of tin cans and coconut shells came gradually and as the need arose.

When not standing in lines for roll-call or food, the internees worked in crews that collected wood, made fires, cooked the small portions handed out for lunch and dinner, sewed, gardened (while it was permitted), cleaned the latrines, and buried the dead. In the beginning they kept up their spirits through a variety of recreational and educational activities—skits on camp life, a glee club, a school for the children, and language and history classes for the adults. (When the Japanese tried to exploit the last, by offering Japanese classes, not a single internee showed up.) On the rare occasion when Red Cross packages were delivered, there was much rejoicing, though the contents were not always practical. One shipment that survived the labyrinth of Japanese red tape turned out to contain long-sleeved British underwear and heavy nightgowns—just the thing for the tropics. The internees made the best of a ludicrous situation by wearing the outfits at an improvised softball match. "The game was called," said a player, "with everyone laughing so hard we could no longer play."

Intrigued by the diversion, the camp commander decreed the internees would play softball against a team of Japanese office staff, an announcement that caused considerable consternation among the prisoners, who were undecided whether to play to lose, and make the Japanese happy, or follow their natural instincts. Unable to forego the pleasure of "whipping the Japs," the Americans routed them through four innings, whereupon the Japanese commander called off the game. Softball was thereafter a taboo subject with the guards, who had other ways of demonstrating their superiority, as, for instance, through mandatory bowing—prisoners who did not bow to the Japanese were roughly slapped and/or fined a meal.

Although food was the most serious problem, the internees also suffered from water shortages and a lack of clothing. On a hillside, "Vatican City" had no running water for most of the time, forcing the priests to haul it up in buckets. At one or two in the morning, when a gurgle in the pipe announced a brief flow of water, the Sisters staggered out of bed to wash clothes, leaving them on the ground to bleach in the morning sun. Everything had to be done in darkness because no lights were allowed in the barracks, a situation that led the internees' internal government committee to establish traffic rules for coming and going at night in the overcrowded barracks. The Sisters learned to go barefoot or wear *bakias,* handmade sandals with wooden soles and tops of straw braid. Most gave up their habits for aprons made from old sheets, the priests and Brothers wearing Huckleberry Finn-style shorts patched and repatched with pieces from the Sisters' veils or laundry bags. Just as priests and nuns helped each other, shared suffering united "Vatican City" and "Hell's Half-Acre" in a single community. Many of those in "Half-Acre" attended both Protestant and Catholic services—in a symbolic gesture of support, the papal envoy to the Philippines declared the camp a diocese.

The setting for such drama was perversely beautiful, in a wide green valley guarded by misty Mount Maquiling and Mount Banahao, covered with luxuriant bamboo forests. Nearby were the southern shore of Laguna de Bay, a large, fresh-water lake, and the hot springs that had given Los Baños (Spanish for "The Baths") its name. But the prisoners were in no condition to appreciate the view, though some spent hours hopelessly staring at the banana and coconut trees clustered outside the camp—the knowledge that the Japanese would not allow them to pick the fruit only added to their despair. As the months went by, and rations were reduced to two thin meals a day, then one and, finally, none, the overwhelming preoccupation centered on food: how to get out of the camp to steal some bananas, how to make a cupful of rice water last two days, how to die with dignity.

Meals in the early months of confinement had never been nourishing, with lunch and dinner consisting of a little rice with a watery vegetable stew and, infrequently, a sliver of pork or water buffalo. But by Christmas the prisoners were reduced to eating weeds, flowers, vines, salamanders, rats, and slugs, as well as "Brownie," a shepherd dog that had been the prisoners' mascot and apparently ended—no one admitted how—in the stew pot. Even worms were not disdained, as one Maryknoller admitted:

> During the last few months our food consisted of two cups of *lugao,* a paste made of four-fifths water and one-fifth rice, one cup of which was served at 9 A.M. and another at 4 P.M. This was filled with worms, sand, and stones. In the beginning we cleaned the rice before it was cooked, but later we were so weak that we hadn't the energy to do even that. The rice was then prepared with all the foreign elements in it. Some people removed the worms from the cooked rice, but when they finished eating, they were still so starved that they ate the worms. The Japanese permitted us to pick the weeds about the barracks. These we boiled and ate with our *lugao.* Personally, though, I never gathered the weeds for myself as I felt the energy expended was not worth the harvest. Some thought that the greens would counteract the beriberi of which everyone was a victim. This was not true as some of those who ate the most weeds had beriberi in its worst form.
>
> Deaths were reaching such a number that the grave-digging crew [composed of Jesuits] had to be doubled in order to prevent the bodies from remaining unburied too long. To watch our men at such work was a gruesome ordeal. Their skeleton frames were clad only in patched shorts, and as they dug laboriously in the clay-like soil, their bones moving painfully with each slow-motion swing of the pick, one wondered if in reality they weren't digging their own resting place. Beriberi was of such long standing that it was beginning to endanger everyone's life. Death also resulted from eating weeds that were not digestible. Operations were performed under the worst possible conditions. As the patients had no resistance, and the doctor no medicine, death was inevitable. One man who was mentally disturbed tried to eat his mattress and mosquito net. He died.

To supplement their meager diet, all the prisoners had garden patches until the Japanese prohibited them, though a few enterprising inmates secretly continued to grow some anemic-looking salad leaves in coconut shells. Others spent their time composing cookbooks or lyrics about food—a typical effort, set to the music of "White Christmas," began, "I'm dreaming of a ham sandwich."

During the garden era, as it was known, everyone guarded his or her produce. One Maryknoll Sister, for example, had three eggplant vines hidden in the tall grass near the barbed wire fence as well as a scrawny chicken that had "escaped" from the Japanese chicken yard and that she fed worms in the hope it would lay eggs. Single men from "Hell's Half-Acre" were blamed for stealing carefully nurtured vegetables or fruit, but on one occasion, a French Canadian nun was tried by the prisoners' internal government committee for uprooting three green onions.

She had spied the blades in the grass along the main path and thought they were growing wild, but it turned out they belonged to an inmate from the single men's section. When he discovered the loss, he stormed into the nun's barracks, wild-eyed and demanding justice. Profuse apologies and the offer of the Sister's sweet potatoes would not appease him—hence the trial, which was presided over by an American judge on a three-legged stool. "Long lanky legs, swollen feet and ankles, gaunt cheeks, and no clothes except his shorts and *bakias*," recorded a Maryknoller, "but he had been a judge for many years in the Philippines and was an expert on American and Philippine jurisprudence."

The owner of the onions was not popular with the prisoners because of his alleged role in the demise of the dog "Brownie," whereas the Sister, who had picked the onions in broad daylight, was believed to have had no evil intent. That moral and legal right was on her side was ably demonstrated by the defense attorney, who happened to be a Jesuit—an ominous sign, had the plaintiff considered it, because Jesuits are renowned for their skill in arguing legal points. The man preferred to defend himself and lost the case on a legal technicality—that the path where the onions had grown was public domain and not part of the garden area marked out by the Japanese.

Despite the awful circumstances, the internees did their best to celebrate Christmas—many said it was the "most moving in memory." "Vatican City" held a midnight Mass, preceded by caroling by the Jesuits. A small green tree, trimmed with "silver" ornaments cut from tin cans, delighted old and young, as did a crib made by a Dutch Brother, the figures molded from mud and baked to a copper hue by the tropical sun. On the altar were a few precious green plants and candles and a huge spray of poinsettia, brought by a Japanese guard who had known the Maryknollers in Manila. After the Mass gifts were exchanged—two lumps of sugar, a bunch of mustard greens, a beautifully polished coconut shell, a tin can with a handle of braided weeds. "It was the most peaceful, happy Christmas," remembered a Maryknoll Sister, "and we didn't have one material thing."

The happy mood did not please the Japanese warrant officer, however, whose Christmas present was the announcement that there would be no more salt. During the early part of their captivity at Los Baños, the inmates had occasionally experienced kindness from the Japanese. One camp commander, after observing how the priests were reduced to using an eye-dropper-full of wine to celebrate Mass, sent six bottles of Mass wine to "Vatican City." On another occasion, a guard took a plateful of rice from the Japanese mess hall to a group of prisoners, who were pawing over refuse in a nearby garbage pail. Silently scraping the rice into a dirty handkerchief held by one of the men, he quickly walked away. But both the commander and the guard were soon transferred elsewhere, as was the Japanese who brought the Christmas poinsettias. For most of the time at Los Baños, the prisoners were ruled by Warrant Officer Sadaaki Konishi, who effectively ran the camp. The major in charge was a weak character in his late fifties—"an old, doddering imbecile," according to the inmates, who "ran around from morning to night in pajamas tending his garden, which was his busiest occupation." Influenced and overridden by Konishi, he left camp matters to the younger man, who despised the Americans—at one point he vowed "they would be eating dirt before he was through with them."

In his late twenties, of medium height and with a scarred face, Konishi was universally despised by the internees because of his deliberate cruelty. On Thanksgiving Day 1944, he turned back Filipinos with wagon loads of food for the prisoners, offering instead to sell a sack of sugar to an internee for an outrageous sum. Later, when the food situation was desperate, inmates exchanged jewelry, fountain pens, and anything else of value for a bit of food from the guards—barter on which Konishi received a cut. When an American prisoner was shot by a guard while trying to slip back into the camp after foraging for food, the inmates begged for mercy, to no avail. Konishi ordered a guard to finish off the wounded man by blowing his brains out. He would later repeat such brutalities against defenseless Filipinos in the surrounding area.

Konishi's rage, the prisoners believed, fed on the string of defeats inflicted on the Japanese by the Americans. Although they could not be certain of the war's progress, numerous signs pointed to the imminent liberation of the Philippines. One was the devaluation of Japanese money. When the internees had first been confined at Los Baños in mid-1944, the price of a water buffalo was sixty Japanese Filipino pesos. By October, when General MacArthur had landed on the island of Leyte, the price was ten thousand. Another indicator was the Japanese newspaper, the Manila *Shinbun,* which was received in camp. According to *Shinbun,* the Japanese never lost a battle, but once the prisoners learned to read between the lines, another story emerged. The Japanese were giving up islands, the paper said, because, like a burnt cigar, they had served their purpose and could be discarded. In another report about the supposed sinking of an American ship, the newspaper concluded: "A squadron of planes dove into the enemy ships and has not yet returned to its base."

Other signs of an American presence were American cigarettes with the inscription "I have returned" and newly minted dimes smuggled into the camp by friendly Filipinos living near Los Baños. In January 1945, when U.S. Navy aircraft were strafing roads and railroads near the camp, Konishi and all the guards abruptly disappeared. Convinced that liberation was at hand, the inmates erected a pole with a historic American flag—the same that had flown over a Manila fort in 1898 after it was taken by an American colonel. His wife was among the internees and had preserved it, hidden from the Japanese, during all the months of confinement. No sooner had "The Star Spangled Banner" been sung than Filipinos poured into the camp bringing food, including chicken, meat, and eggs. Breaking into the Japanese storage sheds, the prisoners found a cornucopia of rice and corn, and for five blessed days they ate three meals daily.

With the gates open, nothing prevented their leaving, but the camp's leaders cautioned against departure, as Los Baños was in an isolated area, and the inmates had no means of knowing where the Japanese army was (at the time, the camp was still behind Japanese lines). Deciding that wandering abroad could prove fatal, they opted to remain in camp to await liberation by American forces.

To their dismay, Konishi and his troops returned before the week was out, restoring the previous servitude and now apparently intent on starving the prisoners to death. In mid-February, they watched anxiously as the Japanese dug a huge hole near the southwestern perimeter of the camp. The rumor quickly spread that the Japanese intended to massacre them all, though in reality the excavation was for a new barracks. Another story then made the rounds: that drums of gasoline had been planted around the camp and at a given signal the Japanese would torch the barracks, shooting all who tried to escape. Whether or not the story was true, the U.S. military command had received "reliable information that the Japanese have Los Baños scheduled for massacre," and after retaking Manila in February, the Americans could well believe it. Retreating Japanese sailors and marines went on a rampage, killing nearly one hundred thousand Filipino civilians and razing most of Manila. Of the Allied cities in those war years only Warsaw suffered more.

Observing American planes flying overhead was a punishable offense at Los Baños, but many prisoners covertly watched their progress. A few minutes before 7 A.M. on February 23, as they were lining up for roll-call, one and then another looked in astonishment at the gold-tinged sky: Floating across the hills were more than a hundred parachutes—American "Angels" had come to rescue them.

Planning and executing the dangerous rescue was no mean military feat. Los Baños was located twenty-five miles inside the Japanese lines, with eight thousand Japanese troops within a few hours' march of the camp. The internees were sick and weak—at least 240 were too enfeebled to walk—and guarded by a well-armed garrison of 243 soldiers. The challenge was to take the camp by surprise, disarm the Japanese, and get the internees across Laguna de Bay to Manila before the Japanese army was alerted.

Some of the internees had earlier made contact with Filipino guerrillas; hence U.S. military planners knew that most of the Baños garrison was engaged in calisthenics in the early morning and that for the period their arms were carefully locked away. A four-pronged plan therefore emerged in which Filipino guerrillas and U.S. infantry would attack the camp at 7 A.M. at the same time that American paratroopers dropped from the sky. Another land force was to set up a roadblock to contain the Japanese to the south and west of the camp, while fifty-four amphibian tanks would cross Laguna de Bay, pick up the internees and paratroopers and return with them to American lines. Calculating that upwards of 25 percent of those involved in the operation might not make it, the army nevertheless set the plan in motion. Even those likely to die, such as the paratroopers, who reckoned it could be a "suicide jump," looked on Los Baños as a special mission—to rescue innocent civilians. Such was the precision of the operation, however, that there was not a single casualty among the internees or their rescuers. As MacArthur later said, "God was certainly with us."

When the internees heard the first bullets whizzing overhead, they hit the ground or dashed for the barracks, diving under beds. A bullet knocked a tin cup from the hand of a Maryknoll Sister, searing her thumb, as another dashed out into the hail of bullets to rescue the Maryknollers' rice, which was burning in a tin can over a brushfire. Twenty minutes later, when the Japanese guards were dead or had fled the camp, an American paratrooper appeared at the door of their barracks. The expression on his face when he saw the place full of nuns was unforgettable. "Won't my mother be proud when I tell her I rescued the Sisters!" he exclaimed.

Getting all the internees out was not so easy, however. Euphoric and devouring their rescuers' rations, many did not realize that the Japanese army could soon be at their heels. They wanted to chat with these American Tarzans—they all seemed so enormous to the starved inmates. One Maryknoll Sister even discovered her nephew among the paratroopers— she had last seen him when he was five. A priest stopped to kneel on the ground to thank God for their rescue, but American soldiers insistently pushed him along. "Come on, Father; let's get the hell out of here."

One way to make the refugees move was to set the barracks on fire, and once the thatched roofs were blazing, they rushed down the road to the amphibian tanks. Undaunted by a deep ditch, the Maryknoll Sisters slid down the incline, then were pulled to the top and into the tanks. Like World War II airplane pilots, the drivers named their vehicles after voluptuous real or imagined girlfriends, and as one tank moved toward the lake with a load of nuns and priests, internees and troops whooped with laughter. The name painted on its side was "Impatient Virgin."

Waddling into Laguna de Bay, the amphibians set off with a roaring clank to make the two-hour journey across the lake, carrying scrawny people and piles of hastily assembled suitcases and boxes. Japanese snipers tried to stop the machines but were too far out of range. Looking back at the lake's southern shore, the internees saw a huge column of smoke billowing over the trees—the last of Los Baños.

At the first stop inside American lines "we began to see something of the magnitude of Uncle Sam's war effort," wrote a Maryknoll Sister:

> Drums and drums of gasoline, trucks and ambulances and jeeps and amtraks. Cans and cans of good food, loaves and loaves of bread, great tanks of coffee. Thousands of Filipinos running here and there, bands of us standing in groups near our stacks of baggage, newspapermen grinding cameras and taking notes. The smells of spilt gasoline, butter squashed into the sandy beach, sweaty men. And over it all a terrific sun burning your eyes and crisping your skin.

On the road to the reception camp throngs of Filipinos cheered under bamboo arches, "Welcome Victorious Americans and Guerrillas." A smiling soldier greeted the internees at the camp with bags of Hershey bars. "I dropped one," remembered a Sister, "but even though it had mud on it, I ate it. The soldier was so shocked. But I was starving."

After registration their first destination was the mess hall:

> No Christmas dinner in any clime will ever taste so good as that first meal—steaming bean soup. In the evening we were given another meal, vegetable and meat mixture and tomato juice! We are told that tomorrow mail will be distributed. Some of us have had no word from home for three years. We have lights and all the water we want, and kindness everywhere. We are all afraid to go to sleep tonight lest we waken and find it a dream. Our last freedom was but a bubble that lasted five days, and this one is so wonderful it might be still more fragile.

The dream proved real. Soon the Sisters were reunited with Brigida and two Filipino Maryknollers, who had been at the Philippine General Hospital during the battle for Manila and narrowly escaped being killed. Their rejoicing was long and heartfelt.

The ending of the Maryknoll war saga should have been a happy one, but the tale was marred by the tragic aftermath at Los Baños and Baguio.

When U.S. troops returned to Los Baños after the rescue, they found to their horror that the vengeful Japanese had massacred fifteen hundred Filipinos who lived in the area near the camp. Men, women, and children had been tied to the stilts beneath their homes, which were set on fire. Others died in a chapel where they were burned to death. Konishi, the despised dictator of the internment camp, led the carnage with other guards who had escaped during the American attack. They also killed an American family caught in the area, including a four-year-old boy whom Konishi ordered bayoneted to death.

With the Americans' advance, Konishi faded into the hills, presumably never to be seen again. Five months later, and quite by chance, he was spotted by a former internee of Los Baños when the American was playing golf on a partially restored course outside Manila. During the war the club had been used by the Japanese as an ammo dump, and after their defeat Japanese POWs were employed in dismantling the anti-aircraft guns that had guarded it. Konishi, who until his unmasking had been just another Japanese soldier, was subsequently tried for war crimes and sentenced to death by hanging. Shortly before he died, Konishi converted to Catholicism. He told the American priest who baptized him that he "had been impressed by the example of Catholic Sisters and priests whom he had encountered during the Japanese occupation of the Philippines."

Hyacinth

When the Maryknoll Sisters were interned at Los Baños, three were left in Baguio, a mountain resort one hundred seventy-five miles north of Manila where the Sisters had a convent and school. The cool, pine-scented air was a welcome change for the heat-weary inhabitants of Manila, and many foreigners and Filipinos had vacation homes there. The Maryknollers had thought the town would be a safe refuge during the war, but it lived up to its name: In the Tagalog dialect Baguio means storm.

Japanese soon swarmed over the area, which overlooked the strategic Lingayen Gulf five thousand feet below. In early 1945, when the Americans were retaking the islands, many Japanese soldiers escaped to Baguio's wooded hills. By that time, there were only three Maryknollers left in the town—Irish Sister Una Murphy, Filipino Carmencita Gabriel, and an American, Hyacinth Kunkel, who was stricken with tuberculosis. A tall, pretty Brooklynite who had once been a secretary in New York City, Hyacinth had gone to Manila in 1927 to work in the dusty, crowded slums. Within a year she contracted TB and was ordered to recuperate at the Sisters' mountain retreat, staying in Baguio for sixteen years and doing as much work as her health permitted. When the war started, she was reasonably well, but bombings, interrogations, lack of food, and the internment of her Sisters took a toll.

In February 1945, when U.S. planes were bombing the area, the three Maryknollers fled to the isolated village of a Filipino friend, Bessie Akop, accompanied by the Maryknoll school gardener, an Igorot from the mountain tribes by the name of Gregorio. The Igorots, many of whom had joined the guerrillas, were good friends of the Sisters, who passed medicine and information to the underground through them. At Bessie's village were a dozen German and Filipino Adoration Sisters as well as a Spanish Dominican who, like the Maryknollers, thought they would be safe in the isolated stilt huts. They were for five weeks, but on a clear morning of the sixth, when the Maryknollers were inspecting a three-foot-deep vegetable bin that Gregorio had dug out of the hillside, planes sounded overhead. Grabbing the Maryknollers, Bessie shoved them and herself into the bin, drawing the corrugated tin door over them and holding to it tightly as it shook from exploding bombs. Then came another kind of pounding—and screaming.

Flinging off the door, they beheld a Filipino Adoration Sister sobbing hysterically, her veil torn off, face and arms drenched in blood. Beyond her was a twenty-foot crater where six Adoration Sisters lay dead. A seventh, in shock, was dragging useless legs along the ground. A piece of shrapnel had lodged in her spine, and she died two hours later. The Dominican Padre buried the women in the crater's soft soil, their mangled faces covered by their veils.

Horrified by the unexpected violence, the survivors fled to nearby caves, but these were soon flooded by swollen streams. Hyacinth, who had survived the mountain hike to Bessie's village and days and nights in sodden clothes, was growing progressively weaker when word came from Igorot runners that they should move out with other refugees to the American lines.

Guided by Gregorio, they reached the assembly point, where five hundred people were milling about—Spaniards, Swedes, Chinese, Belgians, Germans, Irish, and Filipinos. The five-day trek over narrow, muddy paths was difficult even for the mountain-bred Igorots—wave after wave of giant ridges had to be crossed, vertiginous gorges circumvented, all this in torrential rain. Somehow, on the third day of the journey, accompanied by her Sisters, surrounded by acquaintances, Hyacinth disappeared. She had dropped out of her place in the line to rest with two Adoration Sisters, but when the Maryknollers waited for her to catch up, she never appeared. The Adoration Sisters arrived, only to report that she had gone on ahead of them. A worried Gregorio spent hours retracing the path, in vain. When night fell, they had no choice but to move on to a river where the rest of the column was waiting for them. Perhaps Hyacinth had taken another, shorter path to the next rendezvous point, the guides reassured the worried Sisters; on the following day, when they reached it, there was no sign of her. Igorot runners had retraced the main path the same night she disappeared, and they went over the shorter one as well. After the column reached American lines, they searched over and over the same routes, checking nearby caves and hills. Five bodies were found but no clue to Hyacinth's whereabouts. When they heard of her disappearance, two Maryknoll Sisters who had been recuperating from their internment at Los Baños immediately set off with American troops to search the mountains, but they, too, failed. Somewhere along the rocky heights the gentle nun had disappeared. How or where, her Sisters never discovered.

Returning to their missions from the U.S. Army reception camp, the Maryknollers found most of their convents and schools in ruins. St. Paul's Hospital lay under the charred remains of Intramuros, which, like most of Manila, had been razed. Tens of thousands were dead; millions were homeless. Among the victims were 257 priests and nuns. Losses in property and equipment belonging to the Philippine Catholic Church alone were more than $125 million.

The situation in China was even more desperate: Whole areas of the country had been devastated, leaving more than thirty million refugees. Hunger and disease stalked the land, even as a new war, between Nationalists and Communists, threatened. Most of Maryknoll's China missions had been destroyed, and the best the missioners could do was to erect temporary shelters to feed and clothe the destitute Chinese.

Yet out of the ashes came a renewed commitment based on a more solid foundation. Before the war, the Americans carried the stigma of the foreign missionary, who, however generous in providing medical and other services, could always return home to a less austere life. By staying at their posts, even when the Japanese were at the gates—by accompanying the people and sharing their sufferings—the Maryknollers changed that perception. A deeper bond was forged between the missioners and their adopted peoples—the bond of those who together have endured a calamity and survived.

At the height of the war, Mother Mary Joseph had played the piano, coaxing her Sisters to sing a happy tune. Don't look backward but forward, was her message. The Sisters in the Orient took the same get-on-with-life attitude. "As we proceeded up the deserted street," remembered a Maryknoller of the Sisters' return to their Manila mission, "familiar faces appeared at doors and windows smiling their greetings":

> With tin cans for pots and beer bottles for glasses, our culinary department reopened in time for breakfast. We split a container of butter and one of the sausages that had survived four years of war and were perfectly good.

In picking up the dishes to carry them to the table, Sister Server upset the delicate balance of an improvised tray, and everything went on the floor. Ah well, anyone who has been trained in an internment camp knows what to do. We washed off the fried eggs, dusted the bread and just did without the coffee.

∼ 5 ∼

The Fifties

―――――――――――――――

I was twenty-eight when I came to Maryknoll and now I am sixty-four; that means that for some thirty-six years I have borne—gladly, I assure you—the heavy burden of responsibility. Now God has apparently blessed me with re-newed health in order that I may serve you in some new way.

IT WAS NOVEMBER 1947, and the Maryknoll house at Ossining was busy preparing for Christmas. After two years of peace, most of the Sisters were back at their missions, sixty had left the previous year to open new mission areas, and the Motherhouse overflowed with enthusiastic young novices. The future seemed to hold nothing but promise—until Mother Mary Joseph announced she was leaving office.

Repeatedly reelected as the women's leader, Mother Mary Joseph had governed for more terms than allowed at that time by church law, as New York's Cardinal Francis Spellman had gently reminded her. Someone else would have to take her place as Mother General, she told the Sisters, many of whom began to weep at the news. Mother Mary Joseph's charismatic personality, generosity, and concern for the individual, as well as the community, had given the Maryknollers an esprit de corps. What would become of them when she was gone?

Mother Mary Joseph was one of the few who did not feel such qualms. Ever since an unexpected financial gift had allowed her to leave home to join the first band of Maryknollers, she had maintained her faith in the hand of God. If the Sisters had survived the difficult pioneer years, the economic hardships of the Depression, and the horrors of war, it was because God wanted it that way, she believed. Reverses and disappointments were also part of God's plan—"She accepted things she could not change," said a family friend. She still had a few good years to share with the community, and she had confidence in her successor, whom she had personally prepared.

It might have been otherwise had Mother Mary Joseph not enjoyed the love of her community. Two decades earlier, when the Sisters were still a small group, the natural leaders had already begun to emerge, the most obvious being Sister Mary Paul, the energetic regional superior for China. Another was Sister Columba Tarpey, who had opened the Sisters' mission in the Philippines and, after her return, served as Mother Mary Joseph's principal adviser, traveling to the missions and acting as her stand-in at Ossining. But though efficient administrators, neither was gifted with Mother Mary Joseph's personal warmth and humanity. Mary Paul was unrelenting at times; equally tough and outspoken, Columba was nevertheless more open, occasionally recognizing mistakes and accepting advice. Of the two, Mary Paul seemed the more attractive to some Sisters, particularly conservative ones, who thought Mother Mary Joseph's reign too relaxed and open, and of course she symbolized the romance and heroic exploits of the missioners in China. Yet that strength was also a weakness, limiting her vision to the Orient, when China by the forties was only one part of the Maryknoll world, which had expanded to Latin America, Africa, and other parts of Asia. Had Sister Mary Paul been elected, said a Sister, the whole community would have ended up in China—a concentration of money and personnel that might have proved highly improvident after the Communists closed all foreign missions. Columba, on the other hand, was a builder with a global vision at a time when Maryknoll was experiencing sudden growth. In the aftermath of the war young Americans in unprecedented numbers joined religious orders, the Maryknoll Sisters receiving groups of a hundred and more each year, compared to thirty or less in the pre-war years. Mother Mary Joseph thought Columba the better leader, and because she was the beloved foundress, her choice prevailed.

After the votes were cast, Columba faced the delegates, silent and with lips trembling, eyes fastened on Mother Mary Joseph with entreaty, apology, and sorrow. "Take it, take it," Mother loudly urged. When the obeisance to the new Mother General was made, Mother Mary Joseph was the first to make hers. A few weeks later, she was gone for a prolonged visit to the Sisters' other houses in the United States, wisely giving Columba the time and space to take up her new responsibilities.

The General

Like many Maryknoll Sisters, Mother Mary Columba was influenced by her mother's religious piety and Catholic schools. At the age of twelve when she heard a Jesuit speak at her Philadelphia school on the Indian missions, she decided to become a missionary. Even as a girl she was strong-minded, and it took considerable parental persuasion to convince her to delay her ambitions. To please her English father, she worked for a time as a bookkeeper, then as secretary to the chief of records at Remington Arms, Inc.

Soon she was in charge of her company's special services department. Had she not joined Maryknoll, said an admiring profile of her in *Time* magazine, she "might easily have become a top industrial executive."

Nine years younger than Mother Mary Joseph, the "General," as Maryknollers nicknamed Sister Columba, came from a different background and generation. Unlike the early Maryknoll pioneers, most of whom had gone to public schools, Columba was the product of a more formal Catholic education. While Catholic schools played a major role in educating and Americanizing the children of European immigrants, they tended to reinforce hierarchical structures in society and church. Although Mother Mary Joseph never questioned the Sisters' role as "handmaidens" of the priests, her upbringing and character enabled her to transcend the social restrictions placed on women and to encourage the Sisters to develop as individuals. Never a stickler for rules, particularly those that seemed silly or unjust, she stressed flexibility and generosity: In her book kindness to others was more important than a blind obedience to the formalities of religious life. Similarly, her idea of woman's role as man's helper was broader than that current in her day. While the early Maryknoll women gladly cooked and washed for the priests and seminarians, Mother Mary Joseph never thought of such work as domestic service but a natural division of labor (the men did the heavy farm work; the women, the picking, cooking, and canning). However, when Father James A. Walsh, Maryknoll's cofounder, indicated that he thought the women should always be confined to such labors, Mother Mary Joseph diplomatically circumvented the trap: Women could be foreign missioners, too, she gently insisted, and as so often happened, Walsh soon found himself in agreement. When Bishop Ford proposed sending the Sisters in twos to live in Chinese villages, Mother Mary Joseph immediately supported the idea, radical though it seemed at the time, because it was another step forward for women missioners, giving them more opportunities to use their own initiative. None of these developments was seen as competition with men but as a way of encouraging the Sisters to develop their gifts in order to serve others. Although Mother Mary Joseph pushed them to do their best, she relied on loving persuasion, not power. Hers was a genuinely feminine rule, and when her Sisters called her Mother, they meant it in the fullest sense of the word. No one ever referred to her as the "M.G.," the shorthand term for Mother General that came into use after she left.

Mother Mary Columba, in contrast, was an experienced executive bent on steady, efficient administration. The same type of discipline that had become the hallmark of Catholic schools began to make itself felt at Maryknoll, where a strict hierarchy emerged. Mother Columba's personality and mode of action, unlike Mother Mary Joseph's, strongly reflected male structures of authority—a natural if unoriginal response during a time of political conservativism. Once criticized for being different, Maryknoll by the end of the fifties was notably similar in its religious practices to most other American communities.

The expansive mood, fostered by the ever-larger number of candidates, was also a conservative one. Mother Columba endorsed Senator Joseph McCarthy, as did many American bishops, and her Republican views influenced the choice of reading materials and speakers at Maryknoll. "We were constantly fed McCarthy's ideas," said one Sister, adding that the conditioning was reinforced by the expulsion of the Maryknollers from Communist China. Although some Sisters who had been imprisoned by the Communists tried to explain that the situation in China was more complicated than that painted by the Republican right, Mother Columba would not hear of it.

Locked into an era when conservative structures reinforced themselves, Mother Columba nevertheless had two advantages—the continuing presence of Mother Mary Joseph, who softened an otherwise rigid hierarchy, and a global vision that enabled the Sisters to move beyond the Orient to new areas in the Third World that would ultimately change their understanding of themselves and mission.

Slender and handsome in youth, with a mischievous twinkle in her china-blue eyes, Mother Columba by her mid-fifties had developed a heavily lined face, evidence of the rigors of an executive's life. She still retained the sweet, tremulous smile of youth, however, suggesting a tenderness behind the exterior. But most Sisters saw only the latter. Stories of her backseat driving were legion among the Maryknollers, many of whom underwent the unnerving experience of serving as her chauffeur. Some got fed up with the constant directions, said Sister Maria del Rey Danforth, a writer who often traveled with Columba. "I particularly remember one who finally pulled over to the curb and said, 'Maybe you would like to drive.' After a pause Columba replied, 'I deserved that.'"

Though usually strict about observing rules, she was practical enough to change them when unworkable. On a visit to the Maryknoll mission in the Bolivian Amazon, she was dismayed to discover that during evening "recreation" (when the Sisters were supposed to relax), the women wore only a flimsy "night veil" instead of the usual well-padded, wire-framed one they endured during the day. Sternly reminding them that jungle heat was no excuse for laxness, she lectured them on the importance of wearing the ordinary veil at all times. The next evening all dutifully appeared in the stifling headdress, only to discover Columba in a night veil. Smiling, she mumbled something about how hot it was in the Bolivian jungle; thereafter, recreation was enjoyed in the lighter veils.

Strictness also applied to accounts. "If you gave her five cents for a sucker, she would give you back a receipt for the amount and an accounting," said Maria del Rey of the former bookkeeper. "When she was traveling, she would send a careful accounting each week regardless of where she was."

Of such discipline are executives made. But corporate chieftains are often feared, and most of the young Sisters were in awe of Columba. "Once she came for a visit to the novitiate," recalled a then-young Maryknoller. "She said, 'Hello, everybody,' in a deep, booming voice and scared the wits out of us." Another remembered the sinking feeling she experienced when placed next to the "M.G." at a dinner table. "I tried to participate in the table talk by saying a few things now and then, until Columba turned to me and said, 'Sister, you have the greatest store of useless information I ever heard.' I was crushed!"

Older Sisters who were more self-assured, such as Maria del Rey, felt no fear in speaking up and consequently got on well with Columba. "It was hard for her to follow in the footsteps of Mother Mary Joseph, who was tremendously loved," said a Sister who was part of the administration at that time. "She didn't have the warmth of spirit of Mother Mary Joseph or the real deep interest in one's family. "Columba's job was cut out for her," added another—"to continue the organization and expansion and leave the charism thing to Mother Mary Joseph, who was still considered the 'heart' of the Maryknoll Sisters."

In that respect Columba did her job well. By the mid-fifties the Sisters had schools, hospitals, orphanages, and religious centers in British East Africa, Mauritius, the Caroline and Marshall Islands, Formosa, Ceylon, Bolivia, Chile, Peru, Nicaragua, Panama, Guatemala, and Mexico, in addition to older missions in Hong Kong, Japan, Korea, the Philippines, and Hawaii. They had also opened schools and social services for minority groups in seven states, including the Chinatowns in New York City, Boston, and Chicago, and black and Hispanic communities in the Southwest.

These works gained wide publicity, thanks to Maria del Rey, who in an earlier life had been a reporter for the *Pittsburgh Press* and had a degree from Columbia University's Graduate School of Journalism. An energetic Maryknoll booster who often accompanied Columba on her travels around the world, Maria del Rey engineered a series of stunning publicity coups, including a flattering story in *Time* magazine, which featured Mother Columba on its cover—a rare tribute to American nuns that included several pages of photographs of religious habits, some demure, others absurd. That Columba was chosen to represent the American religious community was due not only to Maria del Rey's efforts but also to the Mother General's well-known political sympathies and the Maryknollers' expulsion from

Communist China. Henry R. Luce, *Time*'s cofounder, was the son of Protestant missionaries who had worked in China and was therefore sympathetic to the Maryknollers' sufferings under the "Reds." His wife, Clare
Boothe Luce, became a prominent member of the China Lobby, a group of
politically powerful Republicans who supported Senator McCarthy's witch-
hunts against China experts in the State Department and made loyalty to
Chiang Kai-shek a test of loyalty to the United States.

Highly visible, because of the Society's mass-circulation magazine and
radio programs, Maryknoll gained more exposure in major articles on the
Sisters in *Look* and *Cosmopolitan*, the latter leading to a book by Maria del
Rey, *Bernie Becomes a Nun*. Turning out a book every two years, she had
completed ten, all hits, by the time she returned to her mission in the Philippines. It was one of these that became the potboiler film about Communist China directed by John Ford and starring Jane Wyman as a Maryknoll
Sister.

The Maryknoll Sisters' sudden popularity corresponded in part to the
apple-pie image of a community that served both cross and flag at a time
when few American Catholics thought to question the incongruities in
such an association. "The Maryknoll Sisters are a product of our own
twentieth-century America [and have gained] immeasurable good will for
America," the Maryknoll literature proudly proclaimed. Strongly anti-
Communist and endorsed by both the Vatican and Washington, Maryknollers also enjoyed a reputation as adventurous and fun-loving, or as
Time observed, "The Sisters know how to drive jeeps (and repair them),
how to administer hypodermics and do major surgery, how to teach
Christian doctrine and how to be gay. When they return from the missions to the Motherhouse on the Hudson, they are received with laughter
and merry chatter."

Maria del Rey's books also contributed to a happy-go-lucky image of
intrepid Sisters who laughed about the multitude of dangers they had to
overcome in order to bring Christianity and hygiene to remote jungles and
islands. Although the missioners suffered loneliness and illness, and some
succumbed to nervous breakdowns, normal frailties were seldom admitted—even among themselves the Maryknollers were not supposed to talk
about such problems, as if denying them would make them vanish. Unlike
many of her Sisters, the small, plump writer thrived on adventures. One
minute Maria del Rey was hanging over the edge of a cliff in a Chinese rice
truck, the next caught in a flash flood in the Andes Mountains. Flying out
of Hong Kong in an ancient DC-3, she felt a cold breeze on her ankles.
"Right next to the floor was a ragged hole in the wall about the size of a
half-dollar. Not only cold air, but light and even wisps of cloud came in.
Good grief! A leak in the boat and we ten thousand feet above ground."

(Believe it or not—Maria del Rey swore it was true—the plane's steward plugged the hole with a huge wad of chewing gum!)

The same breathless enthusiasm characterized *Bernie Becomes a Nun,* a photo essay about a young woman's entry into Maryknoll. Published in the mid-fifties, the book substantially increased applications to the Maryknoll Sisters, although, like Maria del Rey's other work, it sidestepped the many problems in religious life. But then the fifties were an upbeat period of national prosperity, idealism, and political naivete. Few knew or cared about a remote place called Vietnam, sexual roles were still clearly defined, and the medieval rules governing religious life seemed immutable. "We didn't question things in those days"—a frequent observation by Maryknoll Sisters applied equally to foreign policy and woman's role as domestic helper. Career women were the exception, and for many Catholic high school girls the choices were marriage or a religious life. At a time when religious piety and simple (or so they seemed) values were still stressed in homes and schools, the appeal of the Sisterhood was considerable. Many candidates could also remember the deprivations and sufferings of World War II—the rationing, a wounded brother, an uncle who had been killed—and the desire to help humanity also played an important part in the unprecedented number of religious vocations. That nuns could achieve a social pinnacle was shown by Mother Columba's appearance on *Time's* cover: She not only ran a highly successful business operation, her Sisters were also doing good for America and the poor in many foreign lands.

Religious idealism and the "can-do" spirit of the times encouraged thousands to enter convents, including Maryknoll. Brimming with energy and not a little self-conscious, they filled every available space at the Motherhouse at Ossining, then another novitiate in Massachusetts and another in Missouri. It was an illusion to suppose that these numbers would continue. But no one could then foresee the sexual, religious, and political upheavals that loomed in the sixties. Like the rest of the country, Maryknoll was intoxicated with the myth of unlimited growth. Mother Columba built more and bigger convents, and another wing was added to the Motherhouse. Since all the surveys pointed to a continued increase in vocations, Mother Columba and other religious superiors could hardly be blamed for a certain sense of security about their way of life. Still, the self-satisfaction that came with success had a built-in weakness—a refusal to alter the formula. Mother Columba might bend a bit in the matter of night veils in the Bolivian tropics, but she refused to countenance any significant changes in the restrictive style of religious life. While she could afford a take-it-or-leave-it attitude, because of the record numbers of applications pouring into Maryknoll, the failure to anticipate change would later cost Maryknoll dearly, in the loss of many members who resented such inflexibility but only realized the extent of their unhappiness when presented with new options in the sixties.

Convent Life

Thanks to the attractions of religious life, nearly 150,000 American women had joined 250 communities by the mid-fifties, or more than three times the number at the turn of the century. Most came from large families from the middle and working classes and had been brought up in an atmosphere of piety and service to others. Catholic schools also played an important role through subtle or open pressures on the most idealistic students, whom the Sister-teachers hoped to attract to their communities. "What do you want to be when you grow up?" was a standard if loaded question put to first graders, who knew the preferred answer: "a Sister" or "a priest." Those who continued to so respond in junior and high school were often singled out for special attentions and favors. While only a minority had a genuine religious vocation, as subsequent dropouts showed, many who entered religious communities did so in the conviction that it was God's will. An additional attraction for those who chose Maryknoll was the possibility of becoming a missionary at a time when opportunities for overseas work with the poor were otherwise extremely limited. But as events later proved, not all who were attracted to mission life were meant to be Sisters.

The announcement of a religious vocation was usually greeted by friends and family with as much joy, or disappointment, as a wedding engagement. Since few people had been inside a convent or knew the intimate details of religious life, all sorts of myths were associated with convent practices, from the sublime to the horrible—convent language was itself ominously off-putting, an example being "cells" for ordinary dormitory cubicles. Many families were convinced they would never see their daughters again or that they would so change as to be unrecognizable. Although most postulants (meaning one who postulates or asks admission) shared their families' uncertainties—"What am I getting myself into?" many asked themselves en route to the convent—they also enjoyed the giddy expectations of the soon-to-be bride, assembling their black trousseaus and a dowry (usually $100) required by church law to enter a religious community. Friends gave them "showers," providing the would-be nuns with countless crucifixes, black gloves, black lisle stockings, and holy water fonts. (Stores actually carried lists of gifts for such occasions.) At farewell parties they stuffed themselves with candy and ice cream in the mistaken belief that never again would they enjoy such treats.

Young women who entered Maryknoll found it was not unlike a girls' college, although discipline was more stringent and they wore a postulant's uniform consisting of a black dress, black veil, and white collar and cuffs. A novice, or post-postulant, was assigned to each newcomer as her "angel" to show her how to dress and find her way about, but the experience of sitting down to dinner the first night with a large group of strangers often proved unnerving. Homesick and bewildered, the postulants wept frequently during their first weeks at Maryknoll. A sympathetic Mother Mary Joseph encouraged, "Go ahead and cry," she would say, "because you will always experience moments of loneliness." Life in a community of women was not easy, as Mother Mary Joseph admitted, particularly one governed by a rigid schedule in which every minute of the postulant's day was organized, from 5:30 A.M. until 9:30 at night, when they were supposed to be asleep. And all the rules! No talking except during short recreation periods. No mixing with the novices or professed Sisters or, heaven forbid, the Maryknoll seminarians and priests across the street. No special friendships—talking or walking in twos was strictly forbidden. No giving or receiving of gifts without permission, no newspapers or magazines and no mail, outgoing or incoming, that had not been censored. No crossing of legs, no gum chewing, no loud laughter, no food left on a plate—the list of no's went on and on. Yet by the religious standards of the day Maryknoll was relatively open and relaxed.

Those who survived six months of such training usually became novices, when they received the community's religious habit and a religious name by which they would always be known thereafter. For two years the novices underwent a regime of spiritual training in preparation for taking the vows of poverty, chastity, and obedience. On average only half of the postulants stayed to make their religious vows, either because those who left or their religious superiors felt they were unsuited to such a life. The survivors were never told why other postulants or novices had left, and it was not surprising, at Sunday dinner, to spot an empty seat or two. "The reasons people left were different," said a former novice mistress. "Some were homesick, some liked Maryknoll but didn't want our life, some had health problems. In general they had a warm feeling for Maryknoll."

"A lot of silly things were required of the novices," admitted another novice mistress. "But that's the way religious life was. If you wanted that life, you had to take the whole thing. What most galled the novices, particularly older ones, was the childish treatment, as if they were incapable of making an adult decision, but professed Sisters also suffered under confining rules. Among the most common complaints was the stricture against talking in twos, which was based on the fear that a close friendship could lead to lesbianism. Since the Sisters were never told the real reason for the prohibition, they had to assume the higher-ups had cause for such a ruling, yet they resented being punished for behavior that would have been normal in any other environment. Although Mother Mary Joseph herself thought the ruling unnatural, she went along with it because there was no way to buck the system.

Equally demanding were public penances exacted for some small infraction: breaking a dish, for example, or refusing to eat certain foods, such as oatmeal. The guilty ones were often required to stand in front of the dining room crucifix, silently holding the pieces of a broken dish throughout a meal. One Sister who accidentally broke an ironing board spent the dinner hour clasping the pieces under the crucifix.

The Sisters were expected to report these and other failings during a weekly "Chapter of Faults" when they confessed their shortcomings in the presence of other Sisters. Most of the faults were trivial—speaking unnecessarily, for instance, or opening a window in the recreation room without first asking if everyone wished more air. Perhaps the hardest admission was a liking for another Sister, a disclosure that immediately led to the separation of the pair. Often, the Sisters had to invent faults because, try as they might, they could not think of any wrongdoing that week. The ludicrousness of the practice was not lost on the early Maryknollers, who, when introduced to the Chapter of Faults by nuns from another order, tried to pretend an edifying solemnity, only to burst into laughter when Mother Mary Joseph described her faults. "Those who followed could hardly speak, it was so funny, and when it was over, no one remembered her penance," reported the Sisters' diary. "Poor Mother! Even she had hard work controlling herself. She could only tell us that she would rather have us laugh than cry."

Still, the novitiate was a happy time for those who could transcend the inanities such as lessons on eating a banana. "There we were in the dining room," recalled a Sister of her failure to remember the prescribed method, "and nobody at my table touched her banana. But I couldn't wait. I peeled it and ate it like I always did. Then everyone else did it the 'correct' way. It was silly, but I was afraid I'd be sent home for that. Our life was permeated with so many rules that God's presence was sometimes shadowed by the learning process. I was always in trouble because I talked so much, yet it was a happy period, too, because we novices felt we were all in it together."

Luckily for the novices, Mother Mary Joseph was still alive, and most of the novice mistresses took their cue from her, bending the rules when necessary and often taking a benevolent attitude toward innocent misbehavior. She did not approve of pointless humiliations, as she made clear from the oft-repeated tale of the Spanish novice who meekly obeyed her superior's command to plant carrot seedlings upside down even though she knew it was foolish. Such practices were a waste of time and energy, Mother Mary Joseph maintained, and the novice mistresses agreed. Although their charges were not supposed to talk, there was no rule against silent laughter, and the novices enjoyed jokes on the older Sisters, as in the laundry, where they held up their darned stockings for hilarious inspection. "We made fun out of simple little things," said a Sister who survived the period, "like breaking the rules about silence and going some place for a little chat."

"There was always somebody doing something wrong," remembered another. One postulant on kitchen duty threw the dinner gravy down the sink; another put soda instead of powdered sugar on the doughnuts. Told to separate the eggs, a postulant spent a busy hour doing just that. "I put them as far apart as possible," she informed the Sister in charge of the kitchen. "Some are in this icebox, some on the table, some near the stove, and I put several outside on the porch."

Literalness was a common failing among the earnest newcomers. One postulant, a tall, gangly redhead who never seemed to be able to drape her veil properly, was chastised by the postulant mistress for breaking the chain on her medal less than a month after receiving it. Ordered to report the misdeed to Mother Mary Joseph, she thought it strange to ask the busy Maryknoll foundress to involve herself in so small a matter but dutifully sent her the broken chain with a short note: "Dear Mother Mary Joseph, I have broken my chain. Please fix it. Thank you." She signed her name, still puzzled and not a little unhappy, and left the packet at Mother Mary Joseph's place at table. A few days later she received an envelope from Mother containing the medal on its mended chain. Who'd have thought it? she wondered, closely examining the chain. She really does fix them, and good.

Then there was the postulant who complained that she never got any clothes from the laundry.

"Where did you put your soiled clothes?" asked the postulant mistress.

"Down the laundry chute," she said.

"But we don't have a laundry chute."

"Oh yes, we do" the girl insisted, showing her the incinerator chute.

Postulants and novices were not the only ones to break the rules. Older Sisters frequently gave candy and other treats to the youngsters and would chatter away when no one in authority was within hearing.

And of course there were always parties to celebrate special feast days—in that respect the Maryknoll Sisters never changed. Under the tenure of a sports-minded house superior, skating, baseball, hiking, and tennis also became popular. "We made a baseball diamond and cookout," remembered one Sister, "and everybody got poison ivy. Even in the dead of winter we would have a picnic by the pond and go down by sleds. The food would be frozen by the time we got there, and we would be black and blue from sledding, but we had a good time."

Best of all, the women agreed, was a growing sense of the experiences and values shared by the Maryknoll missioners. During meals, the diaries of the missioners were read to the postulants, novices, and Sisters, giving them a glimpse of other worlds and peoples. "It was the beginning of constantly expanding horizons," said a Sister, "of a growing awareness of what it meant to be a woman of Maryknoll."

It was the missionary facet of religious life—the going out to others—that marked the Maryknollers as different. Ruled by some of the same stifling regulations as other American nuns, they were still freer and less inhibited, because of the need for adaptability in mission life. "The community I entered was semicloistered," said a Benedictine nun. "That meant that ministry was brought to you; you didn't really go to it. People came in for services, such as schools, but the Sisters did not normally go to other places." The Maryknoll Sisters, in contrast, had to go out in order to evangelize others, and that openness applied to relations with other religious communities as well. "Before the sixties, it was forbidden to have communication with other communities," said a Daughter of Charity nun who worked in Bolivia. "The Maryknoll Sisters were a great revelation because they didn't have those prohibitions. I love them because they gave me a moral support I badly needed, by making me see there was nothing wrong in such relations."

"We were spontaneous and welcomed other Sisters into our community, but they seemed so formal," recalled a Maryknoller of her experience of a convent on Long Island. Though allowed to spend the night there, she and her companion could not eat in the convent dining room nor enter the Sisters' quarters. Mother Mary Joseph told a similar story about a pair of Sisters from another community who, at the end of a meeting at another community's school, discovered they had lost the purse with their fare home and were in dire distress:

"Come across the street, and I will give you your fare home," the local superior told them when she learned of the problem.

"No, our holy rule will not let us go into another house without permission."

"Then you may stay here all night in the school." Well, of course, the Sisters decided to go into the house, and as it was a cold night, the superior had tea prepared for them. They came into the house; they had lost their train by that time and had to wait for another. They could not sit down without permission; they couldn't take a cup of tea without permission. Those Sisters did take the tea, but they were frightened to death. And how did their superior react to this situation? The Sisters who had given them their fare home received back the next day railroad tickets in an envelope with the money they had given the Sisters with not one word of thanks or apology for the trouble they had caused these other Sisters. Now, how displeasing such a thing must be to Almighty God. They were not keeping their religious rule. No founder ever meant any rule to be kept in such a way as that.

Mother Mary Joseph did not believe in exaggerating the vow of poverty. Though she constantly reminded the Sisters of the need to economize, she did not agree with those who criticized vacation houses—for example, a beach house near Maryknoll and another for the mission in Hawaii, both gifts. Sisters had a right to keep up body as well as soul, she insisted, and given the hard living and working conditions, she saw nothing wrong with a vacation retreat for the recuperation of sickly or exhausted Sisters. While the furnishings were austere, some Sisters objected to the purchase of a twenty-dollar chair, even though countless missioners would use the chair over the years, as Mother Mary Joseph pointed out:

> What would be the use of going to the beach house if when you got there, you found ugly, uncomfortable things when you had gone down there to relax your poor body? How much more sensible to have comfortable, attractive things. Such things are really essential to our health. They are not a violation of poverty. So if you find yourself inclined to be critical, please be kind in your interpretation and more thoughtful of what has been done. At Maryknoll we try to have beautiful things even though those things are simple. There is no reason in the world why we should not be surrounded by beautiful things. God has filled the world with beautiful things. Why then pick out ugly ones? Some Sisters say poor Sisters get much more than we do because we look more prosperous. I don't like that sort of beggary. It is not in keeping with our position as children of God.

Lay people tended to agree. Maria del Rey, the Maryknoll Sister-writer, told a telling story about a New York City policeman who stopped her at a corner. Like other Maryknollers, she was accustomed to wearing a neat, clean habit with carefully darned stockings, hardly a picture of wealth but not one of extreme poverty. She looked what she was, the cop said, but did she think that other nun begging by the department store was for real? "I don't know the habit," Maria del Rey told him, "but that is not good proof (I was willing to give the poor woman the benefit of the doubt)."

"Well, I'm going to chase her," said the policeman. "I feel sure she's an imposter. There's a hole in her stocking."

Twilight

In her last years, before she was permanently bedridden, Mother Mary Joseph typically devoted herself to the youngest members of the Maryknoll family. When the Motherhouse at Ossining could no longer hold all the novices, the Sisters opened other novitiates, including one near St. Louis, Missouri, to which Mother Mary Joseph traveled for the inauguration in 1947, making the new branch her home for a couple of years. Willing to undertake any task—cooking, painting cabinets, or teaching Maryknoll history—she achieved instant rapport with the postulants and novices, who made themselves at home in her two rooms, playing her records, listening to football games on her radio, emptying boxes of candy she always had on hand for them, arguing with one another, and giving her their frank views on a multitude of subjects. Not quite appreciating who she was but feeling comfortable with her, the newcomers chatted happily with Mother Mary Joseph about family, studies, and expectations. A faithful attendant at their improvised entertainments, she laughed at their skits and joined in their discussions. After one impromptu show in which a postulant gave a robust imitation of Al Jolson singing "Maa-a-a-my," an argument developed among the postulants over Jolson's singing style. When Mother Mary Joseph mildly agreed with those who disliked his singing, one jumped up and thrust out her hand. "Shake on that, Mother," she said. "Shake."

The dark eyes of the postulant mistress grew darker. " 'Shake, Mother Foundress, shake,'" she quoted. "Now I have seen everything!"

Commuting between Missouri and New York, Mother Mary Joseph gave retreats to the novices and spiritual talks to the community. She was always in demand for her down-to-earth advice and spiritual vision. In 1950, on the forty-fifth anniversary of her graduation, Smith College gave her an honorary degree as "one of the first ladies of the Catholic church in America."

The degree brought the circle full round, to that heady evening in 1904 when a young Mollie Rogers, watching Protestant girls celebrate their call to mission, had dreamed of "work to do, little or great, God alone knew." Though the story was not yet finished, Mother Mary Joseph already knew by the end of that year that death was approaching. As she wrote her Sisters, "May I in this New Year be allowed to love you, pray for you, and serve you a little while."

In 1952, she suffered a cerebral thrombosis that left her permanently paralyzed on one side and for some time unable to speak except in a whisper. Accustomed to illness, she gave way in this final sickness to bouts of weeping yet still struggled to prevent the Sisters from feeling sad or depressed. "Tears don't mean a thing," she would whisper. "I'm just an old softie."

That the long struggle had not been easy she admitted to herself when she had recovered enough to sit in a wheelchair. As a nurse was straightening her room, she mused reflectively, as though thinking aloud, "I don't know why everybody thinks I have had such an easy life. I haven't." Yet she could still smile for the young sisters, and "her sense of humor carried her through and helped those around her to be patient with her and themselves," said one of her nurses. Homesick postulants continued to find a welcome retreat in her sickroom, and novices and Sisters were often reminded of her love by small presents, a pin box or medal, for example. A keen pinochle player, she refused to allow partial paralysis to prevent her from enjoying a weekly game, and on one occasion she managed to get herself transported, wheelchair and all, in the back of a truck to visit the Sisters in the Maryknoll cloister at the top of a nearby hill. But as the months passed, she showed increasing tiredness, her now gaunt face lined with suffering. In October 1955, she was rushed to a New York City hospital where surgery revealed an almost total gangrenous condition. She died a few hours later. Even at the last Mother Mary Joseph continued to show concern for others. In the recovery room after surgery, she said to the doctors, "You must be very tired. Why don't you get yourselves some ice cream."

Ice cream! The highlight of celebrations on the feast of St. Teresa; the inspiration for the early soda fountains that marked the occasion; a time of simple joys for the Maryknoll pioneers. There was little Miss Shea spraying soda water all over the kitchen, the others laughing at gooey concoctions of "Ningpo Sundae" and "Chop Suey." And Mollie herself, young and vibrant, shaking with laughter as she hopped across the lawn in a sack race. It all passed before her like a brief candle flame. Mother Mary Joseph had always liked the inspirational verse, "As one lamp lights another nor grows less, so nobleness enkindleth nobleness." The flame would continue to burn, she believed, so long as others shared her dream.

Encore

Reelected for a second term, Mother Mary Columba governed the Maryknoll Sisters until 1958, when she was succeeded by Mother Mary Coleman, who would have the difficult job of steering the community through the turbulent sixties. Though Mother Mary Coleman's administration was characterized by the same understanding of the role of authority and the response of obedience in religious life as in Mother Mary Columba's time, she was in many ways the opposite of her predecessor—a frail, gentle woman who was well-educated and preferred academic subjects to administrative tasks. Chosen for the job because of her twelve long years of experience on the community's general council and her reputation as a dedicated and successful teacher and missioner, Mother Mary Coleman had been among those at the Los Baños internment camp in the Philippines during World War II. That experience gave her an aura of fragility. Actually, she was tougher than she appeared to be. Prior to Los Baños, when the Sisters had been confined to the Assumption convent in Manila, she had doggedly continued her studies to obtain a doctorate in literature. Later, as Mother General, even though she had a bad heart, she would often travel to Maryknoll's far-flung missions.

Mother Mary Coleman was chiefly interested in the formation and education of Maryknoll Sisters for the rapidly increasing mission works around the world. A teacher herself, she naturally encouraged Sisters to obtain advanced degrees in education, though her efforts were not always appreciated. Some Sisters did not want to become teachers and felt somewhat pushed into education, while a growing number began to criticize the fact that some of the Maryknoll schools attracted mostly middle- and upper-class students. Indeed, the Sisters in many countries were becoming more and more aware of the large majority of poor children who often could not attend any school. A few of the older Sisters were also offended because it seemed to them that younger ones with better academic credentials were given more responsibilities than those who had labored long in the mission areas.

Mother Mary Coleman was always sensitive to these requests and complaints, but she was sometimes frustrated by the enormous number of challenges presented by the changing times. Confronted by a young Sister who wanted to leave an upper-class girl's school in southern Mexico, Mother quickly responded, "What are we to do with all the schools we have—knock them all down with a hammer?" "When she heard that some of us were not saying the rosary daily," said this Sister, "Mother wept. A few Sisters and priests had decided to leave and marry. She may have felt the whole thing was coming apart."

By 1963 the Maryknoll Sisters numbered nearly 1,669 (including novices) and the Sisters were running more missions than ever before. But already religious life was undergoing radical changes because of the reforms wrought by the Second Vatican Council (Vatican II) in the early part of the decade. Signs of change had been evident since the fifties, when Pope Pius XII attempted to encourage women religious to play a more relevant role in the world. Such reforms were not widely known, perhaps because Pius had a reputation for ultraconservativism. Convinced that nuns needed to adapt their dress to the times, he founded a Dominican community of Italian women who wore ordinary clothes and taught in secular universities, the aim being to enable the Sisters to approach young people without the social barrier that a religious habit often imposed.

Though in tune with the Vatican's emphasis on higher learning, Mother Mary Coleman was reluctant to apply such innovations too quickly to the religious "rule" of community life, such as questioning of the need for weekly confession or daily recital of the rosary. Still, she was wise enough to bend with the winds of change that swept through the Catholic world after Vatican II, and during her second term, which ran through 1970, when she had to reconcile the extremes of conservative and liberal opinion within the community, she prudently ruled with a light hand, holding the Maryknollers together until they were able to work out a consensus. When the Sisters opted to do away with the habit, she dutifully donned a suit yet made a gesture to more conservative Sisters by continuing to wear a modified veil.

By the early 1980s the once traditional former Mother General had become an outspoken critic of the Reagan administration, particularly its policies in Central America—Mary Coleman told a group of Sisters she wanted to take on Jeanne Kirkpatrick, an apologist for Reagan's hard-line policies in Latin America, in a public debate, a contest she might well have won.

Though unable to embrace all the changes that were to occur in religious life, particularly those affecting prayer forms, Mary Coleman began Maryknoll's break with the past by accepting the need for renewal. More significant than details of dress, or whether a Sister should use her own name, was the political implications of such changes. By the end of her term of office, the Maryknoll Sisters no longer automatically identified their interests with the American flag. Having flown for years with the American eagle (literally, by obtaining free rides on U.S. military airplanes), the Sisters began to question such uncritical support. Constantly exposed to the injustices suffered by the poor in third-world countries, the Maryknollers were more immediately affected than Sisters who worked exclusively in the United States, and by the end of the sixties, they were rapidly moving toward a position that would bring them to confront the foreign policy of the U.S. government in some instances.

At the time, however, few Maryknollers could have explained such changes or were even aware of them, including the highly articulate Mary Coleman, perhaps because, paradoxically, they represented a continuum with the past. Mother Mary Joseph had always emphasized the importance of adaptability, a strength that characterized the Maryknoll Sisters from their very beginnings. Even though institutionalization had taken a toll on the Sisters' earlier free-wheeling spirit, enough survived, thanks to Mother Mary Joseph, to enable the Maryknollers to welcome the "updating" of Vatican II. Had Mother Mary Joseph been alive, many Sisters later agreed, she, too, would have accepted such changes, particularly since they presaged a return to the openness and flexibility that had distinguished the early Maryknoll community. Though a woman of her times, Mother Mary Joseph had possessed a visionary capacity that allowed her to transcend the enclosed parameters of religious life to communicate to her Sisters the essence of a dedication to God—love of others. Such, too, was the motive of John XXIII in convoking the Second Vatican Council.

Mary Josephine (Mollie) Rogers before she went to work for Father Walsh.

October 1912, the first Secretaries. Front row: Mary Louise Wholean, Ann Maria Towle, Mollie Rogers, Sara Sullivan. Back row: Mary Augustine Dwyer, Nora Shea, Margaret (Gemma) Shea.

St. Theresa's, first home of the Maryknoll Sisters, in 1912.

Father James Anthony Walsh, co-founder of the Catholic Foreign Mission Society of America, with an early group of Maryknoll Sisters. Mother Mary Joseph (Mollie Rogers) is seated to his right.

Maryknoll Sisters preparing copies of *The Field Afar* for mailing.

Sisters performing calisthenics on the Maryknoll grounds.

Sisters kneel to receive first blessing of newly ordained Maryknoll priests, June 13, 1926.

Groups bound for Korea and China pose with Mother Mary Joseph (third from left) on Departure Day, September 8, 1925. Gemma Shea is fifth from left. Agneta Chang is looking over her left shoulder.

Sister Rosalia Kettl in Kaying City in 1936. Sr. Rosalia was later imprisoned and expelled from China after the Communist Revolution.

Sister Mary Andre gives a reading lesson at the mission in Fushon, Manchuria, in 1938.

In 1924, the first group of postulants for the Sisters of Our Lady of Perpetual Help, Pengyang, Korea, pose with Maryknoll Sisters Sylvester and Francis Teresa.

Sister Agneta Chang, left, with other incoming Korean novices, in 1924. Sister Agneta was later killed in North Korea in 1950.

Sister Maria del Rey, one of the forty-seven Maryknoll Sisters liberated from Los Baños internment camp in 1945, lines up to receive American Red Cross supplies.

Some of the twenty-one Maryknoll Sisters repatriated in 1942 from Japanese -occupied Hong Kong, Manchuria, and Korea aboard the Swedish ship *Gripsholm*. Sister Herman Joseph is at top left.

Mother Mary Joseph in
Honolulu.

Departure Day at the
Motherhouse, 1952.

Incoming postulants, 1957.

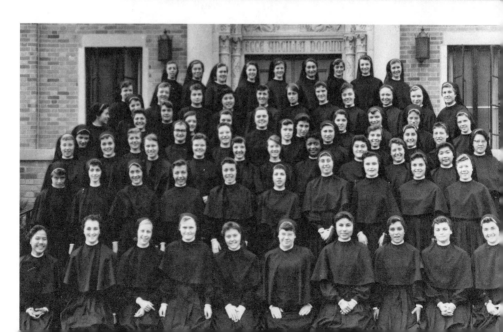

Motherhouse of the Maryknoll Sisters in 1932.

Mother Mary Columba Tarpey, successor of Mother Mary Joseph, featured on the cover of *Time* in 1955.

On their way to visit Sisters in Africa, Mother Mary Coleman (left) and Sister Maria del Rey, author of *Bernie Becomes a Nun* and many other mission tales.

Sister Mercy Hirshboeck, M.D., in her clinic in Pusan, Korea, during the Korean War.

Sister Mercy in the 1940s visiting a blind girl in Riberalta, Bolivia.

Sister Mercy in 1977, when she lived in a contemplative community among the urban poor on New York's Lower East Side.

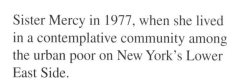

Maryknoll Sisters in Siuna, Nicaragua, on a sick call in the bush.

Sister Marian Peter (Marjorie Bradford Melville), as she appeared in the yearbook of Colegio Monte María in 1965, two years before she was linked with a planned guerrilla uprising.

Sister Dorothy Erickson, M.D., greeting a girl whose leg she saved at the hospital in Jacaltenango.

Maryknoll Sisters John Christine Donnelly and Madeline Dorsey (both wearing plastic scarves over their veils), join Civil Rights demonstrators on the 1965 march in Selma, Alabama.

Sister Barbara Hendricks, at her first profession of vows in 1948, and at the time of her election as the first president of the Maryknoll Sisters in 1970.

Sister Xavier O'Donnell, whose vision served to bridge the "old" and the "new" at the Sisters' 1964 General Chapter.

Sister Gabriella Mulherin, founder of the modern cooperative movement in South Korea.

Sister Mary Grenough, who precipitated a crisis with her community when she sided with striking sugar workers in Negros, the Phillippines.

Sister Joan Kirsch
in Tanganyika in the
1950s.

Maryknoll Sisters
celebrate the indepen-
dence of Tanganyika
in 1961.

Freed from prison in
1977, Sister Janice
McLaughlin boards a
plane in Salisbury,
Rhodesia after the white-
minority government
orders her deportation.

Sister Carla Piette, who drowned an an accident in El Salvador in 1980.

Maryknoll Sisters Ita Ford and Maura Clarke in El Salvador, November 1980, a month before they were killed.

Nuns pray over the disinterred bodies of the four church women slain in El Salvador in December 1980.

Newly elected Central Governing Board in 1978: Sisters Gertrude Vaccharo, Peg Hanlon, President Melinda Roper, Regina McEvoy, and Josephine Kollmer. Only Roper and Kolmer survived their term in office.

Sister Nancy Donovan in Nicaragua, where she witnessed up close the war between the Sandinista government and the Contra rebels.

Sister Luise Ahrens teaching in Indonesia. In 1984 she was elected president of the Maryknoll Sisters.

Sister Luise Ahrens
with three new
Maryknoll Sisters
in 1988: (from left)
Miyoko Kudo, Maria
Colabella, and Elvira
Ramirez.

Maryknoll Sisters
serving in Guatemala
pose in 1985.

Sister Gemma Shea,
one of the original
Maryknoll Sisters,
in retirement in
Monrovia, California.

Sisters Elinita Barry and Anastasia Lee.

Sisters Susan Baldini and Madeline McHugh from the Contemplative Community, Southern Sudan (now South Sudan).

Sister Susan Nchubiri departing for China.

Sister Kim Yoo Soo dancing.

Central Leadership
Team, 2010. (Sisters
Ann Hayden, Rebecca
Macugay, President
Janice McLaughlin, and
Bitrina Kirway.)

Women of all ages
continue to serve.
(Former President, Sr.
Claudette Laverdiere is
second from right.)

6

The Dawn of Change

As the Vatican Council unfolded there was great excitement. We had a chaplain come in for Mass everyday. He would read aloud from the New York Times *whatever was being said about the liturgy that day and say, "That's what we're going to do from now on," whether it was saying the Our Father in English or receiving Communion standing up. It was enough to make your head spin.*

IT WAS OCTOBER 11, 1962. An American had recently orbited the earth six times, the governor of Mississippi had just blocked the admission of a black student to a state university, and the United States and the Soviet Union were moving toward the Cuban missile crisis.

And in Rome on that day, an eighty-year-old Italian, born Angelo Giuseppe Roncalli on a poor farm still worked by his equally elderly brothers, addressed the world, and twenty-six hundred assembled Catholic bishops, in words that would touch the hearts and souls of millions of people. His listeners were amazed, many reacting with deep emotion, as they heard Pope John XXIII, head of the Roman Catholic church, dispense with all triumphalism and declare in humble terms:

> Divine Providence is leading us toward a new order of human relations which, by man's own efforts and even beyond his very expectations, are designed toward the fulfillment of God's superior and inscrutable design.

Among the millions hearing these words, were the sixteen hundred Maryknoll Sisters around the world, Sisters whose lives would be transformed by the implications of this message for all people in mission, as Pope John continued:

> We see in fact, as one age succeeds another, that the opinions of men follow one another and exclude each other. And often errors vanish as quickly as they arise, like fog before the sun ... Nowadays, the

Spouse of Christ prefers to make use of the medicine of mercy rather than that of severity. She considers that she meets the needs of the present day by demonstrating the solidity of her teaching rather than by condemnation . . . ever more convinced of the paramount dignity of the human person.

In Hong Kong and Taiwan, when Maryknoll Sisters, working among refugees and slumdwellers, heard these words, they had the ring of truth. For the Sisters who had served among the poor in Korea, in Hawaii, in the Chinatowns of the United States, these phrases were putting words to their own experience and feelings. To Sisters in Bolivia, concern for "the paramount dignity of the human person" was the definition of their work. Yet this warm, unselfconscious pope had more to say, and—despite the vocabulary common to the time—many of the women religious who heard his words and understood the content knew that what he was saying was about to change the church and, in great measure, their world: "It is time that something decisive was done. For men *are* brothers, and, We say it from a full heart, all sons of the same Father."

No one at that point could have anticipated the full extent of tumult unleashed by the decade of the 1960s. But few listening to the words of Pope John, as he convened the historic Second Vatican Council, could doubt that for the Catholic church it would be a decade of change. As the pope himself declared: "The Council now beginning rises in the Church like daybreak. It is now only dawn."

Pope John's Council

In ways then unforseen the Council marked a turning point in the life of the church. Councils of the past had been convened to address a particular crisis. The previous council, Vatican I, had met nearly a century before, in 1870, to define the dogma of papal infallibility, while the advancing armies of Italian unification reduced the once expansive papal states to the confines of the Vatican palace in Rome. Before that, one would have to reach back to the sixteenth-century Council of Trent, convened to address the Protestant Reformation. In the centuries in between the church had increasingly retreated to a posture of defensive reaction against "the world" and the forces of modernity.

John XXIII changed that. Chosen in 1958 with the expectation that he would serve as a transitional figurehead between papacies, he stunned the Roman Curia with his intention to convoke the Second Vatican Council, announced a mere three months after he assumed the papacy. What was needed, he proclaimed, was to "open the windows" and let in fresh air (and perhaps the Holy Spirit, as well), in other words, to use the pope's Italian term, *aggiornamento*, or "updating."

Pope John believed that the church could no longer exist in holy isolation. It was part of the world—indeed it existed for the sake of the world—and it must join with others of good will in the search for a more just political and social order. He didn't want the Council to revert to the usual theological nitpicking, since basic questions of faith were not at issue. He was concerned primarily about "the way faith is presented." Furthermore, with prophetic insight that was only partially realized by the assembled bishops, he expressed his hope that the Council would help the church to realize its true identity and vocation as a "church of the poor."

The great Jesuit theologian Karl Rahner later called Vatican II the first council of a "world church." The presence of so many representatives of the churches of Asia, Africa, and Latin America (slightly more than half) reflected the reality of a global church incarnated in every language and culture—not simply a European church with branch offices throughout the world.

The Council continued its work over four sessions, from 1962 to 1965. Never had the inner workings of "Rome" been so visible to the outside world, nor attracted so much avid attention. During the Council sessions the Rome-based press corps covering the Council never dropped below several hundred. People everywhere, and not just Catholics, found themselves entering into the debate. In the United States top journalists of the electronic and print media were in close competition as nightly news programs and weekly summaries analyzed the significance of Council proceedings in political, social, as well as religious terms. It was scarcely surprising that some of the most incisive reporting would be published in a secular magazine, the *New Yorker*.

Despite the controversies, all the world seemed to join with Catholics in affection for the large, smiling, and open pope, John XXIII, who became the new image of what a Catholic pontiff should be. In the Council's second year, 1963, and not long before his death, Pope John issued his encyclical letter, *Pacem in Terris*, "Peace on Earth." It was an impressive address to an entire global audience, and it was also seen by some as the summation of what John wanted his Council to be. "Good Pope John" saw world peace in terms of mutual human trust and human rights. World unity could be achieved only if both God and individuals were respected.

He did not live to see his project completed. This would fall to his successor, the Archbishop of Milan, Cardinal Giovanni Battista Montini, who, as Pope Paul VI, would lead the church for the next fifteen years. And as the trials and tribulations of these years unfolded, it became conventional wisdom that, while it took a John XXIII to call a Council, it would take someone as skilled in diplomacy as Paul VI to implement it.

For Americans at this time, Rome was not the only focus of attention. For American Catholics the decade began with a new sense of "arrival" in the election of the handsome, articulate, and *Catholic* president, John F. Kennedy. But the following years brought social and political upheaval so challenging to the domestic status quo that the impact had scarcely declined three decades later. While Catholic bishops in Rome were debating reform and renewal in the church, Americans were embarking on an even more tumultuous analysis and reform of their own society. This volatile reappraisal of accepted facts of national life reduced to tinder many of the restraints that had held fast the prevailing social mores, including racial codes and the rules governing sexual behavior.

Simultaneous to this social and cultural self-examination, many young Americans began to conduct a searing examination of U.S. policy around the world. This was forced by a revolt against the nature of American involvement in Vietnam. The desperation of the urban poor erupted in riots and death; colleges and universities around the country were convulsed by protest and often violent reaction; suddenly everything seemed subject to question, literally "up for grabs."

But if innocence was being shattered, so was complacency. If selfishness was being questioned, it was in part being done by ordinary people committing themselves to new avenues of service. If the nation was at war in Vietnam, never previously had so many campaigned so boldly and, possibly in the final analysis, so successfully for peace.

And so while the Catholic bishops in Rome were examining the church, Americans of all faiths and convictions were examining their social conscience. The two examinations were not cause and effect, but for Catholic Americans, at least, they were inevitably intertwined—and for none more so, as it transpired, than the Maryknoll Sisters. For them, too, it would be a decade of change.

As the 1960s opened, all Maryknoll Sisters looked alike in identical habits. By the end of the decade, with Sisters wearing ordinary clothes appropriate to their geographical setting and work, their unity in a common vision would no longer be reflected in a uniform appearance. In 1960, all women religious were known by specially chosen, more often designated, religious names; ten years later, most had reemerged with their original baptismal names. In this decade, the Maryknoll Sisters went from rule by a Mother General and General Council to a more representative style of governance with a Sister-president and central governing board.

Whereas previously the church had been reluctant to trust lay people with the Bible except under the closest supervision of a priest, the Vatican Council would encourage Catholics to immerse themselves in Sacred Scripture. Sisters, who previously knew Scripture only in a limited way through daily prayer and worship, would begin to sit down together, to reflect on their experiences in the light of God's Word. And out of that reflection would come new senses of direction and commitment, as well as the strength to carry on.

Because the Council in Rome was an ecumenical event, with invited observers from all faiths, various words would disappear from the Catholic, and Maryknoll, vocabulary. In 1912, the Maryknoll Sisters' Constitutions spoke of Sisters being "sent to pagans" in "heathen lands" for "personal sanctification" and to convert others to Christianity. By the 1970s, the Constitutions would speak of "identifying with the poor in the Gospel sense" in "world situations where divisions and barriers have marginated, alienated, or dehumanized people" in order "to develop community through mutual sharing and deeper understanding of the ultimate meaning of life: building the community of God."

A new Christian vocabulary would develop during these years. Words and concepts such as "empowerment," "dialogue," "mutuality," "liberation," "lived experience," and "option for the poor" became shorthand terms for new understandings of mission and religious life.

Perhaps most dramatic of all, in terms of how the Maryknoll Sisters changed their approach to mission, was that when the Council began most Maryknoll Sisters were engaged in various kinds of institutional work—in schools, orphanages, colleges, and hospitals. But before the Council ended, in October 1965, the first few Sisters had begun to move out of the institutions to work alongside the people. In some ways this represented a return to the style of the earlier Sisters in China. In any case, this change was to be the preeminent harbinger of the Maryknoll Sisters' future.

The Council produced sixteen documents, many of them—particularly those on the renewal of religious life, on the relationship of the church to non-Christian religions, on religious freedom, and on the missionary activity of the church—addressing topics of direct relevance to the Sisters. Was it surprising that the Maryknoll Sisters found themselves especially attuned to the document dealing with the church in the world—*Gaudium et Spes*—rather than with those documents dealing specifically with religious life? Not really, because by the time those documents were issued, the Sisters were often ahead of the Council in the process of renewal and reflection. In contrast, the opening words of *Gaudium et Spes*, perhaps the most remarkable passage from the entire Council, charted a path that the Sisters would eagerly follow:

The joy and hope, the grief and anguish of the men and women of our time, especially of those who are poor or afflicted in any way, are the joy and hope, the grief and anguish of the followers of Christ as well. Nothing that is genuinely human fails to find an echo in their hearts. For theirs is a community composed of men and women, who, united in Christ and guided by the Holy Spirit, press onwards toward the kingdom of the Father and are bearers of a message of salvation intended for all. That is why Christians cherish a feeling of deep solidarity with the human race and its history.

Such words would offer impetus to the Sisters' increasing engagement with socially active work among the poor. But there was another, less dramatic directive of the Council that was to have enormous significance for the Sisters. The Council urged all religious orders to reexamine their constitutions to bring them up-to-date. In particular, religious orders were instructed to hold a special conference or, to use the monastic term, Chapter of Affairs, to reexamine their founding inspiration, or charism. The Maryknoll Sisters convened this watershed Chapter in 1968. But in retrospect, some suggestion of the dramatic changes to come were hinted at during the earlier, regularly scheduled General Chapter of 1964. This was the Chapter that opened the door on renewal and invited the Sisters to enter afresh into what it was that Mother Mary Joseph had created.

Considered that way, it was difficult to avoid the fact that Mollie Rogers had been innovative and flexible, exuberant and expansive (and fond of ice cream parties). In her view of mission, she had been a product of her time; but in her flexibility, she had been well ahead of it. In returning to their heritage, the Sisters were to discover resources that prepared them to envision new horizons. But it was the 1964 General Chapter that was the first severing of ties, the cutting loose that was required for a "new creative break."

The 1964 Sixth General Chapter

If it was to be a decade of change, the Maryknoll Sisters were both capable of it and, in some respects, ready for it. Due to the early initiatives of Pius XII and the emergence of the Sister Formation Conference, the women religious of the United States, as a group, were among the best educated women in the world in terms of professional preparation and personal commitment to their work.

For years quiet discussion had been taking place about the future and meaning of religious life. The publication in 1962 of *A Nun in the World*, by Belgian Cardinal Leon Joseph Suenens, gave further impetus to the cause of renewal. It is significant that in preparation for the upcoming Sixth General Chapter, Mother Mary Coleman sent a copy of Suenens' book, along with a bound collection of the writings of Mother Mary Joseph, to each Maryknoll community around the world.

Sister Barbara Hendricks was one of the youngest of the thirty-two delegates to the 1964 Chapter. The major issues of the time, as she recalls, were the updating of religious life—"everything from the religious habit to freedom of choice about recreation"; evaluation of the community's work, "especially the schools and other institutions"; better preparation (in theology, biblical studies, human relations, and catechesis) for transforming the social world outside the schools; and the clarification of goals.

The Chapter opened up a thoroughgoing review of the "externals" of religious life in an effort to distinguish between the apostolic mission of the Congregation and the encroachment of unnecessary monastic forms. Looking back on life before the 1964 Chapter, Sisters remember, with little nostalgia, such rules as leaving outgoing letters unsealed in the Mother Superior's box to be read and censored; the enforcement of the Great Silence between 9 P.M. and Mass the next morning; the rule against leaving the grounds with visiting family or kissing one's brother goodbye. These were seemingly small yet vital signs, indications that personal privacy, freedom, and responsibility were breaking through. As Sister Dolores Geier puts it, "The big thing is that we felt like adults."

This "last of its kind" Chapter was held from July 5 to August 18, 1964. Among those present was Maryknoll Sister Mary Xavier O'Donnell, by that time almost sixty-two, who impressed a group of mainly younger Sisters with her "missionary vision."

She was also a constant sign of contradiction. Born in Cambridge, Massachusetts, as Mary Rose O'Donnell, she gave little evidence of physical strength, yet she lived to be eighty-six. She had joined the Maryknoll Sisters in 1924 and served as secretary to Father James Anthony Walsh. As Mistress of Novices, responsible for orienting and guiding new entrants, she had worked closely with Mother Mary Joseph. In her long career she worked among the Mexicans in San Juan Battista, California, among the blacks in Walterboro, South Carolina, the Hispanics of Chicago, and later with Cesar Chavez and his fledgling Farm Workers Union. Throughout her life, Sister Mary Xavier remained open to the Spirit as she listened to the varied voices of her experience, especially while working with the poor. Yet she bore quietly the fact that year after year, throughout her religious life, she had hoped to be assigned to the overseas missions.

Nevertheless, her special gifts did not go unnoticed. Recognized, in one Sister's words, as a person "amazingly free in her ability to move forward theologically and socially," she was elected in 1964 and then again in 1968 to serve as a Chapter delegate, serving in both cases as a calming link between old and new.

Typical of how forward-thinking she could be is her address to the Sisters on August 14, 1964, in which she said: "The present Church in South and Central America has begun to think of the situation there where social revolution is taking place. Those bishops can see the need for the Church to penetrate the situation of terrible poverty. Unless the Church can send missioners, and lessen the misery of the people, it will not give witness of real concern."

Sister Mary Xavier spoke these words four years before the Latin American bishops, in their historic meeting in Medellín, Colombia, declared their preferential option for the poor. But such sentiments were already in the air, and part of the experience many Maryknoll Sisters were living. Translating her words back to the Maryknoll situation, Sister Xavier continued: "Many of the proposals from our Sisters show great concern and are very thoughtful about the situation. We have to realize that the Holy Spirit moves in the individual Sister and in the Community so that as one family we can perceive just what our mission is in the Church today. This concern for arriving at a deeper sense has come from Sisters in every single country where we have schools. I believe that this questioning of the schools is what we are trying to discern."

Such words, coming from the frail and elderly Sister Xavier, did not seem quite as controversial as they might have from one of the younger Sisters. But in fact what she was proposing was a new model of church, mission, and religious life. When the question of continuing the Catholic schools in Hawaii was discussed, Sister Xavier intervened: "I don't think anybody questions that education is an important part of the apostolate. But I think we should get the question down as to what we are considering. When we went to Hawaii it was definitely a mission territory, there was a missionary bishop and we were badly needed. Under the action that made it a territorial part of the United States, it has now obviously become part of the American diocesan school system." The "precise question" that should be addressed, therefore, was the fact that there are "comparatively few missionary communities for less developed areas."

As Barbara Hendricks observes, "Xavier O'Donnell always dealt with the underlying, bigger issues, and did not waste her energy on nonessential items." Sister Anna Marion Pavao, who served with Sister Xavier as a delegate in 1968, adds: "She was ahead of her time and tended to stand with the 'far-outers,' those who were thinking new thoughts about religious life and mission. She was always trying to push us forward into the new."

There were prices to be paid for pushing "into the new." The changes in consciousness that found expression in Vatican II, while invigorating, left others questioning the meaning of religious life altogether. In 1962, the year the Council opened, 132 young women entered the Congregation of the Maryknoll Sisters. In 1970, when the Sisters' first General Assembly was closing, there were to be only three new entrants. And yet in the intervening years there would be a different form of growth that would belie such numbers. That growth, in a new awareness of what it meant to be a

Maryknoll Sister, came out of the Sisters' interpretation of the Council documents in the light of their own experience and process of reflection.

The Council's demands and liberating changes, in league with dramatic social and cultural shifts occurring throughout the world, led many Catholics to leave the church. Some conservatives quit in protest of the changes in traditional discipline and liturgy: Latin was dropped along with the obligatory Friday abstinence, the familiar disappeared, and the new became mandatory. At the same time many progressives quit because the changes were not coming fast enough or because they believed they could live their "Catholic" faith in other ways. Throughout the world there was a rapid exodus of priests and men and women religious from clerical and religious life. In many cases, the departure reflected no crisis of faith but the simple fact that Vatican II had opened up new possibilities for living out a gospel commitment in the world and erased the negative view of the laity as an inferior Christian station in life.

Speaking of the "identity crisis" felt by many missioners, Maryknoll Sister Betty Ann Maheu, a member of the Central Governing Board from 1971 to 1979, describes the variety of reasons many Sisters left the Congregation. "Before Vatican II we felt totally secure. Religious were in many ways happily and innocently dependent. Then, suddenly, to be told that you have to be responsible for your own decisions, made in discernment with your local community, was enough to cause some Sisters to ask: 'What am I doing here?' And they left. Some said to me, 'I had no choice but to join a religious order if I wanted to serve the church and do missionary work. The culture did not allow me as a woman the opportunity to otherwise devote myself to these things. Now I can serve God in all kinds of ways, or even join the Peace Corps.'"

Because the United States itself was going through rapid cultural change, says Maheu, "many people who left Maryknoll, perhaps most, got caught up into that swiftness. Some left because they had never really bought into religious life—they had wanted the missionary life. Others left because they came to terms with the fact that theirs had been a temporary commitment; still others decided they did not want to remain celibate all their lives. But if there was a crisis in the lives of those who left, there was no less a crisis for those who stayed."

Maheu continues: "Those who remained had to muster up all kinds of energy and resources that most didn't even know they had just to keep going. Every so often you still hear someone say, 'You should have been there and gone through it.' It really does something to you to see your best friend leave; it's like seeing your sister get a divorce. Seeing one after the other opt out really has an effect on you."

The 1964 Chapter left the Sisters pondering the meaning of mission in its deepest sense. The objective had to go beyond simply going into a country and establishing the local church. Increasingly, the Sisters thought in terms of witnessing to the Reign of God—a reality that extended beyond any exclusive understanding of religion to embrace the ultimate and transcendent possibilities of human existence. To be representatives of Christ's church must also mean engagement in the liberation of peoples from oppression, recognition of the contribution of the poor themselves in the process of evangelization, analysis of the interaction between faith and culture, and dialogue with persons of other religious faiths.

"One thing you soon realized," commented Maheu later, "was that as a missioner you had brought the cultural baggage of Western Europe and the religious piety of the Western church with you. Vatican II committed you to have respect for other people's religion and culture."

Symbolic of the changes instigated by the 1964 Chapter was a brochure produced by the Sisters in 1968, which proclaims, "Our changing style of dress is merely one way to adapt to a fast-changing world." Behind the brochure's smiling faces of Sisters dressed in a variety of modified habits, the Sisters were moving faster than they themselves at first realized.

"The assumptions I had not only about mission but about the United States, assumptions about social structures, about class, all those sorts of things were tested during that decade," said Maryknoll Sister Marie Moore, who during the 1960s was among those who moved from institutional work to "being with the people."

"In 1968," she said, "I began working among women in one of the poor neighborhoods on the outskirts of Merida, Mexico. That was a whole open door, which led to many questions. The experience relativizes things instead of letting you be comfortable with absolutes; it even relativizes the question of religion. You think, 'How do other people experience God or the transcendent? How does it work out in their lives?' It definitely does not become a case simply of transmitting patterns, but more a sharing of experiences of how God operates in the lives of us all."

As the Sisters began to explore their original charism, they found themselves reexamining their earliest experience in the mission fields in terms of the new post-Vatican-II language. "The Sisters in China (in the 1930s) would not have thought of their work as a preferential option for the poor," said Sister Betty Ann Maheu, "but it was."

Although some would see the greater immersion of the Sisters in active social work among the poor as a trend away from traditional "religious" life, in fact many Sisters experienced this as the recovery of a deeper spirituality, less concerned with institutional good works and closer to the lived experience of people. As Luise Ahrens, who was later to serve as president of the Maryknoll Sisters, explains, the church had long presented itself as the "bringer of packaged schooling, health care, and social services." As a result, "we were not able to receive. We dealt with poverty by taking steps to wipe out its manifestations. We often missed seeing the hearts of the people who came in to us, as we reached out to heal their wounds and educate their minds." As a result, she recalls how a friend of the Sisters, a Muslim professor in Indonesia, asked one day "why we thought anyone would become a Christian. As he said: 'Christians are nurses, social workers, and teachers, and not interested in the things of God.'"

As Ahrens reflects on "that precious moment of dialogue," she says, "He did not see in our desire to do good the missioners' interest in the spiritual and the transcendent; the incarnational aspects of our missionary approach were not for him visibly grounded in the worship and praise of God."

Looking back, Sister Betty Ann Maheu saw the problem in somewhat different terms: "For that period we dealt with the effects of poverty, but because we did not question the structures that sustained it, we became ourselves part of the problem."

Increasingly the Sisters would begin to question the structures. For some the most difficult and most widely publicized wrenches would come when they questioned the behavior of what was, for most of them, their own government. But for all the Maryknoll Sisters, the cost of those changes—in personal anguish, in departures, in hurt feelings—came high, and they came, as it happened, during the term of Mother Mary Coleman. It was her fate to serve during the difficult years of transition as the Congregation moved from the placid and conformist late 1950s into the reformist fever of the mid-1960s. During her first term (1958–64) the new theological vision of Vatican II was only just emerging, the small changes in lifestyle were being introduced at the 1964 Chapter, and inside religious life as a whole things were still relatively calm. But by Mother Mary Coleman's second term (1964–70), the process of change had gained its own momentum.

It is hard to encapsulate in any anecdote the distance traveled by the Congregation during Mother Mary Coleman's period in office between 1958 and 1970. But a poignant story from her early period in office serves as a vivid reflection of her starting point. In her visit to Jacaltenango, a remote village in the Guatemalan highlands, we see the older institutional form of service, in this case medical care, being established in an area of great need.

∽

It was to be an arduous trip, yet the petite Mother General felt obliged to make it. Elected two years earlier, in 1958, Mother Mary Coleman, the head of the Congregation, was on a four-month visit to the Maryknoll Sisters' Latin American missions, 143 Sisters in seven Latin American countries. This particular segment of the journey was made in order to visit Sisters Regina Johnson and Rose Magdalen Collins in Jacaltenango, and Sisters Elsie Monge and Rose Anna Tobin in Huehuetenango.

To reach mountainous Jacaltenango meant taking the workhorse DC-3 flight from Guatemala City to Huehuetenango, the easiest one hundred miles of the journey. Next came two rough hours in a jeep, to the trail's end. There the two Sisters, Mother Mary Coleman and Sister Martina Bridgeman, transferred to horses led by José León Silvestre, nicknamed "Chepe," for the final, arduous leg: a rough six hours up—as high as twelve thousand feet—and down some of the world's most rugged and beautiful terrain.

Six hours in the saddle for a woman who had not ridden for more than twenty years was a tough trial, but a tougher one was ahead. In Jacaltenango, or Jacal, as the small town was known to the Maryknollers, Mother Coleman had presumed the people would ask for a clinic and a nurse. But no, what they actually requested was a doctor.

As Maryknoll Sister Maria del Rey Danforth reports in her book, *No Two Alike*, Mother Coleman told the Jacaltecos, "I cannot send you a doctor, but I will send you a nurse, maybe two nurses. They can set up a clinic, teach your women, bring your babies into the world with safety."

The Mother General said this knowing that the wife of the man, Chepe, who had been the Sisters' guide, had lost twelve of their thirteen children at birth or shortly after. But the Mother General made her decision, reluctantly closing her eyes to the obvious needs of the indigenous people around her, on the basis of the Sisters' own resources. The Congregation had insufficient doctors only twelve-for the commitments already made to countries around the world.

Jacaltenango was only an overnight visit, one more mission in one more country in four months that had begun to run together. The following morning, Mother Mary Coleman and Sister Martina would make the return trip down the mountains. The farewell to pastor Maryknoll Father Jim Scanlon and to the people was to be in the main plaza. The entire town turned out, but the two Sisters could not depart, they were told, until Chepe was present.

Maria del Rey takes up the story as Chepe arrived:

"Madre," he gasped, as he handed her a long roll of paper, "here is what we want to say to you."

She let the roll lengthen out to the ground. It was cheap paper, crumpled, with dark smudges rhythmically down its length. She read in tortured script:

"Dear Mother,

"We need a doctor, we will give her a hospital." The rest of the paper was covered with thumbprints. There must have been a thousand or more.

"Thank you," she said, rolling up the petition. "I'm glad you got here with this. Believe me, we will do our best to help. But . . ." José "Chepe" Silvestre interrupted. "I tried, Mother. I did not mean to be late, to delay your trip. My wife was delivered this morning. She did not do well and the child died."

A tear rolled from behind the thick lenses down Mother's cheek. She found it hard to talk, but when she did, she said: "You will have your doctor, Chepe, I promise you that."

~

Mother Mary Coleman would deliver on that promise. Later it would fall to her to deliver also on the larger promises of Vatican II. Her own challenges, trials, and decisions during this period are part of the tale. She moved a long way from the day when she set out for Latin America, heavily cloaked in the Congregation's traditional traveling cape and habit, to the moment a few years hence when she astonished the Sisters by walking out into the Center, not in habit, but dressed simply in modern clothes, and with her gorgeous white hair revealed for all to see.

Coleman retained vivid memories of her trip to Guatemala. As the years rolled forward, that country would present her with a far different and more public challenge. In the late 1960s, three Maryknoll Sisters and three Maryknoll priests in Guatemala decided that conditions in the country were so bad that an alliance with the fledgling guerrilla insurgency was a legitimate course for Christians to follow.

This was the "Melville Incident."

The Maryknoll Sisters have their own hymn, "Maryknoll, My Maryknoll." The words have been revised several times down through the years. When Maryknoll Sister Joan Metzner wrote some new verses, she included the phrase, "daring to care." The "Melville Incident" would test the challenge and the ambiguities reflected in those words.

~ 7 ~

Under the Volcano

THE SPANISH CONQUERORS WHO first arrived in Guatemala five hundred years ago came looking for gold and silver. Finding these precious metals in scarce supply, they had to content themselves with exploiting the region's main resources, the land and its people. In the centuries that followed, Guatemalans of Spanish ancestry maintained an unbroken rule over a predominantly Indian population.

The richness of the land—cotton and sugar on the coastal plains, coffee on the mountainous highlands—contrasts starkly with the desperate poverty of the Indian peasants. What the conquistadors began, later nineteenth-century governments completed: the effective transfer of all communally held property into the private hands of the coffee planters. In this country of eight million, roughly the size of Tennessee, 2 percent of the population owns 72 percent of the land and wealth. Beneath the surface of these statistics there is a simmering volcano that has erupted with frequency in Guatemala's tortured history. In the twentieth century a new economic force entered the scene, as North American investors, particularly the United Fruit Company, became the largest landowners in the country. In the 1950s, when a new reform-minded president, Jacob Arbenz, announced plans for sweeping land reform, including the expropriation of idle lands owned by the United Fruit Company, he discovered the limits of just what the United States was prepared to tolerate in its own "backyard." Denounced as a Communist, he was overthrown by a CIA-sponsored coup in 1954. Democratic government gave way to military dictatorship; this was to be the rule in Guatemala for the next thirty years.

The leader of the coup, Colonel Carlos Castillo Armas, was hailed as a savior by many, including the Archbishop of Guatemala City, Mariano Rossell, who saw in Arbenz a harbinger of Communism. For the previous century, a succession of anticlerical governments had restricted the activity of the church, ensuring that there were practically no foreign missionaries in Guatemala. Now, after the coup, the new military government realized that a strong church could provide a bulwark against Communism and so encouraged a new wave of missionaries from Europe and the United States. Within five years of the fall of Arbenz there were 531 priests in the country, only ninety-seven of whom were Guatemalans. They were joined by over 700 foreign women religious, among them twenty-one Maryknoll Sisters.

The missionaries who arrived had little understanding of the complicated history into which they were entering. What was happening in Guatemala in the 1950s would become the chilling norm for many Latin American countries—an increasingly authoritarian government, utilizing military force to maintain tight control over the population on behalf of the oligarchy, including foreign economic interests, in the process eradicating without mercy any movement for social justice or democracy. And behind the scenes, in country after country, the trail of intrigue and manipulation would lead to the United States.

Generations of blood would be spilled in Central America as landless people, denied their rights and trapped in abysmal poverty, would sporadically erupt in an effort to achieve some measure of dignity and control over their lives. For the Maryknoll Sisters, increasingly immersed in the world of the poor, such conditions would pose challenges never before contemplated in the history of the Congregation.

The Melville Incident

The first project of the Maryknoll Sisters in Guatemala was the Colegio Monte María, a school for upper-class young women. It was the archbishop's idea. Although typically conservative in his fear of Communism, he believed it was the responsibility of the church to raise up the needy from their poverty. He reasoned that if young upper-class women, who often traveled abroad for schooling, were instead educated by the Sisters in their own country, their social awareness as Christians would be developed. These young women, in turn, would influence the young men they would take as husbands from Guatemala's ruling elite. In time, through this indirect influence, a climate of social awareness could be established that would lead to the eventual amelioration of conditions.

This approach of providing education to wealthy women as a strategy for social progress was not unique to the Maryknoll Sisters in Guatemala. A similar institutional approach to social progress lay behind church-sponsored projects around the world, including, for example, the Maryknoll College in Manila.

In addition to Colegio Monte María, the Maryknoll Sisters' presence in Guatemala would eventually include the parish of Villa de Guadelupe in Guatemala City (with its school, clinic, social center, and catechetical work), the tiny pioneering hospital and health promotion work in Jacaltenango, as well as pastoral work in the mountainous region of Hueheutenango.

Nor were the Maryknollers alone. By the time Pope Paul VI brought the Second Vatican Council to a close in 1965, the number of foreign priests and women religious in the country had swollen to more than twelve hundred. In this thriving church the number of Maryknoll Sisters, forty-eight, was relatively small, but from the Congregation's perspective it was a large commitment.

Increasingly, as the reforms of Vatican II were discussed and attempts made at implementation, the connection between Christian mission and social justice was drawn in ever clearer lines. In Guatemala, the Sisters were deeply affected by what they saw: In a land of agricultural abundance, four out of five peasants, according to United Nations' standards, were subsisting at the level of destitution. By the mid-sixties conditions were reaching a boiling point, and many awaited the inevitable explosion.

At that time, Sister Mildred Fritz was the regional superior of an area extending from Mexico to Colombia. She was an experienced missioner, with nine years in Guatemala and another thirty before that in the Hawaiian Islands since joining Maryknoll. All of her considerable wisdom, compassion, and experience would be put to the test.

Describing the situation in Guatemala in the mid-sixties, she wrote:

> Maryknollers—priests, Brothers, and Sisters—have been restive. They have been concerned about the socio-economic problems of their people. More than two thousand people were killed last year (1966) in the undeclared civil war between extreme rightists and extreme leftists.

It was in this context in late 1967 that there occurred what became known as the Melville Incident, involving three Maryknoll Sisters and three Maryknoll priests who became involved in an intended guerrilla uprising. It made headlines worldwide, created an uproar within Maryknoll, invested both the Society and the Congregation with a politicized image it proved difficult to shake, and jeopardized the work of the church in Guatemala for years to come.

Revolutionaries in Latin America hailed this example of militant commitment by Christians to the cause of the oppressed. For most Maryknollers, however, it would appear as a naive, dangerous, and unwise action that neither benefited the poor nor served the overall mission of Maryknoll. But it did raise the question: Was the institutional path to social progress adequate? If not the way of the Melvilles, then how in a world of injustice to make Christ's gospel concrete?

For the Maryknoll Sisters, the center of the story begins with Marjorie Bradford. Born in Mexico of American parents in 1929 and raised in Chihuahua, she had attended the Loreto Sisters' boarding school in El Paso,

Texas. That was where she heard about Maryknoll. She joined the Congregation in 1949 and, as Sister Marian Peter Bradford, arrived in Guatemala in 1954, the year of the coup. Like other Sisters of the time, reared on the anti-Communist sermons of Bishop Fulton J. Sheen, she didn't question the official story: "I believed my country had helped overthrow a Guatemalan government that was Communist," she later wrote. "It took me five or six years to find out it wasn't true."

With the other Sisters, she taught at Monte María-grade school at first, then high school social sciences. Mainly at Bradford's instigation, Monte María had established a school for poor children on the Colegio grounds. The Maryknoll Sisters were also sponsoring consciousness-raising courses and weekend retreats with a focus on social awareness and Christian social doctrine. Out of these programs there emerged a group of very dedicated young people. In 1964, with help from the Maryknoll Fathers, they rented a house downtown for meetings and a low-cost lunch. The students called it "the Crater"—because, as Bradford put it, "they felt that our spirit should be like a volcano that erupts forth in love."

When Monte María had its first graduates, the young women were asked to volunteer for one of the missions in Huehuetenango. The idea was to encourage the privileged girls to have the experience of sharing with those who had less. At the same time they would be breaking new ground in providing peasant girls with an education beyond the grade school level.

As Sister Mildred Fritz later saw it, the Melville Incident had its beginnings in those years: "Students went into the mountain villages giving classes in literacy, nutrition, and sanitation," she said. "Later we found out that this wonderful group had been infiltrated by some who had ideas of violence as the solution to Guatemala's troubles." Bradford, reflecting on the lessons of that experience, characterized it differently: "We saw a movement exploding like a volcano."

By 1965, some Sisters were talking about moving out of the institutional convent lifestyle and into a small apartment in Guatemala City. Marjorie Bradford was allowed to teach in public schools and work with the Crater group, but Mother Mary Coleman, who visited Guatemala City at that time, rejected the idea of a separate apartment. Bradford, like the other Sisters, was feeling the impact of the Vatican II documents, struggling to discern where, in the Guatemalan context, true faithfulness lay. Exploring the slums of Guatemala City, she recalls, "I began to understand and to show the students what life in Guatemala City was about. Through working with the students I began to realize my country's involvement in Guatemala." But her Sisters had little idea of where her struggle was leading.

"I couldn't consult or tell the others what was going on," she later wrote. "One of the cooperative leaders whom we had taught to lead was killed, and that was the beginning of the *Mano Blanco*," the White Hand—a dreaded right-wing death squad.

What was going on was that conditions were leading a group of men and women religious as well as their students to consider some form of revolutionary commitment. Among the priests were Maryknoll Fathers Arthur and Thomas Melville, brothers, who had been working in the highlands of Huehuetenango to set up cooperatives with the Indians. They had begun to feel the limitations of this approach as the leaders they had trained were murdered or intimidated into passivity. Gradually they had come to the point of contemplating more radical solutions.

The connection was made at the Crater, the student gathering place in Guatemala City, through a former member of the group, Juan Lojo. After joining and then breaking with the principal guerrilla group, the Fuerzas Armadas Rebeldes (FAR), Lojo had drifted back to the city in 1967 with the idea of forming a new, "Christian" guerrilla group. A key meeting, which would include priests, Sisters, and members of the Crater, was planned for October 1967.

Sister Marian Pahl, the only one of six Maryknollers involved in the Melville Incident who stayed on with Maryknoll, had been in Guatemala only a year when the meeting was set. She had arrived in the country soon after the death of the guerrilla-priest Camilo Torres, in the mountains of Colombia. Reading his letters, she remembers feeling a powerful logic in his statement: "The Christian community cannot offer the sacrifice [of the Eucharist] in an authentic form if it has not first fulfilled in an effective manner the precept of 'love thy neighbor.'" Now she was working with another Maryknoll Sister, Mary Leo (Catherine Sagan), in rural San Antonio Huista, where the pastor was Father Art Melville.

In the summer of 1967, Marian Pahl recalls, "Art came to the convent and said he wanted to talk to me about something. He had received an invitation to go to a meeting where there would be some guerrillas. I immediately said, 'Well, I think the church should be with the oppressed, and we are struggling for the oppressed.' I had no details. But in the month that followed we began to talk. In August, I was invited into the group, with Lojo as the leader. Soon after Sagan was also invited."

In October, the Crater group, along with a few priests and Sisters, met for several days on a farm in Escuintla. It was the first time so many in the widely dispersed and informally structured group had gathered in one place to agree on principles, policies, and tasks to be done, as Sister Marian Pahl later put it, "before we disappeared into the jungles of Peten to begin to live as guerrillas."

Among those present was a Spanish priest who was at first enthusiastic about going to the mountains, but who later got cold feet and reported the meeting to his superior. It was not long before the news had reached the Maryknoll regional superior, Father John Breen, and the U.S. ambassador, as well as the conservative bishop Cardinal Casariegos, who served, among his other capacities, as chief chaplain to the military.

Since everyone present at the Escuintla meeting had used code names, not all could be identified. But among those who were recognized were Marjorie Bradford and the Melville brothers. Enraged, Breen called them in and insisted that they leave the country immediately. The ambassador had said their lives were in danger, and Breen felt their continued presence would endanger others. The three had little choice but to comply, and flew to Miami. But then, instead of reporting to Maryknoll, New York, they took a plane to Mexico. The other three Maryknollers, Sister Marian Pahl, Sister Catherine Sagan, and Father Blase Bonpane, planned to remain as long as they could in Guatemala, arranging to meet with the other three on the Mexican border. But as their identities were gradually discovered, they also departed the country.

In the meantime, the students too had realized the precariousness of their situation. Lojo and some of the others slipped out of the country to join Marjorie and the Melvilles in Mexico City. There, on January 16, 1968, the trio learned that FAR had assassinated two U.S. military attachés in Guatemala City. Two days later, Tom Melville went out to buy a newspaper only to find his own and Art's ordination photographs staring back at him on the front pages of Mexico City's daily newspapers. The headlines blared, "GUERRILLA PRIESTS HIDING IN MEXICO."

Back in Guatemala, news of the six Maryknollers' activities hit the headlines on January 17. For more than three weeks, local newspapers kept the story on the front page. One of them, *La Hora,* called for the expulsion of all Maryknollers from the country, an option that was apparently discussed in a government cabinet meeting.

Most missionaries in the country had known nothing about the conspiracy and were horrified when they discovered what was going on. Rumors were afloat that the Maryknollers' social work was simply a front for subversive activity. The six individual Maryknollers had taken what they believed was a stand of conscience, prepared to lay down their lives in solidarity with the oppressed. Perhaps they did not calculate that others might have to bear the consequences of their actions. As Marjorie Bradford said, "My commitment had reached the point where the Guatemalan people were more important than Maryknoll."

After several months in Mexico City, Bradford and the Melvilles returned to the United States to publicize American involvement in Guatemala. By this time all three had left Maryknoll and Marjorie and Tom had married. Soon thereafter, Marjorie and Tom were once more in the headlines. With seven others, including Fathers Daniel and Philip Berrigan, they had poured homemade napalm on Selective Service files in Catonsville, Maryland, using the occasion of their subsequent trial to make connections between Guatemala and the war in Vietnam. In her final words to the sentencing judge, Marjorie Bradford Melville said, "We do not ask for mercy. We do not ask that history judge us right. That is a consolation for more visionary souls than ours."

Sister Marian Pahl, who had agreed to return voluntarily to the United States, was asked by Mother Mary Coleman to write up her concerns about conditions in Guatemala and send it to Congressman Tip O'Neill, nephew to Maryknoll Sister Mary Eunice Tolan.

That done, Pahl started another letter to Mother Coleman, informing her of her intention to leave Maryknoll. But before sending it she sought out the advice of a Guatemalan friend, who told her, "We need Sisters like you in Latin America." She tore up the half-written letter.

Marjorie Bradford and Tom Melville were married in January 1968. They served one and two years in prison, respectively, for their part in the "Catonsville Nine" action. Arthur Melville and Cathy Sagan were also wed, and still later divorced. Blase Bonpane left Maryknoll to continue speaking out about Guatemala, and later married. Within a year the guerrilla movement in Guatemala, which had failed to set down roots in the countryside, was effectively annihilated.

Looking back two decades later, Marian Pahl admitted that the adventure had been romantic and naive; they would all have been killed had the plot not been exposed. But Marjorie Melville said that, given the chance, she would do it again. "How long can you stand around and see people being massacred?" she asked. "I did not want to bring hurt upon myself but there comes a moment when you decide that some things should not be. Then you have to act to try to stop those things." Still, she admitted that "the hardest thing was trying to understand and search out what was right."

Others who looked back saw it slightly differently. The issue had become not whether one was for the poor, or one's willingness to take a stand, or even the question of violence, but the nature of one's responsibility as a woman religious missioner to her Congregation of Sisters. This was echoed in the words of Mildred Fritz in her later reflections:

All of us were deeply interested in helping the poor and we talked about aspects of this in community. I know how Margie was feeling. I drove up to Huehue and back with her so she could talk to me. She was adamant that the way they were going was the way to do it. I said to her that the Sisters didn't feel it was the thing to do. I think she was adamant because she didn't look at the consequences and what could happen to the whole mission effort, or that everybody could be expelled.

The emotionally charged memory of the Melville Incident has not faded for many Sisters, even after many years. The pain of this episode can be detected in Fritz's judgment:

I had great admiration for Margie. She is a very intelligent person. But she had poor judgment. The people involved were fine women. We feel badly that they could not participate in the Maryknoll group effort but placed their decision above the group decision and yet did not withdraw from the group when they felt they could not accept the commitment of the group.

The concern of Fritz and other Sisters was not just the effect of the Melville Incident for Maryknoll, but the potential loss for the people of Guatemala whom they had sought to serve. The incident severely impeded the potential for the Maryknoll Sisters and perhaps other Catholic organizations to have any long-term impact on Guatemala's viciously unjust social structures. Monte María became a marked school; the painstaking work of establishing connections between the privileged young women of the city and the peasants in Huehuetanango was derailed. In the view of Mildred Fritz, "I don't think you can exaggerate the negative effects of the incident. If it hadn't happened, there would have been fifteen years of positive ripple effect on the students—boys and girls and peasants—that could have avoided the repression and bloodbath of the 1980s. Her final word: "It was a dream that was destroyed."

A Hospital for Jacal

The revolutionary path represented one option for Guatemala, but it was hardly representative of the work of Maryknoll. Elsewhere in the country, Maryknoll Sisters were pursuing other dreams. By the time Bradford and the Melvilles left Mexico City for the United States, it had been almost eight years since Mother Mary Coleman had taken her arduous trip to Jacaltenango and promised Chepe and the other townspeople she would send them a doctor and nurse. She had found both: Maryknoll Sisters Dorothy Erickson (or "Madre Rosa," as she became known), a medical doctor, and Bernice Downey, a public health nurse, who arrived on February 6, 1961. In fact, the Maryknoll Sisters medical team was at work even before construction started at the hospital site, using a tiny room off the church sacristy as a makeshift clinic.

As Erickson recalls, "There was so little space in the clinic room, we gave the vaccinations outside. Water was boiled for sterilization on a two-burner kerosene stove. We saw at least forty people a day, even then." When the priests were out in the highlands, Erickson also oversaw construction. "I remember one time the men were just about to saw through a main beam when I stopped them," she said.

In the Maryknoll archives stored in the New York Center, there is preserved the sheet of thumbprints of the Jacaltecos who begged Mother Mary Coleman to send a doctor to their town. So too the spirit of those years has been preserved in the telling and retelling of how the hospital was built.

The nearest town to Jacaltenango accessible by truck was Rosario, six hours by horse or mule from Jacal. A truck would, deliver materials to Rosario where, for two or three days, a man would sit to guard them until the Jacaltenango men arrived. When word came that the material had arrived, the Jacaltenango townsmen, organized in small groups of volunteers, would set out at hourly intervals, beginning at dawn, leading their mules on the difficult passage down the mountain.

On the return trip, mules could not balance the fragile fittings, the window frames, the glass, the hospital equipment that needed to be turned, tilted, and jiggled to get them past the rocky overhangs, through the narrow points, and around the sharp and precipitous curves. Mules could carry the cement and heavy material; men had to carry the rest.

In Jacal each Sunday, on the way to church, each man brought two or three rocks for the hospital foundation and walls. People donated local materials and manual labor; most men gave two weeks a year to make the adobe bricks from which the hospital was built.

Statistics do not tell this story, but they do give an impression of what occurred: fifteen hundred volunteers built the hospital, and when it was opened in 1964, though only half finished, it had two ten-bed wards and an X-ray room (with no equipment). The townspeople sat down in the hospital courtyard to feast on five hundred pounds of beef and two hundred pounds of potatoes.

For the Sisters, if Jacal was hard to get to, it could also be hard to get away from. As Erickson explained, "In the early 1960s it took two days to get from Jacal to Guatemala City, so we didn't go out very often, maybe once every two months. I remember being in for seven months at a time," she said, "but we kept adding on to the hospital with new rooms and wings, *poco a poco*"—little by little.

With the hospital being built, the first rooms opened, and the health program under way, the Jacal medical service began to expand. A second doctor, Sister Jane Buellesbach, and a nurse, Sister Pat Nolan, were new additions to what would become a long line of Sisters who worked with the people of Jacal.

During the early days, Erickson also made medical history. One night, about 7 P.M., a telephone message came through on the less than reliable line from San Antonio Huista that there was a badly cut child. A drunken father, who had gone after his wife with a machete, instead hit his nine-month-old child and practically severed her leg at the ankle.

When, eventually, the child was brought to the hospital, Erickson decided to stitch up the wound and hold it together with bandages. There was a terrible risk of infection, but they filled her with antibiotics, realizing that if it got too bad, they'd have to amputate.

For two weeks the mother and child stayed in the town auditorium behind the clinic, and each morning Erickson and Downey would examine the foot. "It was getting blacker and blacker, but not infected," said Downey, "and we kept shooting her with penicillin."

"I would say, 'Maybe we should amputate'; Rose would say, 'This afternoon.' Then she would say, 'Let's wait 'til tomorrow morning,' and would postpone it again. We went through this I don't know how many days," said Downey. "One morning I am on the horse and she comes running out; the bottom of the foot was turning pink because the circulation had restarted. The wound had begun to heal." Eventually the child was able to walk, fully recovered.

The incident was written up in Boston area newspapers, but some doctors were skeptical of the report. "Rose was such a straightforward and simple person," said Downey, "And didn't they [in the United States] have a train accident about that time in which a severed limb held, and the same thing happened!" Justification. Years later, in Riberalta, Bolivia, Downey persuaded a doctor not to amputate a severed thumb. "The thumb healed," rejoiced Downey, "and the mother brought me a big tamale as a gift! You do a lot of things that cannot be done," she said, "and the Lord wills a lot of things that help, too."

After the arrival of Sister-Doctor Jane Buellesbach in 1963 the health program expanded out of necessity; the small medical team could not reach the majority of people who needed health care. In a pilot program, they trained fourteen men, catechists and village leaders, chosen by the community or selected by the parish, in basic first aid and hygiene. This would be the first wave of Promotores Rurales de Salud, the rural health promoters.

Over the years, the Maryknoll Sisters had acquired a slightly romantic image as the women on horseback. It lent a heightened sense of adventure to work that could be tedious and unending. Buellesbach, jokingly referring to her years as a "cow nun," does not deny that it could be fun. "But there were times when it was excruciatingly boring and frustrating—when case after case of worms, backache, leg cramps, malnutrition came into the clinic due to generations of neglect and lack of health care."

To Buellesbach, there was a drivenness about the Sisters in the late 1960s, "impelling us to do as much as we could as soon as possible. The political climate was terrifyingly electric and we often felt, as did the other people, that at any moment we would be thrown out and find ourselves looking for another place to work. Many of us were in accord with the ideas that Margie Bradford and Tom Melville held. We were in the struggle together. But remember," cautioned Buellesbach, two decades later, "we were a lot younger then and perhaps not as aware as we are now of all that a revolution involves."

In that decade of change, said Buellesbach, the Sisters reflected the conflicts present in the church and North American society. "One can become anesthetized to human misery or terribly sensitized to it," she said, "aching more and more with each new encounter. We were committed to God—through God's people. Close friends were opting for marriage or other lifestyles; yet there always remained that intangible, inexpressible mystery that blocked out any other choice but the mission of Jesus, and Christ crucified in his people."

By 1972 there were 160 health promoters serving the region of Huehuetenango. Some were barely literate, others were grade-school graduates, but all had gone through six one-week courses and received a government certificate. The Ministry of Health had formally approved the program in 1967. The health promoters served their communities' health needs in a variety of ways, after their daily farming was done. They had been taught to diagnose common illnesses and to recognize those who needed further medical treatment. They had learned about hygiene, nutrition, and local medicinal plants. They also prayed with the sick.

Because more men were literate and spoke Spanish, the health promoters were usually men. But women also had a role. Under Sister Jean Roberts' guidance, Jacaltenango hospital established a school for practical nurses, which functioned until the government centralized its own school in the capital in 1972.

"One of my personal joys," said Roberts, "is seeing what has happened to the nursing students in their personal growth. In Jacal alone we trained over forty-five practical nurses with official titles and about thirty-five nurse's aides."

"For me, the most difficult part of being in Jacal wasn't the living conditions or the language, but the cultural differences. There was the conflict between Western efficiency and this-is-the-way-it-should-be-done and the other's seeming inability to see the need for efficiency and for carrying it out. The struggle to let go and give them authority without controlling them—it is an internal conflict, letting them make their own mistakes."

Simultaneously, the health workers, many of whom were catechists and village leaders, became the catalysts of a popular awakening. By 1980 there were as many as 410 health promoters.

But then tragedy. A wave of violence directed by the Guatemalan military and paramilitary forces against the Indian population reached new heights. Twenty-one community leaders in Jacal were killed; about sixty became refugees in Mexico, and another sixty decided it was too dangerous to continue. By the end of 1982 only 250 health promoters were still working in Jacaltenango.

It had been thirty years since the U.S. government, through the CIA, had set out to destabilize a legitimately elected government. The operation had been a perfect success, not only thwarting the immediate plans of President Arbenz to impinge on the interests of the United Fruit Company but also deferring for decades any popular threat to the system. But the cost of maintaining such a system of injustice grew ever higher. Not only "leftist" movements but any organization or voice devoted to justice and social progress received the label of subversive or "Communist," and found itself the target of repressive violence. Throughout the years, the United States government rarely wavered in its support for the Guatemalan government.

As the 1970s ended, nearly one thousand people a year were being killed for political reasons, many of them assassinated in gruesome fashion by the White Hand. By the early 1980s, under the military junta of General José Rios Montt, the violence reached genocidal proportions. In an effort to "pacify" the countryside whole villages were decimated, with the survivors herded into "strategic villages" or fleeing into exile. By the army's own count, it destroyed 440 villages, some dating to pre-Columbian times. Between 1978 and 1985 it is estimated that between fifty and seventy-five thousand persons were killed. Over a hundred thousand fled to Mexico. Because the Catholic church was known as a strong promoter of human rights as well as a defender of the Indians, Catholic priests, nuns, and lay catechists, as well as countless simple believers, were targeted for persecution. Among those who died was Maryknoll Father Bill Woods. Woods had been helping the Mayan people from the crowded highlands get title to farmland; because of this work he received frequent death threats. In 1976, a small plane he was flying suddenly swerved off course and crashed into a mountainside under full power. The Indians believe his plane was sabotaged or shot down.

In 1954, the Maryknoll Sisters had little reason to question the policies of their government or to suspect that their evolving understanding of mission might put them on a collision course with such policies. In time, and in several countries, the Sisters would pay a high price, indeed the highest, for their opposition to U.S. government policies. They would find themselves branded as "leftists" by some high-ranking officials of their own government. But their actions could not properly be understood in political terms. They had understood the cry of the poor in gospel terms. They had sharpened their focus through chapters and assemblies, believing what the documents of Vatican II, the papal and episcopal statements, and their own mission experience was teaching them about the church's role in the world.

Though none was to emulate the example of the Melvilles, there would be plenty of soul-searching in the Congregation as its members embraced ever more consistently the mystery of "Christ crucified in his people."

~ 8 ~

New Habits

<hr>

NOT ALL THE DRAMA that marked the Maryknoll Sisters' renewal was played out in mountainous mission fields or in their schools and clinics in the developing world. In the Sisters' first major post-Vatican II gatherings of 1968 and 1970, there would be a subtler drama enacted around conference tables, in impassioned conversations over coffee breaks, and in quiet exchanges after hours.

"In the coming Chapter," Mother Mary Coleman wrote in 1968, "we want to take a prayerful look at every aspect of our Maryknoll life and try to 'adapt more suitably to the needs of our own times those institutions which are subject to change.'" If the accent of this statement was on change, there were many Maryknoll Sisters eager to hasten the day. But for others, the underlying challenge was how to remain essentially *the same* in a time of change—in other words, how to remain faithful to the founding vision. If there could be consensus about what, in essence, it meant to be a Maryknoll Sister, many nonessentials could go by the wayside. But no one could clearly foresee the outcome, nor what the cost might be.

The word "Chapter" has a venerable ecclesiastical history. It is said to come from the monastic custom of reading a chapter from Sacred Scripture at the openings of official assemblies. The Maryknoll Sisters had held a Chapter every six years. These early congregational assemblies gathered appointed regional superiors and delegates from around the world to reflect on regional as well as congregation-wide issues and to deliberate on future policy. Although the next Chapter was not due until 1970, the Second Vatican Council had mandated a special Chapter of Affairs for all congregations within a certain time period. Each congregation was to study its origins and the unique inspiration or "charism" that underlay its foundation. In rediscovering their roots the religious congregations were to update and renew themselves in the light of the gospel, the signs of the times, and the guidelines of Vatican II. In response to this mandate, the Maryknoll Sisters held this special Chapter in 1968. No former Chapter had ever been charged with such a sweeping and open-ended agenda.

In studies on religious life, it appears that a congregation typically experiences a crisis after fifty years and has to recapture its original charism. The Maryknoll Sisters were facing a dual challenge; not only were they at the normal half-century crisis point, but with Vatican II the church as a whole was experiencing an enormous burst of renewal.

Nor could the Sisters remain unaffected by a world in turmoil. If the 1960s was a decade of testing, 1968 was high noon. The war in Vietnam reached a new peak with the Tet Offensive, forcing the retirement of an incumbent U.S. president and provoking a torrent of protest and reaction. In Latin America the continent's Roman Catholic bishops, meeting in the Colombian city of Medellín, denounced "institutionalized violence" against the poor and proclaimed a prophetic role for the church as the champion of justice and human rights. American society witnessed the assassinations of Martin Luther King, Jr., and Bobby Kennedy, riots in Chicago and around the country, and, with the arrest of the Catonsville Nine, the new spectacle of priests and nuns as prisoners of conscience. For a time, in the United States, it seemed as if there was nothing firm and familiar on which to fasten. The Maryknoll Sisters were not exempt from the stress and the questioning. The turmoil of the period is reflected, tellingly, in the serious decline in the Congregation's numbers. The Sisters would lose nearly a third of their membership in less than a decade, from 1,430 professed Sisters in 1966 to 993 in 1974—a loss of 437 professed Sisters, only 58 of those by death.

The impact of these events of the 1960s and the documents of Vatican II had reverberated out to the far corners of the world. And now, like a pond's ripple bouncing off the shoreline and returning to the center, the Sister delegates arriving in Maryknoll, New York, were bringing back to their Center the reactions of Maryknoll Sisters around the world to what they had seen, heard, and lived.

The Last Chapter

Months of preparation went into the Chapter; dozens of papers were drafted and circulated. While some focused on specific changes in structure or discipline, others explored more fundamental questions. It soon became clear that the Sisters were being asked not simply to rethink structures but to reexamine their very identity. The major underlying issue facing the 1968 Chapter was a tension in understanding of the Maryknoll Sisters' charism. In essence, the question was this, "Which has priority—mission or religious life?" The dual identity of Maryknoll Sisters as both religious and missioners presented two poles with a powerful magnetic field between them.

So serious were the tensions, according to Sister Anna Marian Pavao, a delegate from the Hawaii Region, that there was fear that the Congregation might split in two. "Essential to the survival of the Congregation would be the discovery of some way to reestablish an integration of both identities— missioner and religious—within the same individual. But this was not easy."

In the heat of one floor discussion on the question, "Are we first of all 'missioners,' or are we first of all 'religious'?" one Sister suggested that the delegates stand and be counted as either "religious missioners or as missioners who happened to be religious." No one moved from her chair.

It helped the Sisters' discussion to return to the vision of their founder, Mollie Rogers. Clearly she had wanted a balance of both identities, but if the emphasis lay one way or another, it had been her intention that religious and community life be shaped by the demands of mission. In the view of Pavao, the prevailing opinion of the Chapter was that "our charism is definitely mission; we needed to identify the key elements of religious life so that we could shape a community geared toward mission. It wasn't easy to identify essentials because each of us had to examine our experience."

Experience varied not just from individual to individual but from region to region. In Latin America, the Sisters had been strongly influenced by their contact with the poor and by their reflection on that experience. It was the early dawn of "liberation theology"—a term that was yet to be coined, but whose basic thrust was already evident in the historic gathering of bishops in Medellín. Many of the Maryknoll Sisters from Latin America were on fire with a new model of religious life, and they brought a vitality to the Chapter that was as refreshing for some as it was threatening to others. As Pavao recalls, "The Latin American delegates felt we should move out of all our institutions as soon as possible. This came as a big threat to those in the Central Pacific and other places where we had schools, hospitals, and other institutions."

If the delegates had much to learn about other regions, they also had to learn about themselves. Sister Blaise Lupo, a delegate from the Philippines Region, discovered she was not as "far left" as many others present—"and I was a firebrand in the Philippines," she said. "My friends, mostly from Latin America, had grown far more than I, and I found I was not prepared for the prophetic ideas they offered."

"To a certain extent I was not included in the wee-hours-of-the-morning strategy sessions held by both sides," she said. "I had great respect for the conservative faction, but was really annoyed by their adamancy. The conviction of both sides was amazing and, if I remember correctly, led to very harsh words, both during the meetings and afterwards." The faction characterized as conservative was holding on to the primacy of religious life in the more traditional mode over mission. Lupo, one of the younger group, spoke of the constant pressure everyone felt. "I remember escaping with some others every chance we got—even walking all the way to Ossining for pizza. Staying in the Center just wasn't relaxing. You either heard that we were 'going too far,' or 'not far enough.'"

According to Sister Rita Ann Forbes, a delegate from the U.S. Midwest Region, "As the whole notion of the Church as Mission emerged from Vatican II there was an identity crisis for us. One dominant interpretation of mission was 'going from local church to local church.' But if that was interpreted geographically, and we were going from the local U.S. church to local churches in other countries—what about those Sisters who never left the United States? Were they not in mission? And what of our Sisters from countries other than the U.S.? Were they not full members? For the group at the Chapter these were basic tensions that could not be resolved."

Giving Up the Habit

If everything seemed to be up for discussion, the Sisters also had to contend with the fact that it was often the external signs or symbols of the deeper internal struggle—a sign such as the changes in the religious habit—that attracted the most public attention. When the 1968 Chapter opened, experimentation with clothing was already under way in the regions and at the Motherhouse (or the Sisters Center, as it was renamed in this period). Few had anticipated the depth of feeling this issue would evoke, as the habits changed and then eventually began to disappear.

The distinctive religious habit worn in the twentieth century was generally patterned on the ordinary clothes worn by women centuries earlier in medieval Europe, adapted from the dress in vogue at the time a congregation was formed. Over the years, custom and familiarity brought a rigidity of costume and a strict adherence to form. A veritable theology of the habit had congealed into a fixed position until 1966, when a very short Vatican Council decree, *Ecclesiae Sanctae*, gave religious communities the mandate to experiment in matters of religious life. The habit became an immediate focus.

For the Maryknoll Sisters, the habit had been the result of steady evolution and a source of mixed feelings from the earliest days. Though the Sisters were affiliated with the Dominican Order, in 1916 Father James A. Walsh had petitioned Rome that the Maryknoll Sisters not be obliged to adopt the Dominican habit. Sister Gemma Shea recalled, "The original dresses, in 1913–14, were gray gingham, long with no veil." There were experiments with various types of headdress, some more successful than others.

Eventually the gray habit, with its white scapular worn as a mark of their Dominican affiliation, became the hallmark of the Maryknoll Sisters. As early as 1915, Father Walsh had said, "The religious garb is, as a rule, an advantage to a community. When a nun appears on the street, she inspires respect among Catholics and often leads non-Catholics to inquire about the faith. [It also] symbolizes your segregation from the world, in, for and with Christ."

Each year at Maryknoll's Reception and "clothing day" ceremonies, the habit's importance was repeatedly stressed. In 1929, for example, Mother Mary Joseph reminded the Sisters: "Tomorrow is the clothing day of two of the postulants . . . The habit should be very dear to us . . . Our great hope is that the habit, reminding us constantly that we are the Spouses of Christ, will give us that desire and strength of will to hold our body in restraint, that our soul may serve perfectly its Lord and Maker."

Nevertheless, Sister Gemma, who was among the first seven pioneer women to join the Congregation in 1912, recalled that "Mother Mary Joseph didn't want us to have a complicated habit. You could take off the cuffs. Ours didn't have a small white band along the bonnet. This was a good thing when I was interned in Japan during World War II, because we had no soap. I liked the gray suits. I didn't follow any particular group regarding the habit, but I would have liked something modern, modified, but religious. Habit is a bad word now."

Yet Sister Gemma, though ninety-five in 1989, was open to change: "I'm not rabid about things," she said, in a conversation at the Maryknoll Sisters' retirement center in Monrovia, California. "It's a different generation." Then she added, with a twinkle in her eye, "I think our Sisters are beautiful no matter what they wear; even if they look awful."

Though some felt pressured to change, the Sisters had been given a range of options. The habit was not actually abandoned. The members could retain the traditional habit, which a few do even to the present; wear a modified habit; or choose contemporary clothes. Most Maryknoll Sisters selected the latter.

Whatever the reasons behind the design of the habit, practicality for the mission fields had not been an evident consideration. There the change in habit was most welcome. "In 'Hong Kong, because of the excessive humidity there, we suffered with those heavy gray woolen habits with their tunic, white scapular, gray scapular, and cape," said Sister Rosemary De-Felice. "I was always scolded for not wearing a cape. One Sister wore a turkish towel under the habit because she would be absolutely wet. Some had heat rash. The gray material was heavy. In 1936 we changed to white habits made out of a thin silkish material and only one white scapular."

But in the tropics, even this did not prove satisfactory. As Sister Mary Shannon from Riberalta, Bolivia, explained, "The Fuji silkish material— there was no polyester in those days—got yellowish with wash. We could only change them twice a week. The worst was the frame for the veil. You would sweat and the pins would rust, and you would have to pull the pins out with pliers. Our hair was ruined. I lost a lot of hair. And the capes around our necks! . . . We had slips with sleeves. We wore a tunic covered by a scapular that came to the ankles and a cape with a high collar that had to be changed every day. You were always sweating."

And yet, for all its discomforts, the habit did immediately identify its wearers as nuns. This could have its advantages. Maryknoll Sister Bernice Kita described the impact of her habit when she took part in the famous march for civil rights in Selma, Alabama.

On March 11, 1965, Kita received a call from School Sister of Notre Dame Margaret Traxler at the National Catholic Council for Interracial Justice. "She [Traxler] had been asked by her office in Selma to call as many convents as possible. The word from Selma was, 'We need Sisters now. One Sister is worth twenty priests. The situation is so bad here in Selma now that violence may erupt at any time, and if that happens, many people will be slaughtered. If the Sisters are here, the violence will be avoided and those lives will be saved.'"

Once in Selma, Kita found herself with a small group that would be guided to its destination, Brown's Chapel, by a courageous local pastor, Edmundite Father Maurice Ouellette. The chapel was surrounded by an angry mob, those inside literally trapped within.

Kita recalled: "As we, five Sisters and a New York Jesuit, Father Philip Hurley, entered the chapel, we were greeted by the sight of a mass of tired humanity, sleeping or just resting on the, pews and floor. As we came down the aisle they seemed to come to life as one and a tremendous applause arose and rocked the church—it is a moment I will never forget. I felt I was a part of something so terribly real and serious that it was almost paralyzing."

At the same time, many Sisters regretted the privileges, the special treatment afforded them because of the habit. Rather than a sign of simplicity and identification with the poor, the habit often created a subtle barrier that set them apart, as if more like angels than ordinary human beings.

By 1973, with most Sisters having chosen contemporary clothing, *Maryknoll Magazine* was responding to the reader backlash. One article headed "Are They Real Sisters?" bore the caption: "They wear no habits, but women of the parish go to them in times of need for advice and consolation."

The article began:

The image of Sisters is undergoing a complete change in Santa Lucia parish in Ilopango, San Salvador. Traditionally the people thought of them in connection with schools and hospitals. Now Maryknoll Sisters are working on a pastoral team, and visiting people at home. "One of the things we had to explain," the Sisters reported, "was that we were real Sisters. Not wearing habits and working on a person-to-person level, we were different."

The general Catholic in the pew did not understand where the changes were coming from; many still don't recognize the Sisters' point that clothes don't make the nun. A segment of the Maryknoll supporters were not slow to join in the "habit" debate, some quite angrily. One complained: "As 'Sisters' you lack the humility and obedience of true nuns. Your lack of a habit means you spend more time and energy on your hair 'permanents' than you do with the homeless. Your clothing requires more expenditure that could be better utilized to help the poor and homeless. Join the Peace Corps if you wish to wear a short skirt."

If there was criticism or confusion, the Sisters were quick to use the changes as a teaching moment. In the street, at church, on the bus, in the markets, when Sisters were asked why they were no longer wearing habits they were able to explain the reason behind their decision. But there were also supportive statements along with the criticism. People said they found the Sisters more approachable now. The habit had intimidated some and created an artificial distance. They seemed more human now, still doing God's work in a special way.

An era *was* ending. The new era, its preparatory work done at the 1968 Chapter, could be said to have opened with the 1970 General Assembly on September 28, 1970.

The First General Assembly

Only twenty months had passed since the ending of the 1968 Chapter, and the Sisters were now feeling an upswing in morale. Not without supreme effort, the Maryknoll Sisters had begun to move beyond the decimation of their ranks and their polarization over issues into matching their lives with the new challenges.

The contrast between the two congregational meetings, 1968 and 1970, is reflected in two books. The 1968 proceedings were compiled into an enormous volume, a thick book bound in bright yellow, with its title, *Missions Challenge*, printed in bold black type. Realizing the depth of disagreement over structural reforms, the Chapter delegates had felt they could do no more than gather all the papers and discussions together to serve as preparation for the next assembly. By comparison, when the six-week-long 1970 General Assembly (no longer called a Chapter) ended, its work was summed up in a very small, fifty-page booklet wrapped in a muted green-beige cover. Its title, *Searching and Sharing*, was an admission, said Sister Rosemary Healy, "that we didn't have all the answers; that we needed to share with one another and the people we serve in order to be in mission."

The anguish and high drama that marked the 1968 Chapter were generally absent from the 1970 General Assembly. The mood was constructive and forward-looking as Sisters from the various regions felt a consensus forming around a new vision and sense of purpose. The joy, the aura of a new day, was echoed in the presence of President Julius Nyerere of Tanzania. Everyone in Tanzania, including the Maryknoll Sisters, called Nyerere "Mwaliumu" (teacher), and that was the impact he had on the assembly. "He evangelized us," one recalled. His deep voice resonating through the auditorium, Nyerere stated:

> Poverty is not the real problem of the modern world. For we have the knowledge and the resources which could enable us to overcome poverty. The real problem—the thing which creates misery, wars, and hatred among people—is the division of mankind into rich and poor.

It was an opening charge the Sisters could not avoid, nor did they intend to. Its urgency was underscored by another speaker, Goa-born Father Jão Coutinho from Sri Lanka. His assembly workshop was based on a series of penetrating questions, such as: "How do you know the Holy Spirit is sending you to the places where you are?" Pointing to the Maryknoll Sisters' stationery, he said, "In all but one of the countries on your letterhead [Tanzania], there is some connection with the U.S. government or U.S. big business." According to Coutinho, the Third World was asking the Sisters, "Why do you come? What do you expect to happen? What are you doing? Who are you? Who is the 'other'?" As one Sister recalled, "These were the questions we were all asking ourselves."

If the 1968 Chapter had been the pivotal meeting, the 1970 Assembly produced the pivotal person, the remarkable first president, Sister Barbara Hendricks. Her selection captured the mood of the Congregation and the desire for change. For one thing, at forty-five, Hendricks definitely represented a younger generation. Mother Mary Coleman was seventy at the time. For another thing, and in contrast to the Asia missioners who had preceded her, Hendricks' mission experience had been in Latin America, the region that at the time stood out front in the renewal of mission and religious life. Not only were the Sisters from Latin America more outspoken about the need for social change, but they had also been among the first to adapt to the new openness regarding dress and other reforms. Hendricks brought this experience, along with a certain mischievous charm.

Only a few days after her election as president (replacing the old term,

Mother General), Hendricks met an older Sister on the way to chapel who smiled and said, "Good morning, Sister Barbara." Then the Sister's face became serious as she said, "I certainly hope you won't continue wearing earrings!" As Hendricks recalls, "I caught my breath and quickly decided that this was to be my first big challenge. 'Of course, I'm going to wear my earrings. They elected me with earrings on and they have to take me with earrings.'" Noticing the older Sister's troubled look, Hendricks decided to soften her remark. "Well, Sister, you see, it's like this. In Latin America even the Blessed Virgin Mary would not be seen dead without her earrings." Nothing more was ever said about the matter. "I guess word got around that I was beyond reform as far as earrings were concerned." Word presumably got around—as indeed it must have been obvious to the Sisters who elected her—that Hendricks represented a different sort of leader.

Hendricks joined Maryknoll in 1945, two days after her twentieth birthday. Having already attended the University of Detroit for two years before joining Maryknoll, she completed her bachelor's degree, studying Chinese philosophy, religion, and art at the New York China Institute with the hope of going to China. She spent five years (1948–53) in New York's Transfiguration Parish in Chinatown teaching grade school, doing youth catechesis, and counseling Chinese and Italian immigrants. But by 1953, with the borders of China closed to the outside world, Hendricks was assigned to similar teaching and catechetical work in Santa Rosa de Lima Parish in Lima, Peru.

Latin America at the time represented a very different field of mission for the Sisters. As Hendricks recalls, "We felt that we had gone to help revive an old church which had fallen on bad times because of neglect. We were to teach the faith and its doctrines, restore sacramental life, and strengthen the structures. It was kind of a revival mission. But it soon became apparent— the situation and cry of the poor was startling—that much more than revival of doctrine and structures and sacraments was taking place."

For sixteen years, Hendricks taught in several Peruvian schools, while also conducting adult religious education and becoming increasingly involved with the Young Christian Worker movement. In those years she came to know the Peruvian theologian and priest, Gustavo Gutiérrez, later famous for articulating the theology of liberation ("He used to come and give courses to the high school and grade school teachers"). In 1969 she was elected Regional Coordinator of Peru. By that time the thrust of the Sisters' work, according to Hendricks, "was beginning to be liberational in the full sense—that is, working with the poor and dispossessed in such a way that they could find the energy and faith to take hold of their own destiny as a people of God." It represented a whole rethinking of the meaning of mission. "The people were telling us what mission was all about in Latin America. It was the people who in a very real sense evangelized us." For many Sisters in this context, agonizing about whether to wear a habit or a veil seemed rather beside the point.

It was these insights and experiences that Hendricks brought with her as a delegate to the 1970 Assembly. Nonetheless, for all her accomplishments, there was no augury suggesting that when Hendricks left Latin America for the Assembly, she would not be back to live there for more than a decade.

As she sat in the assembly room waiting for people to arrive, she found herself beside Sister Mary Aulson from Bolivia. Both had entered Maryknoll together and felt free to speak their minds. Both wore lay clothes selected mainly from boxes of clothing shipped to the missions for distribution—"In other words, although we thought we looked fine, others would have thought otherwise."

Practically all the Sisters coming through the assembly hall door wore "hand-me-downs" or "I-made-it-myself" clothing. Suddenly, Aulson grabbed Hendrick's arm. "Hey, get a load of the Hong Kong twins—they match."

"Be quiet," cautioned Hendricks. "You're going to get us in trouble. Besides, you're just jealous of that lovely dark blue gabardine material."

Aulson instead poked her companion and said in a stage whisper, "The material is nice, but look! They're exactly alike and so are the veils they're wearing. Imagine—two Maryknoll Sisters who still look alike!"

Six weeks later Hendricks was elected the first president of the Maryknoll Sisters, a term in office that would last eight years, after her reelection in 1974. It was a difficult adjustment for a missioner who had had no real experience in the United States since 1953. She felt somewhat like Rip van Winkle. "Picture if you can someone getting elected head of a volunteer organization without having written a check since I was in college in 1945, not knowing how to make a long distance call since the number of digits had been doubled, and never having had the opportunity to turn on a television set!"

Hendricks and the four other Sisters of the Central Governing Board quickly adopted a collegial model of decision making, beginning each day with a half-hour of prayer and reflection on Scripture. According to Hendricks, those half-hour meetings, sustained for eight years, "cemented our relationships, built trust among us, increased our faith, and kept us laughing. We never felt alone in the job and always knew that we could count on each other for anything, anytime, anywhere." More than simply a change in names, the new governing structure represented a profoundly different model of leadership. "As far as I can remember," says Hendricks, "I never made a community-wide decision on my own; we made it together, even if we had to prolong the discussion to get enough input."

After years of the traditional top-down style of management and decision making, the Sisters eagerly seized on the Council's affirmation of collegiality and subsidiarity. The democratic spirit was probably ingrained in Maryknoll from the beginning. According to Hendricks, "I once heard Mother Mary Joseph say, with a smile on her face, that with all our beautiful qualities, we were not too good at obedience. I heard her say this more than once, and each time she smiled as if to say that might not be such a bad thing. In any case, our community took to these principles of Vatican II like a duck takes to water."

With the election of Hendricks and the new governing board, the work of the first General Assembly was done. The renewal was on course. Meanwhile the regions were having their own assemblies, wrestling with the local implications of all that had been set in motion.

When the 1968 Chapter was closing, the Sisters' external sign of identification as Maryknoll Sisters, their habit, was disappearing. The 1970 General Assembly approved as the only external sign of commitment a simple silver ring, worn by all members since their profession day on the third finger of the left hand. It is engraved with the Chi-Rho, whose Greek letters represent Christ and whose circle represents the world to which Jesus was sent.

~ 9 ~

Mercy

===

THE STEAM LOCOMOTIVE OF the South Manchurian Railway blew a loud departure blast on its whistle and slowly began to ease its train out of the Peng Yang (Pyongyang today) station in Japanese-controlled Korea. The journey to Shingishu would take six hours.

It was 1931, over twenty years since the last emperor of Korea had officially ceded his land to the Japanese. The Japanese regarded Korea as strategically vital in their expansionist feud with Russia, a feud that had culminated in Japan's 1904 victory in the Russo-Japanese war. To aid their war effort, the Japanese had applied their considerable industry to building and managing the railroads of Korea and neighboring Manchuria. As a result, the South Manchurian Railway generally ran on time.

In one carriage sat an American woman religious who could speak, read, or write neither the Korean language of the people nor the Japanese of their overlords. Yet, this twenty-eight-year-old missioner, who had never previously been outside of the United States, had set herself two enormous tasks. The first was that she had come to Korea as Maryknoll's first Sister-Doctor to bring whatever health services she could to poor country people, who were wary of modern medicine. The second challenge was even more formidable. There was no medical-license reciprocity between the United States and Japan, and as a result Tokyo insisted that any American doctor who wanted to practice in Korea, its colony, would first have to pass the Japanese medical examinations. Yet if Elizabeth Josephine Hirschboeck, now known as Sister Mary Mercy, was worried, it was only about her chances in the month-long medical examination. For the rest, she had placed herself in God's hands—as she would for the rest of her long life—with calmness and good humor. Yeng You was a town of hovels and poverty, bitingly cold damp winters, and parched, dust-laden summers. Late fall was setting in as Mercy stepped from the train for her first look at what would be her home—possibly for the rest of her life—if she could only satisfy the Japanese examiners.

The first Maryknoll Fathers had taken this same train journey in 1923.

The Sisters had arrived the following year. By the time Mercy stepped off the train, there were nineteen Maryknoll priests, two Maryknoll Brothers, and fourteen Maryknoll Sisters in Korea. Her first assignment was in Yeng You, where the dispensary, located in the church basement, was known as The Dressing Station. Japanese colonial law required a doctor's presence in such a facility.

For a short time, working through interpreters while she grappled with the Korean language, Sister Mercy practiced medicine before setting off again for Tokyo. There Father Henry Felsecker and Sister Agneta Chang, both fluent in Japanese, plus a Japanese priest-doctor, Father Vincent Totsu-ka, were all willing to help any way they could as Sister Mercy prepared for the oral examination, which fortunately was offered in English. If she passed the orals, two weeks of written and practical examinations would follow.

Tokyo was filled with tales of "Americans who have failed." Mercy presented herself at the examination site and went through a week of oral grilling. When she was notified to appear for the written tests, it meant she had cleared the first hurdle. Now it would be two weeks of written tests, followed by ten days of practical examination, followed by silence. Then she would return to Korea, for it would be months until she would be notified whether she had passed or failed.

Elizabeth Hirschboeck was born in Milwaukee on March 10, 1903. She and her two brothers attended SS. Peter and Paul Grammar School and St. John's Cathedral High School. In December 1922, when she was nineteen, Mercy was traveling with her friend in a car driven by the friend's father. There was an accident, and the friend died. Mercy was convinced God had spared her life so she could consecrate it to Christian service as a nun. But the determined Miss Hirschboeck also wanted to be a doctor, so she decided to be both. When she wrote to Mother Mary Joseph, the Mother General suggested that she get her medical degree first and then enter. There was sound reason for this advice. In those years, once professed, a Sister would have to ask permission from Rome to become a doctor, and it might be refused.

Mercy graduated from medical school in 1928—one of the first women graduates of Marquette University School of Medicine—and shortly after entered the Maryknoll Sisters Congregation. By 1936, the Congregation would have three doctors, forty-three nurses, plus several pharmacists and laboratory technicians. That year, Sister Ramona Maria Tombo from the Philippines entered, as the Congregation's first Sister-dentist.

Shingishu

The next time Mercy stepped from the train in Shingishu, it was to start work in earnest. Work would keep at bay the anxiety over the examination results—and as every mission doctor quickly discovered, among the poor there was never any end to the work of medical care.

All parents want their children cured, all spouses are concerned when their partner is sick, all children suffer anguish when their parents are in ill health. Even so, for the Koreans of Shingishu, what proof was there that this strange "big nose," bedecked in the long black cape, white gown, and pointed headpiece, could cure people? No one spoke for her skills. Quite the reverse.

But then one day, when a young Korean boy, Chang-ju, was sick, his father went for this unusual doctor, despite the imprecations of his superstitious wife: "Asking a foreign woman into the house! A doctor at that! To doubt fate!" But it was too late for Chang-ju's mother to prevent the visit. The father discreetly absented himself, and the woman-doctor arrived and stood, smiling, in the doorway, her doctor's bag in one hand, her traveling dispensary in the other.

She was a blue-eyed stranger with large, warm hands. Mercy was five feet six inches in height, tall by then-Korean standards, a woman who always appeared taller than her height even when, in later years, she became somewhat stooped. At twenty-eight she was well built rather than slender, with no trace of the plumpness that would later attend her fondness for sweets. In the more than half-century of life that still lay ahead, friends and strangers would all remark on the same attributes in this Maryknoll Sister about to enter Chang-ju's tiny Korean dwelling: the calmness, the barely contained humor, the compassion.

To that would be added, as her life in mission as a doctor unfolded, her unending capacity for hard work and long hours. And as her life as a woman religious missioner developed, her friends and colleagues would see her faith deepening. She would spend her life spiritually "open," allowing people and events in it to evangelize her.

Mercy stepped into Chang-ju's house and approached the boy's mother who had retreated half fearfully, half angrily into a corner. There was something about Mercy, however, that simply encouraged trust, and within moments the mother was "smiling and gesticulating and explaining and displaying and agreeing and bowing." Now, with her rudimentary Korean, Mercy questioned the mother and examined not only the sick Chang-ju, but his sister To-hong's naked and wasted body, as well as the twins, for whom she gave instructions. Chang-ju had measles, the other three were weak and malnourished. Mercy said she would send food and clothes.

She also examined the mother, who had a persistent cough, and made the woman promise to attend the dispensary for a more thorough examination. As Mercy left, Chang-ju's mother accompanied her to the door and waved until Mercy met up with her companion, who had been visiting the sick in other similar poor homes. At the end of the crooked street, Mercy turned and smiled at Chang-ju's mother, then set off into the city.

The Sister-doctor, though trying to find a calm patience in her soul as she worried about the results of her Tokyo qualifying examinations, began to develop a routine: house calls in the morning, clinic at the dispensary in the afternoon. Weekends frequently included the hour-long train ride to Father Stephen Hannon's mission at Hiken, to conduct a dispensary there, or to visit Gishu, where other Maryknoll Sisters ran a dispensary.

Several months passed until, as an account in *The Field Afar* reported, "the Peng Yang Post Office disgorged a document which told the world that *Lizabutu Yosapino Horsebacku* might practice the science of medicine anywhere in the Japanese Empire." She was qualified, and the document was hung on the dispensary wall, close to its only other decoration, a crucifix.

Mercy wrote home to the Maryknoll Sisters about that crucifix. A young boy, left on his own in the dispensary while Mercy examined his mother, stood looking at the crucifix, below which was a cabinet. Alongside the cabinet was a chair. "Quick as a flash," said the account in *The Field Afar*, "the boy scaled the chair to the cabinet and with his gay blouse endeavored to wipe away the bloodstains from the feet of Jesus."

The account was a reminder, though none was necessary, that whatever their "trade," the Sisters' real purpose was mission work—evangelization and catechesis. In fact, on one occasion, *The Field Afar* carried an article entitled "Every Trade a Mission." Mercy wrote a letter (published in the magazine in 1936) that illustrated the evangelizing work quietly under way:

> Our most urgent call today is to the home of a young man whose mother, a catechumen, hurries us along lest her son die without baptism. We find the man in a dark room about four foot square. There is no furniture and only a few worn quilts, stowed away on a crudely made shelf in one corner of the room, give the only suggestion of anything like comfort. The man's condition is serious, and a prayer for him comes spontaneously, as we watch the mother and wife, and even the eight-year-old daughter, finger his hands and feet under the covers, a sure sign of their anxiety.
>
> To the Korean, "coldness" of hands and feet is an indication of approaching death. The man had been well and able until a few weeks ago when he followed the advice of some well-meaning friends to inhale mercury fumes to cure a mild skin infection. Twenty cents worth of mercury was a cheap medication, but it gave the man mercury poisoning.
>
> We have some medicine that will relieve the symptoms and we impart some hope of the man's recovery to the distraught little family about him. The catechist will call later to instruct him in doctrine. It is good to see the sunshine stream into the room as we step out to don our shoes. Sad faces brighten as they bid us "Go in peace and

return again." As we leave the house, little Sil Tani, with a baby brother bobbing on her back, runs to meet us, bows and greets us, asking if we "came out peacefully," but wastes no time with formalities in telling us that her mother is no better since our last visit. The mother has peritonitis, with little hope of recovery.

We find the patient alone in a room smaller and darker than the one we had just left. Her lips are parched and she looks about for water to moisten them.

Sil Tani, attentive to her mother's wishes, places the spout of a small tea kettle to the woman's mouth and pours water to quench the burning thirst. Drinking straws are unknown in Korea, but the tea kettle serves the purpose well.

There is little we can do, but we kneel to pray for the sick woman, grateful, that she has been baptized and prepared for the death which seems inevitable.

The "dispensary Sisters" in Korea dealt with death, poverty, disease, and much superstition. Existing care consisted of acupuncture, burning, herbal cures, and practices of shamanistic rituals. Mercy and her colleagues quietly worked to confront and eradicate the worst practices. For Mercy even to become a Maryknoll medical doctor—indeed, for any American woman in that era wanting to become a doctor—she had had to confront quite some suspicion, if not superstition, in her own church and the society at large.

Shingishu, a city of six thousand people, was perched alongside the untamed Yalu River, surrounded by dikes that kept the waters at bay. But floods were a constant danger, especially during the annual rainy season. Each year the inhabitants would watch anxiously, as the river rose inch by inch, then foot by foot up the dikes. Water that seeped through the dikes forced the inhabitants to wade knee deep in water; one crack in the dikes and the entire city could be swept away.

One particularly bad year, after fifteen days of solid rain, the view from the top of the dike in any direction was water as far as the eye could see. If Mercy worried about death from flooding, she was equally worried about the risk of epidemics; clean water was scarce, sewage had nowhere to go, food was desperately short, medicine was practically gone. Then, late on the fifteenth day, the rain ended. The fierce Yalu stopped rising. The river level remained constant and the dikes were holding until, finally, the watchers could see the damp mark showing that, almost imperceptibly, the water had started to recede. This time, Shingishu was spared both flood and epidemic.

For three more years Mercy continued her work alongside pharmacist Sister Rose of Lima Robinson, who had come down to Shingishu from Gishu in 1933. But the damp Shingishu climate began to make inroads on Mercy's health—not the tuberculosis that afflicted so many of her Korean neighbors and patients, but a debilitating asthma from the constant dampness and mold. In 1940, Mercy became seriously ill and was ordered home.

Three years later, on September 17, 1943, Mother Mary Joseph sat down to write a troubled letter to the 667 Maryknoll Sisters in forty-four convents around the war-torn world. For many, she said, it would be a "Christmas letter" by the time they received it.

In the Philippines, in Japan, in Korea and China, Maryknollers and other Western missioners were in prison camps under the harshest and most brutal of conditions. Mother Mary Joseph wrote:

> My most dear Sisters—near and far—what an overflowing measure of love we must bring to the Crib in this season to compensate in some small degree for the lack of it in a merciless, hate-dominated world. We are specially grieved these days at the Nazi invasion of Rome and the virtual imprisonment of our Holy Father.

It was in this letter that Mother Mary Joseph disclosed the next stop on Sister Mary Mercy's journey. As she continued:

> The first South American group has left. [Aircraft] priorities for the four had been arranged on very short notice. They went by train to Miami, and by plane to Panama, where Sister Paula [Sullivan, a registered nurse] and Sister Mercy are remaining for a month or so to observe tropical medicine. The other two [Maryknoll Sisters Magdalen Mary McCloskey and Joan Peltier] went on by plane to Lima, Peru and La Paz, Bolivia.

Riberalta

Mercy had swapped the Yalu River for the Beni River, Korea's northern hills for dense Bolivian jungle, Shingishu for Riberalta where, in a tiny ramshackle hospital, the medical and catechetical work would begin again. When the aircraft finally touched down on the rough strip that was and is to this day Riberalta airport, Mercy must have realized that her mission work was rarely going to mean comfortable travel. Her taxi into town from Riberalta airport was an oxcart.

Landlocked Bolivia shares borders with five surrounding countries: Paraguay, Chile, Argentina, Peru, and Brazil. About 30 percent larger than Texas, Bolivia is a geographical anomaly. Half the country is more than two miles above sea level—the famed altiplano, or "high plateau," and the mountains. The other half includes deep valleys—the jungled north, and the eastern savannah. Eighty percent of the population lives in the western third, in the major cities, on the altiplano, and in the mountain valleys. Riberalta, in the northern jungle, has been called a "Green Hell," for its intense and stultifying heat.

In 1942, the Vatican created the Vicariate of the Pando, a fifty-five-thousand-square-mile region, and entrusted it to the care of the Maryknoll Fathers. The first priests arrived later that year. By the time Mercy's plane touched down in Riberalta, there were thirteen priests in Pando Vicariate. Focused clearly on pastoral work, they were engaged in five parishes—Cobija, Riberalta, Porvenir, Cachuela Esperanza, and Guayaramerin. Sister Mercy and the three other Sisters had come to a town of perhaps five thousand people that boasted of four gasoline-powered vehicles. Riberalta was the largest settlement in the Pando and was the center of the mission outreach. There would also be a small outpost in Cobija. With its two thousand inhabitants accessible to the Sisters only by plane, Cobija was the district capital on the Brazilian border.

"Riberalta," said Sister Elizabeth Altman, who arrived there in 1946, "was Maryknoll's Bolivian boot camp. And it was as hot as hell. I said anyone who lives in Riberalta should go straight to heaven to get out of the heat." The inhabitants, then as now, were subsistence level poor. The men tapped the wild rubber trees, and picked Brazil nuts in the jungle. Along the river, the Beni, and the major tributary that fed into it, the Madre de Dios, were encampments, communities of a dozen or slightly more people, eking out the barest of living. These rivers were the main highways.

Altman recounted, "I used to go out for a month at a time, and we also took day trips. We visited as far as Cavinas on the Beni, an Indian village where the Maryknoll Fathers served. The Indians disappeared because we were wearing our long white habits. It was the first time they had seen Sisters."

Maryknoll Sister Ann Catherine Ryan arrived in the Beni area in 1945. "We did a little bit of everything," she said. In Cobija, she did catechetical work for two years and then established a girls' vocational school in Riberalta, which immediately attracted many young girls.

Maryknoll Sister Mary Aulson went out on horseback giving religious programs in one-room schools in the bush. "I learned to ride down there," she recalled. "I only fell off once. A young girl usually accompanied me, and always lagged behind. I had a beautiful horse. On the way back I would sing a Western tune and the horse would have a little dance step." Describing herself as a "vagabunda," Aulson said she would go out with another Sister in a dug-out canoe or motorboat or walk to do the catechetical work.

To Sister Mary Shannon, who was assigned to Bolivia in 1952, "Riberalta and Cobija were like Wild West towns." In time, she, too, left school teaching behind and "started going out on the rivers," to do catechetical formation of the small communities.

"We had two houses," she said, "the school house and the hospital house. When we went from one to the other we had to take a flashlight. Once I forgot my flashlight and ran into the horns of a cow."

"By boat there were quite a few places we could visit within a day's journey," said Maryknoll Sister Catherine Heilig. "We cooked on the boat, though sometimes people invited you for a meal, yucca or platano with a little shredded 'charqui' [dried meat or fish]. But it's so salty. They don't have bread because they don't have ovens. They usually don't eat fruit at a meal. They go out and pick it during the daytime. Usually we slept in the school," she said, "though now I stay in people's homes. Some put their sleeping bags on the floor, but there are ants, cockroaches, and snakes and rats. I like to take a hammock."

For Mercy, Riberalta would have several things in common with Shingishu, but in the rainy season, one was most obvious: mud. Nonetheless, the day after Mercy arrived in 1943, the work began with a vengeance. Next to the Sisters' residence, a dispensary "hospital" was created, with a borrowed examination table and some crates, on which were empty and sterilized butter tins to hold cotton and medicines. A curtain was strung across the one room to provide a modicum of privacy. By 1945 the Maryknoll Fathers, through the efforts of Maryknoll Bishop Escalante, had built a modest twenty-seven-bed hospital. Maryknoll Sisters administered the hospital until 1974 when it was turned over to the Bolivian government.

Riberalta's health statistics were dreadful: 90 percent of the people suffered from amoebic dysentery, 100 percent had verminosis, 60 percent had malaria, most had hookworm from going barefoot in places where there were no sanitary conditions, 30 percent had tuberculosis, and malnutrition was the norm.

The routine began again, house calls—now by canoe or horseback—and work in the dispensary. Mercy was soon writing back to Maryknoll, New York:

We are in the depths of the rainy season, and by "depths" I mean an abyss of mud. The natives say it is pure mud, implying I suppose, that it is all that mud should be.

Very often we go on sick calls by canoe, because the fields are flooded. When traveling this way, the passenger either stands in the canoe, or sits in the water which invariably seeps into the boat. My choice of posture is usually the perpendicular. In the dry season, horses are popular vehicles of transportation. You can see that wheels are more or less useless in our part of the world.

Nearly all Maryknoll Sisters in Bolivia have their snake stories. Riber-alta, explained Sister Virginia Stivers, "was a land of heat and snakes." Bats in the rafters, mosquitoes and biting bugs everywhere. Snakes? The local pucarara was said to be the deadliest snake in all South America. This jungle rattler has fangs strong enough to penetrate the rubber workers' boots and the coiled strength to spring eight feet toward its adversary or prey.

Sister Ann Catherine Ryan told of the 5:20 A.M. meditation in the candlelit dawn of the tiny hospital chapel when she was nudged by another Sister who said, " 'I think there's a snake under your kneeler.' We had only candles because there was no electricity. I picked up the kneeler and there was a three-foot snake. In silence, the house superior, Sister Rita Bonnin, backed out the door, brought in a dust pan and brush, hit the snake on the head with the brush, scooped it up and went out with it. Nobody said a word. We went right on with meditating and no talking until after breakfast."

As always, for these Maryknoll Sisters, the medical work served a larger mission, ministering to an unsophisticated people whose practice of the Catholic faith was fairly rudimentary. As Mercy explained:

> In the homes, almost every adult patient leads us to a marriage that needs to be rectified. We find out each day about what little opportunity these people have had to learn their religion. We judge that ninety percent or more have never received their first Holy Communion.
>
> The homes are very poor—of bamboo adobe, with mud floors. They have one or two rooms, with several beds and hammocks, a table and a chair or two as the only furnishings. Pigs, dogs, and chickens are ubiquitous. However, there is almost always to be found a crucifix or a faded picture of the Blessed Virgin.

As in Korea, superstition and fear of modern medicine again compounded the problem of health care. Yet again, Mercy would show she could outwit the opposition. The instance best known in Riberalta concerned a young woman who, for seven years, had been confined to a makeshift bed in a hut behind her parents' shack.

As a ten-year-old girl, this woman had developed a severe skin rash. The family feared that it was Hansen's Disease (leprosy) and that if the girl was discovered she would be sent to a distant river island where sufferers of Hansen's Disease were kept. On the few occasions when a doctor visited Riberalta, the diagnosis was always the same: no hope of improvement. The girl would be a cripple all her life.

One day, early in her Bolivian experience, Mercy visited the tiny hut in the jungled backyard where the girl was kept. It was not leprosy, Mercy insisted, but a curable skin disease. Nor would the girl be a cripple once she was no longer confined to her bed. After seven days of ointments and medicines, the girl was cured of the sickness that had cost her seven years of her life.

Sister Pauline Frei, who arrived not long after the first contingent of four, reminisced, "We were not prepared for the heat of the Beni when we landed—we were in our gray woolen habits. We walked in from the airport because there was no transport. It was September 24, a big holiday and Sister Mercy's feast day. I can remember sitting around for hours in those gray habits, smiling at people." Frei was one of many who would later say, "Mercy influenced my spiritual life. She was a simple woman and never preached, but she was a wonderful superior. She didn't act like a superior—I think that maybe sometimes she was so generous and at the service of the people that they came first, rather than us. You felt she was holy—not that she prayed a lot, but her whole demeanor."

God's two major gifts to Mercy were her generosity of self and her love for people. In these years, Mercy had an "old-school" attitude toward the priests. Frei was put in charge of the two girls who cooked for the priests and Sisters. Mercy, a product of her generation, felt the best should go to the priests. "If we had cake," said Sister Pauline Frei, "the priests were the first to receive it."

As in Korea, "Madre Mercy" was always available. "They would come at any time of the night and get her, and they would awaken us all." The years began to pass in daily medical rounds and weekly canoe or launch trips. The dispensary's fame spread along this Amazonian region's waterborne telegraph. One man arrived by canoe with his daughter after days and days of travel. His wife and three of his sons were dead, and two other sons remained at home. Malaria was killing them. Mercy treated the two and sent them back with medicine for the two boys.

In Bolivia, the image of Mercy was fixed—to the Bolivians, an angel of Mercy in white; to visitors, an angel of mercy in mud. "My first, last and in-between recollections of Sister Mercy in Bolivia," said a U.S. Public Health Service official, "vary not a whit. I can still see her, plodding through mud, knee deep, the skirt of her otherwise white habit splattered and splashed, as she makes her way from hut to hut."

Sister Ann Catherine recalled her this way. "She was a very much loved person here and I know she worked day and night. People would come to the house at any hour, and she would go with them, slide down the barrancas, the hills, and all the mud, to take care of sick people. She never said no to anybody. She was so service-oriented, very loving and kind. Sometimes she would get so tired. I remember one night at supper, her hand dropped into the mustard dish. She had fallen asleep at the table while we were eating. She was a hard, hard worker."

By the end of the 1940s, the Maryknoll presence in Bolivia had grown to approximately twenty-eight priests and three Brothers and twenty-three Sisters. Fourteen priests, one Brother and eighteen Sisters were in the Pando. But by that time, Sister Mercy's next challenge was already being formulated by politics half a world away. In Asia, the Korean War had started. Instead of hundreds of patients from a sparsely populated region, Mercy would soon administer and work in a clinic that would handle a phenomenal seven hundred thousand patients in two years and bring Mercy worldwide headlines.

Pusan

Mercy had written to General Douglas MacArthur requesting permission to return to Korea—after the Sisters had been evacuated to Japan—to work with refugees. It was granted. And on March 19, 1951, Mercy—with her two companions, Sister Rose of Lima Robinson and Sister Mary Hock—was once again in a light plane, landing amid misery, this time in Pusan. Along the Korean refugee telegraph, word of this tiny clinic in Pusan reached hundreds of miles.

A mass of humanity, waves and waves of individual human beings, had rolled down the Korean peninsula to Pusan, in the south. In the few months since June 1950, when the Korean civil war had begun, Pusan's population had quadrupled to one million, and still more would come. Refugees from communism plus the displaced of northern South Korea, whose homes were destroyed by the fighting, were fleeing the carnage.

But the drama was just outside the Sisters' door. In an alley, a rattle of newspapers in the trash piles near the clinic gates revealed an abandoned baby. "Mercy stooped to pick it up," said a companion, "holding its face to her cheek before gathering it under her gown for warmth." If Bolivia had sapped Mercy's energy because of the heat, travel, and conditions, Korea would test it because of the work: sixteen and eighteen hours a day, day after day. At first, hundreds of refugees lined up outside the clinic each day. Then one thousand, then two thousand. It became known as "the longest charity line in the world," an orderly line stretching off into the distance.

Poor families traveled four hundred miles as refugees from Seoul to stand in line for medical care with the widows and orphans, the remnants of families wrecked by war. Mercy requested, and soon received, additional Sisters from around Asia and the United States.

In Pusan Mercy saw her Maryknoll Sister staff grow to three doctors, several nurses, two pharmacists, two lab technicians, and one X-ray technician. In addition there were twelve Korean Sisters, whom Maryknoll Sister Agneta Chang had trained, also refugees from the North, and who now lived on the Maryknoll compound and helped in the clinic. There were also five trained Korean nurses, who were soon to be joined by five Korean doctors.

The medical staff marched along the refugee line, seeking out the most seriously sick. The staff went on sick calls to refugees on the Pusan mountainside shanty towns of cardboard boxes marked Del Monte asparagus, Schlitz beer, Chesterfield cigarettes; the Sisters crawled into smoke-filled shacks where charcoal stoves were the source of warmth and heat for cooking. Meager water supplies were polluted, sewage ran riot, typhoid, typhus, smallpox, and tuberculosis were almost the norm.

The team set up vaccination tables, often out in the open, sometimes on a street corner, working days that began with the morning light and extended well into the darkened evening. In addition to the sick to be treated, there were also baptisms and then catechism classes and, in time, entire families joining the Catholic church. Years later, the priests in the newly established parishes in Pusan would tell the Sisters that the nucleus of Catholicism in the area had their first contact with the Catholic church at the Pusan clinic.

There were thousands of wandering children, abandoned, orphaned, lost, straying from tents that housed as many as thirteen families, all needing assistance. But if there were tears among the children, there were sometimes tears in the eyes of the Sisters too. One day Mercy approached two emaciated young boys, brothers, waiting in the clinic. She gave them each three crackers, but the younger boy had not seen her give the older brother some crackers, so though gnawingly hungry himself, he immediately gave two of his three crackers to his older brother. The Sisters who witnessed this act had to turn away quickly to hide their tears.

Maryknoll Sisters were among many beneficiaries of the American G.I.s' help. The soldiers came to the children's rescue by helping to build orphanages. They also volunteered at the clinics, repaired buildings, and donated time and money.

After the Sisters had worked for three and a half years in a makeshift building, the U.S. Army planned to build a hospital for the Maryknoll Sisters in Pusan. On July 29, 1954, General Maxwell D. Taylor came from his headquarters in Seoul to turn the first shovel of earth. It was one of seven private hospitals built by the army. With the war over, rather than ship surplus military materials back to America, the army built hospitals for the Baptists, Seventh Day Adventists, Swiss Benedictines, Australian Presbyterians, and others.

The ground-breaking for "The Maryknoll Sisters-Armed Forces Memorial Hospital," to give it its full title, was a signal, too, of Mercy's departure. After three and a half years, her health was again suffering. But there was also a call to an entirely different mission, no less challenging than her overseas assignments. She was to create and administer the first nonsegregated hospital in Kansas City, Missouri.

Queen of the World

In 1951, around the time Mercy was en route to war-torn Korea, a group of Black doctors in Kansas City was meeting with the city's Catholic bishop, Edwin V. O'Hara. The physicians, who had completed their residency requirements under white surgeons, obstetricians, and radiologists, wanted to practice medicine in a hospital with the same standards as white hospitals.

All that Kansas City really offered black patients and doctors was segregated General Hospital #2 and Wheatley Hospital. The first was characterized by one Maryknoll Sister as a "rat trap, and the second one was worse than that." And then there was a Catholic maternity hospital, St. Vincent's, built in 1906, which was facing closure as new hospitals in the suburbs siphoned off the supply of patients. The board of St. Vincent's wanted to reopen. After a survey of the hospital needs of Kansas City's black citizens, a program was endorsed to combine St. Vincent's with the neighboring St. Anthony's Home (for unwed mothers), to create a general eighty-five-bed hospital open to doctors and patients regardless of "race, color, or creed." Fundraising for $300,000 began in 1953. The Daughters of Charity, who staffed St. Vincent's, said they were not able to staff a general hospital and requested that (now Archbishop) O'Hara approach other religious congregations. On May 8, 1954, the archbishop offered the hospital, unencumbered, to the Maryknoll Sisters. It was a Marian year, and, as part of the agreement, which included a nurses' training program, there would be a name change: Queen of the World Hospital.

The Sisters ran the hospital from 1954 to 1965, but its start was extremely slow. First there were builders' strikes, which delayed the actual opening until May 22, 1955, when the first twelve Maryknoll Sisters, along with the Black medical staff, were ready for business.

Next came unanticipated opposition to the plan from the black Protestant clergy, many of them affiliated with Wheatley Hospital. Their cry was, "Negro hospital for Negroes; a Catholic hospital for Catholics." The archbishop thought he had already dealt with this when the black doctors had first approached him. When asked to provide a Catholic hospital for Negroes, O'Hara had replied, "I am not interested in a Negro hospital, but I am interested in a hospital to care for *all* the sick, Negro or white."

Worse, the patients did not come. Two months after its opening, O'Hara was recommending that the hospital be closed for a few months and re-opened later for a fresh start.

However, a 1958 report on the hospital's first three years explained that "the Sisters, fortified by prayer and confidence, were able to convince him that it would be better to continue in operation, but to put greater effort into a public relations program, which would bring more patients and, probably, financial aid."

To the determined Maryknoll Sisters, this was one more mission venture, and things always got tough in the missions. Their determination won out. A nonsegregated School of Practical Nursing opened in 1956, the census of patients began to improve, and the city and nation could look on at a well-integrated highly qualified medical staff working with nonsegregated patients. "Though the percentage of white patients is small," said the 1958 report, "a decided disappearance of prejudice and an open friendliness toward the (Catholic) church" prevailed.

In 1965, the hospital was closed—not because it had failed, but in part because it had served its purpose. Pressure from federal Medicare requirements forced the other hospitals to become nonsegregated. So Queen of the World donated its equipment to a Maryknoll hospital in the Philippines, and Mother Mary Joseph's dictum—when the work is done, the Sisters move on—was honored.

So much for the surface story of Queen of the World. The internal human and spiritual dynamics at the hospital were another story altogether.

Even before the memories had faded of the farewell messages from the Mayor of Pusan, the Commander-in-Chief of U.S. Forces, the hospital staff, and the Korean community, Mercy took up her Queen of the World post in the office that overlooked the outpatient-emergency waiting room. It was the only entrance, which meant that Mercy saw everyone who came into the hospital.

Queen of the World Hospital was part of the Maryknoll Sisters' work for only eleven years, but it has many claims on the community's history and affections.

First, it was an archetypical Maryknoll Sisters' endeavor: a call to serve, the enthusiastic response, building up the required institution, witnessing to Jesus through presence and example, then moving on when the institution had run its course.

Next, the Sisters who worked at the hospital developed a special camaraderie, even long after Sister Mercy had left. It came about because Maryknoll Sisters who needed to get back into the medical field, especially after the novitiate, were sent to Queen of the World for various periods to resharpen their skills. Two and more decades later, in many places around the Sisters' world, a name could come up in conversation and trigger the comment, "Oh, we were in Kansas City together." Dozens upon dozens of Sisters passed through the same door that Sister Mercy could see from her office near the hospital entrance.

As always, Mercy touched many of the Sisters' lives personally. "This great lady," as medical technologist Maryknoll Sister Gloria Ruiz called her, "was Superior most of the time I was there. She worked so hard—she didn't have any time, other than to work and pray. You don't normally get to know superiors too well, but Mercy was a motherly person, attuned to your changes: 'Are you okay?' she would ask, not as a superior, but as a concerned person. She was special in my life. She tried to evoke the deep holiness that was in people."

The person in charge of the practical nursing school was Sister Jean Roberts, a self-described "independent cuss" and a convert to Catholicism against her Mennonite family's wishes. The former army nurse, with a masters in nursing education paid for by the G.I. Bill, arrived in Kansas City in 1954 after novitiate and work at the Motherhouse infirmary—where she had met Mercy—and at Bethany, the nearby Sisters' residence.

"Mercy could read you like a book—at least me," said Roberts. "My relationship with her was that of spiritual mother, not an ideal to be followed, but one of the early relationships that touched me to the core. I was working at Bethany, she was back from Korea, sick with a heart condition, recuperating en route to Kansas City. I used to go to see her. 'How are things at Bethany?' she would ask, and I would just open my heart to her. Then, and for the next thirty years, she either knew what was going on in my life, or I would share it with her at a very deep level."

Mercy's presence at the hospital touched everyone. When Mercy briefly left Kansas City for New York for heart treatment, "everyone was on pins and needles," Roberts recalled. "One Black doctor said, 'I find myself walking down the corridor and going into her office, even though I know she is in New York. There's something about that woman that gets to you.' The doctors would spend hours talking to her; so would the women who mopped the floors, the X-ray technicians, the patients."

Another Queen of the World contribution to the Sisters' future was the effect of a spiritual meeting between Mercy and Sister Regina McEvoy, who became very close friends. While at Kansas City, Sister Regina decided to enter the cloister—a decision that so dismayed the Queen of the World doctors that they practically petitioned her not to do it.

Yet it was during Regina's cloistered experience that she arrived at an entirely different view of what a cloister should be—a contemplative presence among the poor. In effect, she helped to broaden the cloister; her vision and proved experience became a key component of the cloistered Sisters' decision decades later to establish cloisters in the Sudan and Guatemala. Sister Regina McEvoy's decision also provided the final chapter of Mercy's story.

In twenty-seven years, Sister Mercy had spent only three years at Maryknoll; in all those years she had led the fatiguing life of the on-call missioner doctor. But in 1958 she was elected Vicaress General, the second highest authority in the Congregation—second only to the Mother General. She spent twelve years in office, during which time she was often able to moderate the occasional rigidity within Mother Mary Coleman's administration.

While Vicaress General, she was present at the 1964 and 1968 Chapters. "Everyone trusted her," said delegate Sister Anna Marian Pavao. "She seemed to bridge the gap between the old and the new, between the older Sisters and the younger Sisters."

After leaving Kansas City, Mercy never practiced medicine again. But her work and example were not finished yet. She wanted more, needed more.

Avenue C

At the Chapter meetings, and drawing on her own experiences, Mercy had absorbed the new mandate to Sisters to live out more directly what they experienced as their mission. The new understanding of mission and the final image of Mercy were due to her long friendship with Sister Regina McEvoy. Along with Sister Eileen McIntyre, Mercy and McEvoy developed a thirteen-year-long new form of contemplative presence in a tenement apartment on Avenue C in a run-down section of Manhattan.

Surely Avenue C was no place for an elderly Sister to be, living with a couple of companions in a Lower East Side tenement? Many of Mercy's Maryknoll Sister colleagues were aghast. Drug addicts, people surviving on their street skills, felons, and the mentally incompetent were among Mercy's neighbors in the shabby building that became their home in 1973.

The Sisters' plan called for "a missionary prayer presence: a Maryknoll Community within the Church in the U.S. among the socially and economically poor in a city." They were to "form a life primarily given to prayer and to a simple, poor lifestyle and presence among the people, hoping to witness to the unity of love through an emphasis on one aspect of evangelical poverty: social poverty."

Day after day, from her third-floor window overlooking Avenue C, Mercy prayed over the area's squalid conditions, the violence, the inhumanity, the disease, and the poverty her eyes witnessed. As her health failed, when even walking across the room became a hazardous trip of frequent falls, Mercy kept up her good humor, her vigil, and her prayers.

Her days would draw to an end here. After a lifetime of being assigned where she was needed, Mercy, now in her eighties, was living a new life, one she had also chosen. Her last mission reflected her radical and lifelong commitment to the poor and marginalized and her own call to share their poverty in a presence of hospitality and prayer. As her friend Sister Jean Roberts said, "Had Mercy not become Maryknoll's first Sister-doctor she would have become a contemplative. On Avenue C, Mercy was not a contemplative high on a hill, but a contemplative in the marketplace."

In many ways, the scene from the Avenue C window was not one that was utterly unfamiliar. The world of poverty, misery, pain, and squalor had been Mercy's accustomed habitat. Around the world, as in this apartment—where initially timid neighbors came for prayer and reflection—there were many who had felt the reassuring kindness of this aptly named woman.

The fame had receded now. It had never been so great as at the moment in Korea when a woman war correspondent's jeep had broken down near Mercy's Pusan clinic. The story was told in *The Field Afar*. While the newspaper correspondent waited for a mechanic, she wandered into the clinic. There was a nun on her knees, cleaning the stinking gangrenous sore on a man's leg.

Said the correspondent, "Sister, I wouldn't do that for a million dollars."

Without stopping the treatment, Mercy replied, "Neither would I."

The account was picked up by wire services and Mercy's story was told around the world. Among her Maryknoll Sisters, however, this was not the basis of Mercy's fame. Rather, she was known for her gentleness, her compassion, her spirituality—gifts no amount of money could buy.

The 1970s gave way to the 1980s and Mercy was slowing down. By the summer of 1986, her health was obviously failing, and in mid-September it was decided she should move back to Ossining and the Maryknoll Nursing Home. She died there a few days later, on September 20.

Whom had she touched?

Fifty-five years earlier, in a Yeng You dwelling, she had touched Changju. Thirty-five years earlier, in the Korean city of Pusan, she had touched hundreds of people each day. In the last five years of her life, she had touched little children of many colors, those who came to the Avenue C apartment for prayers and, when Maryknoll and other priests stopped by, to share the Eucharist.

In the Bolivian jungle encampments, as in the homes of now better-off Koreans, among black families in Kansas City, perhaps stories of Mercy are still occasionally told. Certainly her memory is kept in Bolivia, where the little girl misdiagnosed as having Hansen's Disease is now a grandmother

~ 10 ~

Rebels with a Cause

═══════════════════

THEY WERE ALWAYS THERE, the Maryknoll Sisters who heard the gospel and who saw the signs of the times, calling them to go further, faster, deeper than the church or their own Congregation's insights and traditions allowed. "I was Vatican II before Vatican II," said Maryknoll Sister Gabriella Mulherin, who in the 1960s started South Korea's successful and nationwide credit union and cooperative movement.

In the Philippines in the early 1970s, Maryknoll Sister Mary Grenough left nursing in the hospital of a sugar milling company, which the Sisters ran, to share in the lives of those whose services the hospital did not reach—the sugarcane cutters, the seasonal workers, and their families.

In their different ways, both Sisters had arrived at a common insight: that the responsibility of the missioner was not simply to provide services for the poor, but also to accompany them on the road to their own empowerment. Though these Sisters took their first steps alone, sometimes uncertain of support from their community members and superiors, they walked a path that others would follow.

A New Name for Peace

The 1960s, a decade of change, was also, in many ways, the decade of "development." That key word, meaning different things to different people, appeared in documents and speeches from politicians, international organizations, and Vatican officials. In the United States, the decade began with President John F. Kennedy and a youthful vision of economic progress in the defense of democracy. The Peace Corps, the Alliance for Progress, and similar United Nations' programs heralded a concerted effort on the part of the "developed" countries to raise the socio-economic levels of countries in the "developing" world. Nations from the former colonial world of Latin America, Asia, the Pacific, and Africa were seen as lagging behind the more prosperous countries of the Northern hemisphere, a difference that could be narrowed through investment, loans, and the sharing of technical resources.

The expressed altruism of such initiatives was often mixed with self-serving strategic motivations, and clouded—as in the case of Guatemala—by covert skulduggery. Nevertheless, these development efforts captured the optimism of the era. The same hopeful trust in progress was also leaving its mark on the church. The final document of Vatican II, "The Church in the Modem World" (*Gaudium et Spes*), issued in 1965, was written in this spirit. While acknowledging the discrepancy between great wealth and terrible misery in the world, the Council Fathers wrote with confidence in the possibilities of good will and international cooperation, and a conviction that "this unhappy state of affairs can be rectified by the greater technical and economic resources available in the world today."

As the decade progressed, there came to be a greater understanding of the difficulties implied in development. In Latin America, social scientists were arguing that third-world countries like their own did not simply "lag" behind their former colonial masters. Their economies had been specially adapted for economic exploitation. What was needed was not more aid and investment but a radical transformation of the world economic structure. Development was not so much the issue as justice.

This insight began to enter the teaching of the church with Pope Paul VI's 1967 encyclical, *Populorum Progressio* ("On the Progress of Peoples"). It was the first papal encyclical to focus on the problems of the Third World, specifically the gap between the rich and poor nations of the world. The key word of the encyclical was "development"—the "new name for peace," the pope called it. But he made it clear that development must not be understood simply in economic terms. The goal was a more human world in which men and women might be enabled to realize their full dignity as children of God. In describing his vision, Pope Paul struck a poignant note:

> The struggle against destitution, though urgent and necessary, is not enough. It is a question, rather, of building a world where every person, no matter what his race, religion, or nationality, can live a fully human life, freed from servitude imposed on him by other men or by natural forces over which he has not sufficient control; a world where freedom is not an empty word and where the poor man Lazarus can sit down at the same table with the rich man. This demands great generosity, much sacrifice, and unceasing effort.

A new Christian agenda was emerging in the pope's words, as he addressed the challenge of global justice for the poor with an urgency previously reserved, in church documents; for the battle against atheism it-self:

The hour for action has now sounded. At stake are the survival of so many innocent children and, for so many families overcome by misery, the access to conditions fit for human beings; at stake are the peace of the world and the future of civilization. It is time for all men and all peoples to face up to their responsibilities . . . For if the new name for peace is development, who would not wish to labor for it with all his powers? Yes, we ask you, all of you, to heed our cry of anguish, in the name of the Lord.

The impact of this document was soon to be felt among the Maryknoll Sisters, as it spoke to the yearnings that evolved from their own experience. It was the key reference for their 1970 General Assembly, as even the most cursory glance at the quotations and references incorporated into the Assembly document, *Searching and Sharing*, reveals. But it was not so much any particular document that posed the greatest impetus for change as it was the impact of the Sisters' evolving experience among the poor. As the Sisters observed, in the operating Constitutions for 1970, "The people to whom we are sent are revealing to us the world . . . and calling forth a response." Sometimes it took a particular Maryknoll Sister to make the first response.

One of these Sisters was Gabriella Mulherin.

A Venture in Trust

"I am a rebel," she said in 1987, when her situation belied the declaration: white-haired, confined to a wheelchair, with severely swollen legs. Yet behind the glasses, the lively blue eyes defied anyone to contradict her statement. This was the Sister whose rebel father had escaped Ireland one step ahead of the British, later to settle as a union organizer in Pennsylvania's coal region. Evidently, he had passed on something of the same spirit to his daughter, Gabriella. As a Maryknoll Sister in Korea, she would set her jaw firm and start out to organize on a scale her father never imagined.

She first arrived in Korea in 1926, two years after the group of pioneers who had opened the first mission at Gishu. Gabriella was assigned to the Yeng You mission, where the ongoing projects included an embroidery-craft workshop. From the beginning she was struck by the condition of Korean women and was filled with desire to do something to help them. Not long after her arrival, she wrote with feeling about "the long years of obscurity in the narrow borders of her home" that faced the average young Korean woman. Through their Yeng You school, the Maryknoll Sisters offered a program that combined several hours of schoolwork each day with embroidery work to provide an income. In Korea, Sister Gabriella wrote that the woman was "considered to have no other purpose than to serve. From her childhood she was prepared for service in the home of her husband: a housemaid for the mother-in-law, a child-bearer for the husband."

For fifteen years Gabriella continued her work in Yeng You. But on December 7, 1941, eve of the feast of the Immaculate Conception, the situation for Americans in Japanese-occupied Korea suddenly changed. All the American Maryknoll priests were taken into custody as enemy aliens. For the time being, the women religious were left in charge of the faith community. In Yeng You, it fell to Sister Gabriella Mulherin, now the superior, to take responsibility for the great number of communion hosts, consecrated in preparation for the Masses for the following feast day. The arrested pastor had instructed the Sisters to distribute what hosts they could and to consume the rest. From Manchuria to Yeng You, the Sisters distributed communion to each other, to seminarians, and to the laity.

This uncertain period did not last long. Pope Pius XII had arranged that all missioners should be withdrawn if a Japanese-American exchange were achieved. In 1942, the Maryknoll groups in Korea and Manchuria were transported to Japan. In Tokyo the assembled missioners were eventually taken aboard a steamer, the *Asama Maru,* which then rode at anchor for a tense week in Tokyo Bay. Finally, it sailed. It was joined in Singapore by another steamer bearing American internees from Shanghai. Together the two ships, crosses painted on their sides, traveled for thirteen days before steaming into port at Lorenco Marques (now Beira) in Portuguese East Africa (now Mozambique). There they were exchanged with Japanese prisoners from the United States. The sixty Maryknoll priests, thirty-four Maryknoll Sisters, and six Maryknoll Brothers were safe and homeward bound. For Gabriella Mulherin there followed seven years of service at Maryknoll and another two years in Hawaii. She was still in Hawaii in 1951 when Sister Mercy returned to Pusan to the medical clinic. Gabriella followed the next year to work with the war widows and refugee women. The destruction and desolation she encountered were overwhelming.

Mercy and the clinic staff were coping with an overload of staggering proportions—sometimes two thousand people were waiting in line for help. Gabriella observed the Korean men working at any task in order to make a few cents for their desperately poor families. While relief supplies kept them from starvation, there was little prospect for these families to improve their lives. With any slight emergency, they were in the hands of moneylenders who charged 20 to 100 percent interest on the meager loans they advanced. Muiherin wondered if some bold initiative were possible to free these industrious Koreans from their new bondage.

Her thoughts turned back to Hawaii and a book she had read at the suggestion of a friend, *Masters of Their Own Destiny,* by Monsignor Michael Moses Coady of Antigonish, Nova Scotia. Coady and St. Francis University in Antigonish had become the center of the North American cooperative movement. During the Depression, Coady had helped Nova Scotia's poverty-stricken fishermen to form their own selling cooperative.

What chance, Mulherin asked herself, of doing something similar in Pusan? At first, thinking back to the old workshop in Yeng You, she tried to interest some of the women in forming a cooperative for their embroidery, but they were not ready to take such a step. But then the answer occurred to her: Why not credit unions? By November 1958, with the Congregation's support, fifty-eight-year-old high school graduate Gabriella Mulherin found herself at St. Francis University with Monsignor Coady, studying the cooperative movement.

The cooperative movement was born in Britain in the first half of the nineteenth century. It is both a theory of life and a system of business: essentially, everything that can be done cooperatively ought to be done that way. There are consumer cooperatives—wholesale buying of goods for "cooperative" members that eliminates the markups of the middleman, the supermarket, or the store. There are manufacturing and selling cooperatives. Farmers' cooperatives include common ownership of expensive machinery, and cooperative marketing enables the group of farmers to sell directly to major buyers. A credit union, in effect, is a cooperative bank. Members pool their common funds, agree to make regular minimum deposits, and in exchange can borrow from the credit union at low interest rates.

Gabriella saw in the credit union a solution to two situations: the loan-sharking of the moneylenders with their exorbitant interest rates that kept impoverished workers in permanent debt and the lack of citizen participation in post-war South Korea. The cooperative movement and credit unions, she knew, were schools for democracy.

In February 1959, back in Pusan from Nova Scotia, Gabriella described her hopes to members of the Korean Association of Voluntary Agencies (KAVA) and sought their opinions and advice. They agreed that the same cooperative methods that had worked in Canada during the Depression were suited to the situation in Korea.

With this support, in March 1960, Sister Gabriella organized a six-week part-time course for the first twenty-eight interested Koreans, all employees of Pusan-based relief organizations. The newness of the concept aroused hesitations. The amount of money members would be required to commit, though barely equivalent to a U.S. cent at the time, was a significant undertaking for the Koreans. The great barrier that had to be overcome, however, was the lack of mutual trust. As Gabriella explained to the first prospective members, "the word 'credit union' means 'I believe in you, I trust you, so I'm going to let you borrow something from my savings.'"

Finally the twenty-eight, plus two others, were ready to take the chance. On May 1, 1960, the feast of St. Joseph the Worker, the "Song Ka Shin Yong

Chohap," or Holy Family Credit Union, was established. Savings would average $20 a member that first year. Chung Ryul Augustine Kang was elected its first president.

Otherwise, it was not an auspicious moment in Korea's history. Students had just toppled the government of Syngman Rhee. A year later, an army coup led to thirty years of military rule. The economy was in shambles, with only the business of the moneylenders flourishing. Nevertheless, Gabriella's credit union was launched, a school for democracy and a vehicle for people's empowerment. By 1963 there were fifty-two credit unions with 6,925 members and more than $70,000 in savings and loans. Sister Gabriella could proudly report that better than 98 percent of all loans "were repaid on time."

Very little more information is needed to tell the rest of the story. Although the expansion of the credit union movement down the years was periodically trouble prone, and always arduous, by 1988 it had so grown in scale that one in every thirty Koreans belonged to a credit union. Korean credit union assets surpassed $1 billion, and South Korea had led the way in encouraging credit unions throughout Asia. Early credit union pioneers in Korea had risen up the ranks in democratic political movements, academia, and labor unions. Gabriella's pride, the Cooperative Education Institute, founded later to explain the cooperative movement to would-be organizers and members, included among its projects consumer, housing, insurance, marketing, and medical cooperatives.

In 1952, with deprivation and the ravaging of war at its worst, Gabriella had tried to interest the widows and refugee women with whom she worked, and who were being kept alive by donations from relief agencies, to form a cooperative for their embroidery and handiwork. They had been too afraid, too suspicious, too poor to take the first steps. But the "rebel" Sister had not been deterred.

On the thirtieth anniversary of Holy Family Credit Union, a stone memorial was unveiled in Pusan on the site of the old clinic. Its words conveyed the values that Gabriella and her mentor Monsignor Michael Moses Coady had worked for.

At this spot in 1958, Sister Mary Gabriella first introduced the concept of credit union action and on May 1, 1960, the first credit union, named the Holy Family Credit Union, was founded.

Holding high the torch of self-reliance, independence, and cooperation, leadership training and guidance in model credit union structure were started.

The credit union members of the entire country erect this memorial in the thirtieth anniversary year to pay tribute to the person and place of the original foundation.

As those words were fashioned, there were some 1.25 million Korean credit union members in thousands of credit unions. Sister Gabriella later explained the details of her driving force—the strength that the inscription on the stone marker did not reveal.

"It is essential to understand," she said, "that my work was motivated by a religious vocation first: my desire to help the people know the true meaning of love of neighbor as we see it in the Gospel. It was not merely the spreading of a particular socio-economic system—it was an expression of God's love for us and our response to it."

Seeking Justice

Two thousand miles due south of Korea, on an island in the Sulu Sea, another Maryknoll Sister's expression of that love took a very different, yet equally challenging form.

In 1971, in Negros Occidental, a middle-sized island in the Philippines archipelago, Maryknoll Sister Mary Grenough was making her second difficult decision in less than two years. The first had been the decision to quit working with the rest of her community in the company hospital of the Victorias Milling Company. Now she had to decide whether to stand firm against her Maryknoll Sister colleagues who wanted her to end her association with the company's striking sugar workers.

Unhappy to be the cause of distress to her Maryknoll companions, Mary Grenough nonetheless felt she must maintain her support for the struggling workers, even if the other Sisters were not ready to understand.

Such tensions were rooted in different perceptions of duty and justice. The Sisters felt a strong obligation to the milling company's management who, through St. Joseph's Hospital, had provided meaningful ministries and financial support for Maryknoll Sister-nurses after their own hospital, St. Paul's in Manila, had been leveled during World War II. In the view of these Sisters, the milling company was offering an opportunity to serve. As Sister Mary Grenough saw it, the question was: Who was being served? Not, as she saw it, those in greatest need.

The service of Maryknoll Sister-nurses in the Philippines began in 1927 when they had taken over St. Paul's Hospital in Manila. It was an old seminary building that abutted the rear of the cathedral, with corridors too wide, rooms too small, bathrooms too few, and operating rooms too cramped. But by the time the war came, it had acquired a reputation as one of the best hospitals in the country.

After the war, all this lay in ruins. Though exhausted and nearly broken by their brutal internment, most of the Maryknoll Sisters in the Philippines elected to remain and to continue their work as best they could. Thus the nursing Sisters were grateful to receive an invitation from the Osario family to run St. Joseph's Hospital, owned by the family's Victorias Milling Company in Manapla. The Osarios, wealthy, pro-American Filipinos of Spanish descent, were reputed to run the best milling operation in the country, the only mill that refined sugar for export. They prided themselves on their modern technology and on the fine sixty-bed hospital that stood in the midst of the endless sugar fields. The purpose of the hospital was to provide medical care for the permanent employees and the mill's industrial workers. Owners of other haciendas who had their sugar milled at Victorias could also send their employees to the hospital. But the vast majority of field workers, those who cut and carted the cane, could use the hospital only if someone guaranteed to cover their debts.

The island of Negros is the fifth largest island in the Philippine archipelago. It has been compared in shape to a Christmas stocking. A spine of high volcanic mountains runs down its eastern side, leaving a wide, rich plain on the western side where most of the population lives. Ninety percent of that rich plain is covered with sugarcane. The sugar trade in the Philippines was established by the Spanish, who relied originally on slave labor. Europe's addiction to sweets fed the fortunes of plantation owners throughout the islands. It was in Negros however, where sugarcane was introduced in the nineteenth century, that the industry achieved its greatest success. Within a hundred years, the waving sugar fields had grown to absorb virtually every acre of arable land—over half a million acres. Most of the population became laborers on the expansive haciendas or plantations. Cutting sugarcane is seasonal work that leaves the laborers idle for much of the year and forces them to rely on credit and handouts that often leave them in a state of debt-slavery.

The Maryknoll Sisters arrived in Negros in 1948. In those days there was little inclination to delve deeply into history or to engage in social analysis. With their commitment both to sound medical care and wider spiritual purpose, the Sisters settled enthusiastically into the work— training and supervising the hospital's three shifts a day, seven days a week, and providing spiritual outreach by training catechists in the surrounding community.

The regional superior considered the hospital a godsend—it paid the Sisters' salaries and provided needed and valued opportunities for ministry, while not burdening the Congregation with the great expense of maintaining the hospital. Yet by the mid-1960s the same winds of change blowing through the church at large were beginning to rustle through the hardworking everyday routine at St. Joseph's Hospital. The tensions within the Maryknoll Sisters' community between pre- and post-Vatican II ideas of mission would be played out in microcosm in the small outpost in Manapla.

While the hospital provided free services to company employees, it gave limited or no benefits to the more numerous and much poorer field workers. Everything depended on the category of hire. Where this affected Maryknoll was that as company employees, the Sisters were not allowed to use working time for health care among the non-company plantation workers. All of these families suffered from preventable diseases; many babies were dying of tetanus and diphtheria for lack of a simple immunization.

The American Maryknoll Sisters did not speak the local languages. According to the Maryknoll superiors, the Sisters could study in their spare time, but work schedules were so tight there was no spare time for intensive study. What "free time was available was often used by the Sisters to travel on the cane car railroad—there was no other road—bringing religious education to more than one thousand public school children scattered over the five company haciendas."

This was the situation in Manapla in 1964, when the new Sister, Mary Grenough, arrived. She was born in 1933 in Louisville, Kentucky, to a family of seven. It was a religious but financially struggling household. As she later recalled, "My parents taught us to share God's blessings." Three of her brothers became priests, and many of her childhood memories included visiting the boys in the seminary. By the time she reached high school, she had "a very strong suspicion and fear that I had a vocation to become a Sister." It was a while before "the call" corresponded to her own desires. But she remembers being very impressed when two Maryknoll Sisters visited her classroom, telling about their life and work in China. "They seemed very happy, and they said that Maryknoll Sisters were supposed to 'be themselves' and be available to go throughout the world to share the love of Christ." She joined Maryknoll in 1956.

Like all young Maryknoll Sisters, she awaited the news of her first assignment with keen anticipation. At the time, she was studying for a master's degree in nursing education and hoped to be sent somewhere exotic— Africa or the South Pacific. Thus, when Sister Mercy confided that she had been assigned to Manila, she was secretly disappointed. Not only were the Philippines already thoroughly Christian but worse, to her mind, they were deeply "Americanized." The Sisters were attempting to build a new hospital in Manila to replace the destroyed St. Paul's. Grenough would head the Sisters' college of nursing. She wondered why another nursing school in Manila was needed—there were already twenty small training facilities concentrated in that city. Nonetheless, she obediently accepted the assignment. "Those were the days when I understood that to obey the superior was to obey God."

An uninterrupted sea voyage of twenty days brought Grenough to Manila in 1963. But circumstances would soon carry her farther than she or her superiors had foreseen. The project to rebuild St. Paul's Hospital was foundering amidst conflict with the Archbishop of Manila, Cardinal Santos. Although the Sisters had brought their own funds to the project, the land belonged to the archdiocese. This entitled the cardinal, as he saw it, to name the hospital board and to claim the last word in hospital policy. Eventually, in 1969, the Sisters would relinquish the project altogether to the archdiocese. Rather than St. Paul, it would open under the name of Cardinal Santos Memorial Hospital.

In these uncertainties Grenough saw an opportunity to escape from Manila, and in 1964 she requested reassignment to the provinces. At the time, the only other nursing outpost was at St. Joseph's Hospital in Negros.

The work at St. Joseph's was very hard. Sisters supervised all departments of the hospital including food, laundry, and maintenance, as well as all the medical services. The Sisters' convent was a separate building about twenty yards from the hospital. It was a comfortable two-story concrete-block construction with a garden and a beautiful view of the mountains in the distance. But the Sisters lived and breathed two realities—the hospital and the company. Outside their windows, at all hours of day and night, they could hear the sirens of approaching ambulances or the sounds of the tractors and heavy-duty trucks hauling sugarcane. An intercom with the hospital meant that the Sisters were always on call.

Despite the abundant work and the scenic view, Grenough increasingly found herself rubbing against the grain, groping for a new way of being in mission. Her constant feeling of helplessness in the face of preventable disease, her inability to communicate directly with patients or their families, the deference and respect that were paid to her simply because she was American, left her feeling discouraged and exhausted at the end of the day. As she recalls, "Patients were crying out for help, and I couldn't even understand them." Before long, she began arguing that the Sisters should not be staying inside the hospital compound but should be out in the haciendas and barrios teaching basic public health. "I thought it was very wrong of us not to find some way to work outside the hospital instead of just admitting dying babies, children, and adults for expensive and usually futile emergency care. If our patients did survive, the family was usually indebted for years and perhaps forever."

Though other younger Sisters shared her concerns, none was so outspoken or persistent. Grenough stuck it out at the hospital for almost six years, trusting that a way would open for a different kind of service. Finally, in 1969, she received permission to leave the hospital to work with the social action program of the new bishop of the Bacolod diocese, in which the hospital was located.

That bishop was Antonio Fortich, a paternal, good-humored, and courageous man, who had been appointed in 1967. Fortich's family were landowners—sugarcane growers and millers—and at first the *hacenderos*, the wealthy owners of Bacolod, had welcomed him as one of their own, rewarding him with a new Mercedes Benz and bottles of Chivas Regal. But Fortich's upbringing had not left him insensitive to the plight of Negros' poor. As a boy he and his sister had taken their turn working in the fields, an experience that left him with a famous bone-crushing handshake.

It was as a boy, while gathering dried cane leaves to be burned to power the mill, that he had "started thinking about the sad plight of the poor." At school and in the fields he wondered about his life and was thinking that his vocation might lie in either politics or the priesthood. One day, when he was twelve, he thought, "Well, if I enter the priesthood, I can preach to defend these poor people."

He was elevated to the episcopacy in the same year that Pope Paul VI issued his historic encyclical, *Populorum Progressio*. As far as the pope was concerned, the church was entering a new era in which the meaning of the gospel must be related to the desperate and dehumanizing conditions of the poor. Fortich was a man well suited for this task. In the coming years, he would survive a hand grenade assassination attempt, he would see his Spanish-era *palacio* residence burned to the ground, and he would be viciously maligned as a Communist by some of the rich landowners of the diocese. Nevertheless, despite these pressures, he would increasingly discover and come to epitomize for others the gospel of the Sermon on the Mount.

Similar commitments had brought Mary Grenough to look for ministry outside St. Joseph's Hospital, and she naturally gravitated to the charismatic Fortich. The bishop welcomed her and was agreeable when she said she chose not to wear the traditional habit. Immediately, Grenough felt liberated. Working with the diocese's Social Action Committee, she organized seminars for church personnel and laity—including sugar workers and the urban poor—dealing with the social, political, and cultural situation. "It was through such work," she said, "that I discovered not only the realities of the poor, but also understood Scripture in a new way. And for the first time in my life I felt integrated as a person who is a Christian who is a missioner."

But while Grenough was resolute in her course, in the Sisters' hospital compound where she still lived, her activism was a source of tension. This only deepened when, on August 9, 1971, 170 hacienda workers went on strike against Victorias, and Grenough set herself to work for their cause. The strike had its roots in the workers' desire to break the grip of their company-sponsored labor union and affiliate instead with the independent Federation of Free Farmers (FFF).

The FFF, which stressed not only wages and working conditions but also the importance of social awareness, had a strong Christian motivation, and many priests served as chaplains. Workshops were arranged for sugar workers to help them to analyze their history and social conditions and to understand their human rights and dignity. Union literature was filled with references to Vatican II, the Bible, and quotations from Bishop Fortich. Many of the sugar workers were actually the descendants of slaves on the same plantations. Now, for the first time, as Grenough recalled, "they understood why they were poor." Through the education and organizing efforts of the union, "they discovered that they had human dignity and personal responsibility and were called by God to struggle for their rights, and that unless they organized and struggled together, the future of their children would be no different from their own or their parents' parents."

The strike lasted for more than a year, putting the Sisters in an uncomfortable situation. "Some of them felt that my presence with and support of the sugar workers was a disloyalty to the Victorias Milling Company to whom we owed so much. Some, I believe, felt I was being disloyal to the Maryknoll Sisters who were still working for the company in the hospital. Some questioned how much pain and anxiety I had a right to impose on the community."

The community asked Grenough not to talk about the strike or to collect money for the strikers on company property. She compromised, promising not to "mount a soapbox" to speak about the strike but insisting that on a one-to-one basis she would not give up her right of free speech or her responsibilities.

The Victorias management began pressuring the Sisters to ask Grenough to desist from her work with the strikers; she said that in conscience she could not. On that position she was rock solid. But then the company decreed that Grenough would be forbidden to enter the hospital compound where the Sisters had their convent. What happened then was a heartwarming instance of the spirit of community that prevailed even during this tense era. The Maryknoll Sisters community superior in Manapla said that the Sisters would stand with Grenough; if the company insisted on refusing her entry to the compound, *all* the Maryknoll Sisters would leave. The company backed down.

Two decades later, Grenough remembered that period with gratitude for the loyalty of her community. Through the whole experience she felt "baptized anew." In those years, she said, "everything came together: the reality of the people, the Constitutions of the Maryknoll Sisters, and the experience of the church around the world. Our Sisters had always helped the poor, but this experience of being with the poor as their consciousness was rising and as they struggled to become liberated from centuries of oppression was very different. It was an education and awakening for me to a new understanding of being Christian."

Within three years of the strike's end, the Maryknoll Sisters had pulled out of St. Joseph's Hospital. The reasons were diverse, including the fact that younger Sisters would no longer accept such institutional work as once they had. But part of the reason was a growing awareness of the "colonial" attitudes represented by such work. The sugar plantation hospital was symbolic of another era. Grenough's resignation from it, like the Sisters' 1968 Special Chapter, had heralded a new one.

As for the strike, it eventually ended in a legal victory for the workers. They were awarded a large settlement. But more than a decade later, with many workers having died or been forced out of the region to find employment, payment had yet to be made, and conditions had scarcely altered. The legal victory was hollow. "The Negros justice system just doesn't work," observed Grenough.

But by that time, the Sisters were no longer part of the structure that gave it credence. The 1972 declaration of martial law by President Ferdinand Marcos hastened the awakening process. The Marcos government began to persecute the church and its personnel for the defense of human rights. In Negros, the military, local police, and private armies backed up by the richest landowners used brutal methods to expand their holdings and to trample anyone who stood in the way. Grenough continued her work with the diocesan Social Action office, now documenting human rights abuses and offering legal assistance to poor settlers and refugees.

By the end of the 1980s Grenough was mainstream in the community, with a significant number of Sisters in similar direct ministries with the poor. The Sisters had grown with the times.

Throughout her sufferings over the hospital, the sugar workers' strike, and the tensions in her community, Grenough never doubted that she belonged to Maryknoll. She survived without bitterness, she says, "gifted, or burdened, with an old-fashioned faith that God had a reason for me being in Maryknoll" and a reason for leading her to Negros. Without Maryknoll she might not have been exposed to the sufferings of the poor and their life-giving example and challenge. They had taught Grenough that to obey one's conscience was to obey God.

Hers had become the Maryknoll Sisters' common experience.

∽ 11 ∽

To Africa

▬▬▬▬▬▬▬▬▬

IN 1948, THE FIRST Maryknoll Sisters went to Tanganyika, the first African country to receive them. Twenty-two years later, Africa came to the Maryknoll Sisters, in the impressive person of Tanzania's first president, Julius Nyerere. It was October 16, 1970, a dramatic day in the history of the Congregation.

At Maryknoll, U.S. Secret Service agents had scoured the Sisters Center, discovering two unexploded shells—World War II souvenirs—that had been placed for years in the foyer. Outside, Ossining, Newcastle, and New York State police provided additional security. In the crowded auditorium the Sisters lined the narrow aisles between the rows of folding metal chairs and the beige-brick walls. The flags of the United States and Tanzania (green and blue separated diagonally by a gold-edged black stripe) flanked the stage, where Mother Mary Coleman, all the Sisters who had served in East Africa, Maryknoll Father William Bergan, Society Vicar-General, and the Tanzanian United Nations delegation stood ready.

Nyerere was in New York to address the annual fall opening of the United Nations. It was a coincidence that his visit coincided with the Maryknoll Sisters' 1970 General Assembly; but it was an inspired coincidence. Nyerere knew the Sisters in Tanzania well—indeed he was a regular and relaxed visitor wherever they worked. Now, in this General Assembly, as the Sisters were struggling to redefine their identity and understanding of mission in light of their experience among the poor, Nyerere's presence spoke to their concerns.

And yet, who was it precisely that they were welcoming? Julius Nyerere was born in Butiama, a village near Musoma, in 1923, a son of one of his father's several wives. He was baptized in his late teen years, after more than a decade of Catholic instruction by the Missionaries of Africa, formerly known as the White Fathers. After completing his education, he worked as a teacher and later assisted Maryknoll Father Arthur Willie, who was ministering among the Wazanaki, Nyerere's tribe. In fact, Nyerere translated the New Testament into Kizanaki. But his true vocation was politics.

Tanganyika, formerly a German colony, had become a British Territory after World War I. According to a United Nations mandate following World War II, Britain agreed to move Tanganyika toward independence. This came about through pressure from the Tanganyika African National Union (TANU), a political party headed by Nyerere. After independence ("Uhuru") in 1961, Nyerere served as chief minister before being elected to serve as the country's first president. In 1964, Tanganyika was united with the newly independent island nation of Zanzibar, thus forming the new nation of Tanzania. It was a country roughly the size of Texas and New Mexico combined, with about nine million people, 44 percent followers of African traditional religions, 24 percent Muslim, and 31 percent Christian, about two-thirds of them Catholics.

In a nation where 93 percent of its widely and often thinly spread population was engaged in agriculture, the government's emphasis was on the absolute basics—health, education, and water. The operative principle was that "the people are the wealth as well as the hope of the nation." Socialism, according to Nyerere, was the way to build the nation. But it was to be a distinctively African form of socialism, based on the concept of family-hood, or "Ujamaa." Rather than stressing ideology, Ujamaa emphasized the time-honored traditions of village life within a deliberate policy of self-help and self-reliance.

Villagers were no longer to be just farmers, but citizens drawn, with government support, into building their own schools and health clinics. Education was a consistent theme of the policy. A "villagization" program meant clustering once widely scattered groups more closely together in agricultural communities, roughly patterned on the Chinese and Israeli kibbutz models. It was a bold and creative model of development that sought to respect African culture while avoiding the pitfalls of economic dependence.

The church, in Nyerere's view, had its own role to play in the challenges facing the developing world. As he told the Sisters, speaking in a low, melodic voice:

> Until quite recently the church was silent on the great issues of man in society, or even sided with those whose exclusive concern was their own power and the accumulation of riches. Even now, despite the teachings of Pope John and Pope Paul, and the deliberations of Vatican II, the most usual practice of the church is the upholding of the established order—regardless of its implications. It is this practice we now have to change.

His words were prescient, too, given the trials for the Sisters in the decade ahead:

Individual church men and women who are working for social justice need the comfort and support of the whole church in their suffering for the teachings of Christ. They are acting according to the dictates of their conscience and, in doing so, they are showing us the way forward. But all too often they find they have to work in isolation from their Catholic brethren. They find that the whole church has not yet committed itself to justice here on earth.

For over an hour Tanzania's president addressed the Sisters on the issues of poverty and the widening gap between the rich and poor, North and South. It was a theme well attuned to the Assembly's deliberations. But first, as Nyerere walked onto the stage in the Maryknoll Sisters' Center he was greeted, to his surprise, by the heart-felt sound of hundreds of well-rehearsed Maryknoll Sisters, singing in Swahili the words to the Tanzanian national anthem, "Mungu ibariki Afrika" (God Bless Africa).

Tanganyika/Tanzania

On December 27, 1948, four Maryknoll Sisters, seated on a raised platform at the rear of a crowded old wartime landing barge and delighted and awed by the blueness of Lake Victoria, felt a mounting excitement as the green hills of their new home in Tanganyika came into view. They were the first Maryknoll Sisters in Africa, a presence that would later extend from Tanganyika to Kenya, Rhodesia/Zimbabwe, and the Sudan. (Some Sisters would later work for shorter periods in Uganda, South Africa, Zambia, Nigeria, Mozambique, and Somalia.)

These first four Sisters included Sisters Margaret Mary Cannon, the superior, and Margaret Rose Winkelmann, both teachers, Sister Mary Bowes, a nurse, and Sister Joan Kirsch, a catechist pastoral worker. Their destination was Kowak, a name that would occupy a special place in the hearts of Maryknoll as the nucleus from which schools, dispensaries, clinics, and a congregation of African Sisters (the Immaculate Heart Sisters of Africa) would grow. At Kowak, the Maryknoll Fathers' superior, William J. Collins, had seen to it that a convent was already under construction, while five African aspirants to the intended African congregation eagerly awaited the Sisters' arrival.

Though Kowak would be a center of outreach to more remote rural areas, it was hardly an urban setting. At night badgers attacked the chickens, while outside, in the nearby bush, leopards kept the baboon population under control. Walking was the principal means of transportation, whether for the men who walked for a day to sell animal skins, or the women who walked all day carrying water and firewood, or the families who thought nothing of walking for days to visit relatives.

It was a new world for the Maryknoll Sisters, who had only recently begun to turn their sights to horizons beyond Asia. It was a new experience for the Africans as well. As the Sisters recorded in an early Kowak diary, to be read back at Maryknoll, "One of the children, Felicita, is darling but very shy of the Sisters. Her mother explained that she fears us because our skin is white."

The Sisters began to get to know these African women, and gradually to understand the cultural practices so different from anything they had experienced. Fertility, whether of fields or women, was a high value. They observed, however, that women were allowed little time to recover from childbirth before returning to work—whether in the fields or gathering wood for the fire. It took half a day's work to gather sufficient wood for one meal.

Frequently the Sisters saw a tribal woman taken reluctantly to the hut of the man she was promised to, because he had given her father twenty or thirty cows. The Sisters would question, the better to understand such customs. They discovered that African women supported the dowry system as giving stability to the marriage and that it remained a matter of pride. Thus, when several Maryknoll Sisters had cows offered for them, they took it as a compliment and not an affront as they politely declined. The Catholic church in Africa did not oppose the dowry system but tried to prevent it from being commercialized. One custom the church did not accept was polygamous marriage, and African women and men were refused baptism because of it.

Polygamy was an accepted form of cultural and economic life in Tanganyika. Society's concept of wealth and stature involved having many cows and many wives. The male gained more cows through accepting dowries for his daughters and then used the cows to obtain more wives. It was difficult for the newly baptized African to accept the idea of using the cows to better his family's living conditions or to provide educational opportunities for his children.

Given the values of their culture, it took particular strength and courage for any young African woman to break with such established tradition and aspire to join the religious life. The five young women who met the Sisters in 1948 were brave beyond words for they were leaping in hope into the unknown. By 1966, however, there were twenty-three professed Immaculate Heart Sisters and many more in the novitiate. Two decades later, by which time the Immaculate Heart Sisters were independent of Maryknoll's mentorship, their numbers had grown to one hundred. The Maryknoll Sisters found that they also needed courage and tact, as they often protected the African novices from irate fathers and prospective husbands who, because of the dowry, demanded their return.

But Africa's first Maryknoll Sisters, initially viewed with curiosity, gradually gained the people's confidence through education and medical work, especially through child care and nutrition programs for women that sharply reduced the rate of infant mortality. The women learned the rudiments of health care and sanitation, such as the importance of boiling water and milk, while also discovering fresh approaches to agriculture. The Sisters could not singlehandedly undo age-old cultural practices that weighed heavily against women, but their influence was gradually felt as the Sisters' programs strengthened in women a sense of self-worth and dignity. Some men, too, came to appreciate the Sisters' work, if for no other reason than because more educated women made for better wives and mothers.

Between 1948 and 1955, the Sisters established new Maryknoll Sisters' communities and projects, including dispensaries and middle schools in Nyegina, Rosana, and Buhangija. The next major step came in 1957, when the Tanganyika Episcopal Conference asked the Sisters to establish a Catholic girls' secondary school at Morogoro, only the second such girls' secondary school in the impoverished nation.

The Morogoro school, situated at the foot of the beautiful Uluguru Mountains, would be called Marian College. Girls traveled from all over the country to enter Marian. Some were en route for more than a week by canoe, by bus, and on foot, to be greeted on dusty arrival by Sisters Margaret Rose Winkelmann, Dolores Marie Jansen, and Marian Teresa Dury. However, when the first students arrived early from distant parts of the country, the classrooms were not ready—no books, chairs, or kitchen. But this was Africa, where people adjusted readily without pouting or panic. The young women simply went to Ngolole, the African Sisters' novitiate, for a couple of weeks until supplies arrived from the capital, Dar es Salaam, 120 miles away.

The school operated, as in all British colonies worldwide, under the complex syllabus of the Overseas Cambridge Examination. It required teaching material to young women whose cultural horizons went little beyond their simple homes, villages, and the necessities of life. The young women were undeterred, however. When given the opportunity for education, they excelled. In time the graduates of Marian College would include many of the most prominent women of Tanzania, including the country's first woman magistrate, a cabinet minister, a number of doctors and nurses, and one woman who later became the first African headmistress of Marian College itself.

After the country's independence in 1961, the work of the Sisters began to change. Nyerere's vision for Tanzania stressed self-reliance and grassroots development. With his own strong Catholic formation, he began to encourage the church and religious communities in Tanzania to set an example for the people and to cooperate with the ideals of "Ujamaa." Tanza-

nia, in Nyerere's vision, would remain a poor country. But by stressing social equality and an economy rooted in communal village life, he hoped
that Tanzania might offer an example of dignified poverty, free of the
squalid urban slums and unemployment that were the typical by-products
of capitalist "development."

In 1969 all schools were nationalized. The Maryknoll Sisters supported
the policy and within a year had turned over the administration of their
schools to Tanzanian nationals, though many Sisters continued to teach
within them. In 1974, however, President Nyerere personally asked the
Maryknoll Sisters to create an experimental secondary school for young
women who had completed primary school. In keeping with Nyerere's villagization program, the emphasis of this school would be on education and
skills appropriate for rural village life. Thus, as part of the curriculum, the
students would work in the fields and grow their own food. The government gave the land (five hundred acres) in Nangwa, a small village on the
slopes of Mount Hanang in the Arusha region.

According to Maryknoll Sister Bernice Rigney, who worked in Tanzania from 1969 to 1983, "It is probably safe to say that almost any Maryknoll Sister who was in Tanzania during the 1970s was involved in and
supported the policy of Ujamaa. When Nyerere called for the church to be
where the people were, in the villages, it was a call to relocate not only
physically but in values as well. Being with the people implied a different
lifestyle, a daily support and involvement in the principles of Ujamaa no
matter where we lived or ministered." Rigney was among the Maryknoll
Sisters who took this commitment particularly seriously. She and a number
of other Sisters chose to live and work in Ujamaa villages.

The villages were the heart of Nyerere's vision of Ujamaa. He wrote:

> Instead of forty different families each living separately and each
> farming their own land, collecting their own water, and sending their
> children miles to school, they will come together and live in a village.
> Then by their joint efforts, they will—in time—be able to bring water
> to the village; they will be able to build their children's school conve-
> niently near all of them; they will build a community center and a
> store for their mutual convenience . . . They will be working in coop-
> eration, and not in opposition to each other; and they will be govern-
> ing their own village affairs as well as being able to discuss together
> national issues which affect them as citizens of Tanzania.

The Sisters who lived in these villages spent their mornings working in
the communal fields while also tending their own gardens, like the other
villagers carrying their own water from the communal well and carrying

rocks for the construction of the village school or other common projects. The rest of the time was spent in "visiting" among their neighbors or teaching sewing classes with the women.

According to Sister Patricia Hafey:

In the first year our ministry could be described as being a Presence. Actually, it was orientation into their way of life. The people were the teachers (and often the teachers were children), and we were the students. They taught us everything, from "kuchota maji"—fetching water, to planting our fields, to eating beans and bananas from a common tray with grace and dignity, to maintaining social relationships with one's neighbors, by preparing from time to time "kabindi," a thick malt-like beer which the people would drink using long reed straws.

As Bernice Rigney recalls, this was a different approach to mission for the Sisters, and it was equally new for the Africans. "They associated Sisters with schools and clinics. They didn't expect anyone who only wanted to share their daily lives. As relationships were formed we could begin to talk about community and what this could mean to us as Catholics." For Rigney, it was a process of "mutual evangelization."

We came to Katerere hoping to give of ourselves as well as our gifts, talents, and professional abilities. We rather quickly learned how much *we* needed them! We learned from them about life as well as the reality of the gospel message in their village. As this process continued, our days fell into a pattern similar to the rest of the village. We rose early to pray before we went to the fields. In the afternoon we rested before going out to visit or meet with one of the Bible reflection groups . . . Interspersed with all of this would be those necessary things we had to do each day to subsist.

We raised our own food and carried our own water. Like everyone else walking was our mode of transportation. It was important to us that we assume even these small details that made up the life of the villagers. Gradually people began to let us know that it was also important to them. In living with them we were doing more than talking about community or unity. Beyond that we were also honoring the sacredness of their life. I have had people stop, as I was working in our field, and thank me for what I was doing, for the care I was taking with the land!

It was an experience that had profound reverberations throughout the Maryknoll Congregation, beyond the individual Sisters involved, for the import was that mission was not only a matter of *doing,* but also a certain style of *being.* This was part of Tanzania's abiding gift to Maryknoll.

As Rigney says, "It can be an uneasy value reversal for an American to be asked to put aside what he or she does and simply share and rely on being who one is. Yet, in this African cultural context even the willingness to attempt this was already the beginning of a growing solidarity with the people. As we grew to understand the centrality and importance of relationships we further understood the truth of this."

Kenya

From Tanzania, the Maryknoll Sisters began to move into other parts of East Africa. Two years after Kenya's independence from Britain, the Maryknoll Fathers had begun pastoral work in adjacent Kenya in 1965. In 1969, the bishop of the Mombasa diocese, on the Indian Ocean coast, invited the Sisters to help staff a government-supported, church-sponsored hospital in Kinango.

In many respects, Kenya was a marked change from Tanzania. According to Maryknoll Sister Margaret O'Brien, who arrived in Tanganyika in 1955, "As soon as you crossed the border there was a world of difference. In Kenya, you found a lush crown colony, while Tanganyika seemed like a poor country cousin." The contrast between the two countries was particularly evident in the capitals. Kenya's Nairobi was a dense African version of a first-world city, cosmopolitan and urbane. But as Sister Margaret Rose Winkelmann remarked, behind the glittering facade there were growing slums, and in the countryside there were conditions as poor and desolate as anything in Tanzania.

Beyond their work in the Kinango Hospital, the ministries of the Sisters in Kenya developed in ever-widening variety: youth work in Kisii, teaching, organizing cottage industries among the urban poor, establishing special schools for street children, staffing Catholic Relief Services, and, later, involvement in a national program of development education coordinated by the Catholic Secretariat in Nairobi. The ministries were less structured and frequently unsalaried.

Maryknoll Sister Jacqueline Dorr, who had worked on and off as a teacher in Tanzania and in Kenya since 1959, in 1982 became one of three Maryknoll Sisters who formed a "development education team" in the diocese of Marsabit. Using Paolo Freire's techniques of adult awareness-raising—the same methods pioneered in Latin America—the team worked with nomadic and seminomadic people in northern Kenya's desert region near the Kenya-Ethiopia border. However, in a pattern not dissimilar to that faced by Sisters in other countries where they were committed to social change and people-empowerment, some of the strongest resistance the Sisters experienced came from other missionaries in allied ministries. As Dorr explains, "They did not like awareness-raising that encouraged people to question the 'whys' of their oppression, since all too often the people focused on the church as their main oppressor." With few if any government services in the area, it was the church that was largely responsible for social services, and as such it became the target of frustrations.

In 1987, Dorr, along with Maryknoll Sister Perla Laurel, began a new project, working with women ex-prisoners in Nairobi. No assistance was offered to these social outcasts, and as a result it was common for many of them to land back in prison, time and again, usually for the same petty offenses. "Most of these women are destitute," says Dorr, "deserted by family and friends, and frequently without shelter. Most were sentenced simply because they were victims of poverty, lacking the essentials of money, education, skills. Trying to eke out a living by whatever means, they often ran afoul of the law. Most had been arrested for such petty crimes as selling garden produce without a trading license, small thefts, handling stolen goods, prostitution, making illegal beer, or fighting and drunkenness."

What did the Sisters have to offer such women? Some skills, yes, but also friendship, a measure of dignity, and, though they would not have used the Swahili word, perhaps a sense of Ujamaa.

Moving to the Front Line

One of the pioneers in Kenya was Sister Janice McLaughlin, a tall, slender native of Pittsburgh, whose mission vocation had been stimulated as a child by her fourth-grade geography book with its pictures of giraffes loping across a scenic plain. Already she felt, somehow, that Africa was her destiny. She joined Maryknoll when she was eighteen (as soon as they would accept her) and, after completing college, she realized her dream with an assignment to Kenya. By 1970, she was settled in her job as Communications Director for the Catholic church in Nairobi.

Her work included running courses in broadcast and print journalism for African communicators through the ecumenical All Africa Conference of Churches (AACC) and running similar programs under the Kenya bishops' auspices at the diocesan level. The AACC courses could last six months to a year, the diocesan one perhaps a week—but they were equal parts of McLaughlin's conviction that communications was a key to social change.

Not long after McLaughlin's arrival in Kenya, one of her first jobs had been to set up press conferences for a priest deported from white-ruled Rhodesia. Father Michael Traber, publisher of the outspoken Catholic magazine *Moto,* initiated McLaughlin into the complexities of the liberation struggle in Rhodesia (now known as Zimbabwe) and the role the church was playing in supporting the rights of the African majority. It was an auspicious meeting that was to change McLaughlin's life dramatically.

For the next six years, McLaughlin deepened her knowledge of the various liberation struggles in Africa and used her position as communications coordinator to champion the rights of the poor and oppressed. She drafted statements for the Kenyan bishops condemning the Concordat and Missionary Agreement between the Holy See and the Portuguese colonies of Angola, Mozambique, and Guinea Bissau (the document had linked church and state in those colonies); she helped to set up the Liberation Support Committee, an ecumenical group of Kenyan church leaders, which raised support for the liberation movements in southern Africa; and she wrote letters of solidarity to Bishop Donal Lamont, the Chairman of Rhodesia's Justice and Peace Commission, who was arrested by the Rhodesian government in 1976.

In 1977, when she learned that the same Rhodesian Justice and Peace Commission was advertising the post of press secretary, she eagerly applied. In February she traveled to Salisbury for an interview and had her first opportunity to meet the courageous Bishop Lamont, who was under house arrest while awaiting deportation. She was captivated by his Irish feistiness and sense of humor. His moving descriptions of the poverty and oppression of the rural African people filled her with outrage, while his commitment to their cause gave her hope that here was a church that was faithfully following in its founder's footsteps.

Lamont also impressed on her the price that the church paid for this stand. He explained that many of his white parishioners had walked out during his sermons and others had lobbied Rome for his removal. Even some of the other bishops openly opposed his confrontational approach with the minority government. Now the Rhodesian authorities had found him guilty of "failing to report the presence of terrorists and encouraging others to do likewise," sentencing him to ten years of hard labor. A few weeks later he was deported.

This brief taste of life on the front line convinced Janice that this was indeed where she belonged. When she returned to Kenya, she succeeded in convincing the Kenyan bishops and the Maryknoll Sisters as well that she was more needed in Rhodesia. The church in Kenya agreed to "lend" her to Rhodesia for one year, where she was expected to launch a newsletter for the Justice and Peace Commission and train a local Rhodesian to take her place.

There were at that time seventy-seven Maryknoll Sisters in Africa: fifty-five in Tanzania, two in the Sudan, and twenty in Kenya. McLaughlin would be the only one in Rhodesia. Before the year's end she would also be the only one in prison—held without bail under the Rhodesian government's Law and Order Maintenance Act.

A Novitiate in Jail

When Janice arrived in Rhodesia, Ian Smith was the premier of a white government selected from among the country's 250,000 whites to hold total sway over the country's six million blacks. For more than fifteen years, while other former British colonies had received—or claimed—their independence, Smith's Rhodesia, like the apartheid government in South Africa, represented an unyielding mindset. After Britain attempted to force Rhodesia to capitulate, Smith had broken away from the British Commonwealth, issuing a unilateral declaration of independence. The whole world refused to recognize this outlaw state, with the United Nations putting mandatory economic sanctions against the white-ruled country in 1968.

Not surprisingly, the majority African population resisted white domination, taking up arms in 1966 after peaceful means had failed. Two main liberation movements arose—the Zimbabwe Africa National Union (ZANU), led by Robert Mugabe, and the Zimbabwe Africa People's Union (ZAPU), led by Joshua Nkomo. By 1977, the war between these two groups on the one side and the Smith government on the other had engulfed the entire countryside. Even the cities were not spared, with bomb blasts in the center of Salisbury and frequent shell and mortar attacks on Umtali, where Bishop Lamont resided.

Government forces retaliated brutally against the civilian population, whom they accused of being "terrorists" or "terrorist supporters." Angry that they could not stem the guerrilla onslaught, the security forces confiscated the cattle of peasant farmers, burned rural villages, detained and tortured innocent civilians, and murdered many people, claiming that they were "caught in the crossfire" or "breaking the curfew." Seven missionaries had been shot dead at one of the rural missions at the beginning of the year, with both sides angrily trading blame.

Documenting these cases had become the chief activity of the Justice and Peace Commission when Janice arrived on the scene. She was able to compile the information that had already been collected into professional reports and press releases that would begin to appear in the overseas media. These documented reports, complete with photographs, were dynamite under Smith's propaganda facade, and his government wanted them stopped at all cost. A showdown seemed inevitable.

It came on August 31, when Janice and three Commission members were arrested: the Commission's lay chairman, Mr. John Deary; his deputy,

Fr. Dieter Scholz, S.J.; and the Organizing Secretary, a Canadian Marist Brother, Arthur Dupuis. The three men were released the next day on $1,600 bail, while Sister Janice was held in detention. She was considered more dangerous because of entries in her personal diary that the police had confiscated from her home.

In the climate of fear and insecurity that existed in Rhodesia, the attitudes and views that Janice brought from independent Africa were seen as subversive by the white minority government. When she was brought to court, days after her arrest, she was refused bail and accused of being a Communist and a self-confessed supporter of terrorism.

Far more than any of her previous media work, Janice's detention served dramatically to publicize the nature of the Rhodesian government. From the moment of her arrest, the glare of international publicity was fast, intensive, and unrelenting. "U.S. Nun Held in Rhodesia" was splashed on the front page of papers across the United States. "Smith Torturers Exposed," ran the headline in the *London Observer.* Janice's day in court appeared on prime-time evening news across the United States.

Meanwhile, Maryknoll's own communications network, formidable when roused, had also sprung into action with letters, telephone calls, and pressure aimed at the political centers in the United Nations, the Vatican, Africa, and the United States. Maryknoll Sisters as far away as Hong Kong demonstrated for Janice's release in front of the South African Embassy, making the front pages in Asia. The media in East Africa united in solidarity with the nun who had trained many of their leading journalists.

Chikurubi Prison, where Janice was held, was, like Rhodesian society itself, segregated into sections for Africans, Coloureds (as those of mixed descent were called) and Europeans (as all whites were called). Treatment varied according to race, with Europeans receiving better food and a single room with a bed. African prisoners slept on the concrete floor, forty women crowded together in one room, and ate a monotonous diet of vegetables while enduring long days of hard labor on the prison farm.

Janice was held in solitary confinement. But she never felt she was alone. She made friends with her two guards, young African women who were working in prison because it was the only job available. "We have to feed our children," they told her, "but we also support the *vakomana.*" This Shona word, meaning "the boys," was how Africans affectionately referred to the freedom fighters.

Janice soon discovered that the prisoners were ingenious in getting around the rules and regulations and the constant surveillance. Stopping perhaps to tie a shoelace in front of her, they whispered messages of support and encouragement. "I felt part of something bigger than myself," she later recalled. "I felt bigger than myself. I was suffering for a cause, and the pain and fear no longer mattered because I was not alone. I was with the oppressed people, and God was there with us in our prison cells." Jokingly, she would refer to her imprisonment as her "novitiate."

The Rhodesian authorities, however, were deadly serious. Her alleged crimes carried a minimum of seven years in prison. At various points there was talk of life imprisonment or even the death sentence. Extracts from her private diary were read in court to prove that she was a "self-confessed supporter of terrorism" and a Marxist deserving the maximum punishment.

"Prime Minister Ian Smith must be deposed and all the Africans allowed to return," she had written. The most widely quoted item from her diary, appearing in headlines in papers throughout Africa, was her passionate declaration: "If I had a black skin I would join 'the boys.'" Far from discrediting her, the glare of publicity and the state's vendetta against her only served to endear Janice to the African majority. "Not only the church supports you, but the whole country," she was told by a long-serving political detainee. Joshua Nkomo and Robert Mugabe each defended her and criticized the government for harassing her and the Justice and Peace Commission. The church too spoke on her behalf, with the Vatican sending its representative from South Africa to visit her in prison, and the bishops of Kenya, the United States, and Rhodesia issuing strong statements of support.

None of this deterred the Rhodesian government in its intent to punish her. Refusing her application for bail, the prosecutor declared, "The picture presented by the defense of an honest, dedicated, harmless nun is a mistaken one. If she is not a Communist, she certainly admits sympathy with Marxist doctrines. Instead of espousing the goals of Christianity indeed she has been fostering the enemies of Christianity."

Janice denied that she was a Communist, but did frankly admit to a courtroom crowded with nuns and priests that she supported the freedom fighters who were not terrorists and that she believed a revolution was needed in the country "to redress the injustices of the present society. There should be a fairer distribution of wealth and equal opportunities for all."

By this time the avalanche of continuing bad publicity was beginning to overwhelm the Smith regime. After a further week in jail, Janice was taken from the prison and expelled from the country. Good publicist that she was, the Maryknoll Sister took the spotlight with her to Europe and the United States, denouncing the Smith regime without cessation. Her imprisonment had opened doors to all the media exposure she wanted.

Finally, as always, the interest faded. But the resolute McLaughlin spent two years in the United States, raising money for Rhodesian refugees exiled in Mozambique. Then, in 1979, she went to the Tete forests in Mozambique to live with the exiles from the war's atrocities. When on April 18, 1980, Jesuit-educated Robert Gabriel Mugabe ushered in his country's independence, McLaughlin was there to celebrate with the new nation on whose soil she had briefly served, but for whose cause she had fiercely fought.

The Shona people have many names for God. McLaughlin's favorite is "Chipindikure"—The One Who Turns Things Upside Down. This was certainly her own experience of God in Africa. She had entered deeply into the hearts and yearnings of the African people, a reality deeper than the school book pictures of giraffes. From the people of Kenya, Zimbabwe, and Mozambique, she had learned "that people are more important than things; that being is more important than doing; that God and relationships are at the heart of everything."

Each region in which the Maryknoll Sisters serve leaves its inevitable mark on the Congregation. In assessing the influence of Africa, different Sisters, of course, have their own particular judgments. Some point to the Congregation's increased concern for racism and the challenge of inculturating the gospel. Others point to the influence of the African approach to decision making through consensus. The Sisters in Africa imbibe a spirit of celebration, in which meetings are enlivened by dance, storytelling, and poetry. They learn to abhor consumerism, adapting to a simpler style of living. They assume a new attitude toward time (plenty of time, no hurry), toward death (the dead ancestors are ever present), toward aging (the aged are the wise and respected people in African society).

Jennieva Lassiter, a Maryknoll Sister of African American descent from Cape Charles, Virginia, and the granddaughter of slaves, served in Tanzania from 1960 to 1978 ("People were always asking me, 'What tribe do you come from?'"). She says of Africa, "It's what you would want for the whole world. They are very poor—and we don't envy that. But the people seem so open. They know how to celebrate, they know how to appreciate. Life is real there. They are free."

Speaking only for herself, Sister Janice McLaughlin said, "I am a wiser, gentler, more outgoing, more religious, and freer person because of Africa."

But perhaps she also spoke for others.

～ 12 ～

Servants of God

═══════════════════

IN THE EARLY DAYS of Maryknoll, before the era of rapid transcontinental travel and communications, there was a finality to the ceremony of departure. Sisters traveling to China and other "fields afar" left behind their families, friends, and other members of the Congregation in the real expectation that they might never meet again. For many this was the case. Whether by illness, accident, or natural causes, they fell where they worked and were buried among the people they had come to serve. A permanent memorial was set up in the Sisters' cemetery on the Center grounds to record their names.

Hardship was an expected part of the life; the annals of mission history were filled with harrowing ordeals, courage in the face of danger, faith in the teeth of apparent defeat. Indeed, such testimonies, like the history of the early church itself, were often written in blood. But generations of missioners, including the Maryknoll Sisters, had embraced such perils in confidence that the blood of martyrs had always been the seed of the church.

St. Paul wrote in 2 Corinthians:

We prove we are servants of God by great fortitude in times of suffering; in times of hardship and distress; when we are flogged or sent to prison, or mobbed; laboring, without sleep, starving.

There were many Maryknoll Sisters whose experience was described in these words. There were the Sisters in the Philippines, Hong Kong, and Japan caught in the net of wartime occupation, and the Sisters in China and later Korea who suffered imprisonment and exile by the Communists. To their stories would be added the names of modern martyrs in Central America, Sisters who found themselves facing "the same fate as the poor." St. Paul had maintained in his letter that apostles of Christ must be prepared for "honor or disgrace, for blame or praise; taken for imposters while we are genuine; obscure yet famous; said to be dying and behold, we live; rumored to be executed before we are sentenced; thought to be most miserable and yet we are always rejoicing." This formidable and prescient testimony would describe the story of Maryknoll Sisters around the world. In war and revolution, wherever the people of the urban slums and poor rural hamlets mourned, Maryknoll also would mourn. But in the light of God's promises, the Sisters would try to leaven their mourning with rejoicing.

Agneta Chang

Ambassador John Chang (Sister Agneta's brother) telephoned Mother Mary Joseph this afternoon . . . Sister Agneta had been in hiding and was not too well, having had pain in her back. October 4 she was taken north in a truck with many other women. All were shot. The mass burial took place close by in a ditch.
> —Sister Mary Paul McKenna, November 20, 1950

The terse announcement of Sister Agneta Chang's death in Korea confirmed the inevitable end of a long and painful vigil.

Agneta Chang came from a distinguished Catholic family in Korea. Her two older brothers were both priests, and she and a younger cousin both entered Maryknoll in 1921. In her application to Maryknoll, she was asked her reason for wishing to enter a religious community. She answered, "In order to become holy and then to help my country and people." After her novitiate, she was assigned to her own country, where she did catechetical and parish work and acted as a language teacher for the Sisters. She enjoyed a relatively peaceful life until the outbreak of World War II. When the American Sisters were imprisoned by the Japanese and then repatriated, Korean Sister Agneta remained behind to guide and assist in the development of the first Korean women's religious congregation. This Korean Congregation, the Sisters of Our Lady of Perpetual Help (OLPH), was started in 1932 by Maryknoll Father John Morris, who had invited the Maryknoll Sisters to help in this ministry. When war came, there were twenty-nine young Korean Sisters. Because wearing the Maryknoll habit marked Sister Agneta as an "enemy alien" in the eyes of the occupying Japanese military, it was decided that it would be more prudent for her to wear the Korean Sisters' habit until her eventual reunion with the Maryknoll Sisters. As it turned out, that time would never arrive.

For the entire period of the war she and her little band of Korean Sisters were cut off from the rest of the world, with little money and often little food. After five years, in her first correspondence to reach Maryknoll, she wrote to Mother Mary Joseph: "How good it was to receive your handwritten letter . . . As for myself . . . the work is quite trying, especially for a nervous type as myself."

With the end of the war, mail began arriving in Maryknoll from their separated Sister, but the news was uniformly bad. Korea was now divided at the 38th parallel, thus trapping the novitiate and Sister Agneta in the Soviet-administered North. After Russian soldiers invaded the convent, threatening the Sisters with guns and swords, Agneta wrote that she had temporarily disbanded the congregation. Later, after they were reunited, the little community lived behind locked doors with the lights covered.

In 1949 the Soviet troops departed, leaving Korean Communists in control. Concern for Sister Agneta increased, because she came from a politically prominent family in South Korea; her brother, John Myun Chang, was ambassador to the United States. The situation was so dangerous for the Sisters that Sister Agneta could not risk appearing on the streets or even in the novitiate vegetable garden.

Mother Mary Columba Tarpey wanted Sister Agneta to leave, but the local bishop, Bishop Hong, as well as the Korean Sisters, wanted her to stay. Communications show the sense of urgency as the Communists gradually tightened the net around the Catholic community.

To the Korean Sisters' letter requesting that Sister Agneta be permitted to stay with them, the Mother General replied:

> We wish you to know that we deeply appreciate your position and the greatness of your need as you see it. However, I can only repeat what has already been told His Excellency, Bishop Hong, that it is the wish of our Mother Foundress as well as mine and that of our General Council that Sister Agneta be not separated from our Congregation. We . . . are happy to let Sister continue wearing the Korean Sisters' habit until she can with safety again put on her Maryknoll habit.

By 1950 the situation was grave indeed, as can be seen from the St. Valentine's Day letter sent to Mother Mary Columba from the senior Maryknoller in Korea, Bishop Patrick Byrne, apostolic delegate to Seoul. By this time Bishop Hong was himself under arrest:

> Bishop Hong and the arrested Korean priests will come to trial soon, and after that it is probable that the [OLPH] house at Sopo will be taken over by the Communists and presumably the Korean Sisters will be ordered, as were the Benedictine Sisters in Wonson, to "go home."
>
> In accordance with your instructions, word has been sent to Sister Agneta to come out to the South. A few months ago this was very dangerous and some were shot trying to cross the line, but of late it has become easier to do in safety.
>
> So we have hopes Sister Agneta may be with us e'er long.

It was not to be. Couriers sent with the letter had to pass secretly over the dividing line between North and South, at the risk of their own lives. One courier who was caught was executed, and the one who followed him had to turn back before completing his mission. By this time the fate of all clergy and religious was uncertain. Maryknoll Bishop Byrne was himself under arrest (he died in captivity on November 25, 1950). Maryknoll Monsignor George Carroll wrote from Pyongyang on October 30, 1950:

> In Huang-Hao-Do only five priests are left and we know for certain one of them was hanged. Two Sisters of St. Paul de Chartres were beaten to death. Missing beside (Maryknoll) Bishop Byrne are 48 other priests and bishops.

The news of Sister Agneta's fate came the following month. The full details of the story, however, came later from OLPH Sister Mary Peter Kang, Sister Agneta's companion and support for fourteen years. Her eventual letter to Mother Mary Joseph is as heartbreaking to read today in translation as it was in 1951:

> I have tried innumerable times to write to you but I cannot say how many times I took up my pen to begin a letter only to find that all turned black before me and I could not hold back the tears that blinded me. I could only end in bitter weeping.

So began her account, after four months of attempted letters. Having finally begun to write, Sister Mary Peter poured out an eight-thousand-word account of events leading to Sister Agneta's death.

She told of how, after the bishops and priests were being arrested in great numbers, the Korean Sisters worked at night hiding, burning, and burying any English-language books or Maryknoll works that might incriminate themselves or Sister Agneta. "Important papers we took to a faithful Catholic's house six or seven miles away like thieves in the night when all was quiet in sleep."

The courage of some of the Korean Catholics was extraordinary. Joseph Pak, a loyal friend to the Sisters, daily risked death by visiting them, especially in the final week of Sister Agneta's life. He had deliberately joined the local secret police as a spy in order to find out what was in store for the Sisters. Because of his information, the Sisters were usually a half-step ahead of the Communist authorities. Pak had already been arrested once, in the company of Sister Mary Peter, only to be questioned and released.

Pak's courage can be seen from the fact that Bishop Hong himself was arrested by a man who had positioned himself outside the convent all day.

Never knowing when they might themselves be arrested, the Sisters frequently wore all the clothes they had on their backs.

On one occasion, Pak sent word through a small boy that suspicious-looking men were loitering around the convent and they would arrest the Sisters once the convent lights were out. The Sisters filed into the church for a final communion—"in extreme tension we had our sacrament," wrote Sister Mary Peter—but that was not to be the night.

With other displaced Sisters of various congregations coming to the convent at Sopo, the authorities' attention was constant, as were the searches and interrogations. Sister Agneta herself was torn between going South or staying with her community. By this time, even her companions wanted her safely gone.

Word came that the convent must be disbanded and the Sisters sent home to their villages. A secret messenger from the South said he would return for Sister Agneta twenty days after the convent was disbanded, for it would be natural then for her to be wandering in the country. Sister Agneta wore a back brace as a result of a serious injury she had suffered some years before. It left her in constant pain. On this pretext, Sister Agneta checked herself into a hospital, reasoning that an escape from the hospital to go South would not bring down official wrath on the local church people. This plan, too, was abandoned. In time she went to a Catholic village where she regained some strength. The villagers openly supported and loved her and Sister Mary Peter. Most of the other Sisters had been tearfully dispersed, the community disbanded. Efforts were under way to obtain a medical exemption for the now bedridden Sister Agneta from conscripted civil defense work.

"Oh please forgive me," wrote the distraught Sister Mary Peter, "but this is how our Sister Agneta departed."

These men said, "We must quickly take her to the mobilization unit hospital in Sunan to be diagnosed." After arguing with them for two hours, they called out all the neighbors who were Catholics, making them carry our mother's bed to an ox cart. None of them said a word but obediently put her on it, covered only in a quilt. As she was pulled along the narrow hill trail she cried, "Lord have mercy on us," and in a loud voice repeating prayers and telling me not to follow but to inform Brother Conrad (a Benedictine).

"The time was about eight in the evening," continued Sister Mary Peter. "The world was wrapped in dusk. The only sound was that of the ox cart jogging down the quiet mountain trail together with the groaning and sound of her prayers. Oh miserable night! My heart seemed to shatter and break into a thousand pieces and it seemed pitiless to me that the ground did not cleave open."

Sister Mary Peter and some other OLPH Sisters made their way to South Korea. Twelve others remained in the North, where their fate was never learned.

El Salvador

Thirty years later, in a small Central American country named for the Savior, a small assembly of priests, nuns, and campesinos watched and prayed as the limp bodies of first one, then two, and finally four North American women were dragged by ropes from a shallow grave on the edge of a cow pasture. They had been shot in the head at close range, and their bruised and broken bodies showed the signs of a horrible ordeal. The faces of the witnesses were contorted with horror and grief. Many of them had known the women—two Maryknoll Sisters, an Ursuline nun, and a young lay missioner from Cleveland—among them the American Ambassador, Robert White, who kept repeating, in impotent rage, "They're not going to get away with this! They're not going to get away with it!"

What road had led these women to El Salvador and finally to this makeshift grave? Indeed, what road had led the Maryknoll Sisters from Korea and China, where they had been persecuted at the hands of Communists, to a time when they would themselves be targeted as Communist subversives and dispatched without pity?

Ironically, it had been the Cuban Revolution of 1959 and the specter of Marxist-inspired revolution that had prodded the church in Latin America to take seriously the horrendous gulf between the rich and poor. The same fears that had inspired such American development programs of the 1960s as the Alliance for Progress caused the church to undertake an active social ministry. Only drastic reform, it appeared, could stand in the way of more radical alternatives. In this light, Pope Paul VI issued an urgent appeal to the church of Europe and North America to send clergy and religious as missioners to strengthen the struggling church of Latin America, an appeal that was answered by thousands of men and women, including, in large numbers, the Maryknoll Sisters. The experience of these missioners among the peasants and urban poor caused many of them to see the world and the gospel with new eyes and to question whether there was any common cause between the church and the anti-Communist defenders of the status quo.

Latin American governments and their allies in the United States spoke of development and reform, but their real interest seemed to be nothing more than containing "Communism"—a label attached to any effort at serious social change. Rather than tolerate any significant affront to the interests of the elite, U.S.-backed military governments emerged throughout Latin America in the 1960s and 1970s, committed to a doctrine of National Security. According to this doctrine, the military was engaged in a permanent war against subversion; at stake was the defense of the family, private property, the honor of God and country. The enemies of these values—who were broadly lumped together as "Marxists"—could be recognized by their identification with the poor and their commitment to such "Communist line" slogans as "social justice," "human rights," and "democracy."

Christians were increasingly conspicuous among these agents of so-called subversion. Under the impact of the church's "option for the poor," thousands of priests, religious, and lay people were proclaiming a vision of God's peace and justice that was at radical odds with the oppression around them. Peasants and workers began citing the book of Amos and the Gospel of Luke in affirming their rights.

The military governments responded with savage force. Torture and methods of assassination achieved scientific refinement, along with a new fate—"disappearance"—that simply consigned its victims to oblivion. First lay people, then priests and religious, and finally even bishops would be added to the list of martyrs. Unlike the martyrs of Korea and China, they were the victims not of left-wing but of right-wing extremists. There was nothing to distinguish the methods, cruelties, or relentlessness of the one extreme from those of the other. The irony, however, was that the generals, the torturers, and the death-squad assassins dared to call themselves Christians. This was the anomaly. Their victims did not die simply for clinging to the faith, but for clinging, like Jesus, to the poor.

In all the suffering witness of the church in Latin America, it fell to El Salvador to expose in glaring relief this modern-day Way of the Cross. With five million people in a land the size of Massachusetts, El Salvador was one of the most densely populated as well as one of the poorest countries in the hemisphere. In 1979, 50 percent of the population was illiterate; three out of four children suffered from chronic malnutrition; three out of five families had no access to water; 250,000 families lived in one-room shacks; less than one percent of the population owned 40 percent of the arable land, most of this dedicated to export crops such as coffee, cotton, and sugarcane.

It seemed that this was the way it had always been in El Salvador, and so the ruling oligarchy was determined that it should remain. A peasant uprising in 1932, suppressed with savage cruelty, was remembered simply as *La Matanza* (the massacre). It had served effectively for forty years as a deterrent to any efforts at social reform. Peaceful efforts at change were brutally repressed. But once awakened, the people's yearning for justice and recognition of their human dignity would not be easily repressed. One man who helped awaken them was Archbishop Oscar Romero.

It would be hard to exaggerate the importance of this Christian prophet in the life of the church in Latin America or as a source of inspiration for the Maryknoll Sisters. A conservative bishop from a poor background, his appointment as Archbishop of San Salvador in 1977 had delighted the oligarchy as much as it disappointed the progressive clergy of his diocese. He would not have been anyone's choice as a man to question the status quo. But with the assassination of his friend, Jesuit Father Rutilio Grande—the first of a dozen priests to fall in El Salvador—Romero underwent a conversion as astonishing to his friends as to his foes. From a once timid and conventional cleric, there soon emerged a fearless and outspoken champion of justice and voice for the voiceless. His weekly sermons, broadcast by radio throughout the country, would feature an inventory of the week's violations of human rights, casting the glaring light of the gospel on the realities of the day. His increasingly public role as the conscience of the nation earned him not only the bitter enmity of the country's oligarchy, but also the resentment of many of his conservative fellow bishops. There were those among them who muttered that Romero was talking like a subversive.

He did not back down in the face of threats. He said:

> I rejoice, brothers and sisters, that our church is persecuted precisely for its preferential option for the poor and for seeking to become incarnate in the interests of the poor . . . How sad it would be in a country where such horrible murders are being committed, if there were no priests among the victims.

His sermon of March 23, 1980, was the last straw. In a passionate voice he chronicled the sufferings of the people at the hands of the military and called on soldiers to cease obeying the illegitimate orders of their superiors: "In the name of this suffering people whose laments rise to heaven each day more tumultuous, I beg you, I ask you, I order you in the name of God: Stop the oppression." The next day, while celebrating Mass in the chapel of the small hospital where he lived, he was shot and killed by a sharpshooter's bullet.

The death of this towering shepherd was a terrible blow to the church of the poor. Only days before his death, Romero had said:

> My life has been threatened many times. I have to confess that as a Christian, I don't believe in death without resurrection. If they kill me, I will rise again in the Salvadoran people . . . Martyrdom is a grace of God that I do not feel worthy of. But if God accepts the sacrifice of my life, my hope is that my blood will be like a seed of liberty and a sign that our hopes will soon become reality.

In the following months, three Maryknoll Sisters would also fall: Carla Piette, Ita Ford, and Maura Clarke. In each case, the example of Romero had posed a personal challenge, disclosing both the radical ideal of God's Reign and the costly path of discipleship.

What were they like, these three women? Ordinary and human: the gregarious, extroverted, pun-loving Carla Piette, who experienced periodic emptiness but found solace during her lowest points in the words of Scripture; the reserved, sometimes uncertain Maura Clarke, who courageously weathered the Vatican II transition to a deeper understanding of mission; the petite, peppy Ita Ford, who wrestled with God, demanding answers with the determination of an Old Testament prophet. They experienced fear, certainly, and doubts at times. They were sustained not only by faith, but also by friendship and love, and so found the strength to answer, when they were finally called by name, "Here I am, Lord."

These were "three women of faith," wrote their Maryknoll president, Sister Melinda Roper, "three women whose faith was a gift that permeated all their personalities, their relationships and their mission." In a preface to Maryknoll Sister Judith Noone's account of their deaths, *The Same Fate as the Poor,* Roper continued:

> They were not blind to the evil and sin in the world, nor were they naive about its causes. The wisdom of their faith was that their lives were not focused *against* evil and sin but *upon* the holiness of human life. Their wisdom flowed from the person, message, life, death, and resurrection of Jesus.

As Roper stated, the manner and moments of these deaths were extraordinary "for most of us from the U.S. because we were not attuned to the reality of martyrdom in our world today."

Carla

Carol Ann Piette was nineteen and a Marquette University student when she entered Maryknoll in 1958. She was described as "friendly, outgoing, jovial, big-hearted and generous, but rather naive and tactless." Six years later she was in Chile where, while being welcomed with a party, she "delighted everyone with skits and songs"—and the next day cried at the cold and strange impersonality of the Immigration Office.

Language school was at the country town of Puçon, where she saw clearly the extreme poverty of the many and the extreme wealth of the few. Rather than refining her knowledge of Spanish, she tended to spend her free time reading the poetry of Pablo Neruda and the works of Nobel Prize-winning novelist Gabriela Mistral.

Chile at that time had two particularly influential bishops, Cardinal Raul Silva of Santiago and Bishop Manuel Larrain of Talca, who were outspoken in their support for economic change. In 1962, the Chilean bishops had issued a farsighted pastoral letter, "Social and Political Responsibility in the Present Hour," which called for agrarian reform and other structural change. The bishops had matched their words by turning over diocesan land to the peasants.

The period of social reform blossomed with the election of President Eduardo Frei, a Christian Democrat and former student of Bishop Larrain. The inwardly sensitive Carla, inspired by the possibilities for change, nonetheless would write home to her sister, Betty, that she would walk home amid the poverty and misery repeating over and over, "I believe, Lord, help my unbelief"—"That poverty of spirit," she wrote, "that comes with the awareness of our own limitations is ever present."

She could embarrass bishops with her uninhibited spontaneity, saying to one who corrected her when she addressed him in Spanish using the familiar *tu,* "You are my father, are you not?" Her openness was disarming, her criticism of clericalism continual, her ability to surprise constant. At the ceremony for her final vows, instead of walking up to the priest who had raised the host for her to receive, after she had pronounced her vows, she gestured to the priest that she would be with him shortly. She then walked to the microphone, where she asked everyone to be seated.

"Because I love God and Maryknoll and you, my dear, dear friends, I am able without wavering to promise to live as a Maryknoll Sister and to serve you until the day I die."

Ita

Ita Ford first joined Maryknoll in 1961, but withdrew for reasons of health in 1964, just two weeks short of her first vows. However, the call never left her, and in 1971 she applied for readmission. The attraction to mission life may have been in her blood. Her father's cousin was the famed Maryknoll Bishop Francis X. Ford, who had died in a Chinese prison camp in 1952 when Ita was twelve.

It was in 1972 at the Maryknoll language school in Bolivia that Sister Ita Ford was confronted by the blatant wealth of a minority, "smelled the poverty of the masses and was amazed how casually and blindly they could live side by side." She was en route to Chile, "to what and where I do not know. Being in South America, I'm learning to live with a lot of unknown factors."

Among the factors, unknown at the time but to a few, was that Chile's military with the aid of the CIA was preparing to dismantle the oldest democracy in Latin America. In the elections of 1970, the government of Frei and the Christian Democrats had lost power to the socialist Salvador Allende. His election enraged Chile's conservative elite and their allies in the United States. Allende's program included nationalization of Chile's copper industry and a broad range of reforms in health care and social welfare. Despite the fact that he was democratically elected, Allende appeared to his enemies as an agent of Marxist totalitarianism. The Nixon administration directed millions of dollars to a covert program aimed at destabilizing his government. It ended in 1973 with the bombing of the presidential palace and the death of Allende in a military coup.

By this time Carla had moved to La Bandera, one of the capital's slums or *poblaciones*, a hastily and crudely constructed shantytown for rural people who had migrated to the city. Ita Ford joined her there. Ita was not long in the country, however, when the coup hit. In fact, it occurred just as she was trying to fly back to the States to attend her father's funeral. The capital was sealed tight for ten days; during that time, thousands of students, workers, and other suspected enemies of the junta were swept up and executed.

Within a few short weeks, Ita and Carla became fast friends. As Judith Noone puts it, "they were opposite and alike: Carla, outgoing, boisterous, argumentative, large in size and presence; Ita, retiring, unimposing, listening, petite—they made an incongruous pair. But what they shared most deeply was a seriousness about life that touched humor and felt pain, and was impatient with anything less than the truth or contrary to the Kingdom of God. In common, too, was a love for the people of La Bandera."

Under the military government life went on, but it was never free of tension. The Sisters' house was searched for subversive materials; close friends were arrested and tortured. For the people of La Bandera, the business of life was simply a struggle to survive.

In 1977, Ita was due to return to New York for her Reflection Year, a year of theological studies prior to taking final vows. She delayed for a year, partly out of concern for Carla and her combined volatility and anguish over the misery around them. Finally, in 1978, Carla gently pushed Ita out of Chile, assuring her friend, "I'll do my best to stay out of trouble; don't worry about me. This is something you have to do."

It was Ita who got herself into trouble; a hit-and-run driver slammed into a car in which she was riding. She was hospitalized for more than a month with a broken pelvis and torn knee, but her determination to return to Chile soon had her exercising and walking to build back her strength in record time.

Repression continued in Chile, but by 1979 a different Latin American country had come under the spotlight of media attention. In Nicaragua, pressure was building to oust Central America's longest-standing dictatorship, the dynasty of the Somoza family. A revolution pitting Sandinista rebels against the country's National Guard was in full swing. The Maryknoll Sisters were caught in the midst of the turmoil, and from outside their colleagues watched and worried. In July Somoza fled the country, leaving the Sandinistas to march triumphantly through the streets of Managua. Out of the darkness of Latin America, it seemed as if the possibility of a new day had dawned in this impoverished country. Carla volunteered to join them.

Ita returned to Chile in time to see Carla off in January 1980. But Ita was already contemplating her own move. From New York she had been transfixed by the voice of El Salvador's Archbishop Romero. She attended to his words:

> I am a shepherd who with his people has begun to learn a beautiful and difficult truth; our Christian faith requires that we submerge ourselves in this world. The essence of the Church lies in its mission of service to the world. The world the Church ought to serve is the world of the poor, and the poor are the ones who decide what it means for the Church to really live in the world . . . The poor are the Body of Christ today. Through them he lives in history.

Such words seemed to epitomize the vision of the Maryknoll Sisters, as reflected in their 1978 General Assembly. The final statement of the Assembly read in part: "The saving mission of the poor is becoming visible to the Church and offering hope to our world. Solidarity with the poor is not an option but a sign of the Kingdom that must be made explicit in our day. We commit ourselves to the cause of the poor through the witness of our lives, our words, and our ministry."

There were only two Maryknoll Sisters in El Salvador, overworked, under constant threat from the death squads, and appealing for colleagues to share the mounting load. Along with Ita, there was another Maryknoll Sister at the Sisters Center, also weighing that appeal as she contemplated her next step.

Maura

When, in 1963, Sister Maura Clarke was notified that she had been named superior of the Maryknoll Sisters' community in Siuna, Nicaragua—a place so small it was not even a dot on many Nicaraguan maps—she said, typically, "there simply must be some mistake."

In 1959, an evaluation prior to her final vows reads: "Sister is the most selfless, generous, outgoing person I have ever known. Her only fault, from my observation, is that she never thinks of keeping her own self together and sometimes goes off in something not quite recognizable as a Maryknoll habit. Just the same, she is an easy person to be with, and a very fine Sister."

Maura Clarke was born in 1931 in Brooklyn to Irish immigrant parents who moved so often that Maura described them as a family of "Irish tinkers." During her freshman year at St. Joseph's College for Women, intending to become a teacher, she decided also to become a Maryknoll Sister. "I am attracted to the missioner's life," she said. "I feel I could do this kind of work. I want to become closer to God. I want to serve Him."

In her book, Sister Judith Noone wrote of Maura Clarke that "while she never really questioned the clarity of God's call, she tended throughout her life to underestimate the quality of her response." Her first assignment was teaching first grade in a parish in the Bronx, a neighborhood so high in crime and low in income that it was classified by the Archdiocese of New York as "mission territory." After five years there, in 1959, she was notified of her next assignment to the parish school in Siuna.

Siuna was a gold-mining town owned by a Canadian company. The miners and their families lived in extreme poverty, at the mercy of company policies and company-controlled law enforcement. Maura found the poverty a marked contrast to the opulence that existed inside "the Zone," the enormous enclosed compound—complete with golf course, private club, manicured lawns—that existed for the mine officials and their families.

Gradually the Sisters began to question their own lifestyle—modest, but still far removed from the condition of Siuna's poorest. Ever-generous Maura, who would give away her hairbrush, toothbrush, and allowance, was an easy and gullible target for a sad story. Her fellow Sisters would sometimes suggest to her that instead of generosity, perhaps the situation demanded attention to the causes behind the people's needs. Maura and the Sisters sought to translate their beliefs into their mission. And it was under an anxious Maura, nine years after she had arrived, that the Maryknoll Sisters decided they would best serve Nicaragua by leaving Siuna.

After a year back home in 1969 to nurse her ailing mother, Maura returned to Nicaragua in 1970 to a slum on the edge of Lake Managua. Protests against the repressive rule of Anastasio Somoza (Junior—his father was assassinated in 1956) were growing, increasingly joined by priests, religious, and Christian lay people.

That year two natural disasters affected the Sisters' lives and altered the course of Nicaraguan history. In October, Lake Managua flooded forcing the Sisters and their neighbors to move to drier ground, a former cotton plantation now dubbed Operacion Permanente de Emergencia Nacional, or OPEN III. The word OPEN would soon become a glaring shorthand for Nicaragua's poverty. Slightly more than two years later, a major earthquake killed ten thousand Nicaraguans, leaving another one hundred thousand homeless. OPEN III swelled to accept them. Maura lived there for three years.

The Somoza family had its hands in nearly every economic enterprise in the country, including the water company supplying OPEN III. In 1976, the Maryknoll Sisters were part of the fight against paying exorbitant rates for drinking water. Writing to her parents, Maura noted, "I enjoyed hearing about the U.S. Bicentennial and the beautiful tall ships. We had planned to get together for a celebration, but it wasn't possible as we are having this big campaign here in the barrio about the price of water. Pray that the poor do not suffer, but gain a little something from this."

Maura returned to the United States in the fall of 1976 to do mission education work in Catholic parishes and schools. She continued to keep track of the "water fight" and Nicaraguan affairs, and prayed for the campesinos and her colleagues at her retreats. As the repression worsened, she participated in Nicaragua awareness programs. In 1978, she spoke during a rally protesting U.S. aid to Somoza's government and urged those present to appeal to President Carter and Congress to recognize the just struggle of the Nicaraguan people.

In 1979, she rejoiced from afar at the downfall and exile of Somoza and the triumph of the people's struggle. The cost had been terrible—as many as fifty thousand had died—and Maura's rejoicing was clouded at having failed to accompany the people through these steps along their journey. Maura's three-year assignment was finishing, and she was eager to return to Nicaragua. "And yet," she wrote, "since El Salvador has been made a priority for Sisters with Latin American experience, I may be going there."

Three Sisters, Carla, Ita, and Maura, were now all facing Central America as the fateful year approached.

The Final Witness

Carla had barely arrived in Nicaragua when she perceived that the greater need was now in El Salvador. Since she was not yet committed to any work, she found it easy to move on, lured by the prospect of working in the archdiocese of Romero. The decision was already made when she received the news that Ita, too, was bound for El Salvador. The friends would be together again. However the reunion would occur under a cloud: Carla arrived in El Salvador on the day of Romero's assassination, while Ita arrived just after his funeral. They found a church in a state of shock, dispirited, and lost.

Under the circumstances, it was no longer clear what kind of work Carla and Ita should do. They accepted an invitation to work in Chalatenango, a rural department in northern El Salvador with a population of two hundred thousand, mostly landless campesinos. Suspected to be an area of rebel strength, Chalatenango had been declared a military emergency zone and as such had been subjected to brutal military "pacification" campaigns. These efforts to "clean out" the countryside of subversion drove thousands of families from their homes and villages. Anyone caught in the army's sweep was a potential target, but community leaders, including teachers and lay catechists, were in particular danger.

Carla and Ita improvised their work as they went about, assisting refugees, shepherding priests on the run, delivering supplies, offering solace to the grieving and support to the isolated and terrified catechists. "This may seem strange to you," Carla wrote in a letter, "but as the repression and genocide continue, it becomes harder and harder to do pastoral work. So what do I do? I drive people places."

The emotional stress of the situation, and the uncertainty of their circumstances, left Carla and Ita relying more than ever on one another for support and encouragement, struggling "to keep walking down this dark road without becoming as dark as the situation." They became a familiar pair in the region—*Carla y Ita* sounded like the single Spanish diminutive, Carlita—"the one large like the strong woman in the Gospel," as one priest described them, "the other fragile like a reed in the desert."

Their travels brought them face to face with the spectacle of death, sometimes in scenes little removed from hell. In one village the security forces had killed twenty-five people and refused to let their families bury them. Instead they had to watch as their bodies were devoured by vultures in the open air. After meditating on the text from scripture, "I will take away your heart of stone and give you a heart of flesh," Carla remarked that she had long ago prayed for a heart of stone.

And yet they were joined in a strange peace, drawing strength from the faith of the people and the conviction of the gospel that where death abounds, there life even more abounds.

In a birthday letter to her niece, Jennifer, Ita wrote:

> What I want to say, some of it isn't too jolly birthday talk, but it's real. Yesterday I stood looking down at a sixteen-year-old who had been killed a few hours earlier. I know a lot of kids even younger who are dead. This is a terrible time in El Salvador for youth. A lot of idealism and commitment are getting snuffed out here now. The reasons why so many people are being killed are quite complicated, yet there are some clear, simple strands. One is that many people have found a meaning to live, to sacrifice, struggle, and even die. And whether their life spans sixteen years, sixty or ninety, for them their life has had a purpose. In many ways, they are fortunate people.

Brooklyn is not passing through the drama of El Salvador, but some things hold true wherever one is, and at whatever age. What I'm saying is that I hope you can come to find that which gives life a deep meaning for you, something that energizes you, enthuses you, enables you to keep moving ahead.

I can't tell you what it might be. That's for you to find, to choose, to love. I can just encourage you to start looking and support you in the search.

On August 23, Carla and Ita responded to a call to transport a prisoner being released from jail. Although he had been jailed as a subversive, the people at the parish center didn't trust him and begged the Sisters to return him to his village. Though night was approaching and rain was expected, they set off for the man's home, some thirty minutes away. They had not gone far when a heavy rain began. Their road crisscrossed a shallow riverbed, normally dry, which they had already crossed four times before the swelling water made them turn back. They deposited their passenger and were setting off to cross the final bend when the waters rose with a sudden fury, turning their jeep on its side. As the jeep filled with water Carla—the "strong woman"—managed to force Ita out the window, where she was immediately swept along with the raging current. Helplessly she bobbed down the river. "You're not going to get up," she remembered saying, adding the short prayer, "Receive me Lord." But eventually, a couple of miles downstream, she managed to cling to some roots and found the strength to hold on. As if from outside her she heard the words, "The Lord has saved you to continue serving the poor and you've got to get out of the river."

Ita was rescued the next morning. Later that day, they found the body of Carla, broken and naked, washed up on a sand bar some nine miles from the scene of the accident.

The days following the funeral were heavy with Ita's grief. She related:

Carla and I had talked lots of times about the possibility of our dying because of things here, very violent things. We talked about how difficult it would be if we weren't together for the one who was left behind. At the very end of St. John's Gospel there is a little scene of Jesus with Peter, and John seems to be in the background. Jesus says to Peter, "Follow me." Peter turns around and says, "What about him?" And Jesus says, "I'm telling you to follow me and he's to wait until I return." If John was within hearing distance, how did he feel? I think we know now.

There was some question of whether Ita should remain in El Salvador, but she was determined to carry on. Maura Clarke, who had been in the country less than a month, volunteered to become her partner in Chalatenango. Ita gratefully welcomed her companionship. No one could replace Carla, but, as Ita recognized, "Maura's great gift of kindness and love will be great for the traumatized, hurting people." And she added, "She'll be great for me, too."

The violence, the sorrows, the daily travels continued. They made constant exhausting trips into the countryside to deliver supplies or to pick up refugees. "The other day," wrote Maura, "passing a small lake in the jeep I saw a buzzard standing on top of a floating body. We did nothing but pray and feel." They found the survivors of military sweeps, people who had been sleeping for weeks in the hills, foraging for food, even bearing children in the open. Such refugees were regarded by the army as rebel sympathizers. If not, why did they flee from the army? And those who helped them—even nuns—were clearly subversives too.

Whenever they could, Maura and Ita enjoyed getting together with a pair of missioners from Cleveland, Ursuline Sister Dorothy Kazel and a young lay woman, Jean Donovan. They used to joke that being among Dorothy and Jean—with their blond, blue-eyed, and obviously *gringa* looks—made them feel safer.

In November, Maura and Ita flew to Nicaragua for the annual regional assembly of Maryknoll Sisters in Panama, Nicaragua, and El Salvador. Maryknoll Sister Maria Rieckelman, a psychiatrist from the United States, had flown in for the week. She found Maura in good spirits, "at home with the old gang again," but Ita seemed withdrawn and distracted. She was grieving for Carla and spoke of how hard it was to be constantly among people burying their dead or looking for missing family members.

Maura, Maria recalled, appeared to be in better shape, "dealing with the horror quite well. She spoke of the mutilated bodies and the little children but it was if she were walking through it with the sense that God was going to bring good out of that tremendous evil, and she was very conscious of her faith."

The meeting in Nicaragua began with a Thanksgiving dinner, which was interrupted by news of the Salvadoran police's brazen murder of five leaders of the opposition umbrella organization, the Democratic Revolutionary Front, who had been abducted from a meeting in downtown San Salvador. There was no escaping the pall of death.

By the last evening of the meeting, December 1, Ita seemed to have recovered her good spirits. The group affirmed their solidarity with the church in El Salvador. Maura acknowledged her fears but entrusted herself to the love of God. Ita, asked to read a prayer, chose an excerpt from one of Romero's homilies:

> Christ invites us not to fear persecution because, believe me, brothers
> and sisters, one who is committed to the poor must risk the same fate

as the poor. And in El Salvador we know what the fate of the poor signifies: to disappear, to be tortured, to be captive and to be found dead.

They finished with a party; Ita joined in the singing, and Maura offered a demonstration of an Irish jig.

The next day, December 2, the Sisters went their separate ways, Maura and Ita back to San Salvador. Their Cleveland friends, Dorothy and Jean, were at the airport to meet them in their white minivan. As yet unknown to the women, their arrival was observed by a group of waiting National Guardsmen, who had been ordered to wear civilian clothes for a special assignment.

Maura and Ita, Dorothy and Jean were never seen alive again.

∼ 13 ∼

A Time To Mourn

THE PUBLIC ADDRESS SYSTEM in the Maryknoll Sisters Center delivered its stark message: "Sisters, please assemble in chapel."

It was almost 1:10 P.M., just after lunch, on December 4, 1980. In the offices, corridors, lounges, and nursing home floors of the Sisters Center, the listening Sisters knew that the news, whatever it was, had to be bad. An immediate call to the chapel was a very rare occurrence.

Filled with foreboding and awaiting news of the events unfolding in El Salvador during the previous twenty-four hours, the Sisters made their way to the long chapel. As they took their places in the chapel, they saw at the microphone near the altar the solemn face of their president, Maryknoll Sister Melinda Roper. Seated near her was Maryknoll Sister Maria Rieckelman, who was just back from the regional assembly of Maryknoll Sisters serving in Panama, Nicaragua, and El Salvador, and attended by Sisters Maura Clarke and Ita Ford.

By now most of the Sisters knew that Maura and Ita had been missing since their arrival in San Salvador. Some of them had been kept busy during the night trying to confirm details from El Salvador and fielding telephone calls from the media. The only special event planned for the day was an afternoon Eucharist and Sending Ceremony for Maryknoll Sister Mary Lou Daoust, to signal her pending departure for Guatemala.

Several generations of Sisters were gathered. A few elderly Sisters, some still garbed in the original habit and others in everyday clothes, brought with them memories of earlier announcements, recalling tragedies from China, Korea, or the Philippines in decades past. All who arrived in the chapel entered past the plaque on the rear left-hand side wall, commemorating the death in North Korea of Sister Agneta Chang.

From the foot of the altar, Melinda Roper told them that the four women were missing and that it was fairly certain they had been killed. Their burned-out minivan had been discovered on the road from the airport. Maria Rieckelman told of being with the Sisters in Managua. She described the manner in which her plane from Managua, when it landed in San Salvador en route north, was searched by the army, who examined all the passports as if they were seeking someone in particular.

After the brief announcement from the altar, many Sisters stayed in the chapel to pray, while others returned to their duties with heavy hearts. By 2:30 P.M. the Maryknoll Sisters knew the worst—that Maura and Ita, Dorothy Kazel, and Jean Donovan, had been murdered. Their bodies had been discovered and identified.

So it was that later that afternoon the Eucharist originally planned for Daoust's Sending Ceremony became, instead, a gathering and grieving for the four women. Before the liturgy began, with Maryknoll Father John Halbert as presider, Rieckelman gave a brief account of her last twenty-four hours with Maura and Ita. Roper again addressed the Sisters, employees, and the many Maryknoll Society members also now assembled in the Sisters' chapel: "As we approach the altar now to celebrate the Eucharist, let us have forgiving hearts."

What type of woman was this who, in a moment of acute tragedy, could immediately move to ensure that no bitterness or thoughts of revenge be allowed to take hold? The clues were in the recent past. When in November, 1978 she had been elected the Sisters' president, Roper had concluded her remarks at the Eucharistic celebration of the day:

> As we read the Gospel there are some qualities that we can't do without, either as persons or as a Community. At this moment in my life I would describe them in the following manner:
>
> —A forgiving heart, or an attitude of forgiveness. In our world it isn't sufficient for you to forgive me or for me to forgive you. We don't forgive out of fear or smallness of heart, but out of the courage and greatness of our hearts.
>
> —And this is what we are about to celebrate in our Eucharist—we celebrate our suffering, our death, and our hope in the new life in the death and resurrection of Jesus. And why?
>
> —"So that sin may be forgiven"—and perhaps one of the strangest mysteries of our faith as Christians is that we celebrate suffering, death and resurrection with GRATEFUL hearts.

Now at the liturgy for the four women, where tears were plentiful and grief tangible, it was difficult to be either forgiving or grateful. But on that day and in the days to come, Roper would continue to provide depth and perspective on the four women's deaths, stressing, on the one hand, that their fate had resulted from their faith and from their option in life to walk with the poor and on the other hand, that the death of these four North American women must not be isolated from the larger tragedy of the people of El Salvador.

In a press release issued on December 4, Roper reminded all that "for some fifty years the Salvadoran people have been struggling for freedom from military rule. Disappearances and killings are nothing new to this war-torn country but have instead increasingly become the order of the day. It is estimated that nine thousand people have been killed in the last year alone, 80 percent of these deaths attributed to paramilitary groups covertly backed by the government."

In the next four years of her presidency, Roper, always a powerful speaker, seemed to redouble her efforts to explain both the "why" and the "risks" synonymous now with the life of the missioner and the Christian. In her role of leadership she had been given a special responsibility to point to the thousands of Salvadorans who had met the same fate and to extract from all that suffering a revitalizing account of Christian faith.

In the sixty-eight years of the Congregation, a number of different women, possessed of contrasting gifts and personalities, had occupied the office of president, and before that, Mother General, of the Maryknoll Sisters: Mother Mary Joseph Rogers, Mother Mary Columba Tarpey, Mother Mary Coleman, and Sister Barbara Hendricks. Some were remembered for their organizational abilities, others for their vision, personal warmth, or spiritual depth. Regardless of the differences, it seemed many times that some inspiration managed to match the leader with the demands of the time. This was never more true than in the election of Melinda Roper.

Before the General Assembly of 1978 that elected her, Roper had spent the previous fifteen years doing pastoral work in Mexico and Guatemala. A simple and retiring person who disliked public speaking, she was respected for her spiritual depth and the strength of her convictions. Steeped in Scripture, she had an ability to articulate both the faith dimensions of the Sisters' lives and to make sense of the political. All these qualities would be in sore demand.

Roper's term of office posed the challenge of leading the Maryknoll Sisters during a time of particularly public visibility. Although only two of the four women killed in San Salvador were Maryknoll Sisters, the name of Maryknoll became indelibly associated with this tragedy, helping to galvanize public outcry and a movement to resist U.S. policies in Central America. The death of the four women prompted a tremendous outpouring of support from the American church. But as the churches in North America became a significant obstacle to these policies, so too the Maryknoll Sisters, for the first time in their history, found themselves publicly reviled from conservative quarters, forced to justify their faith and mission. That was the public challenge that Roper met. But there was another, more intimate role to fulfill: comforting, consoling, and ministering to the Congregation during a time of stress and sorrow. For the death of Ita and Maura was only the beginning of a series of losses, great and small, that befell the Congregation in these years.

Roper's experience among the poor of Central America gave her a special sensitivity for the experience of the Sisters in that region. No one who had worked in Guatemala during those years could avoid wrestling with the reality and meaning of human suffering. And this would be one of Roper's particular themes, both in the aftermath of the Sisters' deaths and in the years to come. Of the poor of Central America, she said:

> Many of them inspired me, taught me to pray and opened my heart and mind to the word of God in ways that I never could have imagined had they not shown me with their lives, words, and prayer. Above all, they called me to life through their suffering. They called me to question, to confront, and to embrace that which is most tragic and most tender in human experience: suffering.

In her frequent reflections on this theme, Roper was able to differentiate the social and religious dimensions of suffering. On the one hand, the death of so many people, like the Sisters in El Salvador, was the result of social structures and political policies that must be challenged and resisted. On the other hand, such deaths were related to the passion and death of Christ; they had the power to draw believers more deeply into the mystery of faith that teaches that life, and not death, is the final meaning and calling of our existence. As the Sisters, in their deaths, had entered more deeply into the suffering of the poor, so too they had been conformed more deeply to the spirit of Christ, who said that there was no greater love than to lay down one's life for one's friends.

While speaking forthrightly about such issues as U.S. military aid to the Salvadoran government, Roper kept insisting that this stance was rooted in a religious vision. And if she posed a challenge to her country's government and its supporters, she posed a challenge as well to those demonstrating against these policies to look beyond politics and to draw their energy from a deeper well:

> Liberation and solidarity with the poor, if they are not to deteriorate into merely economic, political, and theological theories, must be rooted in the lived experience of hungering and thirsting for justice and of actively pursuing truth and justice with forgiving hearts. Liberation *from* unjust systems, structures, and relationships and liberation *toward* just societies where the human community is free to live in God's peace, respecting the dignity and beauty of each person, are integral to the coming of the Reign of God.

One of the greatest dangers that I, personally, experience in the process of liberation in solidarity with the poor is that of becoming so absorbed in struggling against the injustice and of naming the evil, that I fail to be creative in searching out alternatives—my dreams and my hope seem to be so vague at times.

For four years, month after month, Roper maintained her steady voice, and maintained too the balance between outrage and hope. Her forthrightness and clarity helped the Congregation to grieve and to coalesce in its sense of what mission demanded. "She was our miracle," says Maryknoll Sister Peg Dillon, looking back on that time. "As fast as we all grew, Melinda was always just ahead of us, calling us to take the next step."

Bearing Witness

One thing that soon became clear to all was that Maura's and Ita's deaths had not occurred in a political vacuum. As it happened, their murder occurred only weeks after the presidential election of Ronald Reagan, who was determined to stamp out the threat of "Marxist Communism" in Central America. In dogged pursuit of this goal, his administration was prepared to bend and bypass national and international law, as well as the U.S. Constitution, to roll back the Sandinista revolution in Nicaragua and to bolster the right-wing government of El Salvador through massive military aid.

There were, however, obstacles to this policy. The murder of the four churchwomen in El Salvador had called attention to the overwhelming violations of human rights in that country, mostly attributable to the Salvadoran armed forces and its unofficial death squads. Public concern, much of it stimulated by religious communities and churches, forced Congress to make military aid to El Salvador contingent on progress in the area of human rights. In the eyes of the Reagan administration, those who protested against human-rights abuses in El Salvador were serving, wittingly or not, the cause of subversion in the hemisphere.

The new administration had not officially taken office before its representatives began making excuses for the four churchwomen's murderers while apparently blaming the victims. On December 16, Reagan's designated U.S. Ambassador to the United Nations, Jeanne Kirkpatrick, told reporters she did not believe the government of El Salvador could be held responsible for the deaths of the four churchwomen.

"The nuns were not just nuns," she told the Tampa *Tribune's* Washington correspondent, "the nuns were also political activists. We ought to be a little more clear about this than we actually are. They were political activists on behalf of the Frente (the Farabundo Marti National Liberation

Front) and somebody who is using violence to oppose the Frente killed these nuns. I don't have any doubts about that and I don't think those people are in control of the government. The death squads are not agents of the Salvadoran government."

In congressional testimony on March 18, 1981, Reagan's Secretary of State, Alexander Haig, went even further, presenting his own fanciful version of events, breathtaking in its departure from all the available evidence:

> I would like to suggest that perhaps the vehicle in which the nuns were riding may have tried to run a road block or may have accidentally been perceived to have been doing so and there may have been an exchange of fire. And perhaps those who inflicted the casualties sought to cover it up. This could have been at a very low level of both competence and motivation in the context of the issue itself.

The next day, again before a Senate committee, he attempted to explain and elaborate on this theory, stating falsely that an autopsy on one of the women showed the presence of glass fragments. This suggested that she had been shot through a car window, causing other soldiers to panic and try to cover up the evidence of this mistake. "I laid that out as . . . one of the prominent theories as to what happened; and I hope that it does not get distorted or perverted emotionally and incorrectly."

Asked specifically about the suggestion that the nuns may have tried to run through a roadblock, Haig responded with a tone of amazement: "You mean that they tried to violate . . . ? Not at all, no, not at all. My heavens! The dear nuns who raised me in my parochial schooling would forever isolate me from their affections and respect."

Senator Claiborne Pell asked Haig what he had meant by the use of the term "exchange of fire." "Did you mean that the nuns were firing at the people or what did 'an exchange of fire' mean?"

Haig chuckled with amusement at the suggestion: "I haven't met any pistol-packing nuns in my day, Senator. What I meant was that if one fellow starts shooting, then the next thing you know they all panic."

Haig's "prominent theory" was evidently a concoction that had little to do with the readily available facts of the case: that the women were picked up on the way home from the airport; that they were killed many hours later in a different place; that they were shot in the head at close range; and that before being killed they were raped. There was no evidence of glass in their bullet wounds. There were no bullet holes in the abandoned minivan or other evidence to support the "roadblock" theory.

As Anthony Lewis of the *New York Times* commented, "Whatever the effect of Haig's comments in El Salvador, they say a good deal about their author. An American Secretary of State, talking about the vicious killing of four American women, suggested that they were responsible in some measure for their fate. The next day, challenged, he tried to slither away, joking and expressing amazement and blaming the press."

The Maryknoll Sisters had known suffering and tragedy before in their history. The deaths of the four missioners in El Salvador was a watershed, partly because it represented such a direct consequence of the model of mission that had been emerging since Vatican II. The Sisters were not singled out because they were perceived as "enemy aliens" or because of any outright hostility to "Christianity" as such. They were killed because they had insisted on seeing and defending in the bodies of the poor the living image of God. Melinda Roper defined this mission vision thus:

> My understanding of our mission today is to bring consistently and perseveringly the perspective and cause of the poor, oppressed, and repressed of our world into all dimensions of life in our society and to do this in the spirit of the gospel.

While there had always been a risk for Sisters caught up in war and social upheaval, now as the Sisters found themselves ever more directly challenging the social structures of the world, they experienced a more general sense of vulnerability. What had happened to Maura and Ita, Dorothy and Jean, might happen anywhere. This realization was sobering as it was potentially terrifying, and the Sisters found themselves acknowledging more openly the stress and anxiety of their lives.

It was no accident that Maryknoll Sister Maria Rieckelman, not only an experienced missioner but also a psychiatrist, had been present for the Sisters' meeting in Managua, attended by Maura and Ita. She had been invited there, as she was to other communities around the world, to help the missioners cope with the pervasive pressure unavoidable in the midst of such poverty and violence. Maura and Ita were not the only ones at the meeting to speak of their frustration, anger, and unresolved grieving. All, to one extent or another, had been exposed to suffering, terror, and death, yet were trying to deal with such violence rather than let it numb them to reality. The presence of Maria Rieckelman represented a progressive change that had taken place in the Maryknoll Sisters' self-understanding. They had long known, despite the public image, that they were ordinary women. But only recently had they begun to realize they needed help dealing with the pressures of their lives. Such had not always been the case. In earlier years there had been no formal process, for example, to debrief the exiled China Sisters or the Philippines survivors of interrogation, torture, and imprisonment. Even later, after the Sisters experienced political violence in Chile, Guatemala, or the Philippines, the need to talk out the emotional trauma or stress with professional counselors was little understood.

But there were deeper questions beyond the Sisters' own problem of coping with a terrible situation. It was natural for them to ask themselves what they could do to change the situation itself. One task, for which they were amply qualified, was to bear witness to the North American people of what they had seen and heard and so raise the consciousness of American Catholics regarding conditions in the Third World.

In the 1980s, the Maryknoll Sisters took on increasingly public advocacy on behalf of the Central American people, protesting military aid to El Salvador and U.S. support for the contras in Nicaragua. The Sisters' longtime presence in Central America gave credibility to their testimony; they became a widely respected source of information about human rights in the region—and thus an irritant to the U.S. administration. In so many ways the Sisters' account of reality contrasted sharply with the version propagated by the U.S. government. According to the latter, the United States was promoting economic stability and democracy in Central America by training and supplying the armies of El Salvador and Guatemala and the contra rebels of Nicaragua in their battle against Marxist subversion. According to the Sisters and many other religious witnesses, on the other hand, the United States was pursuing a war against the poor, supporting corrupt oligarchies in the ruthless suppression of the people's hopes for a just and peaceful life. As Melinda Roper put the matter simply: "I attempt to view our government's policies from the perspectives of the poor. As a result, my perspective is obviously different from that of the U.S. government."

The public advocacy of the Maryknoll Sisters was broader than Central America and included other work on behalf of peace and disarmament, opposition to militarization in the Philippines, and support for a Nuclear Free Zone in the Pacific. All of these efforts involved criticism of U.S. government policies. But nowhere was the contrast in perspective more acute than when it came to assessing the meaning of the Sandinista Revolution in Nicaragua.

Nicaragua

The Maryknoll Sisters had a great deal of experience in Nicaragua, having arrived there in 1944. The first group was honored by an invitation to dine in the presidential palace with the dictator, Anastasio Somoza, and his wife. The Sisters found Somoza "a very amiable person, educated in the States and speaking fine English." By the 1970s, however, they had traveled a long road in their estimation of the Somoza family. From their original work in the mining town of Siuna to their later presence in the slums of Managua and the rural countryside, the Sisters had come to see up close the impact of four decades of Somoza rule on the poor of that country. Anastasio Somoza, killed by an assassin in 1956, was succeeded by his son,

Anastasio, Jr. Both maintained their rule through the brutal arm of the National Guard and used their power to amass fantastic fortunes.

The 1972 earthquake in Managua had been a turning point. The capital city was devastated, with a loss of ten thousand lives and many more left injured and homeless. Maura Clarke and other Sisters had shared the terrible first moments of the quake, barely escaping from their collapsing convent, and then witnessed the subsequent suffering and orgy of greed. While the poor were crowded into "temporary" settlement camps like OPEN III and downtown Managua was left in rubble, millions of dollars in donations for earthquake victim relief and rebuilding found its way into the Somoza family's pockets. It was out of the growing dissatisfaction triggered by this outlandish corruption that a broad consensus emerged in the country that the Somozas must go.

It was another seven years before the end finally came. In the meantime, popular support had turned to the Sandinista guerrillas as the best hope of driving Somoza from power. Formed in the 1960s, the Sandinistas were named after Augusto Sandino, the peasant general who fought against the occupying U.S. Marines in the 1920s and 1930s before his assassination by Somoza, Sr. Now, through their audacious challenge to Somoza and their idealistic program for social change, the Sandinistas had won support not only from the poor but also from many business leaders and even the Nicaraguan bishops. By the summer of 1979, the country had erupted in open civil war, with the National Guard indiscriminately bombing the cities and countryside in an effort to forestall the inevitable.

On July 19, 1979, with Somoza on a plane to Miami, the Sandinistas marched into Managua amidst a cheering throng. Maryknoll Sister Peg Dillon was among the crowd gathered in the central plaza to meet the triumphant "boys and girls," as they were popularly called. "The enthusiasm was tremendous," she recalls. "There was a feeling that this victory belonged to the entire Nicaraguan people. And at the same time, I noticed these mothers holding up pictures of their children as the trucks rolled by, asking 'Have you seen my son?' 'Have you seen my daughter?' Even in the midst of the euphoria you couldn't forget the tremendous price that had been paid."

Many of Dillon's friends and neighbors had helped pay that price. She had lived for nine years with a community of Maryknoll Sisters in OPEN III, the vast slum and squatter settlement on the outskirts of Managua. The barrio was reputed to be a hotbed of subversive activity, and the Sisters had earned the suspicions of the National Guard, not only for their part in community protests against exorbitant water and transportation rates, but also for their work in organizing "base communities" in the parish. According to Dillon, "In the base communities, we would read stories from Scripture and then ask the people to relate those stories to the stories of their lives. Inevitably, as people grew in faith, they grew in their desire to serve their neighbors and the wider community, just as they grew in their criticism of injustice in society." When Dillon arrived in OPEN III in 1970, she found people ready for Basic Christian Communities. By July 19, 1979, the day the barrio was renamed Ciudad Sandino, the number had grown to hundreds. It was people like these, long schooled in thinking not only of their own interests but also of the good of society, who immediately committed themselves to the work of the revolution.

One of the distinctive features of this revolution had been the widespread involvement of Christians at every level in the struggle. The new government included four priests in the cabinet—including Maryknoll Father Miguel D'Escoto as foreign minister. Many priests and religious Sisters enlisted themselves in the grassroots tasks of rebuilding the country and supporting the projects of reform. Among the first projects of the revolution was a massive literacy campaign organized by Jesuit Father Fernando Cardenal. The purpose of this campaign, which employed tens of thousands of volunteers, including many Maryknoll Sisters, was to equip the poor to become conscious participants in transforming their lives and the society. Similar programs were begun in health education, land reform, and urban renewal.

The glorious promise of these early days did not last. Conflicts soon erupted within the new coalition. Not all who had supported the ouster of Somoza had necessarily reckoned on a full-scale revolution. Middle-class and wealthy Nicaraguans were alarmed by the pace of change and challenged the Sandinistas' claim to legitimacy. Conservative church leaders were not at all happy about the high-profile presence of priests in the government and accused the Sandinistas of manipulating religion. Somocista exiles in Miami charged that the revolution was in the hands of Marxists. And with the election of Ronald Reagan in 1980, there was soon an unbridgeable gap between those who saw the Sandinistas as well-intentioned champions of the poor and those who saw them as devious agents of international Communism. Reagan, for his part, regarded the defeat of the Sandinistas as the critical priority for his administration. He imposed an economic stranglehold on Nicaragua and with the CIA and elements of the exiled National Guard set about forming and supplying a rebel army known as the "contras."

To generate public support for this program, the Reagan administration engaged in unrelenting demonization of the Sandinistas, portraying Nicaragua as the worst violator of human rights in the hemisphere and even—in the most hysterical scenario—as a staging ground for a possible Soviet invasion of the United States. It was typical of U.S. officials to insist that all rebellion in the hemisphere was the result of Soviet subversion rather than the product of generations of oppression and frustrated hopes for peaceful change.

While Americans were deluged with Sandinista horror stories, there was little awareness of the growing horror of the contra war. The contras' principal weapons were sabotage and terror. In the countryside, all those identified with the revolution—whether as teachers, health workers, or community leaders—were targeted by the contras for kidnaping and assassination. Maryknoll Sisters working in the northern provinces shared the people's tension in face of the encroaching violence. In January 1985, one of them, Maryknoll Sister Nancy Donovan, had a brief but close encounter with the contras.

It happened when the bishop of Esteli called a meeting for all religious working in that northern diocese. San Juan de Limay, where Donovan worked, had been under siege for six months, caught in the crossfire between the government and the contras. "We had spent most of the time either in the cemetery or saying novenas for the dead," she said, and under the circumstances the Esteli meeting sounded like a welcome relief.

Donovan had just started the trip, traveling on a pickup truck crowded with refugees from a recent contra attack, when they were stopped by an armed patrol of uniformed contras. She was detained all day with about twenty others. Over the contras' walkie-talkies they could hear screams and gunfire from another nearby ambush. The contras knew Donovan by name, and knew too that she was an American religious. Eventually they let her go, possibly prompted by her reminder of the consequences if she were harmed. After walking back to Limay, she learned that ten people had been killed in the shooting she had heard over the walkie-talkie. One of the refugees detained with Donovan, a seventeen-year-old boy named Freddy, was not found for another three days. His fingernails had been removed and acid had been thrown in his face before he was killed.

Back in the States, Nancy Donovan took her story to the American public, describing the positive aspects of the Sandinista revolution, and decrying the human costs of the contra war. She received particularly wide exposure when she appeared on the Phil Donahue television show.

"The fact is," she told the television audience, "I had to tell the people I talked to that I had seen a lot of good things happen to the poor with the Sandinista revolution. I did not see anything good that the contras had done. There was [during the Sandinista years] much more sense of dignity and of purpose among the people in Nicaragua than in Mexico or Guatemala. There was a feeling of hope despite the blood, the shortages, the fear. There was a purpose, a target we were striving for. We are working for the poor. When I worked in those other countries I worked against the system; in Nicaragua we were working as much as possible within the system."

The Sisters were not uncritical apologists for the Sandinistas. But as Donovan explained in radio and newspaper interviews during the course of a six-week national tour, the World Health Organization had declared

Nicaragua "a model country" in health care. In five years infant mortality had dropped from 121 per thousand to 58 per thousand, a change that reflected the revolution's commitment to those at the bottom. It was achievements such as this that were under assault by the contras.

Nevertheless, it was difficult to communicate such facts to an audience bombarded with anti-Sandinista rhetoric. Donovan, driving toward an interview at a Denver radio station, could hear herself described on the car radio as a "self-avowed Marxist." On the air, she told the show's host, "I don't look much like a guerrilla," as indeed she did not. "But this contra war," she would insist, "is just not right. And you have to tell people because they haven't seen it—they haven't been there."

But the Sisters had been there. Their presence in Nicaragua and throughout Central America gave them considerable exposure and credibility during this period of national debate. They found themselves serving as witnesses to what they had seen and experienced. Sister Peg Dillon, who had returned to the States in 1980, devoted the next four years to speaking to whoever would listen about her experiences in Nicaragua. "I must have spoken to hundreds of groups—church groups during the summer, elementary, high schools, and colleges during the school year." In each talk she tried to challenge her audience not just to understand what was happening in Nicaragua, but to think about "how in their own lives they could connect their story to God's word, and how they could learn to express their love not only on a personal and interpersonal level, but on a social level"—as the poor in Nicaragua were trying to do.

Congressman Thomas Downey (D-NY), who represented a heavily Catholic Long Island district, experienced first-hand the impact of the Sisters' testimony. When Downey was visited by several Maryknoll Sisters just returned from Central America and unhappy about the Reagan military buildup there, Downey suggested they take their message to his constituents. He recalled that for months afterwards, people would visit his New York office to discuss Central America. "I would ask them how they'd heard about it," said Downey, "and they'd say, 'Well, this nun came to talk.'"

By speaking in churches and public gatherings, the Sisters were not simply raising consciousness about political policies and their effect on the poor—there was also an element of "reverse mission." By bearing witness to the faith and suffering of the world's poor, the Sisters were delivering an urgent spiritual message to their relatively affluent audience in North America. As Melinda Roper put it, the poor of the world are in mission to the affluent: "They are inviting us to repent and believe; to enter into the living parable and paradox of the Reign of God in our moment in history."

But there was a price for this public exposure. With the 1980s, the Sis-

ters found themselves the object of considerable criticism and even vilifica-
tion by the conservative and right-wing supporters of Reagan's policies. In
1981, Pat Buchanan ran a syndicated column that read, "Maryknoll Order
Dyes Its Roots Red." William F. Buckley told readers of the New York *Daily
News* that Maryknoll was pro-Marxist and antipope. When House Speaker
Tip O'Neill admitted that Maryknollers had influenced his opposition to
Reagan policies in Central America, he was rapped by the syndicated col-
umnist Cal Thomas with the headline, "O'Neill listens to wrong voices on
Nicaragua."

Increasingly, the Sisters became experienced and sophisticated in getting their message across. The Congregation's Office of Social Concerns
(OSC), founded in the mid-1970s, increased its staffing in order to facilitate and coordinate responses by the Sisters to issues of peace and justice.
Sister Helene O'Sullivan, director of the OSC from 1981 to 1985, worked
alongside family members of the four slain churchwomen, the Lawyers
Committee on Human Rights, and the Washington Office on Latin America to push for a thorough investigation of the 1980 murders. That painstaking work, undertaken with support from many church people and others
of good will—including some in the U.S. Congress—finally led to the 1984
prosecution of the five National Guardsmen who committed the crime.
(This was only a partial victory; the high-ranking military officers who ordered the crime and participated in its cover-up were never punished.)

The public voice of Maryknoll Sisters on behalf of peace and justice
continued throughout the 1980s. This voice was further strengthened in
the Sisters' 1984 General Assembly with the election of Maryknoll Sister
Luise Ahrens as the new president of the Congregation. The Mission Vision of the 1984 Assembly said: "As we are received in different lands, we
are invited to journey with the people, especially the poor, the oppressed,
the abandoned . . . and we encounter God's saving love in ways that are
new." In January 1988, at a gathering of American religious congregations
on the eve of a showdown vote in Congress on continued U.S. assistance to
the Nicaraguan contras, Ahrens declared: "We cannot keep silent. We cannot keep silent while the United States pursues a course of violence, injustice, and immorality."

Reflecting on this period, Maryknoll Sister Sandy Galazin, director of
the OSC from 1985 to 1989, observed that the 1980s made the Sisters more
aware of the public dimension of their vows and of the enormous credibility and name recognition that Maryknoll had developed within the U.S.
church. "We want to be faithful to what we have experienced in walking
with God's poor," said Galazin, "and to be precise in the language we use to
communicate that experience. The 1980s showed us the wisdom of Jesus'
words, 'be wise as serpents and gentle as doves.'"

Signs of the Cross

This was the public and at times controversial face of Maryknoll during those years. But there was another side, less visible to the public, but so painful that this period would be remembered by the Sisters not only as an age of social action but as an age of grief.

The grieving did not begin with the murder of the Sisters in El Salvador. That event had simply brought home the terrible fact that the Sisters in many countries were surrounded by ineffable suffering. The burden of seeing church people tortured and murdered, of working with refugees and families dying from the effects of repression and poverty, contributed to an often overwhelming environment of sorrow and loss.

Besides the terror and warfare in El Salvador and Nicaragua, there was the situation in Guatemala, where violence against the rural Indians and the church had become a raging storm. The army's hostility toward the church and its efforts to promote the welfare and consciousness of the Indians was such as to recall the days of the Roman catacombs. Catechists were resorting to burying their Bibles in their cornfields or carrying consecrated hosts hidden between tortillas. Maryknoll Sister Bernice Kita and other Sisters caught in the midst of the violence eventually joined the thousands of refugees who were escaping from the terror into southern Mexico.

At the same time, Sisters were living under dictatorships in Chile, Bolivia, and South Korea. In the Philippines, under Ferdinand Marcos's martial law, Maryknoll Sister Helen Graham was compiling testimony on torture and human-rights abuses, only to be accused on national television of being a Marxist. In the Sudan, Maryknoll Sisters were surrounded by a civil war.

In the midst of this turmoil, the Congregation was visited by a series of personal losses. On July 22, 1981, Maryknoll Sister Pam Beans, only twenty-eight years old, was struck and killed by a passing car as she got off a bus. A beautiful and talented young woman who had only just concluded her first year of work in Chile, she was called by the bishop who presided over her memorial service "a gift of God to each of us." In her evaluation of the past year she had written, "This year's experience has strengthened my belief that all things, no matter how difficult they seem, work together for good for those who have faith. The faith of others—the Sisters, my friends, and the Chilean people—has given me faith and hope through their love and example to live out my commitment to Jesus here in Chile with them."

In December 1982, there came a terrible shock that again, ominously, called for a summons to the chapel. The Sisters gathered with a chill of dread, expecting a repetition of the news of Maura and Ita. But this time it was the news that a plane in Chile bearing two members of the Central Governing Board, Maryknoll Sisters Peg Hanlon and Gertrude Vaccaro, along with forty-four other passengers, had crashed and exploded, leaving "no survivors."

Their bodies, identified in part by their "dear old rings," were returned to Maryknoll for burial. Their coffins were draped with an Andean and an Oriental cloth, to signify the regions—Bolivia and Hong Kong—where Hanlon and Vaccaro had worked. After the Mass the Sisters processed to their nearby cemetery under a pouring rain. As one Sister wrote, "I'd like to be poetic and say that the heavens wept, but in reality it wasn't romantic or poetic. It was muddy and drippy and sloppy and miserable, and maybe that expressed how most of us felt. So, in the pouring rain, under a gray sky, we said goodbye to our Sisters, friends and leaders, Peg and Gert."

And then a third member of that fated Governing Board, Maryknoll Sister Regina McEvoy, succumbed to cancer in December 1983. McEvoy had entered Maryknoll in 1955 and worked with Sister Mercy at Queen of the World Hospital in Kansas City. In that time she and Mercy had become good friends, and they were later reunited in their experiment in contemplative community in New York's Lower East Side. McEvoy had lived there among the poor, offering her witness of prayer, until the 1978 General Assembly that elected her to serve as vice president of the Congregation. As a woman immersed in prayer and the love of God, and at the same time possessed of a playful, teasing touch, she had helped to sustain the Congregation and the Governing Board during a difficult period.

Now faced with this loss, Melinda Roper could only recall the words of Jesus:

> "Blessed are you who mourn, for you shall be comforted." Mourning is not the same as feeling sorry for ourselves and for others, nor is it one step away from discouragement and despair. To mourn is to be moved in the depths of our being by the fact that we are limited; to accept that fact is the key to letting go of ourselves. It is the initiation to human freedom and joy.

But this was not the end. One month later came the news from Bolivia. Two Maryknoll Associate Sisters—Sister Geraldine McGinn of the Sparkill, New York, Dominicans and Sister Gilchrist Conway of the Indianapolis Sisters of Providence—were caught in a flash flood in Charamoco and drowned along with two other women. The Maryknoll Associate Sisters program, which enabled Sisters from other congregations to participate in mission with Maryknoll Sisters, had begun in 1974. At the time of the Charamoco accident, forty-three women from thirteen other congregations had shared the Maryknoll Sisters' life in mission. Both McGinn and

Conway had joined the program in 1981, inspired in part by a desire to replace the fallen Sisters in El Salvador. They had taken up this challenge well aware of the risks. At a ceremony at which Gerri and Gilchrist received their mission crosses, they had been told that "the cross is a reminder of the life, death, and resurrection of Jesus, and that those who wear it, do so as a sign of their willingness to live, to suffer, and even to die with and for the people among whom they are sent in mission."

No Maryknoll Sister had ever entered the Congregation because she looked forward to death. Each had been drawn to mission out of an experience of God's promise of life and a desire to share that with others. With every new loss—whether by accident, or assassination, or the common mortality of the flesh—the Sisters were reminded that each of them, in accepting the ring of Maryknoll, had made a commitment to give everything and to go wherever God's Spirit might call. The burden of the cross was easier for being shared, and so life went on. New members of the Governing Board were selected. The pastoral work among the people continued, and there were still moments in that dark time when a glimpse of God's Reign and the promise of the resurrection illuminated the path ahead. Still, the loss of beloved friends, talented colleagues, and trusted leaders could not but take its inevitable toll.

And it fell to Melinda Roper, as it had so often during her administration, to offer some word of grace, to articulate the meaning of this time for the Sisters, and to call them all to take the next steps:

> Our journey is and will be much like that of those who have preceded us. We may grow weary of pursuing justice with forgiving hearts. Some of us will be tempted to substitute ritual for life and to multiply our prayers, sacrifices, and fasts, instead of embracing the mystery of God's wisdom in Jesus Christ. Others of us will be tempted to abandon ritual, prayer, and fasting as hypocritical and false until that day when the poor, the widow, and the orphan experience justice.
>
> It seems to me that since our 1978 General Assembly we have grown in our understanding and in our pursuit of justice in the spirit of the gospel. Now may be a moment in our history when we are being called to a new understanding that, just as there is no true worship without justice, so there is no true justice without worship.
>
> As we contemplate the mystery of God's wisdom and as we come before God made poor through our suffering, we continue our journey into the night. Our eyes are not fixed on the star because for some of us it has disappeared—but we know that it is there. We must wait with the patience of the poor. We must be free to travel when it appears. As a community of faith, we peer through the darkness anxious for a glimpse of the road ahead.

Seventy-one years ago, three women of faith began the journey through Maryknoll. Many have lived and died in mission through Maryknoll during these years. We continue the journey—sometimes moving with heavy, weary steps; sometimes moving with swiftness and joy; sometimes waiting in darkness.

Today we continue our journey together with simple, loving trust in our hearts. We go with many peoples around the world—beyond this place, beyond this moment, beyond our visions and dreams: to worship the living God.

～ 14 ～

Saving Grace

═══════════════════════

There is nothing more astonishing than life, just as it is, nothing more mirac-ulous than growth and change and development, just as revealed to us. And as happens so often when we stop to regard God's work, there is nothing to do but wonder and thank Him, realizing how little we planned, how little we achieved, and yet how much has been done.

—Mollie Rogers, 1936

MANY OF THE WOMEN who were attracted to enter Maryknoll have shared the experience of having met Maryknoll Sisters whom they admired as women involved in meaningful ministry and community. Others, especial-ly among the older Sisters, first encountered the Maryknoll vision through reading *The Field Afar* or later *Maryknoll Magazine*. But all have easily iden-tified with Mollie Rogers' description of the ideal Maryknoll Sister:

I would have her distinguished by Christ-like charity, a limpid sim-plicity of soul, heroic generosity, selflessness, unfailing loyalty, pru-dent zeal, gracious courtesy, an adaptable disposition, solid piety, and the saving grace of a kindly humor.

It is a statement that transcends cultures and nationalities. But if such qualities of character represent the common ideal, Mollie Rogers was just as committed to the individuality of each Sister. She wrote:

Each one of us, in her own work, with her own particular attrac-tiveness is to be used by God as a particular tool to do a particular work ... That explains our spirit, an attempt to keep our individ-uality, casting out what is objectionable in it, finding what is good and beautiful, and using them not for ourselves, not for any honor or distinction, but only with the thought that they will be used for God's honor and glory.

It was this respect for individuality that attracted one of the youngest Maryknoll Sisters, Miyoko Kudo of Japan, who joined the Maryknoll Sisters in 1987. "I didn't want to be a 'nunny-bunny,' living a restricted life," she says with a mischievous smile. "I was attracted to the Maryknoll Sisters who have so little pretense, who keep their own lifestyles, respecting each other's differences." Kudo arrived at Maryknoll after years of thinking about religious life, having lived with Mother Teresa in Calcutta, studied nursing, and worked with famine victims in Ethiopia. It was in Japan that she met her first Maryknoll Sisters. But she admits that it was the deaths of Sisters Maura Clarke and Ita Ford that made her think seriously of Maryknoll: "I asked myself, what congregation is it that would have women murdered for peace and justice? That event really opened my eyes and my heart."

Miyoko Kudo represents not only a new generation of Maryknoll Sisters but another emerging trend—the increasing proportion of Maryknoll Sisters from outside the United States. The ideal of a crosscultural Congregation is also rooted in Mollie Rogers' vision. After her first trip to the Far East, she welcomed women from Japan and Korea who were called to mission within the charism of the Maryknoll Sisters. So from the earliest years of the Congregation, the Maryknoll Sisters have welcomed women from all nationalities. In fact, this is one of the distinctive differences between the Congregation and the Maryknoll Society. In accord with the Society's efforts to assist in building up the local diocesan clergy in its mission areas, membership in the Society is, in principle, open exclusively to men who are citizens of the United States. The Maryknoll Sisters, in contrast, include women from twenty-two countries. Apart from North America, the largest numbers are from Asia: thirty-six from the Philippines, eight from Japan, five from Korea, three from Taiwan, three from Hong Kong, two from Indonesia, and four from China. Though the majority of Maryknoll Sisters are from the United States—the percentage from other countries is just over 16 percent—among new entrants the percentages are reversed, with the majority of new vocations entering from what were once considered "mission lands."

The effect of this movement has been that the Maryknoll Sisters—who were founded with the ideal of foreign mission—have come to recognize mission not exclusively in geographical terms but in the sense of crossing cultural boundaries. In the past, as the Sisters recognized in their 1984 General Assembly, "religious life was a culture all its own; we all became women religious and cultural blending was superficial." But increasingly the Maryknoll Sisters affirm the cultural diversity within their own Congregation as a sign of the universality of the gospel and a gift to the wider church.

If there is cultural diversity within the Congregation, there is greater diversity than ever before in the forms that mission takes for the Maryknoll Sisters today. Although the center of mission remains evangelization—the proclamation and witness to the gospel—the Sisters have traveled a long way from the early documents of the Congregation that spoke of saving souls in heathen lands. As one Sister commented, "Mission is the proclamation of the Good News of Jesus Christ that human life has meaning." This mission is a total way of life that assumes various shapes. Many Maryknoll Sisters are involved in some form of pastoral ministry, whether helping to form local Christian communities among the poor and marginalized, training lay catechists, or promoting a richer knowledge of Scripture and the life of faith. This is rarely detached from an effort, at the same time, to promote social awareness and a concern for justice. In 1987, the Sisters in Bolivia described their region's priorities as "accompanying the poor by choosing a simple lifestyle and striving to understand their culture and language, deepening our awareness as women, and working for the change of oppressive patriarchal structures, empowering youth, promoting a participation and liberating missionary pastoral focus in the Bolivian church."

Of course, mission still takes the Sisters to the periphery. In 1988, the Congregation opened a new mission presence in Nepal. Work with refugees around the world remains a particular focus. In the 1980s, the Sisters were working with refugees in El Salvador, Guatemala and Mexico, Nicaragua, Hong Kong, Thailand, the Sudan, and elsewhere. In 1987, four Sisters went to Somalia in response to the refugee crisis there. At the same time, Sisters Maria Colabella and Pat Maher were working with Central American refugees in Brooklyn and Pennsylvania, respectively.

The latter point to another important area for the Sisters—Mission USA, now explicitly recognized as one of the significant fields of mission work. The very first mission assignment of Maryknoll Sisters in 1921 was among the Japanese immigrant population in Los Angeles, California. That assignment was soon followed by another to Seattle, Washington, and then over the years to many locations in the United States, usually among cultural and racial minorities. Even so, mission within the United States was often regarded as a stepping-stone to "real mission." But with the Sisters' growing understanding of mission in transcultural and not just geographical terms, there is less inclination to differentiate between mission "at home" and mission abroad. Crossing from one culture to another does not require a passport to another country, as the ongoing influx of refugees and immigrants to the United States has made evident. However, one of the things that distinguishes Maryknoll Sisters from other pastoral workers in the United States is precisely the experience of overseas mission and cross-cultural ministry that they bring to their work in the United States. Most of the Sisters in Mission USA still work with ethnic and cultural minorities—like Maryknoll Sisters Noel Chabanel Devine and Eugenia Marie Jautz, who work in Chicago's Chinatown, or Patricia O'Meara and Theresa Lisak, who minister to the Hispanic community in San Diego. But others work with organizations promoting peace and justice or global solidarity—Sisters like Bernie Desmond, who served as director of Eco-Andes, a group promoting solidarity with the Andean peoples, and Blaise Lupo who, after many years in the Philippines, served for ten years as codirector of Clergy and Laity Concerned in New York City.

Dialogue of Life

For some Sisters, mission takes the form of interreligious dialogue. A number of Sisters have become involved in exploring the common elements between Zen meditation and Christian contemplation. Maryknoll Sister Kathleen Reiley in Japan has been given permission from her teacher to offer guidance to practitioners of zazen meditation, while Sister Mary Little, a missioner in Seoul since 1976, participates in activities at the Lotus Lantern International Buddhist Center there. Her "experience of entering another religious tradition," she says, has become a call to conversion, "not conversion to Buddhism, but conversion to following Christ more faithfully."

The 1984 General Chapter brought a new president to the Congregation, Luise Ahrens, whose experience of having worked in Indonesia, a predominantly Muslim land, reflected the strides the Sisters had taken in the years after Vatican II toward a broader view of the world community.

"I went to Indonesia in 1973, as part of Maryknoll's first significant venture into the world of Islam," Ahrens explains. "It is the fifth largest country in the world, and its 165 million population will surpass that of the United States by the end of the century. Ninety percent of the people are Muslim, so that also makes it the largest Muslim population in the world."

Ahrens had no special training for her new reality—only the encouragement of a bishop who advised the Sisters that the church must witness to the Muslims and to the government that Christians were willing to work together with Muslims. Of the original group of four, two worked in government institutions and two in pastoral work. All of them lived among the Muslim poor.

It is against the law to proselytize in Indonesia, and so the Sisters had to ask themselves just what their presence in this country meant; what did mission mean in such a setting? Slowly Ahrens learned that it must mean, at the very least, a commitment to interreligious dialogue.

"Most people involved in dialogue with the great religions of the world understand dialogue in many different ways. Scholars generally recognize three modes of dialogue: of word, of collaboration, and of life." The dialogue of word involves the verbal exchange of views and ideas with the effort to arrive at a higher level of mutual understanding. The dialogue of collaboration promotes mutual respect through the commitment to a common task—the welfare of the community or the wider pursuit of peace and justice. In the dialogue of life, understanding is the fruit of a witness rooted in everyday experience; rather than proclaim that Christianity is a religion of love, for example, one communicates this point by being a loving friend and neighbor. All three approaches have their place in the Sisters' efforts.

And then Ahrens tells her favorite story:

> "Dahyan was a ten-year-old boy who lived next door to us in Bandung, Indonesia. Since our walls are contiguous, we live quite closely and share a great deal; Dahyan was a special friend of mine. One morning as I was praying in my room, his head appeared in the open frame.
>
> "'What are you doing?'
>
> "'Praying,' I responded.
>
> "'I'll come too,' he said quickly. I heard water splash, as all Muslims wash before they pray, and Dahyan appeared with his rolled-up prayer mat. He sat beside me on the floor. I had on my wall that wonderful picture from Chartres Cathedral, the creation of Adam. Adam and God are clearly in a warm, loving relationship in that picture.
>
> "'Who's that?' he asked.
>
> "'Adam and God.'
>
> "For a Muslim Adam is a very clear figure, loved and revered in the Qu'ran. But Muslims do not image God in a representational way. Dahyan stared at the picture for a long time. And then he said:
>
> "'Sister, I fast for twenty-eight days every year, sometimes more; I pray five times each day; and when I can, I give alms for poor children'—and this family has sixteen children and the father sells cloth from door to door—'but, Sister, I don't think my God loves me the way your God loves Adam.'"

Ahrens, raised as a child on thoughts of saving pagan babies, now experiences a different world. "For me, for all Christian missioners," she explains, "we *have* to share the consummate joy that is ours in a God who has in Jesus come to be one of us, who has entered into a relationship with us of friendship." But the missioner cannot assume that she has all the answers.

From the Muslim people among whom they live there is a challenge to question, to explore assumptions, and to enter more deeply into the meaning of faith. Ahrens was teaching English to engineers in Indonesia's most prestigious educational institute. "About a half-hour into the class, one young man stopped me and said, 'I cannot concentrate, Dr. Ahrens, on what you are talking about with the symbol of hatred and conquest in front of me. Your people killed thousands of my people under that sign.'"

Ahrens was wearing a simple cross.

"For us Christians," she says, "the cross speaks of life, suffering, death, and resurrection—the paschal mystery. To this Muslim man it speaks of hatred, violence, injustice. But the road of dialogue was opened—we talked long and seriously about what the cross was to me, to him. History for him is close; to me, the Crusades are a distant date in the history book. He spoke of his anger and hurt; I spoke of my sorrow at violence and death—and we both could speak of other current situations where fanaticism on both sides is creating mistrust.

"And in this way, we missioners in Indonesia learned to use our occasions to speak, to dialogue at the depths of our experience, rooted first in trust and friendship."

Women in Mission

Since the decade of the 1960s, the Maryknoll Sisters had come to a new understanding of their mission in terms of accompaniment and solidarity with the poor and oppressed. Of course, from the very beginning the Sisters had focused on the poor. But it was only gradually, initially through the experience of the Sisters in Latin America, that this had been joined with any kind of social analysis. An understanding of the structural causes of poverty had led to the conviction that evangelization must incorporate a commitment to social justice. In addition to providing charitable services to the poor, there arose a commitment to "walking with the poor," learning to see the gospel and the world through their eyes, identifying with their yearning and struggle for liberation. This growing "option for the poor," chronicled in the documents of successive General Assemblies, had enormous impact on the ministries of Maryknoll Sisters around the world.

In a similar way, with the 1980s, there began to develop among the Maryknoll Sisters a more articulate understanding of themselves as *women* in mission, with a conscious spirit of solidarity with women around the world and a commitment to their empowerment. Again, this represented more of a change of consciousness than any startling shift in focus. Long before the issue of the inequality of women had achieved widespread concern, the Maryknoll Sisters had *chosen* to teach and engage in pastoral work among women. Future Maryknoll Bishop James Edward Walsh, one of the first four missioner priests assigned to China in 1918, had written back to Maryknoll that "we need women missioners to work with the women in China." Indeed, the experience of the early years in China had demonstrated the relative ease with which the Maryknoll Sisters, as women, established intimate and informal relationships with the people. Unencumbered by clerical authority, the Sisters often seemed more approachable, more at ease with children, women's work, and the ordinary realities of daily life. Encountering the stark oppression of women in many societies, the Sisters endeavored in all their ministries to promote the equal worth and dignity of women. The tangible effect was to prepare many women in Asia, Africa, the Pacific, and Latin America to assume new roles and responsibilities in their societies.

As with their early work with the poor, however, this commitment to women was not yet accompanied by any social analysis or feminist critique. But with the growing influence of the feminist movement, the Maryknoll Sisters were inevitably challenged as women to identify with the developing consciousness of women around the world.

During the post-conciliar period and the 1968 General Chapter, the Sisters had based their future approach to community and ministry on a new understanding of their original charism and on principles promulgated during Vatican II—participation, mutuality, subsidiarity—principles also close to the heart of the women's movement. In trying to live out these principles, the Sisters became increasingly aware of the way structures in the church and society impede the full participation of women.

In their 1978 General Assembly the Maryknoll Sisters resolved "that we choose ministries which promote the equality of women and raise awareness of women's role, contribution to and status in the church and society." They also recorded this significant implication: "Our consciousness of what it means to be women will deepen and we will discover new roles in society."

Reflecting on this statement in their 1984 General Assembly, the Sisters could observe:

> This implication was indeed far-reaching. Through ministries with women and the mirroring effect they have had on our own lives, many of us have grown in awareness of our identity as women. Today we recognize that the faces in the mirror are ours as well as theirs. In 1984 we look at our entire life from the perspective of our identity as women missioners; we name a new consciousness.

Part of this new consciousness was a recognition of the oppression and powerlessness of women "in a world society that has been conditioned to the social inequality of women. We need to discover the extent to which we have internalized the violence resulting from unjust structures and oppression in society and church."

By the early 1980s, Sister Rose Marie Franklin was writing in *Maryknoll*

Magazine: "Even given the present discipline of the Church precluding female ordination, most women find it unreasonable and unconscionable that full participation in Church planning, consultation, and decision-making is still denied us. The linkages among gender, sacrament, and power in the Church continue to favor men."

As with the earlier "option for the poor," not all the regions, nor indeed all Maryknoll Sisters, were deepening in their consciousness about women's roles at the same pace. Maryknoll Sister Rose Guercio, a delegate from Korea to the 1984 General Assembly, remembers the painful struggle:

> There were radical delegates who were way out in front of the majority. In Korea, for example, the role of women was not at that time a burning issue. When the Assembly finally issued a paper on women my feeling was that it didn't move as far as some would have liked; but we did move everyone a little bit on the continuum and opened up some Sisters who hadn't given this much thought. By nature, I am more of a compromiser. I lived through the 1968 Chapter and 1970 Assembly, when there had to be a lot of trying to move everybody a few steps forward without everybody going the whole way.

The process continues. As Sister Sandy Galazin, director of the Sisters' Office of Communications, describes it: "Our 1978 Assembly emphasized that we will work *for* women; our 1984 Assembly that we will work *with* women. At the next assembly I would like us to be able to say, 'We *are* women,' with a fuller consciousness of what that self-identification means personally and as a group." Still, by 1986 the Sisters could report that "the priority ministries mentioned by eleven Regions, or 52 percent of those responding, had to do with some type of mission with women."

One example can be seen in Korea, where two Maryknoll Sisters, Jean Maloney and Dolores Geier, operate a hospitality house for women involved in prostitution. Magdalena House is located in Yongsan, a desperately crowded section of Seoul where, in an area of six blocks, three to four hundred women are involved in prostitution. It is only one such area of the city; throughout Korea, it is estimated that about one million women are involved in prostitution.

In the neighborhood of Magdalena House, scantily-clothed women sit in tiny glass-fronted rooms and call out to the passing men. These rooms, where the women live and work, belong to an owner, to whom the women are bound under endless debt. Magdalena House is a place for the young women to visit, to talk, and to find friendship and help—whether health care and legal assistance, skills training, or an emergency shelter. The Sisters spend a good part of their time visiting the women in the neighborhood—to see how they are, to let them know there is someone who cares, and to try to encourage a sense of community among neighbors. Out of such relationships there may come the hope and strength to create a different future. According to Dolores Geier, "These women are alienated from society, from their families, from old friends. So part of what we try to do is break down that alienation by fostering friendships."

Each woman has been drawn to prostitution through a variety of circumstances. There is "Miss Lee," brought up in a strict Confucian home, who chose to marry a man against the wishes of her family. After several years of marriage there were no children, and she was abandoned because of her inability to bear a son. There is "Miss Kim," who at age seven was abandoned by her mother along with her brother and sister at a U.S. army camp, and ended up in an orphanage. At fourteen she was hired from the orphanage to work as a housemaid. At sixteen she was raped by the man of the house. When this became known she was denounced by the orphanage as a bad girl and put on the street to fend for herself. There are hundreds of these women, each with her own story. But the basic story, in Maloney's words, remains the same: "Patriarchy, and the system in society that supports it."

Says Dolores Geier:

These women are survivors, but they are often despondent, filled with repressed anger. They will do drastic things—try to kill themselves, set themselves on fire. It is hard for me to face this reality. Yet it is balanced by seeing them survive, reach out, celebrate their friendships. It is not a constantly depressing environment. There is a lot of grace. In Magdalena House each woman comes with a huge problem, and yet they can come together, plan their meals, sit and talk for hours without fighting, and really care for each other. And for me that's just a big grace—to see people who you wouldn't think have the strength reach out to each other.

As in so many areas of renewal, the Sisters' deepening consciousness of themselves *as women* has prompted many of them to return to the example of their founder. Of course, Mollie Rogers did not have recourse to a sophisticated critique of women's place in society and the church. And yet, she was prepared to push the limits of conventional understandings of women's role in the church by her insistence that the Maryknoll Sisters be allowed into the overseas mission field. Certainly there were those, even in Maryknoll, who felt that women's contribution was to stay home and "hold down the fort," or, if permitted overseas, to serve as helpers or auxiliaries to the missioner priests. Mollie Rogers was not satisfied with such limited roles.

Sister Barbara Hendricks notes:

She wanted us to be carriers of the gospel or, as she expressed it, "messengers of the Word." She early sought permission from Rome for us to live in communities of two Sisters in places where rather often we would not have the benefit of Mass and the Sacraments because there were no resident priests. This was an innovative role for Catholic women at that time. They traveled frequently in South China from village to village, forming Christian women, teaching the women how to pray and praying with them. It was an apostolate of friendship, and within the friendship, faith and hope blossomed for many.

Looking back on Mollie Rogers, Maryknoll Sister Nonie Gutzler says:

As a woman at Smith College, she had a vision of what Catholic women could do. She had a vision that went beyond what was accepted then and she didn't let the church stop her or hamper her. Nor did she leave it. That is a point we are at now as we struggle at being women in the church. It is the same struggle: how to be a creative woman in the church. Of course, the whole picture of women has changed. That means that we have to struggle to articulate a vision for women today, just as she did for her time.

Charting a Future

The membership of the Maryknoll Sisters peaked in 1966, with 1,430 professed Sisters in a total membership of 1,629, including Sisters in formation. By 1988, the number of professed Sisters was 851, plus 6 candidates and 17 Associate Sisters. Of these 540 are in active mission.

These diminishing numbers are not unique to Maryknoll; most religious congregations in the United States have faced a similar decline, as have the Maryknoll Fathers and Brothers. There are, of course, a variety of reasons. On the one hand, there is no longer the same Catholic immigrant culture that once proudly channeled pious children in the direction of religious life. On the other hand, since Vatican II there are increased opportunities for lay people to express their religious commitment—even to serve overseas as lay missioners—without making lifelong vows. For women, especially, there are simply far more options available to develop their talents and abilities within the church and society. At the same time, there are certainly pressures in American culture that resist the ideals of voluntary poverty, lifelong celibacy, and the hardships of mission life.

Sister Barbara Hendricks contends that another reason for decreasing vocations might be the change in mission theology since Vatican II. "If you no longer have to go overseas to save souls, if people can be saved in their own culture, if somehow Christ's redemption is available to all people—whether or not they have explicit knowledge of Christ's redemption of them—then what is the motivation for missioners to go out overseas?" Her answer: "We go to announce the Good News that God's Reign has come and is available to us. It is present and must be 'preached' through a life of witness. People must see signs that something is happening as a result of God's Reign—evidence that disease, ignorance, cruelty, injustice, alienation are being challenged and overcome."

Although there was a large surge of vocations to religious life in the United States just after the Second World War, the Sisters accept the reality of a smaller—and perforce older—congregation. Though new Sisters join each year—thirty-three in the decade of the 1980s, with slightly over half from countries other than the United States—the overall decline in numbers raises questions about the future that cannot be ignored.

In some ways, there are resources in Maryknoll's past for confronting these uncertainties. The closing of China after the Communist Revolution represented the end of one era for Maryknoll, while it opened doors to new ventures in Africa, Latin America, and elsewhere in Asia and the Pacific. The shift after Vatican II out of major institutional responsibilities—hospitals, colleges, and other large-scale educational endeavors—demonstrated again the capacity of the Maryknoll Sisters to let go, to move on, as the needs of the time demanded. Their mission was wider than any particular ministry—as teachers or doctors, for example. Instead, the trend over the years was to move toward smaller, grassroots ministries, where the missioner might serve as a leaven or catalyst, assisting the local church, and not as the foreign professional in charge of dispensing services.

Reflecting on her Korean experience, Dolores Geier notes:

In Korea after the war there was a huge need for medical response for refugees, so everyone sent there had some kind of medical background. But I don't think any Maryknollers in Korea today are doing medical work. Once that emergency was over other social problems came to the surface, and the tendency was no longer to respond to these in an institutional way but as individuals. What we brought wasn't money or buildings or any of the traditional kinds of mission response, but our own interests, virtues, talents—and a heart to love people and a desire to be present with them.

There is really little else to work with than the lessons of the past, the vision of the founders, a lively engagement with the present, and a trust in the Holy Spirit. But it was always thus. Mollie Rogers once wrote: "Love, work, prayer and suffering will sustain us in the future as they have in the past. All who are here now, all who will come after us, will have no other tools than these with which to build."

At their 1968 General Chapter, the Sisters illustrated their document with a traditional navigational map from the Marshall Islands. Hundreds of years ago, without recourse to modern navigational instruments and using only simple vessels, the Islanders were able to travel vast distances throughout the Pacific. They were adept at reading ocean currents and interpreting the various qualities of the waves to guide them in their search for land. For the Sisters, facing an uncertain future, it was an apt metaphor.

In discussing the future with various Maryknoll Sisters today, one finds a number of common themes: acknowledgment of uncertainty, recognition that the future size, shape, and organization of the Congregation may be different from the past, and at the same time enthusiasm for the challenges ahead, faith in God, and confidence that their own experience, creativity, and imagination will create a future.

According to Sister Nonie Gutzler, who joined Maryknoll in 1964 and worked in Tanzania and Taiwan before becoming director of personnel, "We are in a hard place, and we are going to have to struggle with it. It is a hard time, we don't know where we are going. But neither did Mollie Rogers. And somehow her heritage for us is to keep on going and not to settle into what we know now and say 'this is enough.'"

Sister Barbara Hendricks, the indomitable first president of the Congregation who describes herself as "an inveterate optimist," nevertheless acknowledges the uncertainty. "This is a time of winter in the church, a time when everything goes down to its skeleton stages. During winter everything seems to die; and yet you know it didn't die. You believe the seeds are there buried in the cold ground. Maryknoll and the church are living through a time of winter, and you can't get excited about that and drop your hands in despair. You keep on going and do what you need to do and work for the spring."

Sister Rose Guercio joined Maryknoll in 1947 and spent five years in Sri Lanka and another thirty in Korea before returning to Ossining for work at the Center. She says, "I personally don't have the feeling that the majority of Maryknoll Sisters are concerned about survival, as if that, and not the Reign of God, is our ultimate concern." She recalls one of Mollie Rogers' ideals, "heroic generosity," and she relates that ideal to the possibility that the Sisters may be called to such generosity in sacrificing fixed preconceptions about religious life. "We have to decide, what are the 'negotiables' that we are willing to give up? All along in the history of religious life people have said, 'That is nonnegotiable'—like the habit, something that turned out to be completely negotiable after all."

There is a palpable sense among the Sisters that they are in the midst of a profound period of renewal in religious life and mission, a time of questioning, of letting go, of listening to the needs of the times, and the demands of the gospel. While images of religious life based on *The Nun's Story* and *The Sound of Music* remain deeply imbedded in the American psyche, the real lives of women religious have long outgrown such images. In such a time, the Sisters are increasingly aware of how much they need one another. The outer journey of mission is being balanced by the call to an inner spiritual journey.

Sister Nonie Gutzler recalls, "Mollie Rogers once told us that we should do acts of tenderness for one another . . . I realize, when I look around, that there is a lot of that tenderness and kindness among us—although we argue and have our disagreements. I think that Mollie Rogers would be at home with our struggles to have a quality life, a tender life with one another . . . We are *for* each other, and we are all in this together."

Into the Evening

The decline in new vocations has been accompanied, inescapably, by the increasing median age of the Sisters. In 1970 it was forty-five; by 1988 it was sixty-four. And yet, the Sisters note that much of the "grayness" in religious life today has little to do with the reality of aging membership; it is a state of mind, a state of the soul. In that light, what matters most is not the age of their senior members, but what they do with the time they have. Of those over the age of seventy, 175 are still living in the regions, continuing their contributions to community life and ministry. There are Sisters like Michael Damien O'Connor, who at the age of seventy-six accepted an assignment to Bangladesh; or Rose McGrale, who at the age of seventy and after many years of mission in the Philippines accepted an assignment to Japan; or Mildred Fritz, who, more than twenty years after her part in the Melville Incident, still carries on her pastoral work in Mexico.

The same spirit lives on in many of those who have retired to the Center or the residence home in Monrovia. Sister Dennis McCarthy writes letters for those who cannot write their own; Magdalena Urlacher volunteers at a local health clinic, corresponds with women in China with whom she worked sixty years ago, and visits infants suffering from AIDS; Ann Elise Gallagher plays piano for the Sisters' choir and for the nearby parish's Korean community.

Sister Peg Dillon, who, after almost thirty years in Maryknoll, feels herself entering mid-life, sees in the older Sisters around her "possible models for me of getting old. Older Sisters are supposed to be introverted, but they are so outward-oriented. There is a contemplative stillness, but I see some of them so interested in mission and in the younger people, so very much a part of this world. I hope I can grow old that gracefully, that much in tune with what is happening in the world, so enthusiastic."

When she entered Maryknoll, Dillon says, there was a toughness about the way mission was regarded—an eagerness to work without resting, to prove one's willingness to overcome all obstacles, and to give everything without complaint. "As we get older, we balance that out with a need for beauty, time for ourselves, space for contemplation. Going to the farthest ends of the earth is part of our charism; but you have to balance that with the inner journey. The future of Maryknoll has to be a combination of action and stillness. For me, it is all simpler than when I started out."

Life must end, and few have captured those moments more beautifully than did seventy-five-year-old Sister Anne Clements, with her poignant remarks in *Maryknoll Magazine* in 1981. The retired Sister, reflecting on her years in mission and religious life, recalled earlier days: "As I left home one of my sisters (there were nine children: six girls, three boys) said: 'How on earth are you going to live with a bunch of women? I can't imagine anything worse.' Frankly, I couldn't either, but I wouldn't admit it to her." Fifty-six years later, in the nursing home, "everyone is full of years or sick, but pervading the home are the supernatural beauties of women who have led lives of joyful courage and are now preparing for death. Sister Ursula Kenkel in her eighties, alert and interested, always ready to supply the name, author and next line of any classical quotation; Sister Mary George Callan, charming and gracious, despite senility; Sisters Jane Ketter, Gloria Wagner, Alice Daly, Constance Wenzel, Anna Hayashi—loving companions going gently together into the evening. My sisters. Living examples, all, of what it means to belong to the community of saints."

Mollie Rogers once wrote of the Maryknoll Sisters: "Ours are to be the labors of the apostolate at home and abroad, hard, unflagging, continuous; we are to expect reproach, ingratitude, weariness of soul and body; to be betrayed—to have our own passion—and in the end, death. All with joy, eagerness, and exhilaration."

Commenting on these words, Sister Sandy Galazin observes: "When I look at the kind of joy I see now among my Sisters I feel that we are really making something new. The language we are learning is not Chinese or Swahili—but a new language for speaking about ourselves, about the Spirit, about life. A whole new consciousness is being called forth, and we are realizing that mission is not simply geographical; it also has to do with the landscape that connects the head, the heart, and the gut."

That enthusiasm before the challenges ahead is clearly present in the younger Sisters. The future? According to Riji Lee, a Korean-born Sister who entered Maryknoll in 1983 and has worked with the Quechua Indians in Bolivia, "I'm not that concerned about numbers. We're going to be fifty or sixty Sisters. But as long as there are a few women who are committed to the same vision and dream—to share our love and faith with people of another culture—Maryknoll will continue."

After all, it began with no more than a few women, among them Sister Gemma Shea, great and gracious to the end and smiling broadly in a photograph taken at the residence in Monrovia—ninety years old, one of the original group from 1912, one of the Manchuria hands, one of the sources for this book, and one of the sources of inspiration for all Maryknoll Sisters. It was to her, little "Miss Shea," that Mollie Rogers spoke those words of invitation, back when it all began: "Let's just go together and see what God has in store for us."

She follows Mollie and so many others, not just gently into the evening, but with spirited beauty, with Christian magnificence. Their joy, not just their work, magnifies the Lord.

～ 15 ～

Closing the Circle

═══════════════════════════

*"As one lamp lights another nor grows less, so nobleness enkindleth nobleness."
... The meaning of these words is clear. We know that if we take a lighted
candle and enkindle another with it, the light of the first does not lessen, although it has given of its light to the second. So it is with us, as we give good
example. Kindness begets kindness, charity begets charity, and the first act does
not grow less because of its begetting ... Our spirit as individual Maryknoll
Sisters, and the very spirit of our whole congregation, depends largely on the
use we make of the abiding truth of these words.*
—Mollie Rogers, 1929

IN A CITY IN southern China in 1985, Maryknoll Sister Maureen Corr was
intrigued to notice, painted on a wall, a sign indicating "Catholic Church."
Beneath the Chinese characters was an arrow pointing down an alley. Without hesitating she strode into the alley to see what she would find. There
was no visible Catholic church. The church building that had once stood
in this spot had been pulled down during the Cultural Revolution of the
1960s to be replaced by an apartment building. But there was indeed a living Catholic community. It turned out that in what had once been the rectory dining room, there was a regular gathering of the faithful—mostly elderly Chinese—who met for Sunday Mass conducted in Latin by a Chinese
priest. By the time Sister Maureen stumbled upon them, the little Catholic
community had been meeting and worshiping in the rectory for two years.

These Catholics were naturally most curious about their visitor. She
was American? Yes. She was working in China teaching English? Yes. She
had no children? No. "If you have no children and you speak Chinese," said
one of them, "then you must be a Sister." Yes. And which congregation? At
the mention of Maryknoll, an elderly Chinese woman came forward and
spoke of the Maryknoll bishop, priests, and Sisters she had known as a catechist forty years earlier in another part of China.

For Sister Maureen it was an extraordinary moment. As she listened to
the names of Maryknollers of the past, most long dead but living on in this
woman's memory, she felt that a circle had been completed. A Maryknoll

Sister was back in China among Catholics, some of whom had been welcomed into the faith by Maryknollers many decades before.

Sister Maureen was not the first Maryknoll Sister to return; she was one of seven in the 1980s who were working in China as professional English teachers. The circumstances were far different from those that had greeted their predecessors. They were present not overtly as missioners but as language instructors. And yet the motivation, the love for the Chinese people, and the desire to bear witness, though in a different way, linked these Maryknoll Sisters to those who had gone before.

"For the first year," Corr said in 1987, "I didn't go to Mass at the rectory every Sunday. The priest was still fearful of what the government would do if the Catholics got too friendly with a foreigner. But this year I have gone there much more often. The Mass is very pre-Vatican II, but I am always deeply moved as I watch this little group of Christians. I feel very close to them, and they have welcomed me to their community, invited me to their meetings, prayed for my father when he was sick." And yet, she added, "I am given no special attention. I am treated just like another member of the community."

During the week, Sister Maureen taught English in a university. In the classroom, if the subject came up, she would acknowledge her Christian faith. Most of her students had never been inside a church. She found it rewarding work, but increasingly Sister Maureen's decision to remain in China would be influenced by "this little group of Christians whom I admire and who strengthen me in my faith. They have asked me to stay with them and be with them as they try to open and build a new church."

The story of this community "down the alley" is one of many examples of a church in China, linked to the old, but on the threshold of renewal. It is still, however, a church subject to strict surveillance and regulation. China's first cautious openings to the West in the 1970s became, in the 1980s, a partially opened door through which passed a steady stream of Maryknoll visitors and teachers. Yet the opening was—and remains—only partial.

China does not grant visas to religious missioners as such. But Maryknollers are present in other countries in which this is also so. In Nepal, for example, it is illegal to convert or to be converted. Even under these circumstances, however, it is possible to be present among the people, to walk beside them, and to share in the dialogue of life.

In China, the earlier missioners had planted seeds. In the 1980s, the Sisters were privileged to see that these seeds were still growing, to see, in fact, that there are more Catholics and other Christians in China now than there were when the missioners left in 1951. Once again religious devotion is expressed openly, and there is an obvious hunger for the moral and spiritual values that faith provides. The missioners and these Chinese Christians are reconstructing a fragile bridge toward the wider church from which these Chinese were for so long cut off. It is a task undertaken with much compassion and understanding of all that China's Catholics have suffered for their faith.

An Enforced Leavetaking

In the late 1940s, as Mao's army continued to advance against the Nationalists, the missioners in China were generally unprepared for the coming furious backlash. Few missioners realized the revulsion of certain Chinese toward a church controlled by Westerners and entangled in so many complex ways with the culture and imperialistic policies of the West. Some Sisters saw the battles ahead but not the extreme treatment that would ensue with a Maoist victory.

Sister Mary Lou Martin recalled, "I went to China in 1947, three months after my twenty-first birthday, to Wuchow, Kwangsi, the province beyond Hong Kong. I was there until 1951. It was simple living and I was happy. There were eight Sisters—six of us who had come after World War II, and two old-timers. We were just beginning to build the two-Sister structures as in Kaying—catechetics, village-visiting, all very traditional parish work." The Sisters also worked closely with a native Chinese community of women religious.

The Communist victory came in 1949. "Before that," said Martin, "there had been small battles between the Nationalists and Communists. When the Communists came into Wuchow in November, 1949, people had great hopes. It was a euphoric time because the fighting was over." But then in 1950 the Korean War began, and with that came a great clampdown. "The order came from Peking to control the foreign missions."

Maryknoll Sister Agnes Cazale was assigned to a rural parish in Szwong with Sister Mary Diggins. She was there at the time of the Communist takeover and explained that because there was little news or information, it was difficult to know precisely what was happening. "If we did get newspapers in China," she said, "we didn't know how to interpret them. We were not aware of what was happening beyond our own situation. We were actually under surveillance all the time. Local people were told by the Communists not to mingle with the Americans. We were not allowed to shop. We relied on the ingenuity of people loyal to us. So we just lived day-to-day, not knowing what to expect. I, like most Americans, was loyal to my president and thought Chiang Kai-shek was a good guy."

Diggins was doing parish work "up in the mountains. It was a very primitive place. We didn't have toilets, just buckets that we dumped every day. In the beginning, we didn't think the Communists would take over when they came from the north. The first group we met was very courteous. They borrowed cooking pans—woks—and they always gave them back. But the more they came through, the less polite they were." From being less than polite, the Chinese Communists began to display their outright hostility. Their strategy, as it became clearer, was to employ increasing pressure and harassment to force the foreign missioners out of China. First came surveillance, then restrictions on movement and travel, and finally confinement to virtual house arrest, as the missioners were accused of being spies for the United States. Possessions were confiscated, contact with the outside world was curtailed, and the missioners were regularly interrogated and threatened with arrest.

The Maryknollers were determined not to abandon their posts, but it became increasingly difficult to hold on. By June 1951, most Maryknollers had voluntarily curtailed their contact with Chinese Catholics, realizing that any relations between them would only result in persecution for the Chinese faithful. When all else failed, the Communists contrived charges against certain missioners, even planting evidence—opium, in the case of mission superior Sister Rosalia Kettl or bullets, in the case of Maryknoll Bishop Frederick Donaghy—to justify their arrest. Kettl, Donaghy, and a young Maryknoll priest, Justin Kennedy, were arrested in December 1950. They would not emerge for six months.

By the middle of 1951, the Maryknoll Sisters in South China, having finally agreed to request permission to leave, were on their way to Hong Kong. Sister Rosalia Kettl followed in July. While she was "terribly thrilled to see the Sisters again," Sister Rosalia recalled her crossing into British territory as "the saddest day of my life, because I was leaving behind all those dear people. I knew I could never go back."

Among those left behind were the many Chinese Sisters in Wuchow. After the arrival of the Communists, Bishop Donaghy had told the Sisters that because they were so young they were to return to their villages and should consider themselves dispensed from their vows. As far as the Chinese Communists were concerned, these young women were expected to marry; otherwise they would not be entitled to food.

As the door closed on China, and with it one chapter in the Maryknoll story, so new challenges opened up. The first of these was coping with the flood of desperate people pouring into the island colony of Hong Kong.

Hong Kong

British Hong Kong, a cluster of islands and peninsulas, is a minute appendage on the mainland of China. Hong Kong Island was a barren rock with a single fishing village and a magnificent harbor when the British claimed it in 1842. As the nineteenth century rolled on, Britain forced treaties upon

China for today's existing 590 square miles. In 1997 those treaties expire, and the Chinese government has made it perfectly clear that on June 30, 1997, at midnight, Hong Kong reverts to Beijing.

It was in Hong Kong, where the Maryknoll Sisters had established their center in South China, that the history of the Maryknoll Sisters in China had begun. Among their earliest projects were two flourishing girls' schools: the Maryknoll Sisters School on Hong Kong Island and the Maryknoll Convent School in Kowloon.

Hong Kong today is a concrete city dominated, as one Sister said, by "the dull roar of humanity." The constant noise from automobiles, radios, aircraft, construction work, and human activity amidst the crowded conditions is, by every account, fierce and without respite.

These days, says Sister Mary Diggins, "the Sisters who come back for renewal at the Center in Ossining and who ask for longer than the usual four months' renewal are from Africa and Hong Kong. Africa because of the excessive isolation; Hong Kong because of the excessive urbanization. The Sisters from Africa, when they arrive in Ossining, say, 'Look how built up it is!' Those who come from Hong Kong say, 'Look at all the land!'"

In 1946, the population of the British Crown Colony of Hong Kong, most of it mountainous and uninhabitable, was around five hundred thousand. Forty years later, it had swollen to at least five and a half million. Much of that growth was from refugees. During a period of barely twelve months after the Revolution in 1949, the population of Hong Kong doubled and then redoubled to absorb two million refugees from the mainland. Such an influx of refugees would have posed a strain under any circumstances, but at the time, Hong Kong was itself still recovering from the ravages of World War II and its three years of Japanese occupation.

The regional superior of that time was Sister Mary Paul McKenna, a strong and outspoken woman who undertook the challenge of recovering control over the Maryknoll Schools. They had fallen into the hands of the British government, after having been used by the Japanese to house troops (and horses) during the war. She was successful on both counts. But it was not until 1947, after being closed for seven years, that the schools reopened.

School was just beginning as the steady trickle of refugees from the mainland began. But then, in 1949, the floodgates opened. Hundreds of thousands of people swarmed into Hong Kong by day and night, by boat and train, some walking and others even swimming. They moved onto the hillsides and built shacks of straw, flattened tin cans wired together, cardboard, tar paper, or anything at hand, anything to accommodate six, eight, or ten people in a few square feet of space.

In the Maryknoll Archives there is a black and white 16-mm film of the Maryknoll Sisters in Hong Kong, entitled "And They Found Him," shot as the refugees were flooding in. In the movie, the Sisters in their habits are seen going about their tasks amidst the masses of humanity. On the hillsides we can see tens of thousands of huts. The film shows the fire that in one day swept six thousand of them away.

The story line of the film is based on an actual account, written up in *Maryknoll Magazine*. The Wong family has arrived in Hong Kong by boat, leaving behind the father, a political prisoner. One son has escaped ahead of the family. With great difficulty the mother, Leelan, begins the search for her son. Often accompanied by her daughter, Leelan takes to the streets. Weary at the end of one day of walking Hong Kong looking for her son, Leelan sits on the curb to rest. Nearby, a young orange vendor rattles his cart along the street. Some of the oranges fall off. And yes, the orange vendor is Leelan's missing son. With joyful embraces the mother and son are reunited. Sometimes it really happened that way. But for every happy ending for these refugee survivors, there were countless stories of tragedy and loss.

By 1952, as the population approached three million, the colony had been transformed. New parishes were opening, and for the Sisters, their own numbers expanded by many of those expelled from the mainland, there were a host of new projects and ministries. Beginning with medical work and other social services, the Maryknollers increasingly added projects that would assist the people in economic self-reliance. In the Chaai Wan refugee settlement area, Maryknoll Monsignor John Romaniello and Maryknoll Sister Moira Riehl had organized a series of noodle factories, making use of the otherwise inedible—to the Chinese—flour furnished by the United States government. At the factory, a customer would bring in two pounds of flour and leave with two pounds of noodles. Refugee women were organized into embroidery teams and encouraged to sell their wares.

As the refugees poured into Hong Kong, the shacks they built on the mountain sides were very vulnerable. The combination of overcrowding, poor materials, and kerosene stoves posed a constant fire hazard. After one especially damaging fire, the Sisters began canvasing business owners, seeking contributions to assist the homeless. One man they approached suggested that the Sisters raise money to build housing that would not be so susceptible to fire. Maryknoll Father Paul Duchesne and Sister Imelda Sheridan pursued the idea, initiating a building program in Tung Tau, one of the first of its kind in Asia, which resulted in a small settlement of modest one-room cottages. Father Duchesne raised funds from among his contacts and supporters while the Sisters sold chances on prizes. "How many bricks can you buy?" they asked the local business owners. Eventually a school and clinic were developed there as well.

Aside from fires, there were also typhoons, mud slides, torrential rains, and other sources of misery. In the 1950s, when the Sanitation Department made its rounds, there would frequently be as many as a dozen corpses a day laid out near the settlements, to be collected like refuse. Gradually, the Sisters set up a network of medical clinics, and by 1961 there was a Maryknoll hospital.

Tiny Hong Kong had nowhere to go but up. By the 1960s, the first of the seven-, then twenty-story high-rises began to mark the Hong Kong skyline. In heavy rains, however, the expanding city had a tendency to slide back toward the center. In 1964, a landslide buried Sister Anne Clements' refugee school near Kwun Tong. Clements, who had begun her mission life in Manchuria and spoke fluent Mandarin, Cantonese, and Japanese, marshalled the children and adult volunteers from throughout the colony and pitched in to rebuild. The work was done, the books dried out, the desks clean but still damp, when Typhoon June buried the school up to the ceilings in a second mud slide. The Sister and her volunteers simply started all over again.

In time new missions became prominent. Four Sisters began living in the Sau Mau Ping government housing project in Kowloon, listening to the needs of its 135,000 residents, often crowded six and eight people to a single room. Maryknoll Sister Teresa Dagdag, an educator from the Philippines, took a job in a plastics factory in the Kwun Tong industrial center along with young and older women from nearby housing projects. As she assembled toys and dolls, earning $2.50 a day as an unskilled laborer, Sister Teresa got to know the women in the factory and to encourage them to assert their rights. Sister Michelle Reynolds administered a nearby parish. Dietitian Sister Anne Marie Emdin lived at a government housing project, worked at Maryknoll Hospital and later in housing with the elderly. Sister Moira Riehl set up a center for the blind. Other Sisters in Hong Kong worked with abused women, the deaf, children with mental disabilities, and the elderly. Whatever the work, its value was in doing it *with* and not simply *for* the people.

Since their departure from China, the Sisters had witnessed an extraordinary transformation of Hong Kong, much of it a reflection of the industry and determination of those early refugees. In the meantime, China too had undergone immeasurable change and turmoil, much of it beyond the gaze of Western eyes. But the greatest surprise for the Sisters, when in the 1980s they began to return to China as visitors and teachers, was to learn that China had as many as three and a half million Catholics, some half-million more than when the missionaries of many lands had been forced out nearly forty years before. The people had kept the faith and had practiced it. Once again churches were opening and seminaries filling up. The seeds of faith planted by the early missioners, women of Maryknoll among them, had taken root, despite the forces determined to see them wither. Despite all, the new Christians had grown in strength and numbers.

The Return—and 1997

A decade ago, when the first groups of Maryknollers and Catholic Chinese from Hong Kong returned to the villages where they had once lived and made contact with their long-separated Catholic friends and kin, the stories of endurance brought tears to their eyes. Elderly lay catechists, Chinese priests thin from harsh prison-camp life, dispersed women religious, some of whom without community, without a church, without support, nevertheless had tried to remain true to their vows, gradually revealed the extent of their sufferings.

Maryknoll Sister Pauline Sticka, with a reporter's eye, returned to the city of Kaying, from which she had been forced out almost forty years earlier. She recorded how the hills had been stripped of trees for firewood, though there were new plantings. She noted the almost nonstop traffic. Cemeteries were gone, the headstones used for roads and buildings. Temples were not to be seen. Yet some routines remained: the women, early in the morning and again in late afternoon, climbed into the mountains to gather the twigs still used as fuel for cooking meals. To the returning Maryknoll Sisters, the faces and eyes of the mainland Catholics told stories of their hardships, yet there was encouragement, Sticka wrote, in the faces of the young, a "hopeful joyousness."

Sisters Pauline Sticka and Magdalena Urlacher, who, after leaving China, had both spent more than thirty years working in Taiwan, met a woman lay catechist who had risked her life decades earlier to take water to a Chinese priest in a labor camp. The priest had later died. A male catechist recounted how it had not been the beatings that had been hardest for the Chinese Catholics to endure; what was most difficult was having no Mass, no rosary, no holy cards to help them pray. As he recalled his work in a Maryknoll parish of four decades before, the catechist broke down in tears and sat with his head in his hands.

As she wandered the streets in the city she had left thirty-seven years before, Sister Pauline was surprised to hear her Chinese name being called out. The Chinese woman who threw her arms around Sister Pauline was a Sister in a Chinese congregation who had never been able to make her final vows. Still, she had not married and had continued to live all these years as she thought a religious life should be witnessed.

The cost of their faith for many Chinese Catholics was high indeed. As the numbers of visitors to China increased, so did accounts of the suffering that had been borne. And with each additional story, the Maryknoll Sisters were able to add to their understanding of what *their* lives in China had represented.

In 1988, a group of Maryknoll Sisters—Rosalia Kettl, Dorothy Rubner, Agnes Cazale, Agnes Virginia Higgins, and Doretta Leonard, all among the Sisters expelled from the country decades before—went back to Wuchow. They found the church building the same. Housed nearby were the few remaining Chinese Sisters, including two who were in the community at the beginning, now seventy-five and sixty-nine years of age. There were two other Sisters who had never married, both in their sixties. During that visit, twelve of the other original Sisters came to visit, the majority of them widows. One had been under house arrest for ten years and had been forced to marry. During the Cultural Revolution of the 1960s, some of them had suffered greatly because they were Catholics and religious women. But it was especially moving to the Maryknoll Sisters to find also eighteen young Chinese women who had recently entered the religious community—preparing to go out "two-by-two," as had the Maryknoll Sisters sixty years earlier in Kaying. Women the Sisters had trained years before were now training others for mission.

Maryknoll Sister Rosalia Kettl was herself one of the pioneers of Kaying, who had endured six months of prison before her expulsion from China, and who had wept at the thought that she would never again return. She was now seventy-seven and had trouble walking. Nonetheless, she found the strength to climb seven flights of stairs to meet a catechist she had once known, now a woman in her nineties. "The woman was so happy," she reported. "It seemed to her—and to us, as well—like a miracle."

As the Chinese Catholics poured out their stories, the Maryknoll Sisters, too, were coming to terms with what their lives in China had meant and with the sufferings and anguish they had experienced. Sister Rosalia recalled a woman she had met in prison who had never met a Catholic but who was moved at the sight of the imprisoned Sister to ask about the Catholic faith. "I was in the process of instructing her in the faith when she was taken out and shot," she remembered. So much suffering. And yet she was not dispirited: "I think that there is nothing that happens in the crises of people's lives that goes to waste. I think God uses it. To be back in China again made me realize that things that happen aren't always for the worst. God has his plans." And what of the circle that the Sisters had set in motion? According to Sister Rosalia, "The church only moves forward one inch at a time; it takes its slow pace, changing hearts. In China we could only move one inch; China is so big, and we were so small. But I like to think it was one inch of splendor."

And as these Sisters gathered in reconciliation and reunion with their Catholic friends and families of decades past, many experienced a heart-warming peace. Said Sister Rosalia, "It was as if we had never left them."

And perhaps, in fact, they never had, and never will. The future of China's Catholics remains uncertain. In 1997, Beijing will resume control over Hong Kong. What this will mean for the millions who fled after 1949, and for the Sisters who accompanied them, remains to be seen. This time there will be fewer Maryknoll Sisters to accompany the people of Hong Kong into a new future. Fewer, but committed to remain.

∾

After the Communist takeover in China, very ordinary people who had been cooks or catechists or held minor positions in Catholic parishes suddenly found that they had to endure endless trials because of their association with the suspect Maryknoll missioners. In the years immediately after the exodus of the Maryknollers, one Catholic woman, a cook in a parish, was constantly being pressured to make untrue statements about the Maryknoll bishop, priests, and Sisters she had known. She steadfastly and loyally refused. Her severe punishment included being deprived of food while being forced to do hard work.

But when she could, she would return to the pagoda in Kaying built by Bishop Ford, and, standing there, she would imagine each Sister, face after face, one by one, acknowledging each in turn. This communion in spirit with the Maryknoll Sisters, she said, gave her the courage to go on.

Around the world there are graves of Maryknoll Sisters, some of them martyrs, and others who simply served and served simply. Who can know the many places where Maryknoll lives on, not only among the hundreds of women still serving, but in the shadows of Sisters who are only seen now by those who knew them at the edges of deserts, in remote villages, in solid stone schools and convents now used by others, in hospital corridors, or in jungle clearings where spindly planes once landed, in overcrowded and slum-ridden urban streets where the Sisters opened a little space and witnessed to a little peace.

The story of the Maryknoll Sisters had its beginnings when one woman decided that other women, too, wanted new ways to be in mission, new ways to be with people and to open their hearts to them. In over thirty countries around the world, in Asia, Africa, the Pacific, Latin America, and the United States, their hearts remain open—and on fire.

∾

There once lived in China a holy woman who knew the location of a sacred tree in a sacred forest. Whenever she prayed at the tree, she received what she wanted.

After the woman died, her daughter also went to pray at the sacred tree in the sacred forest, but, try as she might, she could not recall the words of the prayer. Yet, because she remembered the importance of the prayer, she, too, was given what she sought.

Then the family moved to the city and the woman died. Her daughter could not remember where the tree or forest were, nor did she know the words of the prayer. But because she remembered their importance, she also was rewarded.

Conclusion to the Centenary Edition

Opening the Circle

The Maryknoll Sisters

~

The love of Christ cannot be confined;
like the flame—our love must expand or it will die.
Mother Mary Joseph Rogers, 1948

MOTHER MARY JOSEPH'S REFLECTION in 1948 was another articulation of the sustained sense of calling reflected in her earlier encouragement to Margaret Shea: "Let's go and see what God has in store for us!" Such is the adventure of the call to mission that each Maryknoll Sister freely chooses— a calling that must, in turn, be enkindled and passed on to the uttermost parts of the earth.

Another generation has passed since *Hearts on Fire* was first published. Nothing changes. Everything changes. The fundamental commitment to meet people where they are and walk with them to a better place continues. It is the journey that inflames hearts and inspires Maryknoll Sisters and our many partners to respond to emerging needs. There is joy in discovering what God indeed has been working in us.

God has been transforming us and preparing us in membership and vision for a very different world from the one that saw Maryknoll's beginnings. Our world is now "globalized." Any development for the good of an individual or of one community potentially affects another. This same dynamic applies with problems as well. Science and other social disciplines and spiritualities have brought us to a level of understanding that all communities of life are interconnected. And our own life experiences from the gift of cross-cultural mission have confirmed that we are all part of that web of life. As religious missioners, the Maryknoll Sisters are influenced by this process and are challenged to nuance its expressions so as to be always about the promotion of life. Our membership is not only living and serving in twenty-five countries but our Sisters are from many different countries and cultures as well.

We find that our Maryknoll charism also has led us to be "on the ground," working on world concerns, oftentimes years before governments and international bodies became involved. A valuable legacy we have from Mother Mary Joseph Rogers was her ability to take bold risks without fear of failure: *"A good missionary must be willing to try anything. Failure is not bad. It can help us to be humble, simple and courageous. So keep that in your minds…have no fear of trying things you are asked to do."* Her openness to innovative ministries and her encouragement of each one of us to cultivate our individuality for a purpose have inspired Maryknoll Sisters over the years and have encouraged us to walk new paths.

What follows is simply a sampling of the many paths that Maryknoll Sisters have walked in recent years.

Mission: A Hand in Nation Building

At the 1984 General Assembly, the Congregation emphasized the urgency of working with refugees around the world. These "people on the move," not by their own choice—refugees, internally displaced people, migrant workers, trafficked humans—are features of a world marred by militarization, war, genocide, and economic exploitation. It was a new situation calling for ministries of compassionate service, from responding to basic needs for health care and education to building capacities for nation building and responsible citizenship. Collaborative efforts with international and government agencies, interfaith initiatives, and civil organizations in the work of transforming societies became a necessary content of the mission enterprise.

Maryknoll Sisters volunteered to minister to displaced peoples of Somalia, Ethiopia, and Sudan in refugee camps in the horn of Africa. In 1990 the impending independence of Namibia—annexed by the South African apartheid regime after World War II—opened the way for the repatriation of its exiled population, and Maryknoll Sisters responded to the needs of nation building and renewal of the long-isolated church.

Similarly, in 1990 a group of Sisters began preparations to work with refugees from Cambodia who were in camps along the Thai border. By the next year, signing of the Paris Peace Agreement opened Cambodia to the repatriation of refugees and the receiving of international aid, long suspended during the era of war and genocide. International aid workers could not choose where they would work and were assigned by the Cambodian government. Assigned to a rural health care center, Joyce Quinn told stories of women who came to the clinic with many ailments that defied diagnosis. So she started a group where they could come together and share about themselves and their experiences. With vitamin pills and story-telling, the women healed themselves together.

Luise Ahrens was assigned to help rebuild the government's premier higher education institution, the Royal University of Phnom Penh. She worked with the World Bank to build a library and cultivated a cadre of generous donors to fund scholarships for training educators and technical personnel to replace those lost to the country during the genocide. On the other end of the spectrum, Regina Pellicore, a primary school teacher, started accelerated learning classes to help older students who had missed the opportunity for primary schooling.

Education toward a Global Community

The Maryknoll Sisters were invited to Bangladesh in the late 1970s to minister in health care with an emphasis on women's development. In early 2000, Miriam Francis Perlewitz and Joan Westhues, with the support of the Archbishop of Dhaka, started an English-language middle school that has successfully trained young people with a method that fosters critical thinking and tolerance of other peoples' views and ideas. It envisions and works toward creation of a generation of Muslim, Hindu, Buddhist, and Christian students who are ready to carry on a tradition of learning that is liberating, provides peer support, and promotes confidence that together they can overcome cultural obstacles that limited the horizons of their parents and elders. Seeing the dedication and enthusiasm of the sister teachers, a fellow educator thoughtfully asked them: "What is it that motivates you and impels you to stay and work in Bangladesh with all its inhibitions and difficulties? Whom do you look to for inspiration and guidance? Is it your prophet, Jesus?" The Sisters could only answer: YES!

As foreign women, they have not found it easy to operate in this strongly patriarchal society where a wife is regarded as a precious possession. As they live among such energetic, resilient, and handsome people, these Sisters come to appreciate their faith in Allah, their hospitality, their deep love for family, their relationship with the earth they cultivate, their care for the animals they raise, and their beautiful language—Bengali, the language of poets like Tagore.

At the end of the 1990s, Mary Vertucci started the Emusoi Center, a learning center for pastoralist young women in Arusha, Tanzania. Traditionally, girls from these nomadic livestock keepers would be married off early. Even with the universal education policy of the country, these young women would barely finish their primary schooling before being pulled out of school for marriage. *"We are involved in a 'pioneer work,'"* she says, *"to build where nothing existed before, to develop a curriculum which suits the people of this area and to help raise the status of women and to help young women realize and develop their own gifts."* Now over 600 women, mostly Masaai, are being educated throughout Tanzania, with their first graduate in Law in 2010. The name of the center, Emusoi, is a word derived from the Masaai language meaning *"a place of discovery and awareness."*

Life beyond the HIV/AIDS Pandemic

Maryknoll Sisters around the world were quick to express concern over the burgeoning AIDS epidemic. Sisters responded at three levels: raising awareness and educating for prevention, promoting innovative community health programs, and creating innovative programs to address the plight of orphans left in the wake of the disease.

In the early 1980s, Maryknoll Sisters in Africa faced the initial AIDS epidemic. The whole structure of society shook, as its productive members—teachers, construction crews, and government and business workers—began dying. As the young adults of their communities died of "Slim disease" and grandparents took over raising as many as twenty grandchildren when all of their adult children died, Maryknoll Sisters looked for ways to respond to the multifaceted challenge of the pandemic.

Veronica (Roni) Schweyen has been on the front line in the battle against AIDS. She founded a parish-based AIDS outreach program in 1992 in Nyakahoja, Tanzania, at first to offer pastoral care to the person with AIDS and to the family, then to help provide for anti-retroviral drug treatment, and later to respond to the needs of a growing population of orphans. Roni had to deal with the shock of the children whose parents died close together…and then with the stigma attached to the disease. "After the parents' deaths, children are often chased away from the family home. A child has to be helped to work through that type of rejection."

In 1993, at the request of the National Health Commission of the Catholic Bishops Conference of Guatemala, Jean Yamashiro began a low-cost HIV testing clinic in Xela. She was soon joined by Delia (Dee) Smith, an HIV counselor and educator. They called the program Project Life (*Proyecto Vida*) to differentiate their vision of the promotion of life from the widely held perception that HIV means AIDS and AIDS means death.

In El Salvador, Mary Annel, a medical doctor specializing in public health, Lorraine Beinkafner and Bernadette Lynch, teachers with decades of experience in popular education, placed all their skills at the service of AIDS prevention, offering innovative workshops to parish groups, schools, and prisoners. AIDS theater groups with pre-adolescents and teens performed for their peers in street theaters. To help transform unjust "machismo" relations among women and men, they developed workshops for groups on masculinity and femininity.

Mary Ellen Kerrigan worked in the National Taiwan University Hospital in Taipei to help the nurses and doctors there, many of whom were very afraid and knew little about the prevention of HIV infection and the care of people with AIDS. Then as now, compassion was sorely needed in the care of patients and family members who suffered from the fears and the stigma that accompany HIV/AIDS. In 1994, Sister Mary Ellen was invited to go to the Taipei Prison in Taoyuan to help answer questions of prisoners living with HIV/AIDS. Before long, it became obvious that besides learning about HIV/AIDS, their coming together accomplished even more; relationships were formed, and soon they were meeting together weekly. She says of her ministry: *"Each week when I sing, laugh, and talk with my friends in prison who have HIV infection, together we experience God's unconditional love for us."*

Throughout the Maryknoll world, responses to the HIV/AIDS pandemic reflected an ethos based on the gospel message of Jesus: "I have come to bring life, life in its fullness." The mission of Maryknoll, to work with the most marginalized and excluded of society can be realized daily in our work with people with HIV and with the most vulnerable and high risk populations.

Contemplative Community

Even as she firmly believed in "the ideal and idea that every Maryknoll Sister is a contemplative," Mother Mary Joseph established the Contemplative Community in 1931, as "the powerhouse of prayer" for Maryknoll's mission endeavors. From its inception, the contemplative community was envisioned to have foundations in countries overseas; each mission presence making an indelible contribution to the local church and the missioners who serve there. The first mission outreach was a prayer presence among the Navajos in Gallup, New Mexico in the early 1970s.

Responding to a request from the Maryknoll Sisters in Guatemala, the Contemplative Community decided to go to the Quiche area, which was badly affected by the violence that swept Guatemala in the 1980s. Settling in Lemoa, their mission was primarily to offer a prayer presence. Nonetheless the Sisters were very much attuned to the basic needs of their immediate neighbors. Connie Pospisil and Helen Werner assisted widows in building simple and sturdier housing, as well as seeking out scholarship funds for deserving students who could never afford to pay for their tuition fees and school materials.

In the mid 1990s the Contemplative Community went further afield, sending Madeline McHugh and Theresa Baldini to offer a presence of prayer and peace in southern Sudan. Amidst the chaos brought about by a protracted civil war, their presence witnessed to God's desire of peace for all. As civil war violence moved around the country, the Sisters were more than once forced to evacuate their locations and hunker down in bomb shelters. With each move they carried in their hearts a deep love and concern for their former neighbors. The courageous Sisters never lost confidence in God's presence and love. In their account of one of these escapes, each harrowing day ended, "and then we baked bread."

Maryknoll Women: For Women, with Women, as Women

At the 13th General Assembly of the Congregation in 1990, we acknowledged the sources of a deeper understanding of ourselves as women religious in mission. There were numerous factors: New theological and biblical insights into Jesus' life, teachings, and relationship with women empowered women for fullness of life and discipleship; countless women and women's groups deepened our consciousness and challenged us to respond to injustice by sharing their suffering and faith; and our reading and sharing about the work of women scholars who contributed a feminist perspective in the arts and sciences, Scripture and theology.

Since the early mission in Yeungkong, China, the Maryknoll Sisters have always worked closely with women. Now that work takes many forms.

Leonila (Nila) Bermisa's training as a lawyer was put to good use in her mission assignments to Indonesia and the Philippines. In Jakarta, she accompanied prostituted women as they tried to get out of prostitution. Nila worked in a transition house for prostituted women and stayed in the house during weekends. In southern Philippines she worked in a women's program that provided skills training and justice and peace education to rural and indigenous women, as well as paralegal assistance to women victims of rape and other forms of violence. From 2002 to 2005, Nila worked on research and documentation of sexual abuse in the Catholic Church in the Philippines, and she was a resident administrator for Talitha Cum, a temporary home for women victims-survivors of sexual violence. Nila reflects on her own growth as a woman missioner: "I've been a Maryknoll Sister for twenty-seven years. The choice was not as much about service as it was a response to an experience that was hard to name then. The choice was, and is, to keep responding to what I would call now as 'the divine call:' to share God's love and compassionate justice with others, which involves encountering unfamiliar faces and realities, constantly crossing boundaries, facing challenges, and embracing many unknowns."

The massive migration of peoples due to the pressures of poverty, economic exploitation, cultural discrimination, and oppressive dictatorial governments has also marked this period of entrance into the third Millennium. This situation takes on special human rights dimensions in regard to the smuggling of immigrants and the trafficking of persons, especially women and children. Helene O'Sullivan works at the Cambodian Women's Crisis Center in Phnom Penh where safe temporary shelter, legal assistance, and monitoring of violence against women are offered. Eighty percent of the trafficking survivors cannot go back to their families and must start a new life for themselves in Phnom Penh. The reintegration and repatriation programs assist women in job training and helps in setting up small businesses. Helene sees the many hurdles that these women have faced on their long road to recovery: "The women are so traumatized by the experiences that they've undergone being handled as commodities that the offerings we have at the Center do not even touch the wound inflicted on them...it takes a long time for the women to even feel physically well ...As long as the demand for humans as objects is there, the inhuman means of supplying that need will continue."

For the past thirty years, Kathleen (Kay) Kelly has worked for *Mujeres Latinas en Acción* (Latin Women in Action) in Chicago. This is a bilingual/bicultural comprehensive social service agency that seeks to empower women, their families, and youth to become self-reliant. Kay works in the Women in Transition program, which serves low-income Spanish-speaking women and children who are homeless or at risk of becoming so. Her fifteen years in Nicaragua give her insights into the culture and a command of Spanish, so that she can be very helpful to these women. Kay's light and happy disposition endears her to the women with whom she works, and she believes in their innate power and beauty: "We learn so much from these women whose faith and sense of hope bear fruit in their efforts to make a better future for themselves and their children."

Making a Difference One at a Time

As HIV/AIDS took its toll on the vital middle sector of populations in many countries, a surprising sector emerged in need: the elderly. As social structures broke down, elderly people—formerly held as venerable and cared for by their families—were left with no support and no resources. They ended up heading again a household with limited resources and with only the support of an older child.

Once a dietician in a hospital formerly run by Maryknoll Sisters in Hong Kong, Anne Marie Emdin now ministers to the elderly in Macau. Serving as a friend and companion to the elderly, especially those who are homebound, Anne Marie provides monthly toenail and fingernail service. "Being with the elderly keeps me fully alive in mission...I've worked with and come in contact with them throughout the years here in Hong Kong, Macau, and even for a short time in China. These elderly are those who faced the ravages of war in China, the Cultural Revolution, and came here to Macau as refugees. They have looked life and death squarely in the face and accepted both with the same spirit. They are survivors and have made peace with the past and the present and look to the future through the eyes of their children. The grandmothers who are seventy or older have for the most part never had an education and cannot read or write but their grandchildren are teachers, lawyers, nurses, and in other professions. I look at them and think, 'Let us continue growing old together. The best is yet to come!'"

Earnest Chung, who early on introduced to the Congregation the concept of Third Age as mission, works with Catholic Charities Hawai'i. "God's call to me is through the elderly, immigrants, survivors of domestic violence, unwed mothers, homeless, victims of child abuse. They come to seek a hand up, an advocate, and equal access to services. As we practice our core values of respecting the dignity of a person, serving with compassion, seeking social justice, and pursuing excellence in our services, we see in each and every one the face of God."

Cybermission: New Ways to Pray, Connect, Minister, and Cross Borders

In order to further efforts in mission education, the Maryknoll movement has long engaged all the available communications media. Throughout the 1990s, interest in the world wide web as a means of mission education grew. Individuals and organizational offices learned to use e-mail, blogs, and emerging social media as a way to spread the word about mission. More than simply a means of communication, this was also a new culture in which to discover a means of approach.

Although the Sisters' website, www.maryknollsisters.org, had long hosted a "post-a-prayer" section, inviting visitors to indicate their prayer intentions, the web as ministry media grew. In Hong Kong, Anastasia Lindawati complemented her ministry with a project to create a twenty-four-hour prayer presence. Her goal is to organize a presence that makes prayer companioning available through a chat-room type environment. More than an on-line perpetual adoration, the idea is to pray together with another person in a moment of need.

Collaboration: We Are All Called to Mission

Historically, the collaborative expressions in Maryknoll started with the initial meeting of Mollie Rogers with Fr. James Anthony Walsh where she saw the galley sheets of the first copy of *The Field Afar*. Their working relationship in the promotion of *The Field Afar* gave shape to the dream of the first foreign mission enterprise of the Catholic Church in the United States. Over one hundred years later, the collaborative nature of mission continues and takes on different expressions as we cross borders on many levels of our being: *beyond appearances, beyond opinions, beyond interpretations and categories.* Ultimately, all our efforts at collaboration coalesce at the core of mission, which is relationship—God's love. As Mother Mary Joseph said, "I like to think of the Maryknoll Spirit as being a reflection of the

Love of God. I truly believe it is the best expression of what it is, nothing more nor less than that, a reflection of the Love of God."

The Congregation, together with the Maryknoll Society (Fathers and Brothers) and the Maryknoll Lay Missioners (Maryknoll Mission Association of the Faithful) sponsor the joint Maryknoll Office for Global Concerns based in Washington, D.C. Staffed jointly by missioners from each Maryknoll entity, salaried personnel, and volunteers, the office brings the experience of Maryknollers from around the world to educate for social justice, peace, and the integrity of creation.

The Maryknoll Sisters non-governmental (NGO) status in the United Nations opens avenues through which the voices of grassroots people from around the world may be heard. Ann Braudis, who initiated the Ecological Sanctuary in Baguio, Philippines, is the Congregation's current representative to the United Nations. Ann was chosen to co-chair the UN's NGO Committee on Sustainable Development, working on issues related to the UN Climate Change Conference held in Copenhagen, Denmark, in December 2009. The conference examined what has been achieved during the past twenty years and what still needs to be implemented globally regarding sustainable development. Asked what is meant by or included in sustainable development, Ann says, "Sustainable development is environmental, social, and economic development that meets the needs of the present without compromising the ability of future generations to meet their own needs."

Collaborative efforts for mission provide the richness of diversity and the strength of unity. We not only learn from and challenge each other to grow but we also endow each other with a spirit of centering our lives in the Gospel for the common good.

In Brazil, Maryknoll Sisters are part of a collaborative unit together with priests, brothers, and lay missioners. Carolyn Moritz notes: "This meant letting go of preconceived ideas of mission as separate groups and working out the new model together. This was a great adventure." As the Brazil mission community, they minister to the indigenous Guarani and other marginalized groups that live on the periphery of the city of São Paulo, South America's largest metropolis.

Connie Pospisil, along with two lay missioners, formed a community and pioneered work with women in a mission in João Pessoa, Paraiba, in the northeast of the country. Two Sisters from Tanzania, Ephrasia Nyaki and Theresia Ndesoma, later joined the mission group and work in ministries that provide holistic health care alternatives. They work with Brazilians of African descent, enabling them to uncover the richness of their cultural roots. They also make efforts to incorporate local religious rites and symbolism into the liturgy. Many Maryknollers have been part of this collaborative approach. There has been a tremendous growth together and richness shared because of this partnership.

In the United States, collaborative ministries have emerged at inter-congregational, ecumenical, and societal levels—in joint endeavors such as NETWORK (a national Catholic social justice lobby) and the Maryknoll Office for Global Concerns, in ecumenical partnerships, and in national movements such as Pax Christi, Call to Action, and the protest vigils at the School of the Americas. In person and through electronic media, Sisters have involved themselves in a variety of social and environmental justice issues related, for example, to human rights, uranium mining, and care of the earth. Although their commitments persist in diverse areas and in varying degrees even as they age and many "retire," Sisters increasingly carry the Maryknoll charism to others now through part-time and volunteer ministries, by home and hospital visiting, in person-to-person and family ministry, in creative visual and written expressions, as well as through association with the Maryknoll Affiliates and Full Circle.

Creating Peace and Justice

Through our evolving history, Maryknoll Sisters have taken part in the movement of active nonviolence for peace, justice, human rights, and equality. In 1989, the same year that Penny Lernoux died, six Jesuits, their house helper, and her daughter were massacred in El Salvador. This spurred a movement of protest at the School of the Americas (SOA) at Ft. Benning, Georgia. SOA was known as an institution that trained Latin American military and police later implicated in using oppressive techniques to terrorize and kill dissenters in their own populations.

Maryknoll Sisters began to participate in the yearly vigil/protest at the gates of this "school." Madeline Dorsey, one of the Maryknoll Sisters who originally witnessed the exhuming of the bodies of the four churchwomen assassinated in El Salvador in December 1980, was one of the first to risk arrest by "crossing the line" at the SOA entrance. In 2004, Lelia Mattingly crossed the line, was arrested, and sentenced to six months prison the following year.

Bernice Rigney worked in a church-sponsored counseling center in Nairobi, Kenya. In 1994, following the tragedy of the Rwandan genocide, she found herself immersed in training counselors from groups of both victims and perpetrators of the genocide who were pouring into Kenya. This experience led her to study and work in the field of peace building, conflict transformation, and trauma healing with men, women, and children affected by war, HIV/AIDS, domestic violence, and dysfunctional situations. Bernice traveled to conflict areas at the invitation of church groups and aid organizations to work with agency personnel in their de-briefing and in developing needed skills in coping with trauma. In 2006, a multicultural team of Maryknoll Sisters, Sia Temu, Teresa Hougnon, and Giang Nguyen, was assigned to Kenya for community-based peace-building ministry. They facilitate relationships among culturally diverse people, and together explore peaceful means of coexistence through their program, "Conversations for Social Change."

Elsie Monge worked tirelessly in Ecuador advocating for and accompanying the families of people who were "disappeared" for having spoken out about injustice. In 2010 President Correa of Ecuador named Elsie, along with two human rights activists (a lawyer and the parent of two persons who were disappeared in 1988), to chair the Truth Commission to Impede Impunity.

Jean Fallon and Rosemarie Milazzo are reservists of the Christian Peacemaker Teams (CPT), an international organization set up to support teams of peace workers in conflict areas around the world. The teams believe that they can lower the levels of violence through nonviolent direct action, documentation, and nonviolence training. In many situations, team members serve as human buffer zones. Jean and Rosemarie have been called to witness for peace in areas of conflict in the Middle East, Congo, Shabat Lake, Canada, and Ethiopia.

"If you want peace, work for justice." Pope Paul VI's words struck a chord in Anna McAnany's heart and she put her own unique expression on it. As a young parish elementary school teacher, the themes of justice and peace shaped her choices and relationships. Whether breaking up fights in the schoolyard or visiting her pupils' families to talk over the children's progress, Anna came to see that violence frequently stemmed from injustices and discrimination. Domestic violence, she soon realized, frequently arose when a spouse was treated badly by his employers. From her earliest years in Hawai'i her heart so ached for the Filipino, Japanese, and Portuguese sugar plantation workers that she became an advocate for them.

Anna devised a curriculum for middle school titled "Peace as a Way of Life," and she fostered a Peace Farm where classes of children from many public schools cultivated their own plots and cared for the soil. She was eighty-eight years old when she received the "Women of Justice Award" in 1996 from NETWORK, the National Catholic Social Justice Lobby sponsored by congregations of U.S. women religious. That same year Anna, and the Peace Education Program of the Wai'anae Coast, published the fruit of her many decades of peace education, *Teaching Peace*, a teacher's lesson plan manual that is still used in Hawai'i schools.

In her preface to the book, Anna wrote, "The root causes of war begin within ourselves. If we can overcome our selfishness and extend a helping hand, if we can appreciate the goodness and talents of others, if we can acknowledge the value and dignity in each human person, and if we can realistically acknowledge and work for resolution of the conflicts that threaten to destroy us, then we can be assured we have done our part to bring about peace on earth."

Ensuring the Rights of the Community of Life

The 13th General Assembly in 1990 was a watershed for the Congregation to act on the awareness that "all creation is a primary source of revelation of the divine Presence and in fulfillment of God's plan is intended to grow together toward fullness of Life." This new consciousness of the interconnectedness and oneness of all the communities of life impelled us to move from a human-centered to a cosmic view of justice.

The global increase in social unrest related to environmental issues is echoed in the realities experienced by Maryknoll Sisters in Peru. Pat Ryan works with a non-governmental organization, *Derechos Humanos y Medio Ambiente* (Rights of Humans and the Environment) in Puno advocating for the indigenous populations' rights to defend their land held sacred from the destruction caused by (mainly foreign-owned) mining companies. The government no longer has exclusive control over exploration, mining, smelting, and refining of metals and fuel minerals. As of 2001, the government had privatized 90 percent of its assets in mining, a greater rate than in any other sector. This move has caused an irreversible destruction of the land, and greatly undermined the people's capacity to use their land for food production and raising livestock, the traditional and sustainable source of their livelihood.

Another face of the on-going ecological crisis is the destruction of the tropical rainforests that form a belt of fragile, intricate biodiversity around our planet. After years of living in the rainforest of Darien, Panama, Maryknoll Sisters were witnessing the continual decimation of the forest around them by settlers and commercial companies, justified by economic and political interests and profit-centered development strategies. Melinda Roper and Jocelyn Fenix began small projects and programs that help conserve and, as much as possible, reverse the destructive trends in relating to the natural world. They started a small organic farm with the surrounding community for food production. With the use of local forest plants they produced soap, medicinal creams, teas, and other natural health products, while also promoting the use of renewable energy and conservation.

Ecology—Mission of Earth Healing

A special concern for ecology was a salient direction from the 16th General Assembly in 2008, which observed, "We seek creative ways to be responsible for the sustainability for all life...." The theories and practices put forth by the science of ecology help us shift our human-centered understanding of life to that which sustains all life. Like increasing numbers of people, we realize that we can no longer regard human activities as over and above other life processes and realities in our planet Earth. We all share the same home and the same system that nurtures and sustains Life.

During an earthquake in 1990 the Maryknoll Sisters' convent in Baguio, Philippines, was destroyed. This prompted a decision to redirect our ministry there away from formal elementary education to alternative environmental education. With a phase-out program of their elementary school, we began the Maryknoll Sisters Center for Justice, Peace, and Integrity of Creation, popularly known as the Maryknoll Ecological Sanctuary. The Center offers workshops and retreats on spirituality and the arts, new cosmology, indigenous spirituality, ecology, global warming, ecological solid waste management, and Earth-based early learning education for the young. The four-acre area of old growth forest features a biodynamic garden and a small coffee plantation where visitors delight in the sight of butterflies and flowers and sound of bird songs. The extravagant beauty and biological diversity of our planet Earth is shared and passed on to future generations so that it will continue to inspire and sustain us.

Mission: From a Worldwide to a Cosmic Enterprise

Since the General Assembly of 1990 when Ecology became an important direction in ministry for the Maryknoll Sisters, there has been an evolution of consciousness, drawing us into a new understanding of the cosmos and our relationship to it. Ecological practices do not only apply to our use of resources, they extend to our relationships with each other and with our environment. The landscape of mission profoundly fashions the drama of our energy and spirit. Maryknoll Sisters in Africa share their experience of developing a new consciousness in the societies in which they find themselves: Their "energy is fed by the beautiful vastness of the lush savannahs, mountains, harsh deserts; the wild animals—claiming their ancestral home of millions of years, delighting all who see them. A continent of hundreds of different tribes, and languages, each with deep ancient heritage—a spirit of freedom and dance; of rituals and protocols; of acceptance and generosity, permeates this Africa, which long ago, found a home in our hearts. We now see Africa has co-created us, gifted us, brought us life. Africa is part of our blood."

This new consciousness deeply challenges our limited language to express or interpret it. One of the projects of the Maryknoll Sisters at the Santa Fe Pastoral Center in Darien, Panama, is an extensive popular art program through which children and young people have the opportunity to see with new eyes the beauty of the forest and ways to relate creatively with each other and the environment. Their emerging lifestyle, prayer, and ministries are a conscious effort to be a living symbol of the human community learning to live in harmony with the whole community of life; to live with the Spirit of Jesus in their relationships with all of creation. They continue to discover how to be contemplatives in living their faith in the tradition and spirit of Jesus, Mollie Rogers, and Maryknoll Sisters who have been faithful to mission and to each other in community. We are convinced that the future of the community of life on this planet Earth and the coming of the Reign of God inspired by Jesus are intimately interwoven, and we pray for the wisdom to live this hope.

Interreligious Dialogue: Seeing as God Sees

In Southeast Asia, the reality of world religions has been a factor in all of the countries where Maryknoll Sisters are in mission. Our expansion into Southeast Asia has brought us into contact with Islam in Indonesia and Bangladesh; Hinduism in Nepal; and Theravada Buddhism in Cambodia, Thailand, and Myanmar. Over and over again, we are stretched by the mutuality of our values in matters "that give life, life in all its fullness." We might call our gods and sacred journeys with different names, with the strangeness of images and expressions of religious rituals that evoke prejudice and fear, yet, when we start speaking to each other from our hearts, we discover, with joy, that we are both naming the one "in whom we move and have our being."

Luise Ahrens, who served in Indonesia from 1973 to 1983, vividly remembers what she learned from her encounters with Muslims when "my heart and religious worldview burst wide open." Now serving in Cambodia, Luise sees that "God opens a different window of grace for me...as I sit in prayer among Buddhist monks at weddings and funerals, I not only experience a feeling of reverence and respect for the beliefs of others but a sure and certain knowledge that God is moving within and among us as we pray together. Buddhism calls everyone to attentiveness, to mindfulness. It is in this spirit/Spirit of peaceful attentiveness that the knowledge of God and of God's way of seeing are rooted within our too active senses. Indeed, all religious experience is holy ground."

In Myanmar, Maryknollers and numerous partners are finding ways to share life, education, and dialogue of life with many students, teachers, families, and people of the diocese. They are able to help bring Christians together with Buddhists, Muslims, Hindus and animists and grow in mutual discovery of deep faith and compassion—especially for the poor and suffering. Through it all they know they are building peace and unity not only in Myanmar but in the whole universe.

Hinduism permeated every aspect of life in the Kingdom of Nepal when our first group of Sisters arrived in the late 1980s. More than a religion, Hinduism is an integral part of the law and the fabric of political, social, and family life. For Nepali citizens to become Christian was a criminal offense resulting in imprisonment. Foreigners entering the country had to work with an approved agency and offer a skill that the government felt was needed. Thus, our first ministries were teaching English with NGOs such as the Jesuit School in Kathmandu and the Notre Dame School in the middle hills.

After 1990, the law against conversion to Christianity was repealed. However, Hinduism is still deeply ingrained in all aspects of the culture, and the restrictions about public teaching of Christianity continued. In 2001, three Sisters began working with the United Christian Mission to Nepal and were involved in hospital administration in an urban hospital, nursing education, and social/pastoral ministry in the distant rural and hill areas of the country. In all these ministries our witness was one of life and service in the compassionate spirit of Jesus, learning from the people and our colleagues the many faces of our loving God.

Dance and Art

When Rosalie Lacorte worked with out-of-school young women in Musoma, Tanzania, in a program that taught them life skills and trades that might enable them to be self-employed, she also encouraged them to plant a flower garden. When asked why they needed to use their time on that instead of focusing on income generation, she responded: "They also need to feed their souls." The different media of communication that artists use are indeed for soul making. Sister artists—poets, writers, musicians, dancers, gardeners—have always been encouraged to develop their gifts.

When she was a new Sister in Maryknoll, Yoo Soo Kim felt some disquiet about her prayer expression until one day, while trying to speak with God, she got up unconsciously and danced what was deepest in her heart. Her prayer has brought her to a ministry of healing through dance. "When *I dance, I can touch people's hearts. Through the healing process, something inside people bursts out when they see my dance; they cry." She invites people to wholeness through sacred dance in workshops and parish liturgies.* "A person's body is an instrument to express beauty, pain, communication, betrayal, joy. It comes out mystically when you dance."

Artist Joanna Chan has also been a prolific playwright and stage director in China, Hong Kong, Canada, and the United States for over thirty-five years. She co-founded Yangtze Repertory Theatre of America in New York in 1992 to produce works for and by Asian artists. Since 2002, Joanna has been working in the Rehabilitation through the Arts Program at Sing Sing state prison in Ossining, New York, directing the inmates in August Wilson's *Jitney and* a critically-acclaimed production of Sophocles' *Oedipus Rex,* hailed by one critic as a work that gave the play "one of its finest hours 2,500 years later."

Engaging the Emerging Dream of God

Almost 100 years ago, the small band of women who came to Hawthorne, New York, dreamed with audacious hope of spreading, preaching, and witnessing to the mission of Jesus to the ends of the earth. They created a life in community that utterly relied on God's providence. That hope, in the loving providence of God, gains depth, courage, and meaning with the realization that the world they vowed to serve and save also calls for an ongoing conversion and transformation.

In 1997, a Congregational Gathering with 470 Maryknoll Sisters in preparation for the 14th General Assembly was held near the Maryknoll Center. The event, called "Gathering the Dreamers," was unprecedented by the attendance of so many Sisters and by the variety of rich activities presented and facilitated by attendees looking to "find God in new ways... to drink deep in the giftedness of diversity and to dwell deep within the sacredness that we discover in each other." We noted with ardor the shifts in thinking and evolution in perspective.

We endeavor to sustain a global focus beyond our regional identities. We are challenged to live out the reality of multiculturality in our relationships with one another as well as in our ministries with others. We seek to adapt structures and ways of communicating to facilitate new kinds of participative discernment and leadership.

Such shifts in thinking and experience bring us to an expansiveness of being that empowers us to recognize that once again, we stand at the edge of an historical moment. Thus encouraged and inspired, we enjoin to continue with the dream. We gather the dreamers, for our dream will more likely become reality when we open the circle. Our search for the sacred leads us to become more global and cosmic persons. The following verse, composed by one of the groups, images the dynamism and commitment of the Congregational Gathering:

"Now is the time to give birth to the dream
Journeying
Holding hearts together

Cosmic fire bursting new energy
Creating life anew
YES!"

Over the years, Maryknoll Sisters have immersed ourselves in cultures and with peoples and governments and geography totally different from our own. We have also continued to experience a God who is always with us and the awesome surprise that God also waits for us in these landscapes of life into which we are sent. The Swahili expression, *"I have eaten your kindness,"* describes the vital relationships and sharing with many peoples and cultures that tremendously enrich us and teach us that *"we are one."*

Again and again, Maryknoll Sisters encounter other dreamers in search of the sacred and the quest for meaning. On this road, we join our brothers and sisters on a pilgrimage to engage in God's emerging dream through Jesus.

Today we are ready to begin our second century of mission with nearly 500 Maryknoll Sisters already in position in and for a globalized world. We have been blessed and hold promise for our church and world! We welcome the future, nurtured by the past. The fire and passion for mission continues to burn steadily within our hearts, lit long ago deep in our souls. So we recall a blessing by our foundress, Mother Mary Joseph, some eighty-five years ago:

"And so tonight, I thought we would drink a little toast to our past, particularly in thanksgiving for all that God has given to us—to the blessed memories of the past, whether painful or pleasant ones—and to our future, to hope that God's blessings will rest upon us and that each and every one of us—individuals, and we, as a Community, will correspond fully to the graces that God will give us."

Silver Jubilee, January 6, 1937

Afterword

Sister Claudette LaVerdiere, M.M.
President, Maryknoll Sisters

~

WHEN PENNY LERNOUX BEGAN THIS oral history of the Maryknoll Sisters, she wrote to Barbara Hendricks that she hoped it would be a thoughtful history, "a work that (would) convert hearts." Penny certainly could write a good story. Her project held such promise—even as preliminary drafts, her first few chapters brought tears to our eyes—until an act of God confounded her dream . . . and ours.

After Penny's death in October 1989, just when it was not clear to anyone what the next step would be, Penny's husband, Denis Nahum, wanted the book finished and Arthur Jones offered to continue the story so that Penny's last work might be completed. He proceeded to transform her notes into a manuscript that Robert Ellsberg, the final editor, brought to completion. In the hands of these faithful story tellers, *Hearts On Fire* reads as the thoughtful history Penny had begun, with the hope that it would convert hearts. When life itself was taken from her, Penny's hopes were definitively confided to God. With the publication of this book we know that God heard her prayer.

Because of her quest for justice in Latin America, we know too, that Penny would be pleased with the establishment and report of the Truth Commission in El Salvador. The murders of Archbishop Romero, the four church women, the Jesuits and their helpers, and the tens of thousands of Salvadorans, are not totally laid to rest. Yet, justice has begun to be served.

Since October 1989, when research for this oral history ended, there have been some important developments in the Congregation. On February 14, 1990, seventy years to the day we were recognized as a new religious congregation, the Holy See accepted our updated Constitutions. Over a period of twenty years, the leadership and members of the Congregation had engaged in a thorough process of study and reflection on the essentials of the call to mission through religious life.

The new Constitutions reflect a significant growth in our understanding of mission as a Congregation. Essentially, at the end of the twentieth century, we respond to the mission mandate to "Go, teach all nations . . ." (Mt 28:16–20), with new ears, new eyes, and new hearts. Over the years we have been humbled by our encounter with people whose lives are imbued with faith in God, regardless of the extremity of their circumstances. We journey with them less as teachers and leaders and more as friends and companions. We yearn to share with them our faith in Jesus so that they also may know the length and breadth of God's love for them. The words of Luke 4:18–19, where Jesus describes his mission, guide us on the way:

> The Spirit of the Lord has been given to me, and has anointed
> me.
> The Spirit has sent me to bring the good news to the poor, to
> proclaim liberty to captives
> and to the blind new sight,
> to set the downtrodden free,
> to proclaim the Lord's year of favor.

Despite decreasing membership we continue to reach for new horizons, beyond the familiar and the comfortable. In the past three years, our experienced missioners have responded to places such as Cambodia, East Timor, and Papua New Guinea. Within the next few months we will have three Sisters in Namibia. Every new endeavor evokes the same spirit of love, excitement, and expectation that characterized the first group of Sisters who went to China in 1921. That same spirit still infuses the Congregation with fresh new life just as it did then.

Visits and our Sisters' newsletters enable us to follow the new initiatives closely. In Cambodia four sisters are working to heal the wounds of the brutal war and to build bridges between people who are now experiencing freedom after many years of enforced confinement in refugee camps. The Sisters describe their experience in a small clinic on the outskirts of Phnom Penh. They struggle to express themselves and to communicate in the difficult Khmer language. They wonder if their Buddhist staff understand anything at all about who they are and why they are there. Then one day they overhear a member of staff tell others: "They are a listening of the heart."

In Papua New Guinea, since 1991, three Maryknoll Sisters offer skills training to young women and animate pastoral leaders. Often this means long journeys on foot to remote villages to pray and read scripture with small groups of Christians. Describing one such trip, Sister Patricia Redmond wrote that it took over an hour of climbing up and down hills, over and under fences and through mud and water to reach their destination. They waited another hour and a half for the people to assemble, then spent the remainder of the day squatting on a sapling laid on the ground as a seat. Pat comments, "The heat and the fatigue were real but the example of the pastoral team and the experience of spending the day with the people are the privileged memories that far outweigh any discomfort. Most of the people I've met have a sincere, childlike thirst for God. What they probably don't realize is how much God is revealed in them."

Our Maryknoll charism inspires us to cross new frontiers—be they distant places, neglected peoples, or modern-day challenges. The AIDS pandemic has been a particular challenge to Maryknoll Sister Mary Annel, a doctor who trained health promoters in Guatemala for more than fifteen years. In 1993 at our Maryknoll Center, she has researched how the Congregation can best channel its response to this global crisis. Her findings point to the need for culturally appropriate AIDS preventive education and pastoral care. A joint AIDS Task Force of the Maryknoll Congregation, Society, and Associate Lay Missioners has been established to continue ongoing education and research among the more than seventy Maryknollers who are currently involved in this ministry around the globe. Mary herself is answering a call to set up a grassroots AIDS prevention program in El Salvador.

Maryknoll Sister Mary Ellen Kerrigan teaches hospital staff and family members in Taiwan how to assist AIDS patients. In a recent encounter with a young man called Chen who asked her to read a letter he had written to his older brother, he blurted out, "Sister, I am afraid to die. You see, I don't believe in God or Buddha or anything like that."

"Please explain then, why you mentioned God so many times in the letter to your brother."

With a shy smile, he pointed to his heart and said: "I should tell you that I have a God in me." His reply took her by surprise.

"Tell me about your God and I'll tell you about mine," she responded.

"Oh, I can't share my God with you because you're a well person and my God is for people like me with AIDS—my God is for sick people."

Once assured that she would not try to change his God, Mr. Chen began: "My God is very forgiving and doesn't keep thinking about the bad things I've done. My God wants to help people like me not to be afraid; my God is beautiful, and the best thing is, my God loves me."

Overwhelmed by his confession of faith and mindful of her promise, she was at a loss for words. While Mr. Chen eyed her expectantly, she took a deep breath and exclaimed, "Well, Mr. Chen, if our God isn't the same God, then—they're twins!"

Such grace-filled moments are not uncommon in our mission journey. These are the people we have come to know and love in Asia, Africa, Latin

America, the Central Pacific, and the United States. They help to teach us the generosity of a loving God. By becoming women of a "listening heart," we find the Gospel message comes to life in the struggles of the poor and humble with whom we walk.

Responding to new moments in history enables us to break new ground. The women's movement, for instance, makes us more conscious of the urgent need to bond with women everywhere, and in all circumstances, so that women's voices may be heard in the public forum. All along and for many years, our Sisters had given special attention to the needs of women. When at our General Assembly of 1978 equality with women was highlighted as a specific direction in ministry for the Congregation, the emphasis gained unprecedented momentum among us.

Prominent in the promotion of women is Maryknoll Sister Virginia Fabella of the Philippines, who is instrumental in encouraging third-world women theologians to develop a women's liberation perspective. Cofounder of the Ecumenical Association of Third World Theologians (EATWOT), she is a key architect of its Women's Commission. "As Third World women theologians we have gradually become conscious that unless the emerging theologies on our continents are inclusive of the women's viewpoint, these theologies cannot be relevant or liberating for ourselves or for the Church or for society at large," she writes in her 1992 book, *Beyond Bonding: A Third World Women's Theological Journey.*

We believe that bonding with the women with whom we live and work around the world is an important step towards recognizing and naming problems so that we may work together for change. From the earliest days of our Congregation we have been joined by women of many cultures. In recent years the trend is significant. We are deeply challenged to examine the implications of what it means to be a multicultural community and to confront our own racism. This on-going call to conversion in a world that is increasingly fragmented along ethnic and racial lines must begin with ourselves.

In addition to the issues of women, racism, and multi-culturalism, we also addressed the subject of ecology at our General Assembly of 1990. Recognizing the interconnectedness and oneness of the universe, we committed ourselves to integrate ecology and environmental concerns into our ministries as a justice issue.

While consciousness of the environment permeates the lifestyle of most Maryknoll Sisters, for several it has become a full-time ministry. When their home was destroyed by an earthquake in the Philippines in 1990, Sisters Carmela Carpio, Ann Braudis, and Amelia Omana, started a Center for the Integrity of Creation on the site. An alternative education center, it responds to the needs of the local community and particularly so in the

Cordillera Mountains where the indigenous people are waging a battle with mining companies to preserve their land.

While the women joining religious life continue to be few in number, we are encouraged by new forms of mission outreach among the laity. The Associate Lay Mission Program, which was established by the Maryknoll Society in collaboration with the Sisters' Congregation in the seventies, has enabled many dedicated young people to embrace a mission vocation. In 1993, the Maryknoll Fathers, Brothers, and Sisters are collaborating with the Associate Lay Missioners in a new venture that attests to our ever-developing mission theology. The call to mission is grounded in our baptismal commitment and is not limited in any way to the clerical or religious vocation. None replaces the other; each is vitally necessary to the total Christian endeavor. The new initiative is an affirmation of the Associates as equal partners in the Maryknoll Family.

The Maryknoll Affiliates is another budding and exciting development on which both Society and Congregation are collaborating. Affiliates are "persons who enter into a special relationship with Maryknoll," initially in the United States and with potential for all countries where Maryknoll is present. That relationship is intended "to foster creative mutuality" and provide opportunities to grow in one's mission spirituality through prayer, reflection on scripture, work for justice, mission education, assistance to the needy at home, as well as support for the work of overseas mission. Having started in 1991, by mid-1993 over thirty Affiliate Chapters had been formed in the United States and Puerto Rico.

At this writing, of all the Sisters featured in this oral history, there are three who are now notably absent among us. At the beginning of 1993, a major chapter in our Maryknoll history ended with the death of Sister Gemma Shea, our last founding member. Gemma, at 98, remained alert to the very end. In her last years, with gracious good humor, she delighted us often with her recollections of the early days. She also shared liberally the wisdom she had acquired in her long cross-cultural experience among the Japanese people.

Early in 1992, Sister Dorothy Erickson, "Madre Rosa" of Jacaltenango fame, died after a short illness. As the doctor who had been promised by Mother Mary Coleman, in response to the "thumbprint" appeal, Dorothy was mourned in Jacaltenango and buried with great honor by all the townspeople she had befriended and served so well for thirty-one years.

Also, we remember Sister Gabriella Mulherin, the feisty woman whose capacity for organizing whole populations was legendary. You may recall from Chapter 10 that she started and developed the credit union movement in South Korea and guided it to international status. After Gabriella died this May at Maryknoll, New York, we received a posthumous award for her from the World Council of Credit Unions sent from their June meeting held in Quebec.

For every Maryknoll Sister whose experiences are described in the text, there are many others whose stories could also be told, for all share in the exhilaration of outreach to our brothers and sisters of the world. To keep before us the purpose of our foundation as a mission congregation, and to encourage one another in mission, a Heritage Photo Exhibit designed by Maryknoll Sister Joanna Chan, now fills the space that was once a museum at the front of the main building at the Maryknoll Sisters' Center. Opened in September 1991, it is to keep in memory all the Maryknoll Sisters who have served and continue to serve in many countries of the world. Joanna captured some photos and narrative in a booklet: *Toward a Distant Vision*.

While some noteworthy events and experiences are preserved in photos, others are highlighted in letters, as this one from a Christian woman in Lukang parish, Taiwan, to Sisters Agnes Virginia Higgins and Maria Etsuko Ogo, dated April 10, 1993. They received it just before their departure, after many years of active ministry in Taiwan:

> These days when I think of your leaving us, my heart becomes full of pain. . . . In order to repay your love for us we will reach out to others as you have taught us, so that others will know we are Christians.

The woman who wrote this letter had grasped the essence of Christian discipleship.

The road ahead stretches further than the eye can see. We know not what new mysteries, challenges, joys and tragedies await us. Like Moses, like the Apostles after Jesus died, we set forth with both apprehension and hopeful desire. We, too, are strengthened by the Spirit and supported by companions willing to walk uncharted paths into the future.

Maryknoll
October 1993

Afterword to the Centenary Edition

Sister Janice McLaughlin, M.M.
President, Maryknoll Sisters

~

IT IS A TIMELY tribute that Orbis Books is reprinting a new edition of *Hearts on Fire* to commemorate the 100th anniversary of the Maryknoll Sisters. This labor of love by Penny Lernoux, a renowned journalist who was inspired by our commitment to justice and peace and to our worldwide mission to the dispossessed and downtrodden, captures the heroic spirit and undaunted courage of generations of Maryknoll women who followed in the footsteps of our pioneers since January 6, 1912.

In the ensuing years the works and locations have changed, as have the theology of mission and the nature of religious life but one thing remains the same—a desire to cross borders to share God's love with all people and a commitment to remain true to the spirit of Mother Mary Joseph, our visionary founder who combined a genuine love for each person, a deep faith, and a down-to-earth wisdom.

We are blessed to be members of a larger Maryknoll family that enables us to extend our missionary outreach, provides companionship, and strengthens our advocacy and action for justice through the Maryknoll Office of Global Concerns, a collaborative initiative of Maryknoll sisters, priests and brothers, and lay missioners. We also are blessed with a worldwide network of friends and supporters who tell us that "Maryknoll is in our blood." Whether they are former members, donors and sponsors, or graduates of our schools, these partners in mission raise the funds that make our work possible and also provide for our retired and sick elderly.

The love and loyalty of our former students in Hong Kong, Hawaii, Marshall Islands, Philippines, Guatemala, Mexico, Bolivia, Peru, and Tanzania to the ideals and values that were taught to them is truly God's love made visible. Many of these graduates have become leading figures in their societies, spearheading the movement for women's rights and initiating projects that serve the neediest members of their communities. Gertrude Mongella, for instance, one of the first graduates of Marian College in Morogoro, Tanzania, headed the African Parliament and also chaired the Beijing Women's Conference. Anna Tibaijuka, a graduate of Rugambwa Secondary School in Bukoba, Tanzania, was the first woman to head the UN

Habitat program, helping to champion low cost housing for the poor and shedding a light on income inequality worldwide. Award-winning film-maker Nancy Tong attended Maryknoll Convent School in Hong Kong, while Carolyn Woo, the Dean of Mendoza Business School at Notre Dame University, attended Maryknoll Secondary School in Hong Kong.

As I travel to different corners of our Maryknoll world, I am struck by how the seeds that were planted by our Sisters in the past have taken root and are spreading. In Manila, Philippines, for example, the President and staff of Miriam College (formerly Maryknoll College) pass on the value of caring for one's neighbor to the students from pre-school to post-graduate level. The Medical Director and staff of Our Lady of Maryknoll Hospital in Hong Kong maintain a caring environment for the patients, including an outreach program to visit them in their homes. "We want to keep alive the ideals that were instilled in us by the Sisters who worked here before us," they told me.

The list of those who are putting into practice what they learned from their Maryknoll predecessors is endless as is the list of Maryknoll Sisters who have followed in the footsteps of our pioneers. They continue to carry the message of God's healing love to the four corners of the earth, creating small miracles wherever they go. These miracles can be as simple as en-abling an orphan to attend school in Zimbabwe, bathing the sores of an AIDS patient in El Salvador, or bringing communion to a housebound el-der in East Timor. Or they can be as far-reaching as helping to re-establish a national university in Cambodia, heading a Truth and Reconciliation Commission in Ecuador and enabling Masaai women to attend school in East Africa.

When our Sisters Ita Ford and Maura Clark were murdered in El Salva-dor in December 1980 by members of the military that was supported by the US government, Maryknoll's leaders exposed the complicity of the United States in supporting a repressive government that was killing its own people. This was a far cry from the unquestioning support of Mary-knollers for the US government in the early days of our foundation when God and country were hailed as one. We continue to ask uncomfortable questions that get to the root of problems, rather than merely dealing with the symptoms. In Peru, for example, we support the protest of the indige-nous people against international mining companies that are taking their land and destroying the environment. In Zimbabwe, we work with Doctors and Lawyers for Human Rights that are helping to treat the victims of vio-lence while exposing the corruption and brutality of those in power.

Our first missionary outreach was to immigrants from Asia living on the West Coast of the US. As globalization increases the movement of peo-ple around the world, Maryknoll Sisters continue to minister to migrants. In Japan, for instance, we assist migrants from the Philippines who number more than one million to adjust to their new home and to overcome the legal and social problems they encounter. In the US many of our members help migrants from Mexico and Central America to get jobs, an education and legal status. While in Asia and Southern Africa, our Sisters work with others to prevent human trafficking and to assist the victims of this modern-day slave trade.

Another priority for the twenty-first century is the movement to protect the earth from environmental degradation. As "development" has come to mean the acquisition of goods, the world's natural resources are being depleted, leading to a crisis of sustainability. From São Paulo to Hong Kong, our sisters help to create awareness of the need "to live simply so that others may simply live."

As the world becomes more violent and polarized, we are called to be peace builders. Whether we are promoting dialog between Christians and Muslims in East Africa, participating in inter-religious dialog in Asia or bringing rich and poor together in Latin America, our goal is to bridge the gap between people that can lead to violence.

Finally, our promotion of the rights of women and girls underpins all that we do. Until women are respected and treated as equals in both church and society, there will never be genuine peace or development.

Our 100 years have taught us the incredible diversity and richness of cultures and the need to preserve them from extinction. It has also taught us that the message of Jesus is as relevant as ever. In the words of our founder, Mother Mary Joseph, "The dominant factor in our lives is love— love of God and love of neighbor." She described our spirit as being "a reflection of the love of God."

Maryknoll Sisters from a multitude of nations continue to express that spirit. Our numbers are fewer and our nationalities more varied but we seek to be faithful to her vision and we look forward to the future with hope. Our founder's words to Gemma Shea, one of the pioneer women, sums up the attitude that will usher us into the next 100 years: "Let us go and see what God has in store for us."

Index

~

Pruitt Dorthea

Mary Low Townsead